Beyond Pluralism

BEYOND PLURALISM

The Conception of Groups and Group Identities in America

Edited by Wendy F. Katkin,
Ned Landsman, and Andrea Tyree

University of Illinois Press

Urbana and Chicago

© 1998 by the Board of Trustees of the University of Illinois
Manufactured in the United States of America

1 2 3 4 5 C P 5 4 3 2 1

This book is printed on acid-free paper.

Library of Congress Cataloging-in-Publication Data

Beyond pluralism : the conception of groups and group
identities in America / edited by Wendy F. Katkin,
Ned Landsman, and Andrea Tyree.
p. cm.
Includes bibliographical references and index.
ISBN 0-252-02385-4 (cloth : acid-free paper). —
ISBN 0-252-06685-5 (pbk. : acid-free paper)
1. Pluralism (Social sciences)—United States—Congresses.
2. Ethnicity—United States—Congresses. 3. United States—
Ethnic relations—Congresses. 4. United States—Race
relations—Congresses. I. Katkin, Wendy Freedman, 1940– .
II. Landsman, Ned C., 1951– . III. Tyree, Andrea.
E184.A1B49   1998
305.8'00973—dc221
97-33747
CIP

Contents

Introduction: The Construction of American Pluralism   *1*
Ned Landsman and Wendy F. Katkin

1   The Legal Framework of American Pluralism: Liberal
Constitutionalism and the Protection of Groups   *11*
Stanley N. Katz

2   Multiple Ethnic Identity Choices   *28*
Mary C. Waters

3   Postethnic America   *47*
David A. Hollinger

4   The Multiculturalism Debate as Cultural Text   *63*
Werner Sollors

5   Pluralism, Protestantism, and Prosperity:
Crèvecoeur's American Farmer and the Foundations
of American Pluralism   *105*
Ned Landsman

6   Pluralism and Hierarchy: "Whiz Kids," "The Chinese Question," and Relations of Power in New York City   *125*
John Kuo Wei Tchen

7   Malevolent Assimilation: Immigrants and the Question of American Empire   *154*
Matthew Frye Jacobson

8   From Jim Crow Racism to Laissez-Faire Racism: The Transformation of Racial Attitudes   *182*
Lawrence D. Bobo and Ryan A. Smith

9   Toward an Effective Antiracism   *221*
Nikhil Pal Singh

Afterword: How Shall We Live as Many?   *243*
Kwame Anthony Appiah

Commentary: Race and the American City   *261*
Senator Bill Bradley

Contributors   *271*

Index   *275*

Acknowledgments

This volume emerged from a conference entitled "American Pluralism: Towards a History of the Discussion," held at the State University of New York, at Stony Brook in June 1992. In putting together the conference, we enjoyed the enthusiastic support of Andrew J. Policano, then dean of Social Sciences at Stony Brook, who assisted us in more ways than we can list here. We also gratefully acknowledge Robert Nathans and Barbara Nathans for their moral and financial contributions to the conference and the State University of New York "Conversations in the Disciplines" program for its grant to help defray expenses. Finally, we thank all those who participated in the conference as speakers or commentators, including Richard Alba, Laura Anker, Amiri Baraka, Mia Bay, Thomas Bender, Lizabeth Cohen, Nancy Foner, Ofelia Garcia, George Fouron, William Harris, E. Ann Kaplan, Gretchen Lopez, William Taylor, Nancy Tomes, and Richard Williams.

Several individuals have made important contributions to this volume. We single out Kenneth D. Katkin for his painstaking and detailed checking of citations and thoughtful commentary. We also express great appreciation to Debra Palmese for the care and attention she gave in preparing the essays for publication and for never losing her sense of humor as we edited and reedited. Thanks are extended as well to Eric Mahoney, Johanna Schneider, and Jamie Pomeranz, who performed an endless variety of tasks. Finally, we express our appreciation to Larry Malley, who has been the most patient of all editors and for whom we have only the highest praise.

Beyond Pluralism

Introduction:
The Construction of American Pluralism

Ned Landsman and Wendy F. Katkin

The conference out of which this volume emerged was inspired by what then seemed to be something of an impasse in contemporary discussions of group relations in the United States, brought about by highly charged and dramatically conflicting conceptions of the appropriate parameters for discussing both group identities and group interaction in America. So great was the divide that separated "pluralists" from "multiculturalists," advocates of the academic "canon" from defenders of diversity, and celebrants of ethnic heritage from critics of racial ascription that there seemed to be no obvious way to mediate between them. Our intention was to try to transcend the overly politicized nature of the debate by historicizing the problem, looking at the parameters within which the discussion had developed and the manner in which those seemingly irreconcilable categories had come about. We therefore organized the conference around the history of the *discussion* of group relations in the United States and persuaded an interdisciplinary mix of scholars to examine the way that American conceptions of group interaction had evolved over time into the particular form that they had assumed. The participation of scholars in diverse disciplines demonstrates the continuing centrality of the issue in the United States and reflects the numerous, complex dimensions of the discussion.

The representation of America as a plural society is a good deal older than many contemporaries realize. As far back as the seventeenth century, American was colonized by European settlers of vastly different cultural, religious, and linguistic backgrounds who were forced to come to terms both materially and conceptually with the native inhabitants of the lands they settled, with the African slaves they brought, and with each other. By the time of the American Revolution such writers as J. Hector St. John De Crèvecoeur already were celebrating the creation of a distinctive American identity, differing from others in that it was made up of diverse cultures. Thereafter some form of pluralism became ingrained in American consciousness and established in its fundamental law, which was written in remarkably universal language.[1] Yet tensions over the relationship between the various ethnic and racial groups and a larger collective identity have existed since the nation's founding.

From the beginning, pluralism as a concept was less than universally applied. Crèvecoeur's America combined only European nationalities, as Ned Landsman's essay in this volume suggests, and overwhelmingly Protestant ones at that. There was little room in his conceptual scheme for those of other than European origin. If most Americans assumed the continuing existence of diverse groups in American culture, Stanley N. Katz demonstrates in his essay that the emerging legal framework did little to support their claims against an entrenched liberal philosophy of individual rights and developing aspirations for national unity.

Over the course of the two centuries, the meaning of pluralism has been adapted to markedly altered social and political conditions, including revolution and nationhood, expansion, civil war and emancipation, and wave after wave of "new immigration," as well as the active claims of excluded groups. The boundaries of the American citizenry have been expanded to include additional religious, national, and racial groups, even as it has sometimes excluded others. Under the various labels of nationalism, assimilation, nativism, multiculturalism, and pluralism, American identity has continually been defined as a composite incorporating diverse peoples. What form that incorporation was to take and even who was to be an American have been debated ever since.

For better or for worse, the last several decades have constituted what might be called an age of pluralism in American public discussion. An often-cited point of origin for that period is the publication of Nathan Glazer and Daniel P. Moynihan's *Beyond the Melting Pot* in 1963, which directly challenged the validity of the older, long-entrenched assimilationist paradigm for understanding group life in the United States. The melting pot, they contended, had never really happened; the history of the United States *was* the history of groups and the group identities Americans maintained.[2]

It is sometimes forgotten in current discussions that the metaphor of the melting pot had represented a considerable advance in its day as a progressive alternative to then-prevalent nativist and racist assumptions about the determinants of ethnicity and group life in America, as well as their consequences. If immigrants could be assimilated, they did not have to be excluded. Their cultures were not genetically fixed but were adaptable to the American environment. An important focus of scholarly inquiry in response to the conceptualization of the melting pot thus became the process by which people and cultures adapted themselves to the process of immigration and to the new conditions that surrounded them.[3]

By the time Glazer and Moynihan were writing, some of the shortcomings of the assimilationist model as a tool for social analysis or as a model of group relations had become all too evident. Moreover, those shortcomings were apparent not merely to obviously excluded groups, such as African Americans, but also to many in the mainstream. If the belief in assimilation mitigated some important causes of social injustice, it created or sustained others. It tended to privilege the customs and values of established British and Protestant strands in the American social fabric, as well as those who adhered to essentially Protestant values. It classified as ephemeral, and thereby devalued, a substantial portion of the experiences of those groups whose cultures were not as easily adapted. It rejected as un-American those who valued modes of coexistence other than assimilation. It also often made distinctions on the basis of national origin and especially race. By the mid-twentieth century, there were simply too many Americans who had come to see the exclusive focus of the melting pot, and its assumption of a uniform "American" character to which all should aspire, as hindering rather than helping further their social ambitions.[4]

Beyond the melting pot lay pluralism. Over the last several decades, pluralism has been an effective byword of American culture. If the primary purpose of assimilation was to deemphasize difference, the prevailing principles of pluralism were to recognize, tolerate, and celebrate it. In academic terms, this has meant historians and sociologists of group experience have shifted their focus from assimilation to ethnicity, from the process of acculturation to the dynamics of cultural development. The trend was exemplified in the academy by the 1981 appearance of the *Journal of American Ethnic History,* by the development of ethnic and African American studies programs and institutes at universities throughout the United States, and by the proliferation of studies of a multiplicity of cultural groups in the United States, past and present.[5] Yet, as almost all the essays in this volume make clear, pluralism has important roots in the American past, building on a broader ethic of toleration that preceded and underlay some versions of the melting pot, as well as democratic politics itself.

The near ubiquity of pluralistic expression in contemporary culture has led to more recent criticism, from very different perspectives. To some critics, pluralism has signified the primacy of the particular over the universal, the negation of the aspiration for a common cultural commitment and even the majoritarian assumptions of democratic culture. This has led to calls for the restoration of a common academic canon.[6] To others, the particulars of American pluralism have implicitly valued the cultures of certain groups in American society, especially certain races and ancestries, over others, while failing to find a place for those whose values have deviated from what have been considered American norms. That has been the thrust of a newer set of conceptualizations collectively labeled "multiculturalism," which has generally distanced itself from pluralism largely in a refusal to privilege the normative values often associated with pluralism in the United States.[7] Yet without such a consensus, critics on the other side have asked, what is the basis for coexistence? More often than not, proponents of the two sides have simply talked past one another, as Werner Sollors's essay in this volume details.

The essays in this collection do not attempt to provide a final answer to the problems that pluralism poses. Nor do any of them propose abandoning pluralism altogether as an interpretive framework. Instead, working from their various disciplinary perspectives, they attempt to examine the pluralistic framework as a historical creation, considering where it has come from and the directions in which it might evolve. The essays collectively ask what the pluralist consensus has shared with older conceptions of group relations as they exist in the United States, as well as the ways that it has differed. They compare the way Americans have *talked* about group relations with the ways that they have *experienced* group identities. What distinguishes this collection from other related works on pluralism or multiculturalism is its attempt to look not only at group relations as they exist in the United States today but also at the fundamental ways that group relations have been conceptualized in the American past.[8]

One essential point on which the authors are agreed is that it is *American* pluralism that they are considering rather than pluralism in some pure and ideal form. Its roots go deep into the American past, to the time when Americans first began to articulate their views of the distinguishing features of their societies, which they identified as toleration and inclusion. Its character is embedded in American law and institutions. Yet its principle characteristics have always been integrally related to the specific needs of the larger society within which it existed. Thus, as we shall see, from the beginning of settler society through the age of "white man's democracy" to the era of ethnic celebration, pluralism has functioned not only to include but also to exclude.

The authors are also united in acknowledging that there have been some important inconsistencies in the way Americans have talked about groups. On the one hand, the language of pluralism from the beginning has tended to treat national origin as something fixed and invariable, one of the primary sources of personal identity. Such a view had no precedent in constitutional law, as Stanley N. Katz explains; nor does its rigidity seem wholly consistent with the flexibility and tolerance on which pluralism depends. It relies excessively on a hereditary and implicitly male model of ancestry, traceable principally by surname. On the other hand, Americans have experienced group identities in ways that have been considerably more complex, voluntary, and multilineal, as Mary C. Waters's essay vividly details; mixed and multiple identities are less the exception than the norm for many Americans. That discrepancy also has a long history; indeed, it was part of the process through which the rhetoric of toleration and pluralism was adapted to serve the particular needs of a New World settler society.

American pluralism has confronted a special problem in addressing groups that have typically been identified by racial rather than national origin; the language of ethnic diversity sits uneasily beside the language of race. The very term *ethnic* has often been reserved for Americans of white, usually European ancestry. If ethnicity implies a beneficial cultural heritage in the age of pluralism, the status of race remains more ambiguous, suggesting a more fixed and unyielding legacy, with a strong genetic component that precludes easy assimilation. Yet recent scholars have cogently argued that race itself is less a matter of genetic transmission than of cultural creation and that the attribution of race is related to its functions in racially divided societies.[9]

The very manner in which Americans have defined groups has helped restrain the aspirations of many nonwhite groups, as the essays by Matthew Frye Jacobson, John Kuo Wei Tchen, and Lawrence D. Bobo and Ryan A. Smith detail. The experiences of the Chinese in New York, discussed by Tchen, and of African Americans in the post–civil rights era, as explored by Bobo and Smith, suggest that that has sometimes been the case, even where conscious racism has not been involved. Even positive images of Chinese Americans as a "model minority," Tchen demonstrates, have often been constructed to serve the needs of others and have reinforced the belief in ethnic distinctions. Moreover, dominant expressions of American pluralism have rarely, if ever, taken into account the long-standing and often illuminating perspectives of those African Americans or others who have remained outside of its framework,[10] such as those Nikhil Pal Singh surveys in his essay.

Part of the problem has been an often excessive focus on an immigration model of American group development: the United States is considered solely as a nation of immigrants. An overreliance on such a model has tended to create radical distinctions between those who came to the United States as free men and women and those who came in bondage or—as in the case of many Native Americans—those whose formative experiences did not involve migration, or at least transatlantic migration, at all. If one of the principal historical by-products of the American settlement was the displacement of huge populations, so the settler model of group culture in America displaces and segregates the experiences of peoples whose identifiable ancestors bore a different relation to the settlement process. In short, the immigration model has reinforced the assumption that the experiences of North America's Indian and African American populations, and perhaps the Asian American population as well, were somehow outside the bounds of the central story of American history.[11]

A final point of agreement is the often unspoken assumption on the part of virtually all of the contributors that the evolution of the discussion beyond pluralism should not abandon the important values of toleration, equality, and freedom of expression from which pluralism evolved; rather, these values will have to be even more fundamental features of whatever new conceptions emerge. Like the census respondents Mary C. Waters describes, the authors generally favor a tolerant approach to group identities that allows individuals to emphasize those aspects of their cultural backgrounds that suit their particular needs. They leave considerable room in their analyses for flexible and multiple identities.

The book is divided into two parts. Part 1 consists of broad overviews of the problems of pluralism and identity in American society. Stanley N. Katz begins with a wide-ranging essay that discusses the concept of the group in American constitutional history and points out that for most of American history, groups as entities were denied any positive status in a constitutional tradition dominated by a liberal defense of the rights of individuals. Only in the last few decades have the courts begun to vest in groups a modest measure of rights. Even now, underprivileged groups seeking protections still confront the legacy of an older, negative tradition that viewed group privileges principally as dangers to be guarded against.

The next three essays move from the content of constitutional theory to the language of group identity. Mary C. Waters discusses the way people identify themselves and are identified by the Bureau of the Census. She finds that most respondents employ a much more complex and flexible system of identification than either the Bureau of the Census or most of the language we commonly use to discuss group identities would suggest. She notes also that the ability to choose one's identity is itself something of a privileged position, more readily available to some—predominantly white—groups than to others.

David A. Hollinger follows with a review of the history of the discussion of group relations over the course of the last century, leading to what he calls a "postethnic option." Avoiding both the excessive ethnic particularism inherent in pluralism and the confining universalism of assimilation, Hollinger would, in effect, extend the kind of ethnic voluntarism that Waters finds among many American groups to all of the groups in American society and, just as important, to our way of looking at groups and group identities.

The final essay in this section is by Werner Sollors, who examines the language of recent debates over multiculturalism in American education. He argues that, in a debate dominated by accusation and anecdote, neither side has lived up to the scholarly standards that advocates of the canon so loudly proclaim. Moreover, both have ignored some serious efforts by an earlier generation of liberal social scientists, including some of those Hollinger discusses, to balance the sometimes conflicting goals of tolerance and self-expression. Many of the arguments now offered have been made earlier, and better, by others.

Part 2 is composed of case studies that consider American pluralism as a historical construction. Ned Landsman looks at the origins of American pluralism in the European settler societies of early America. Focusing on one of the earliest and best-known expressions of pluralism, by Crèvecoeur, he explores the connection between the particular character of toleration and group identity as it emerged in early America and the needs of the Protestant, settler society within which it existed. He also notes the limits that both the language of pluralism and the needs of the society imposed on toleration and inclusion.

John Kuo Wei Tchen examines a long history of the depiction of Chinese Americans in popular art forms and the media in New York City. Although those portrayals have varied considerably, Tchen finds that most of the representations, whether positive or negative, have been constructed principally to serve the needs of white American culture and pay scant attention to the actual experiences of Asian Americans. Even the most flattering and welcoming images have often served purposes other than easing Asians into American society.

Matthew Frye Jacobson's essay, like Landsman's, is concerned with the functions of pluralism and assimilation in American culture. Focusing on the experiences of three groups of European immigrants, Jacobson examines the role of foreign affairs in the formation of ethnic identity in the age of the Spanish-American War, noting in particular that the cultivation of American patriotism allowed some European immigrants to make the transition from non-Anglo-Saxon to white American. In the process, the language of inclusion was often replaced with the language of race.

Lawrence D. Bobo and Ryan A. Smith further the discussion of the relationship between pluralism and racism by considering the transition from the Jim Crow racism of an earlier era to what they call "laissez-faire racism." Bobo and Smith contend that recent political economies have attributed the economic marginality of African Americans not to racial but to cultural inferiority, a situation less susceptible to legal remedy within the constitutional traditions that Katz described. The result has been to leave African Americans very much outside a pluralist mainstream still defined by the kind of settler society that Crèvecoeur originally envisioned.

Nikhil Pal Singh shares with Bobo and Smith an interest in the persisting importance of racial categories in American pluralism, even after the decline of the formal trappings of racism. Indeed, Singh might well have borrowed the phrase "laissez-faire racism," but where Bobo and Smith apply it to economic policy, Singh is concerned with cultural politics. The same era that has witnessed a pulling back from a serious antipoverty policy has seen in both the academy and the larger public the emergence of an opposition to all forms of racial preference, including those designed to counter the legacy of formal racism in its legal and cultural forms. The purpose, Singh suggests, has been less to create a truly pluralist culture than to make the "Negro problem," including its principal victims, disappear from public view. Like Hollinger, Singh draws on a long-standing discussion, this one by African American writers, to work toward what he calls an effective antiracist alternative to American pluralism.

Kwame Anthony Appiah supplies an afterword in which he applies the lessons of African history to American pluralism. On the basis of his observations of the recent African past, Appiah argues for both the importance of group constructions as expressions of personal identities and the dangers of reifying and using them as instruments for exclusion. His proposal, much like Hollinger's, is to emphasize the voluntary aspects of group identity, to give all Americans the opportunity to choose the nature of their own identifications, a privilege that Waters suggests many Americans have long claimed for themselves. The goal of choosing traditions and establishing composite identities brings us somewhere near Senator Bill Bradley's closing vision of a society in which groups would be able to acknowledge and experience each other's celebrations and their pains.

Notes

1. Werner Sollors, *Beyond Ethnicity: Consent and Descent in American Culture* (New York: Oxford University Press, 1986), surveys the discussion of ethnicity and pluralism in American culture. Useful collections on the subject of ethnic diversity in early America include Bernard Bailyn and Philip D. Morgan, eds., *Strangers within the Realm: Cultural Margins of the First British Empire* (Chapel Hill: University of North Carolina Press, 1991); and Frank Shuffleton, ed., *A Mixed Race: Ethnicity in Early America* (New York: Oxford University Press, 1993).

2. Nathan Glazer and Daniel P. Moynihan, *Beyond the Melting Pot: The Negroes, Puerto Ricans, Jews, Italians, and Irish of New York City* (Cambridge, Mass.: Harvard University Press, 1963).

3. A classic statement was Oscar Handlin, *The Uprooted: The Epic Story of the Great Migrations That Made the American People* (Boston: Little, Brown, 1951). See also Milton Gordon, *Assimilation in American Life: The Role of Race, Religion, and National Origins* (New York: Oxford University Press, 1964).

4. For discussions of earlier, often similar critiques of assimilation, see David A. Hollinger, "Postethnic America," herein; and Philip Gleason, "The Melting Pot: Symbol of Fusion or Confusion," *American Quarterly* 16 (Spring 1964): 20–46, reprinted in his *Speaking of Diversity: Language and Ethnicity in Twentieth-Century America* (Baltimore, Md.: Johns Hopkins University Press, 1992).

5. James Stuart Olson, *The Ethnic Dimension in American History* (New York: St. Martin's, 1979), was an early attempt at synthesis; the volume of such studies has by now outstripped easy generalization, but see Stephen Thernstrom, Ann Orlov, and Oscar Handlin, eds., *Harvard Encyclopedia of American Ethnic Groups* (Cambridge, Mass.: Harvard University Press, 1980).

6. See, for example, Arthur M. Schlesinger Jr., *The Disuniting of America: Reflections on a Multicultural Society* (New York: W. W. Norton, 1992).

7. See, for example, David Goldberg, ed., *Multiculturalism: A Critical Reader* (Boston: Blackwell, 1984); and *American Quarterly* 45 (June 1993).

8. Other recent collections on diversity that have moved beyond a simple compilation of ethnic profiles to explore discussion and representation include Werner Sollors, ed., *The Invention of Ethnicity* (New York: Oxford University Press, 1989); and Shuffleton, ed., *Mixed Race.*

9. See especially Barbara J. Fields, "Ideology and Race in American History," in *Region, Race and Reconstruction: Essays in Honor of C. Vann Woodward,* ed. J. Morgan Kousser and James M. McPherson (New York: Oxford University Press, 1982), 43–77; Herbert Gans, "Symbolic Ethnicity in America," *Ethnic and Racial Studies* 2 (January 1979): 1–20; and Richard D. Alba, *Ethnic Identity: The Transformation of White America* (New Haven, Conn.: Yale University Press, 1990). Winthrop D. Jordan, *White over Black: American Attitudes toward the Negro, 1550–1812* (Chapel Hill: University of North Carolina Press, 1979), remains the classic analysis of racism, although not of race itself.

10. Interesting examples include Mia Bay, "'The Proud and Selfish Anglo-Saxon': African-American Ideas about White People in the Nineteenth Century" (Paper delivered at the Stony Brook Conference on American Pluralism, June 1992); and Nikhil Pal Singh, "'Race' and 'Nation' in the American Century: A Genealogy of Color and Democracy" (Ph.D. diss., Yale University, 1995).

11. There have been some interesting recent attempts to interpret both Anglo-American and Native American history in ways that bring the common experiences of adjustment and displacement to center stage. See, for example, James H. Merrell, *The Indians' New World: Catawbas and Their Neighbors from European Contact through the Era of Removal* (Chapel Hill: University of North Carolina Press, 1989); and Richard White, *The Middle Ground: Indians, Empires, and Republics in the Great Lakes Region, 1650–1815* (New York: Cambridge University Press, 1991). For the new immigration history that works to integrate immigration into the larger parameters of American history, see especially Virginia Yans-McLaughlin, ed., *Immigration Reconsidered: History, Sociology, and Politics* (New York: Oxford University Press, 1990).

I The Legal Framework of American Pluralism: Liberal Constitutionalism and the Protection of Groups

Stanley N. Katz

The problem considered in this essay is the way the American constitutional system over time has—and has not—accommodated itself to the claims of groups. Traditional legal analysis in the United States has always focused on the individual. When Americans talk about "constitutional rights," they speak almost entirely about individual rights. The basic principle for the protection of individual rights in the American constitutional tradition can probably be described quite simply as the tradition of anti-discrimination: the protection of individuals against discrimination on the basis of violations of what Americans take to be their constitutional rights.

During the past decade Americans devoted considerable effort to celebrating two centuries of American constitutionalism, culminating in 1991 with the commemoration of the two-hundredth anniversary of the Bill of Rights.[1] Yet if one thinks hard about that document, one will recognize how limited it is. The celebrants, of course, did not call attention to its limitations. Justice Thurgood Marshall, to be sure, did note the limitations of the constitutional structure itself in addressing the problem of slavery,[2] but neither he nor anyone else did it very effectively with reference to the Bill of Rights.

The problem is, very simply, that our Bill of Rights, in contrast to every other modern bill of rights, is almost entirely procedural. It has virtually no substantive protections. It is designed for very particular purposes, reflecting especially the concerns of its principal author, James Madison, that it protect personal rights without harming the structure or the strength of the government.[3] The simple solution was to put in place a structure of government and append to that structure a long list of procedural rights.

One could argue that the First Amendment provides substantive protections for speech in several forms and the exercise of religion but not much else. Considered in an international context, the Bill of Rights consists almost entirely of what could be called civil and political rights. In contrast, the U.N. rights regime includes both the International Covenant on Civil and Political Rights[4] and the International Covenant on Economic, Social and Cultural Rights.[5] The idea of social and economic rights is not built into our constitutional structure, nor do we subscribe to a broad universalism of rights.

Not only is there very little content in the Bill of Rights, but even our procedural rights relate almost exclusively to individuals. That has led to our current position on pluralism and group rights. Except for a few instances of groups colliding with the Constitution, mainly in the context of group protection of free speech such as in the famous case of *Near v. Minnesota* or in the more recent instance of the Nazis in Skokie[6]—the United States as a nation has not really come to terms with this sort of problem. An understanding of these issues is essential if we are to move into an era of genuine pluralism, similar to the constructive and integrative view of pluralism that David A. Hollinger has espoused.[7] The critical question is whether it is possible for the legal structure to come to terms with the problem of groups—that is, whether groups will be able to obtain protection and recognition in the legal system in a way that they currently do not.

I review our history in three lengthy and entirely unequal periods, beginning with the long period before the Civil War. During this period pluralism in the sense of protection for groups was entirely outside the constitutional structure. The reason is fairly obvious if one goes back to the original Federalist theories of politics and of representation in political life. The federalism of the Constitution embodies a liberalism prevalent at the end of the eighteenth and the early nineteenth centuries, which was concerned principally with individuals and with rights: "life, liberty, and property," in John Locke's famous formulation, or the right to pursue that form of social peace and prosperity that the eighteenth century referred to as "happiness."

For the most part, what has come to be called "classical republicanism," emphasizing not the freedom of individuals from the intrusions of government but rather the freedom of citizens collectively to participate in defending and governing the state, finds very little place in the actual constitutional structure, particularly as it is interpreted by the courts.[8] Moreover, whatever republicanism there was very quickly disappeared as an effective constitutional mechanism. A principal reason for that disappearance lies in constitutional practice. Until the Civil War, constitutional rights were limited to citizens, and the definition of who were citizens was very restrictive.[9] Citizenship was limited to members of the political community, which was designed quite explicitly to be exclusionary, consisting of only adult white males—and not all of them either. In other words, the assignment of citizenship did not start from the point of inclusion; the nation granted rights only to those who were explicitly included in the political community.[10]

Citizenship denoted the right and obligation of members of the political community to take part in the political process. Constitutionalism itself was defined as the conduct of political right—the right to participate in the political process. This view is consistent with minimalist notions of constitutional rights. The only effective way in which groups functioned in this structure was in federalism itself, in the notion of states as groups. There was not even a way to constitutionalize political parties in the United States, which have been among the most important groups.

Among the most striking aspects of the Constitution is its nonrecognition of one important group, African American slaves. The framers were quite worried about the issue of slavery. The Constitution refers to slaves as a group five times, always euphemistically.[11] As the legal tradition—not so much the constitutional tradition—began to develop in the early nineteenth century, it was difficult to find ways even to justify corporations and other kinds of legal groups, but of course we did. Voluntary groups—business corporations, churches, charitable organizations of the one sort or another—most of them incorporated, began to find their way into the legal tradition. When the Supreme Court finally found a way to talk about them, it did so largely in terms of business or contract. In other words, a key element of the country's constitutional history in the early nineteenth century was the inability of the constitutional structure to address group rights. All of the reform movements of the period confronted difficulties that resulted from the inability of the legal and constitutional structure to break out of its liberal foundations.

The second period to be considered lasted from 1865 to 1954, from Reconstruction until the famous Supreme Court decision *Brown v. Board of Education.*[12] This period began with the enactment and ratification of the Thirteenth, Fourteenth, and Fifteenth amendments, which started to come to terms with the legal structural problems that groups in the United States faced. Section 1 of the Fourteenth Amendment, ratified in 1868, provides that "[a]ll persons born or naturalized in the United States, and subject to the jurisdiction thereof, are citizens of the United States and of the State wherein they reside." That made birth and naturalization the primary qualifications for citizenship to a degree that they had not been previously.[13] Toward the end of section 1, the Fourteenth Amendment also provided citizens with new kinds of protections that would become absolutely critical later, but it granted these protections in particular terms. No state was to "deny to any person within its jurisdiction the equal protection of the laws." The Fifteenth Amendment expanded on the Fourteenth Amendment by endowing all citizens with the right to vote.[14]

In principle, the Fourteenth Amendment should have begun to solve the problem of group rights through its prescription of "equal protection," which could have provided the basis for aggregations of individuals to obtain constitutional protections. At the very least, African Americans—the group the three Civil War amendments were primarily enacted to protect—should have obtained such protection. To some extent, they did.[15] But in a group of five civil rights cases decided jointly in 1883, the Supreme Court effectively took the teeth out of the ability of the Fourteenth Amendment to protect the rights of African Americans by holding that the Fourteenth Amendment did not empower Congress to enact civil rights legislation designed to eliminate "private" discrimination.[16] Focusing on the words, "No State shall," with which the amendment began, the Court held that the amendment empowered Congress to legislate only with regard to *state* action, not *private* conduct. In so holding, the Court editorialized, "When a man has emerged from slavery, and by the aid of beneficent legislation has shaken off the inseparable concomitants of that state, there must be some stage in the progress of his elevation when he takes the rank of a mere citizen, and ceases to be the special favorite of the laws, and when his rights as a citizen, or a man, are to be protected in the ordinary modes by which other men's rights are protected."[17] So much for special protections.

The Court's ruling created a situation in which the equality provision in the Constitution could be (and was) used by the Supreme Court mainly for a very special category of groups: business corporations. There was a special legal irony in this situation, since Anglo-American law considered the corporation as an individual in order to confer the privileges and protections of individuals on those groups the law permitted to be incorporated. By and large those were the groups favored and protected by the Fourteenth Amendment through much of this period.[18]

In the jurisprudence of the Fourteenth Amendment, there were two principal results. The Supreme Court had to find a basis for permitting useful state legislation that was discriminatory against groups. It did that by allowing any state legislation rationally related to a legitimate state purpose, and effectuating that purpose, to survive constitutional scrutiny, even if the legislation had an unfavorable impact on groups.[19] On that basis, the Court allowed all kinds of group discriminations to survive.

The Court also continued to apply the "state action" threshold laid out in the *Civil Rights Cases* to any group protection claim.[20] To prevail when claiming unconstitutional discrimination, a group needed to show that the discrimination was the direct result of state action. Such a standard did not exist in the language of the Fourteenth Amendment,[21] and it proved to be an incredibly hard threshold to pass, but it was quite consistent with the persistence of group discrimination in the United States in the late nineteenth century. The most obvious examples are the long-standing immigration restrictions imposed on Asians;[22] the anti-Mormon discrimination in the *Reynolds* decision, which ruled that polygamy was not protected by the free exercise clause of the First Amendment;[23] and, in the twentieth century, the Japanese relocation the Supreme Court condoned in the *Korematsu* case.[24]

Our tradition, in other words, became at least partly one of constitutional discrimination against groups rather than protection of them, and it was based on the growing prescription of individual equality and equal protection of the laws. (The major exception to this generalization is the law of affirmative action, discussed later.) This prescription persisted into the twentieth century, and the discrimination is against a great variety of groups. To give an example, in 1921, responding to a 1913 Arizona statute passed to protect labor unions, the Supreme Court ruled that Arizona had no right to enact such protection.[25] The law was intended to protect the right of labor unions to engage in peaceful picketing, but the Court decided that picketing was a violation of property rights and that the Fourteenth Amendment would therefore not apply. The Fourteenth Amendment, the judges reasoned, was intended to give equality of protection not only for all but against all similarly situated. Protection, the Court argued, is not protection unless the state meets this equal obligation to everyone. In other words, it was not the group that needed protection, but rather everyone who was not in the group needed to be protected against the group. That ruling was characteristic of the prevailing constitutional way of thinking about groups. That is a very strong element in our constitutional history. *Plessy v. Ferguson*—the decision that allowed the provision of "separate but equal" public facilities—was another example of the same sort of thing.[26]

Occasionally, the Court did act to protect groups. Perhaps the two most interesting cases involved religious groups: *Meyer v. Nebraska* and *Pierce v. Society of Sisters*. In *Meyer,* the court struck down a Nebraska statute that prohibited teaching modern foreign languages to children in elementary schools. The court grounded its decision on the Fourteenth Amendment, particularly its guarantee of liberty—liberty in this case was the liberty to bring up one's children in accordance to the dictates of one's own conscience.[27] The *Pierce* case involved an Oregon statute that required all children between the ages of eight and sixteen to attend public schools. The Society of Sisters claimed that children ought to be able to go to religious schools or private schools instead. The Court struck down the statute for violating the rights of the parents, without considering whether it also violated any rights of the children.[28]

Cases involving group rights were usually decided under the First or Fourteenth amendments and were often resolved on curious and narrow grounds. The shift in thinking toward a more modern and progressive conception of groups really did not take place until the late 1930s. Prior to World War II, there was little constitutional basis for protecting groups, except that African Americans were to be protected for some purposes and in some situations.

The change in the conception of groups was foreshadowed in 1938 in the most famous footnote in the history of U.S. constitutional law, at least

until 1954. In a footnote in the *Carolene Products* case, Chief Justice Harlan Fiske Stone asserted the need to protect those groups that might not
be able to protect themselves in the political process:

> There may be narrower scope for operation of the presumption of consti-
> tutionality when legislation appears on its face to be within a specific pro-
> hibition of the Constitution, such as those of the first ten Amendments,
> which are deemed equally specific when held to be embraced within the
> Fourteenth. . . .
>
> It is unnecessary to consider now whether legislation which restricts
> those political processes which can ordinarily be expected to bring about
> repeal of undesirable legislation, is to be subjected to more exacting judi-
> cial scrutiny under the general prohibitions of the Fourteenth Amendment
> than are most other types of legislation. . . .
>
> Nor need we enquire whether similar considerations enter into the re-
> view of statutes directed at particular religious, or national, or racial mi-
> norities, whether prejudice against discrete and insular minorities may be
> a special condition, which tends seriously to curtail the operation of those
> political processes ordinarily to be relied upon to protect minorities, and
> which may call for a correspondingly more searching judiciary inquiry.[29]

Chief Justice Stone's remarks have become the primary basis for all
subsequent attempts to provide protection for groups in U.S. constitutional law.[30] It is significant that Justice Stone used the term *minorities.*
Under Madisonian Federalist theory, groups were "factions," seeking to
advance their parochial interests at the expense of the public interest and
were therefore to be resisted.[31] But another goal of the Constitution was
to counter the tyranny of the majority. In *Carolene Products,* Chief Justice Stone sought to conceive of groups and to assign a special claim to
protect certain kinds of them, based on the failure of political and constitutional processes. The groups to which he referred were "discrete and
insular minorities," what lawyers and some sociologists would call "involuntary groups,"[32] groups to which individuals belong, not by choice
but because of their gender, race, or other attributes derived from birth.
Those groups might be able to claim special protection.

In the fifteen years following *Carolene Products,* very little case law drew
on Justice Stone's thinking. Some protection for involuntary groups was
achieved through legislation, but little came from the courts. The most
hopeful sign came at the end of this period, in 1943, in *Shelley v. Kraemer,*
which involved an attempt to overturn a racially "restrictive covenant."[33]

The plaintiffs, who sought to purchase the property at issue, claimed that judicial enforcement of the restrictive covenant would violate the Fourteenth Amendment. Ever since the *Civil Rights Cases* of 1883, such claims against the actions of private parties had normally failed, on the ground that no state action was involved.

In *Shelley,* however, the Court held that enforcement of the contract violated the Fourteenth Amendment because "the purposes of the agreements were secured only by judicial enforcement by state courts of the restrictive terms of the agreements."[34] The Court carefully noted that the cases before it were not ones in which states had merely abstained from action. Rather, the Court saw the cases as ones "in which the States have made available to such individuals the full coercive power of government to deny to petitioners, on the grounds of race or color, the enjoyment of property rights. . . ."[35] By implicitly redefining "state action" to include action taken by state courts enforcing private contracts as well as action taken by state legislatures, the Court offered some victims of private discrimination a way around the burdensome "state action" requirement. Perhaps this decision marked the beginning of the Court's recognition that there had to be a bridging of the state action threshold if groups were to be effectively protected by the Constitution.

This line of reasoning was pursued more rigorously in 1954 in *Brown v. Board of Education.*[36] *Brown* represented the first time in American history in which substantive equality entered the Supreme Court's jurisprudence. The potential for enforcing equality had inhered in the Constitution since 1868, but, except for a few scattered cases,[37] it was not effected. In *Plessy v. Ferguson,* for example, the concept of "separate but equal" represented a beginning toward equal protection of laws of the Constitution,[38] but from 1954 there is substance to "equal protection" and thus potential constitutional protection for the rights of certain groups. Although there is actually nothing in *Brown* itself that would indicate it ought to have gone in this direction, the Court did extend these protections to groups other than African Americans. Two groups ("suspect categories") brought thoroughly under the rubric of what is known as "strict scrutiny"—the highest level of protection for groups deriving from Justice Stone's *Carolene Products* footnote—were illegitimate children and aliens.[39] After the late 1950s, aliens received precisely the same constitutional protection that citizens did—a quite staggering development in the light of our original political and constitutional theories of citizenship.

During the 1960s the Supreme Court seemed to be moving in the direction of providing equal protection to women as a group, but in the next decade it drew back. There were many cases testing whether discrimination against women would be judged by the harsh standards of "strict scrutiny," but by the late 1970s it became clear that while some protection would be given to women as a group, gender would not be considered a "suspect" category,[40] deserving the "strict scrutiny" that imposes a heavy burden of justification on the state. The same was true for certain other groups that tried to get in under the tent. Arguments were made that the economically deprived, for example, should be recognized as a suspect category.[41] Such claims of group protection represented a way of thinking of pluralism that was very different from anything in our historic constitutional tradition. Significantly, however, the most effective protection for groups came not from the Court but from the Congress, in the form of the Civil Rights Acts of 1964 and the Voting Rights Act of 1965.[42] There had not been any civil rights acts from the 1880s until 1957, when very weak legislation was followed by a whole series of acts.

It was a combination of statutory language and judicial lawmaking that produced the most socially significant type of group protection—affirmative action. This concept permitted "affirmative discrimination" in favor of those "discrete and insular minorities," which were also the primary beneficiaries of constitutional protection against negative discrimination. Affirmative action plans in the contexts of employment, business opportunity, broadcasting, admissions to educational institutions, and other areas of life in which minorities had been discriminated against provided special access for those who were underrepresented in proportion to their numbers in the general population. For political liberals, affirmative action offered an opportunity to compensate groups that had previously suffered discrimination for the harm they had suffered, and it helped them to make up lost ground. For political conservatives, however, affirmative action seemed to contradict the liberal antidiscrimination principle that lay at the heart of the *Brown* revolution.

For a decade or so, in such cases as *Griggs v. Duke Power Company,* the Supreme Court upheld the constitutionality of affirmative action plans, although not in all instances.[43] By 1976, however, in the case of *Washington v. Davis,* which involved a challenge to a police force entrance examination in Washington, D.C., the Court began to reverse itself by holding that the test of constitutionality for affirmative action schemes should be the nature of the intention of the alleged discriminators rather than the real-life effects of their actions.[44] In this case, for instance, since the African American applicants for the police force could not show that the test that had disqualified them was intentionally racially discriminatory, they were denied relief, even though they could demonstrate that the test effectively screened out blacks. To this day, the *Washington v. Davis* intentionality test has served to limit the effectiveness of affirmative action and thus affirmative protection for group rights.

Apart from affirmative action, there have been few constitutional cases in the Supreme Court since the civil rights acts that were explicitly protective of groups. One of them, *Wisconsin v. Yoder,* goes back to religious tradition before *Brown.*[45] It involved a claim by Old Order Amish people in Wisconsin to the right to remove their children from public schools after the eighth grade because they considered the entire high school curriculum to be sacrilegious. While the Court in *Yoder* decided that the Amish did have this right, Justice Douglas, dissenting, observed that there was a fundamental conflict hidden in the case. Specifically, he feared that in deciding in favor of the Amish, "the Court's analysis assumes that the only interests at stake in the case are those of the Amish parents on the one hand, and those of the State on the other."[46] Noting that "[r]eligion is an individual experience," however, Justice Douglas suggested that the court might be protecting the rights of Amish parents rather than those of their children.[47] His concerns reflected the bind the Court confronted in deciding religious freedom cases. Given the First Amendment tradition and its emphasis on freedom from interference by government, that is not very surprising.

In a relatively recent case, subsequently overturned, the Supreme Court defended legislation giving preference to minorities in the assignment of broadcasting outlets, on the grounds that the market was likely not to produce a sufficient diversity and that the Federal Communications Commission was therefore entitled to favor minority applications.[48] This short-lived ruling was one of very few decisions supporting group rights in recent years. Another, less happy, case was *Moose Lodge No. 107 v. Irvis,* a Pennsylvania case in which an African American sued a local Moose Lodge that refused to allow him to be a guest of the lodge or to have a drink there because of his race.[49] The Court decided that, as a private association, Moose Lodge Number 107 was entitled to exclude Irvis on the basis of race, even though in this locality there were only a limited number of liquor licenses. In this case, the group protected was the white membership of Moose Lodge 107, against a member of another group.

On the whole, the period from 1964 to the present has been one of retreat from the group protections of the post–World War era and the Warren Court. A good example was the famous Virginia case *City of Richmond v. J. A. Croson.*[50] Richmond had a program that gave preference to minority contractors. The Supreme Court ruled that that preference unconstitutionally discriminated in favor of a particular group. Its rationale was that unless a plaintiff could show explicit discrimination against members of a group, there were no constitutional grounds to favor that group. That line of reasoning, of course, underscores the whole affirmative action problem. The Court's actions in withdrawing protection from groups unless the group can show intentional discrimination is a radical shift back in the direction of 1954.

It seems clear that for the foreseeable future, the Supreme Court is likely to move only backward, not forward, on this question. We are unlikely to see any expansion or fulfillment of what was to be the promise of the *Brown* decision. In practical terms, that means that groups other than those already embedded in the special protection of the Fourteenth Amendment are not likely to be included in it and that the contest is likely to be fought out in the Congress rather than in the Court.

The difficulty is that we now are thinking about groups differently than we did a long time ago. The pattern is much more complicated. While there is a good deal of thinking and writing about the need to rethink pluralism in the context of a United States that is becoming increasingly nonwhite and non-English-speaking, there is also growing popular sentiment for immigration restriction (such as Proposition 187 in California)[51] that sometimes seems to verge on nativism (as in Patrick Buchanan's rhetoric in the February 1996 New Hampshire presidential primary).

How to think about groups has become a real challenge for people who think about constitutional law. The commitment we have to the distinction between public and private is likely to continue to discourage the constitutionalization of voluntary rights, despite the rhetoric of support we have for this in the public sector. In real life, the distinction between public and private is not very strong. We have drawn arbitrary lines between them that have taken on a legal reality and have completely confused our general perspective on the subject. We have also distinguished (constitutionally) between involuntary groups and other kinds of groups.

We privilege voluntary groups in our thinking for many purposes, but we do not know how to incorporate them in the constitutional structure. That is because of the radical individualism of the way our legal system is articulated.

The question, then, becomes, what theory can be used to justify public status protection for voluntary groups as well as for those involuntary groups? Kathleen M. Sullivan, a Stanford law professor, has used the expression "Rainbow Republicanism" in criticizing the scholarship of two other celebrated law professors who have rediscovered republican political theory in American history.[52] Yet American society is made up of groups, and groups do require legal and constitutional protection to defend their integrity.

The key point is that "the people" are not necessarily coextensive with "the citizenry"; communities are composed of several peoples linked politically. A people is an internally unified collectivity standing between individuals and the political community. We will somehow have to incorporate that sort of definition into constitutional notions of pluralism and equality if we are to transcend the liberal individualism of the constitution and achieve the kind of postethnicity that David A. Hollinger posits.[53] That seems to me to be our most significant constitutional challenge. Our purpose has always been to privilege the individual and individual rights, but always from one of two points of view: as an actor in the political process or as an actor in the economic process. If we want to promote values other than the political or the economic, we are going to have to find a way to articulate other kinds of rights within the constitutional community. Democracy has been defined as "having faith in strangers." The question is, can constitutional democracy in the late twentieth century operate on the basis of having faith in groups other than one's own?

Notes

1. U.S. Constitution, Amendments 1–10.

2. See Stuart Taylor Jr., "Marshall Sounds Critical Note on Bicentennial," *New York Times,* May 7, 1978.

3. Alexander Hamilton, *The Federalist,* No. 84 (New York: Bantam Books, 1982), 438.

4. International Covenant on Civil and Political Rights, opened for signature, December 16, 1966, U.N.T.S. 171, 6 I.L.M. 368 (entered into force March 23, 1976), in *International Bill of Human Rights* (New York: United Nations, 1978), 21–39.

5. International Covenant on Economic, Social and Cultural Rights, opened for signature, December 16, 1966, 993 U.N.T.S. 3, 6 I.L.M. 360 (entered into force January 3, 1976), in *International Bill of Human Rights*, 10–20.

6. *Near v. Minnesota*, 283 U.S. 697 (1931), upholds the right of a "scandal sheet" to publish anti-Semitic attacks on local politicians.

7. David A. Hollinger in his essay argues for a "postethnic" America, in which "affiliation on the basis of shared descent would be voluntary rather than prescribed." See also David A. Hollinger, *Postethnic America: Beyond Multiculturalism* (New York: Basic Books, 1995).

8. On the republican tradition, see especially J. G. A. Pocock, *The Machiavellian Moment: Florentine Political Thought and the Atlantic Republican Tradition* (Princeton, N.J.: Princeton University Press, 1975); on its relation to the U.S. Constitution, see Gordon S. Wood, *The Creation of the American Republic, 1776–1787* (Chapel Hill: University of North Carolina Press, 1969).

9. See, for example, *Dred Scott v. Sandford*, 60 U.S. (19 How.) 393, 404 (1857), which held that African American slaves and their descendants "are not included, and were not intended to be included, under the word 'citizens' in the Constitution, and can therefore claim none of the rights and privileges which that instrument provides for and secures to citizens of the United States." See also James H. Kettner, *The Development of American Citizenship, 1608–1870* (Chapel Hill: University of North Carolina Press, 1978).

10. At the same time, although suffrage was extended to only propertied white men in the early days of the United States, other rights of citizenship (e.g., the common-law rights of property, contract, and tort and the protection of the criminal laws and law enforcement) were extended to *all* white men and to unmarried white women and even children.

11. See the "three-fifths compromise," U.S. Constitution, Article 1, §2, cl. 3: "Representatives and direct taxes . . . shall be determined by adding to the whole Number of free Persons . . . excluding Indians not taxed, three fifths of *all other Persons*" (emphasis added); the "grandfather clause," U.S. Constitution, Article 1, §9, cl. 1: "The Migration or Importation of *such Persons as any of the States now existing shall think proper to admit, shall not be prohibited* by Congress prior to the Year [1808] . . ." (emphasis added); the "fugitive slave law," U.S. Constitution, Article 4, §2, cl. 3: "No *Person held to Service or Labor* in one state, under the Laws thereof, escaping into another, shall . . . be discharged from such Service or Labor, but shall be delivered up on Claim of the Party to whom such Service or Labor may be due" (emphasis added); constitutional amendments, U.S. Constitution, Article 5 (constitutional amendments are valid after being ratified by three-fourths of the states, "provided that no Amendment which may be made prior to the year [1808] shall in any Manner affect [the 'grandfather clause' in Article 1, §9, cl. 1]"); and African American suffrage, U.S. Constitution, Amendment 15, §1: "The right of citizens of the United States to vote shall not be denied or abridged by the United States or by any State on account of *race, color, or previous condition of servitude*" (emphasis added). The word *slavery* does

not appear in the Constitution until the Thirteenth Amendment, which abolishes it (U.S. Constitution, Amendment 13, §1).

12. *Brown v. Board of Education,* 347 U.S. 483 (1954), supplemented by 349 U.S. 294 (1955).

13. Prior to this provision, it was unclear exactly who qualified for U.S. citizenship, and states were free to set their own criteria for state citizenship.

14. Section 1 of the Fifteenth Amendment provides that "[t]he right of citizens of the United States shall not be denied or abridged by the United States or by any State on account of race, color, or previous condition of servitude."

15. See, for example, *Strauder v. West Virginia,* 100 U.S. 303 (1880), which holds that the equal protection clause forbids a state from excluding African Americans from jury service and overturns the conviction of an African American criminal defendant by an all-white jury; and *Ex Parte Virginia,* 100 U.S. 339 (1880), which affirms the criminal conviction and prison sentence of a Virginia county court judge for purposely excluding African Americans from jury service.

16. *Civil Rights Cases,* 109 U.S. 3 (1883), 25.

17. Ibid., 25.

18. See, for example, *Allgeyer v. Louisiana,* 165 U.S. 578 (1897), striking down a state statute making it illegal for any person to contract with an insurance company not licensed to do business in the state; *Lochner v. New York,* 198 U.S. 45 (1905), striking down a state statute requiring bakers to be paid time-and-a-half after working a sixty-hour week; *Adair v. United States,* 208 U.S. 161 (1908), striking down a federal law making it a criminal offense for a railroad to fire an employee simply for joining a labor union; and *Adkins v. Children's Hospital,* 261 U.S. 525 (1923), striking down the District of Columbia's minimum-wage law for women. But see *Muller v. Oregon,* 208 U.S. 412 (1908), upholding a state maximum-hour law for women; *Bunting v. Oregon,* 243 U.S. 426 (1917), upholding a state maximum-hour law for men; and *Nebbia v. New York,* 291 U.S. 502 (1934), upholding a state price floor for milk.

19. See, for example, *Plessy v. Ferguson,* 163 U.S. 537 (1896), upholding the Louisiana statute requiring segregated railroad cars on the grounds that the statute protected the public health and morale; and *Cumming v. Board of Education,* 173 U.S. 528 (1899), upholding the local school board's discretion to not fund a black high school, on the grounds that intervening would constitute unjustifiable federal interference with local school authorities.

20. *Civil Rights Cases,* 109 U.S. 3 (1883).

21. Section 1 of the Fourteenth Amendment states, "No *State* shall . . . deny to any person within its jurisdiction the equal protection of the laws" (emphasis added).

22. See, for example, the Chinese Exclusion Act of 1882, chap. 126, 22 Stat. 58 (repealed in 1943); the Chinese Exclusion Act of 1888, chap. 1064, 25 Stat. 504 (repealed in 1943); and the Exclusion Act of 1902, chap. 641, 32 Stat. 176 (repealed in 1943). These acts were upheld by the Supreme Court in *Ping v. United States,* 130 U.S. 581 (1889), and *Fong Yue Ting v. United States,* 149 U.S. 698, 730 (1893), which upheld the depor-

tation of Chinese laborers under the Chinese Exclusion Act. The exclusion acts were finally repealed by Congress on December 17, 1943, chap. 344, 57 Stat. 600.

23. *Reynolds v. United States,* 98 U.S. 145, 166 (1878), held that while laws "cannot interfere with mere religious belief and opinions, they may with practices."

24. *Korematsu v. United States,* 321 U.S. 214 (1944) upheld the World War II military order requiring all Californians of Japanese descent to relocate to detention camps for the remainder of the war. See also *Hirabayashi v. United States,* 320 U.S. 81 (1943), which upheld a wartime curfew order that applied only to Japanese Americans.

25. *Truax v. Corrigan,* 257 U.S. 312 (1921).

26. *Plessy v. Ferguson,* 163 U.S. 537 (1896), was overruled by *Brown v. Board of Education,* 347 U.S. 483 (1954).

27. *Meyer v. Nebraska,* 262 U.S. 390 (1923).

28. *Pierce v. Society of Sisters,* 268 U.S. 510 (1925).

29. *United States v. Carolene Products Co.,* 304 U.S. 152–53n4 (1938).

30. See John Hart Ely, *Democracy and Distrust* (Cambridge, Mass.: Harvard University Press, 1980), 75–88, who presents a fully developed, process-based "representation reinforcement" theory of judicial review that is essentially a book-length exegesis of Chief Justice Stone's footnote four in *Carolene Products.*

31. James Madison, *The Federalist,* No. 10 (New York: Bantam Books, 1982), 43, defines a "faction" as "a number of citizens, whether amounting to a majority or minority of the whole, who are united and actuated by some common impulse of passion, or of interest, adverse to the rights of other citizens, or to the permanent and aggregate interests of the community."

32. Kathleen M. Sullivan, "Rainbow Republicanism Symposium: The Republic, a Civic Tradition," *Yale Law Journal* 97 (July 1988): 1713.

33. *Shelley v. Kraemer,* 334 U.S. 4 (1948). Restrictive covenants were described by the Court as "private agreements . . . which have as their purpose the exclusion of persons of designated race or color from the ownership or occupancy of real property."

34. Ibid., 13–14.

35. Ibid., 19.

36. *Brown v. Board of Education,* 347 U.S. 483 (1954), supplemented by 349 U.S. 294 (1955).

37. See, for example, *Strauder v. West Virginia,* 100 U.S. 303 (1880); and *Gibson v. Mississippi,* 162 U.S. 564 (1896), both of which held that the equal protection clause forbade a state from excluding African Americans from jury duty and overturned an all-white jury's conviction of an African American; *Yick Wo v. Hopkins,* 118 U.S. 356 (1886), which struck down a municipal ordinance regulating the laundry industry that was neutral on its face but was administered in a way that discriminated against Chinese American cleaners; and *Steele v. Louisville & Nashville R.R. Co.,* 323 U.S. 192 (1944), which held that a labor union acting under authority of the Railway

Labor Act as the exclusive bargaining representative of railway employees had a duty to represent *all* railway employees without discriminating on the basis of race and that courts had jurisdiction to protect minorities from the violation of such obligation.

38. *Plessy v. Ferguson,* 163 U.S. 537 (1896), overruled by *Brown v. Board of Education,* 347 U.S. 483 (1954).

39. For illegitimate children, see *Weber v. Aptna Casualty and Surety Co.,* 406 U.S. 164, 175–176 (1972). (But see *Matthews v. Lucas,* 427 U.S. 495, 505–506 [1976], which reduces the protection of illegitimate children to intermediate scrutiny.) For aliens, see *Graham v. Richardson,* 403 U.S. 365, 372 (1971), citing *Carolene Products Co.,* 304 U.S. 152–53n4 (1938), which holds that "classifications based on alienage, like those based on nationality or race, are inherently suspect and subject to close judicial scrutiny. Aliens as a class are a prime example of a 'discrete and insular' minority for whom such heightened judicial solicitude is appropriate."

40. See, for example, *Reed v. Reed,* 404 U.S. 71 (1971), striking down statutory preference of men over women as administrators of estates; *Frontiero v. Richardson,* 411 U.S. 677 (1973), striking down a military benefits scheme that allowed servicemen to claim their wives as dependents but allowed servicewomen to claim their husbands as dependents only upon showing their husbands were actually dependant; and *Craig v. Boren,* 429 U.S. 190 (1976), striking down a state "drinking age" statute that allowed women to purchase beer at eighteen but made men wait until twenty-one.

41. See, for example, *Maher v. Roe,* 432 U.S. 464, 471 (1977), rejecting such a claim.

42. Civil Rights Act of 1964, Public Law No. 88–352, 78 Stat. 241 (codified as amended at 2 U.S.C. §1311, 28 U.S.C. §1447, 42 U.S.C. §§1971, 1975a to 1975d, 2000a to 2000h-6 [1994]); Voting Rights Act of 1965, Public Law No. 89–110, 85, 79 Stat. 437, codified as amended at 42 U.S.C. §§1971, 1973 to 1973ff-6 (1994).

43. *Griggs v. Duke Power Company,* 401 U.S. 424 (1971), which held that the Civil Rights Act of 1964 may require private employers to engage in some affirmative action as a remedy for past employment discrimination. It should be noted, however, that the *Griggs* case was not decided on constitutional grounds. In *Griggs* the changed plans were claimed to have violated not the Constitution but the Civil Rights Act of 1964.

44. *Washington v. Davis,* 426 U.S. 229 (1976).

45. *Wisconsin v. Yoder,* 406 U.S. 205 (1972).

46. Ibid., 241 (Douglas).

47. Ibid., 243 (Douglas).

48. *Metro Broadcasting v. FCC,* 497 U.S. 547 (1990), overruled by *Adarand Constructors v. Pena,* 115 S. Ct. 2097 (1995).

49. *Moose Lodge No. 107 v. Irvis,* 407 U.S. 163 (1972).

50. *City of Richmond v. J. A. Croson Co.,* 488 U.S. 469 (1989).

51. Proposition 187: Initiative Statute—Illegal Aliens—Public Services, Verification, and Reporting, 5–8, 1994 Cal. Legis. Serv. Prop. 187 (West) (approved by voters November 8, 1994, and codified in scattered sections of the California Code). A tem-

porary injunction against enforcement of most of the provisions in Proposition 187 was granted in *League of United Latin American Citizens v. Wilson,* 908 F Supp. 755 (C.D. Cal. 1995), and is still in effect.

52. Sullivan, "Rainbow Republicanism Symposium," 1713. See also Frank Michelman, "Law's Republic" and "Beyond the Republican Revival," *Yale Law Journal* 97 (1988): 1539, 1574–75.

53. Hollinger, "Postethnic America," herein.

2 Multiple Ethnic Identity Choices

Mary C. Waters

An increasing proportion of the population of the United States can claim multiple ethnic or racial identities, and the proportion of the population with multiple identities is bound to increase in the future because of rising intermarriage rates. The existence of people with multiple identities has important implications for American cultural pluralism. A pluralist society is predicated on the existence of separate ethnic and racial groups and on specific modes of political and social accommodations among those groups. Since 1965 the American accommodation among groups has increasingly involved counting and classifying our racial and ethnic minorities. This essay explores some of the implications of mixed-race and mixed-ancestry people for such procedures and speculates about the long-run tensions between political and social pluralist ideologies and such social processes as intermarriage.

Although ethnicity and race were sometimes conceptualized as biological or fixed characteristics of individuals, there is now general consensus in social science writing on the subject that ethnicity and race are social constructs.[1] Racial and ethnic identities are socially constructed through a complex interaction between individuals and their societies—between self-identification and other identifications. The boundaries between groups are consequently variable—both across societies and in particular societies because of different historical circumstances. The sharp division between black and white in the United States thus contrasts with the finely graded distinctions among different shades and admixtures in the Caribbean and Latin America.

One of the most important factors affecting the social classification system of race and ethnicity in a society is the system of rules governing the identities of people of mixed ethnic and racial backgrounds. Historically, in the United States, the offspring of black-white unions have been forced to identify as black through the "one drop rule." The offspring of those belonging to other races, such as Native Americans and Asians, married to whites have generally been classified as nonwhite, but with far less vigilance and certitude. The offspring of mixed ethnicities—German and English, for example—have had no formal societal pressures to identify one way or another.[2]

Currently the social rule in the United States governing racial and ethnic identity is self-identification. It is generally accepted that individuals are allowed to choose their own identification for administrative purposes, for reporting to the Census Bureau, and the like. For a large portion of the population, this involves some degree of choice. There are three types of multiple racial and ethnic identities that involve some degree of individual choice.

First, some people are of mixed racial or ethnic ancestry. These are individuals who are the offspring of an intermarriage or the progeny of individuals who were of mixed ancestry. For instance, a person who is part Italian and part German and Irish can identify with one, all, or none of these ancestries in everyday life or when queried in a survey. Those who have origins defined racially in the United States, for instance a person who is part Native American and part black, also have a degree of choice in their identity but generally less choice than those who are defined ethnically. David A. Hollinger illustrates this point clearly in his discussion of the constraints Alex Haley faced in finding his "roots" in his African American heritage and not his Irish American heritage.[3]

Second, there are people of unmixed origins but those origins can be defined in various ways and on different levels of inclusiveness. For instance, black immigrants from Jamaica to New York City can identify as Jamaican, West Indian, or black. People from Puerto Rico can identify as Puerto Rican, Latino or Hispanic, and white or black.

Finally, there are people who feel free to choose to identify with an ancestry or ethnicity or to choose to be just American. In general in the

United States, those who are nonwhite racially have not been granted this opportunity by society but have been identified racially *by* others even if they wanted to disregard their racial or ethnic identity. However, some in the white population who may or may not know where their ancestors came from have the choice to call themselves white or American or merely to be "unhyphenated."[4]

While all three of these sources of many identities can be significant in shaping the future of racial or ethnic groups, I focus on the first category—people who have mixed racial or ethnic ancestries. What are the implications of mixed ancestries for the subject of this volume—American pluralism?

The sociologist Milton Gordon has defined pluralism in the following way:

> Pluralism refers to a national society in which various groups, each with a psychological sense of its own historical peoplehood, maintain some structural separation from each other in intimate primary group relationships and in certain aspects of institutional life and thus create the possibility of maintaining, also, some cultural patterns which are different from those of the "host" society and of other racial and ethnic groups in the nation. . . . Racial and ethnic pluralism can exist without a great deal of cultural diversity; it cannot exist at all, however, without structural separation.[5]

Gordon's formulation of the distinction between cultural pluralism—the existence of separate cultural groups—and structural pluralism—the lack of intermarriage between groups to maintain the structural integrity of the groups—has been enormously influential in sociological studies of ethnicity.

Gordon specifically stated that logically it was necessary to have structural separation of the groups in order to have cultural separation. He reasoned that if groups intermarried on a wide scale, the integrity of the groups would be broken down. Parents with "diluted" backgrounds would be unable to pass along to their children specific cultural practices that set groups apart from each other.

Gordon acknowledged that it is possible to have structural integration and maintain separate groups if somewhat rigid rules about the "reaffiliation" of the children of intermarriage are maintained and if intermarriage and intermixing remains relatively low. This has been the historical experience of racial intermixing in the United States. Although there was some voluntary intermarriage between blacks and whites and much rape and forced intermixing of blacks and whites, the rigid enforcement of the one drop rule maintained the structural division between blacks and whites.[6] The boundaries between groups defined racially in the United States—such as Asians, Hispanics, and Native Americans—also meant that the offspring of intermarriages were generally defined in terms of the "nonwhite" parent, and the children of the generally infrequent intermarriages were reabsorbed into these racial groups.

Historical Influences on the Groups in the United States

Different historical and political circumstances have created different expectations and official reactions to groups defined as ethnic groups of European origin and groups defined as minority or racial groups of non-European origin. The United States currently has four federally designated minority groups: Native Americans, blacks, Asians, and Hispanics. The Office of Management and Budget issued a directive in 1978 that officially defined and designated these groups as minority groups. These groups correspond roughly to an important distinction the anthropologist John Ogbu makes between voluntary immigrants and involuntary minorities.[7] The treatment of involuntary minorities in our history has been very different from that afforded European voluntary immigrants. Although the European immigrants faced some discrimination and prejudice, non-whites were treated much more harshly. Asians were allowed into the country only under certain conditions and then were almost completely restricted until 1965. They were not allowed to acquire citizenship and, in the western states, were prohibited from owning land. Native Americans were removed from their lands and settled onto reservations or brutally repressed. Mexicans in the Southwest and Puerto Ricans on the island were brought into the United States as a result of a war and then were forced to adapt to an Anglo society. Blacks were subject to the most brutal and exclusionary treatment. Brought to the United States as slaves, after Emancipation they were kept separate and unequal through extralegal terrorism and Jim Crow laws, as well as severe discrimination and economic and social exclusion.

These groups were basically kept separate from the white majority throughout U.S. history. Although European immigrant groups at the height of immigration at the turn of the century were practically as segregated from one another as from these groups, this changed over the course of the twentieth century. The descendants of these European groups now have very high intermarriage rates and growing rates of marriage with some racial minorities.[8]

The one drop rule was strictly enforced with black-white children, but it was also used in extreme cases with Japanese-white children. In World War II the Wartime Civil Control Administration specified that people with ¹⁄₁₆ Japanese ancestry were to report to the internment camps. In practice this was not enforced completely, but when there was some question about whether a person was covered by the order because of mixed ancestry, it generally was decided on the side of Japanese ancestry.

Because American Indians have had a generally high degree of intermixing with non-Indians, a "blood quantum" has been used in the past, and is still used by many tribes, to decide who is an Indian. The federal government decreed that "any person with less than ¼ degree of Indian blood was for administrative purposes not an Indian and therefore not entitled to Bureau of Indian Affairs services."[9] Different tribes now state their own complex rules for determining eligibility to claim membership. These rules specify anywhere from ½ to ¹⁄₁₆ "Indian blood" to belong.

As long as minority groups were legally excluded from immigration and kept separate by law and custom and as long as the status of those children who did result from an intermarriage was rigidly defined, the definition of the categories and the conventions by which people were assigned to the groups were relatively straightforward. The long-run existence of the groups could be therefore assumed and easily ensured.

Since the 1960s, however, there have been some major changes in American society that are altering the nature of the definition of these groups. The removal of laws enforcing segregation as a result of the civil rights movement, most notably the Civil Rights Act of 1964 and the Voting Rights Act of 1965, and the removal of racist restrictions on who can immigrate to the United States through the Immigration Act of 1965 have led to a different milieu in which racial and Hispanic groups interact in the United States. Increasing interactions among individuals of different groups and growing social and geographic mobility have characterized the situation of minorities in the United States in the last thirty years. At the same time, the legislation passed to remedy past and current discrimination required these groups to be counted as mutually exclusive categories.

Current Intermarriage Levels and Patterns

Among the four federally designated minority groups—blacks, Asians, Spanish origin, and Native Americans— intermarriages and thus mixed-race children are increasing. Census data are not good indicators of precise intermarriage data because they record only intermarriages at the time of the census, not the incidence of intermarriage, thus missing marriages that break up before they are counted. For that reason, and because of the types of data collected on marriage records, some scholars use administrative records in studies of intermarriage.[10] Studies done on these four groups using either census data or the more precise marriage license record data report rising intermarriages for all groups.

Gary Sandefur and Trudy McKinnell, using 1970 census data, report that 33.0 percent of Indian men had white wives and that 35.0 percent of Indian women had white husbands.[11] Akemi Kikumura and Harry Kitano analyzed data on intermarriage in Los Angeles in 1979 and report that 41.2 percent of Chinese, 60.6 percent of Japanese, and 27.6 percent of Koreans marry exogamously.[12] If marriages to other Asians are excluded, there is still a high rate of intermarriage, with 30.2 percent of Chinese marrying a non-Asian, 49.9 percent of Japanese marrying a non-Asian, and 19.2 percent of Koreans marrying a non-Asian. Using marriage records in New York City for 1975, Douglas Gurak and Joseph Fitzpatrick report high rates of exogamous marriages for Hispanic groups, except Puerto Ricans. They disclose that 29.5 percent of Puerto Ricans married exogamously, while 56.1 percent of Central Americans, 63.4 percent of Cubans, and 37.9 percent of Dominicans married exogamously.[13]

Blacks still have extremely low rates of intermarriage. Stanley Lieberson and Mary Waters, using 1980 census data on race and ancestry, report that 98.7 percent of American-born black women in their first marriage are married to other blacks.[14] However, even among blacks there has been a sharp rise in intermarriage, albeit a rise from an almost microscopic base. M. Belinda Tucker and Claudia Mitchell-Kernan report that while overall black-white marriage rates remain much lower than any other interracial marriage rates, there is considerable variation by region and gender.[15] Since 1970 black men tend to marry white women at a much higher rate than black women marry white men. Interestingly, in 1960 equal numbers of black men and women married whites. By 1970 the number of black men marrying outside their race was double the number of black women who did so. By 1980 four times as many black men as black women married outside their race.[16] Interracial marriages are much more common on the East Coast and the West Coast than they are in other regions of the country. Tucker and Mitchell-Kernan, using 1980 census data, point out that if "the focus is limited to first marriages occurring between 1970–1980, the western black male intermarriage percentage is 16.5 percent." Overall the national rate in 1980 was 1.2 percent for black females and 3.6 percent for black males.[17]

Determining Identities of Mixed-Race People

The requirement to count minorities in the United States means that there must be rules about how to deal with people whose identity straddles the categories. The Census Bureau and most other statistical agencies of the government rely on self-identification. The Office of Management and Budget issued a directive advising that in the case of people who are of mixed origins, "the category which most closely reflects the individual's recognition in his community should be used for purposes of reporting."[18] Since the Census Bureau does not have information on how individuals are recognized in their communities, they designed a procedure to assign a single race to an interracial child if the parents had disobeyed the instructions and checked two separate boxes or had written in something like multiracial as a response. If an unacceptable response was given to the race question, the Census Bureau assigned the child to the mother's race, providing the mother was in the household. In other cases, when mother's race was unknown, multiracial individuals were assigned the first race that they reported (i.e., the first box checked on the form). This represents a change in policy because in 1970 when the classification of persons with parents of different races was in doubt, the father's race was used.

The National Center for Health Statistics uses a different procedure in determining the race of mixed-race babies for their birth certificates. Until recently birth certificates in the United States were decided in an intricate algorithm: if both parents were white, the baby was white; if one parent was Hawaiian, the baby was Hawaiian; if only one parent was white, the child was assigned the race of its other-than-white parent; if both parents were other than white, the child was assigned the father's race. Death certificates were in some cases decided differently. In a 1983–85 study of babies who died in their first year researchers found that whites received different racial classifications on their birth and death certificates only 1.2 percent of the time. Blacks were inconsistently identified 4.3 percent of the time, and other races were inconsistently identified a whopping 43.2 percent of the time.[19] This occurs when a baby is, for instance, defined as Filipino on its birth certificate, but the death certificate, often filled in by an attending physician or funeral director, classifies the baby as white or Asian.[20] This disparity in identification can affect aggregate statistics on outcomes such as life expectancy, because this baby would not be counted in the numerator in calculating infant mortality rates by ethnic group for Filipinos.

The way mixed-race individuals are classified is different from the way mixed-ethnic individuals are recorded in the census. Because of the need for unambiguous data for legislative reasons, mixed-race people and mixed–Spanish origin people must be put into only one mutually exclusive category. Mixed-ancestry people are permitted to report multiple origins. In 1980 among those reporting at least one specific ancestry, 37 percent reported at least a second ancestry as well. Work by Stanley Lieberson and Mary Waters, who used 1980 census data, and special studies conducted by Richard Alba in 1990 and Waters in 1990 indicate that there is considerable fluidity and even inconsistency in the reporting of ethnic origins of white families in the United States.[21]

This ethnic flux is somewhat surprising if one assumes that ethnic categories are fixed entities. It is also quite a headache for census takers and others trying to define groups by assigning individuals to mutually exclusive categories and assuming continuity over time. It is an accepted fact that ethnicity for many white Americans is increasingly variable, the subject of a personal choice, which may change over the life-course, in different situations, and from one generation to the next. In effect, as David A. Hollinger points out in this volume, white Americans have the freedom to be "postethnic" in choosing which of their grandparents' identities to accept as their own.

The discussions about racial and minority groups in the United States generally do not take into account the fact that intermarriage, ethnic flux, and changing individuals' identity choices might alter the nature of the groups themselves. In April 1990 *Time* magazine asked in a cover story, "What will the U.S. be like when whites are no longer the majority?" Quoting a Census Bureau population projection, they report that by the year 2000, Hispanics will increase by 21 percent, Asians will increase by 22 percent, blacks will increase by 12 percent, and whites will increase by only 2 percent.[22] It is notable that they did not include in their predictions the increase in Native Americans. Although Native Americans are a small part of the national population in the United States, their numbers are increasing very rapidly. Since 1960 the number of people reporting an American Indian race on the census has grown from about half a million to just under 2 million in 1990. The rate of change has been rising as well, with the category of American Indian, Aleut, and Eskimo increasing by 38 percent between 1980 and 1990. This growth rate is four times the growth rate of the population of the country as a whole and far beyond what one would expect based only on natural increase. The change is actually due to an increase in the number of people who identify as Indian.[23]

If one had begun in the year 1900 and estimated the number of people in white ethnic groups a century later without taking into account intermarriage and identification choices, one would have under- or over-estimated the size of groups. Michael Hout has shown that the 40 million Americans claiming Irish ancestry in 1980 could not possibly have descended only from the Irish immigrants recorded in the United States. Instead, the ninefold increase in the number of Irish Americans in U.S. history is partly because of a high intermarriage rate and a high retention of Irish identity among the descendants of part-Irish people.[24] This high rate of identification comes at the expense of identifications with the other parts of these individuals' ancestries, so that while the Irish are a larger group than one might expect, the Scottish are probably a smaller group.

Discussions of current racial and Hispanic groups in the United States, however, tend to assume that the groups are static; they will marry only each other and will have little generational change. This is of course an open question, but given the rising intermarriage rates for all racial groups described here, it is an increasingly important question. Mixed-race children now make up 3.2 percent of all annual births in the nation, up from 0.7 percent in 1968. This represents an increase in absolute numbers from 22,100 in 1968 to 110,500 in 1989.[25] It is also reasonable to expect that intermarriage and thus the numbers of interracial births will also be quite high for the descendants of the post-1965 immigrant group because they face a society with a higher degree of interethnic contact and mixing and less discrimination and segregation than did earlier immigrants.

Relying on self-identification, the Census Bureau requires mixed-race people to choose an identity and requires the parents of mixed-race children to choose for them. A growing number of people are refusing to choose and are checking two or more boxes or are writing in a mixed-race identity in the category called other. As stated earlier, the Census Bureau does not allow this choice to stand and reassigns these individuals into a racial category whenever possible. In effect, the Census Bureau is creating ethnicities—or enforcing them—much as the law has, as Stanley Katz describes in this volume. The Census Bureau reports that it received many phone calls during the 1990 census from mixed-race people requesting aid in answering the race question. It has also stated that one of the major questions in planning for the census in the year 2000 is going to be deciding what to do with interracial people.[26]

In counting the nation's minorities to comply with the legislative requirements of the Voting Rights Act and affirmative action legislation, it is necessary to act as if all people neatly fit into one racial or Hispanic group. The long-run existence of these minority groups is thus assumed and partly reinforced by compelling people to classify themselves into preset categories. In the case of mixed-race children, this involves an actual choice of identity by the parent completing the census form. If there are rigid rules governing the reaffiliation of the children of intermarriage, one could assume that these high levels of intermarriage are compatible with the long-run existence and integrity of the groups. But if a large proportion of the children of these intermarriages are adopting majority identities or if they are choosing neither identity and forging a new hybrid identity, then intermarriage is gradually eroding the existence of racial and ethnic groups as we know them and breaking down the boundaries between groups. At the same time our societal requirement to count the groups reinforces their existence and reinforces rigid boundaries between groups.

The paradox is that by allowing self-identification in an era of rising intermarriage and shifting socially constructed boundaries, the government record-keepers are acknowledging the rights of all Americans—those defined racially or ethnically—to the "postethnic" future Hollinger describes, where people are free to choose an affiliation based on the principle of revokable consent rather than descent.[27] By requiring people to choose a racial identity and disallowing the choice of affiliating with multiple ancestry, however, the government is in effect forcing people to reaffiliate with an identity and thus creating an ethnic America for racial minorities—one in which descent rather than consent still determines identities.

Census Data on Mixed-Race People

The overall distribution of the race and ethnic origins of the U.S. population is presented in table 2.1. This table combines the race and Spanish-origin question results into mutually exclusive categories. Non-European groups constituted over 20 percent of the nation's population in 1980, whereas blacks made up approximately 12 percent.

Census data on the children from intermarriages suggest that there are no clear social rules for assigning a race to people of mixed parentage. Although the "one drop rule" might suggest that an identity as a racial minority would always take precedence in assigning a child's identity, the actual choices parents make when filling out the forms do not conform to this prediction. The choices made by parents show that no simple rule governs the identities of these children.

Table 2.1. Race and National Origins of the U.S. Population, 1980

Group	Percent of Population	Total Population
White, not Hispanic	79.60	180,330,461
Black, not Hispanic	11.80	26,732,405
Native American	0.70	1,585,821
Japanese	0.30	679,637
Chinese	0.30	679,637
Filipino	0.30	679,637
Korean	0.10	226,546
Indian	0.20	453,092
Vietnamese	0.10	226,546
Hawaiian	0.08	181,237
Asian	0.10	226,546
Spanish Origin[a]	6.30	14,272,386
N (total population)	226,545,805	226,273,950

Source: Calculated from the 1980 United States Census Public Use Data Sample A (5 percent sample).

a. Includes people who said they had Spanish origin and reported any race, including white, black, and all other races listed in the table.

Both the race and Spanish-origin questions on the 1980 census were fixed choice in format, and a person was required to choose among the possible alternatives. The "race" question did not have the heading "color or race" (as it did in 1970 and again in 1990) but just stated, "Is this person . . . ," and then provided fifteen categories for the person to check off: white, Negro or black, Japanese, Chinese, Filipino, Korean, Vietnamese, American Indian, Asian Indian, Hawaiian, Guamanian, Samoan, Eskimo, Aleut, and other—specify. A person was required to pick only one category. A person with a black mother and white father would therefore have to choose either black or white on the race question and could not claim a mixture of both backgrounds. The Spanish-origin question asked, "Is this person of Spanish/Hispanic descent?" The possible answers to check off were five: no (not Spanish/Hispanic); yes, Mexican, Mexican American Chicano; yes, Puerto Rican; yes, Cuban; and yes, other Spanish/ Hispanic origin.

Although it is impossible to tell from the census what percentage of adults are of multiple racial origins, it is possible to look at intermarried couples and the decisions they are forced to make about their children's identities because of the design of the census. To examine the patterns of these choices, I drew a 5 percent sample of the Public Use Microdata Sample (PUMS) of 1980 census data at the individual level, restricting the sample to married parents, both spouses in their first marriage, with no more children present in the household than the mother reported giving birth to.[28] This was done to control as much as possible for blended families, stepchildren, and adoptions.

The Choice between Paternal and Maternal Ancestors

The race of the father seems to prevail over that of mother, especially when the father is white, for all groups considered here except for combinations involving a black and a white parent. The legacy of the one drop rule is evident in these instances, because the child is most likely to be labeled black, regardless of whether it is the child's mother or father who is black. Although the influence of the one drop rule is present, the erosion of its effects can be seen because black-white parents do label a minority of their children white and a significant proportion "other."

The choices made by interracial couples in identifying the race of their children can be seen in table 2.2. In families where the parents have different racial origins, 56 percent of the children are labeled by the parents (who filled out the census form) with the father's race, 38 percent are given the mother's race, and 6 percent are given a race that is different from the mother's and the father's. Undoubtedly, if the U.S. census allowed for multiple responses to the race question, some proportion of these parents would choose that option for their interracial children.

Table 2.2. Racial Identities Given to Children Whose Parents Have Different Racial Origins, United States, 1980[a]

Children's Identity	N	Percent
Same as father's	61,180	56.0
Same as mother's	41,180	38.0
Different from mother's and father's	6,520	6.0
Totals	108,880	100.0

Source: Calculated from the 1980 United States Census Public Use Data Sample A (5 percent sample).

a. Restricted to families where both husband and wife are in their first marriage, there are no more children at home than the mother gave birth to, and the census did not allocate race response.

Children Who Match Neither Mother's Nor Father's Response

What about the 6 percent of the children in these households whose reported race was different from that of both their mother and their father?

To control for adoption and blended families, this analysis was restricted to husband-wife families in which both spouses were in their first
marriage, and there were no more children living at home than the mother reported giving birth to. Not very many nonwhite children are reported
living with white parents.

In general when both parents share the same race, the children are likely
to be given the same race as their parents. For instance, when both parents are white, very few of them report having nonwhite children (only
0.1 percent). Nonwhite parents who share the same race slightly more
frequently report that their children are white, but this is still rare. When
parents each report a different nonwhite identity, 2.9 percent of their
children are labeled "white" in the census. When parents report the same
nonwhite identity, only 0.7 percent of their children are reported as white.
Very few of children in these families are reported as "other" race.

Tables 2.3 and 2.4 provide information on intermarried households. In
the situation in which the mother is white and the father is some other
race, compared to all the other groups, children with black fathers are
much more likely to choose the black race—69.1 percent of the children
are reported as black. Another 8.0 percent are reported "other," and 22.0
percent are reported as white. The remainder, less than one-half of 1 percent (0.47 percent) are given yet another specific race from among the

Table 2.3. Race of Children Whose Mother Is White and Father Is Another Race,
United States, 1980

Father's Race	Percent "White"	Percent Father's Race	Percent "Other" Race[a]	Percent All Other Race[b]	Totals
Black	21.92	69.10	8.51	0.47	55,020
Native American	50.99	48.21	0.65	0.15	85,620
Japanese	42.58	43.93	11.56	1.93	10,380
Chinese	34.96	48.73	15.25	1.06	9,440
Filipino	54.25	39.23	4.64	1.88	18,100
Korean	57.89	31.58	10.53	0.00	2,280
Asian Indian	74.13	20.22	3.48	2.17	9,200
Vietnamese	45.71	48.57	2.86	2.86	700
Hawaiian	42.89	53.95	2.89	0.27	7,600
Other Asian	55.46	36.24	6.11	2.19	4,580

Source: Calculated from the 1980 United States Census Public Use Data Sample A (5 percent sample).
   a. Includes children whose parents selected "other race" from among the options given to them by the
Census Bureau.
   b. This is a residual category including all children whose parents chose a specific race that was not
the same as the father's race, the mother's race, or the category "other race." These children were given
one of the other specific races recognized by the Census Bureau.

Table 2.4. Race of Children Whose Father Is White and Mother Is Another Race, United States, 1980

Mother's Race	Percent "White"	Percent Mother's Race	Percent "Other" Race[a]	Percent All Other Race[b]	Totals
Black	21.89	70.82	6.04	1.25	15,900
Native American	51.27	47.48	0.73	0.52	88,000
Japanese	67.19	24.87	6.68	1.26	38,040
Chinese	61.53	26.43	9.54	2.50	13,620
Filipino	63.04	32.62	2.73	1.61	37,340
Korean	73.64	21.33	4.45	0.58	24,280
Asian Indian	93.31	5.20	0.74	0.75	5,380
Vietnamese	64.44	29.78	5.33	0.45	9,000
Hawaiian	56.06	42.86	1.08	0.00	9,240
Other Asian	63.92	32.66	3.42	0.00	12,860

Source: Calculated from the 1980 United States Census Public Use Data Sample A (5 percent sample).
   a. Includes children whose parents selected "other race" from among the options given to them by the Census Bureau.
   b. This is a residual category including all children whose parents chose a specific race that was not the same as the father's race, the mother's race, or the category "other race." These children were given one of the other specific races recognized by the Census Bureau.

Census Bureau's other thirteen possible responses, such as Native American, Asian Indian, or Japanese. In contrast, 50 percent of the offspring of white mothers and Native American fathers are reported to be white, 43 percent of Japanese-white children are reported as white, 35 percent of Chinese-white children are reported white, and 58 percent of Korean-white children are reported *by* their parents to be white. In sharp contrast, when the father is Asian Indian and the mother is white, only 20 percent of the children are reported as Asian Indian. A much lower percentage of children of Japanese, Chinese, and Filipino fathers married to white mothers are given their father's Asian origins. Although these Asian groups do show a large proportion of the children as "other" race (11.56 percent for children of Japanese fathers, 15.25 percent for children of Chinese fathers, and 10.53 percent for children of Korean fathers), there still are far more children identified as having their mother's white race.

Table 2.4 shows the intergenerational transfer rates for situations in which the father is white and the mother is nonwhite. The differences here for the Asian groups are even more striking. For instance, in families where the father is white and the mother is Asian Indian, 93 percent of their children are labeled white. In households where the mother is Japanese, only 25 percent of the children are labeled Japanese. In households where the mother is Chinese, only 26 percent of the children are Chinese.

At this level of aggregation, it is not possible to determine whether parents of mixed Asian heritage are more or less likely to report their children are Asian. In other words, we do not know whether parents reporting themselves as Japanese or Chinese are themselves the offspring of an intermarriage.

These tables thus show that there is no one rule governing the choices made by parents about mixed-race children's identities. There is evidence that some parents try to choose neither parent's identity by checking "other." Parents do not completely choose on the basis of either the maternal or paternal identity, and some parents choose "majority white" identities while others choose "minority nonwhite" identities.

Conclusion

Overall, these data show that the one drop rule does not determine the choices intermarried parents made about their children's identity. Even black-white couples do not automatically report their children as black. Among some interracial couples—Asian Indians married to whites, Native Americans married to whites, and Koreans married to whites—over 50 percent of their children are labeled white. A sizable number of people report their children as "other" race, thus trying to tell the census that the child should have its own category—different from the mother's or father's.

Of course, these data do not tell us how these children will identify themselves when they are grown, and they also do not tell us how society in general will identify them. Some of these children may identify themselves very differently, and some who wish to be considered one identity will probably find that others in society continue to identify them differently.

These data do show the socially variable nature of racial identity in the United States. Even the racial division most rigidly defined throughout our history—between blacks and whites—is beginning to be challenged by increasing intermarriage and variable identity choices for the offspring of these intermarriages. Perhaps it is a reflection of a move toward acknowledging the social construction of race as well as ethnicity that in the 1990s Alex Haley's ancestry was explored in a miniseries called *Queenie.* It is clear that we have not yet reached a "postethnic" America where it is unremarkable that someone could be both African American and Irish American, but these census figures show that the days of automatic assignment of interracial children to a minority identity are over.

However, the need to assign people to a racial identity for public policy reasons and the growing acknowledgement that identity is not primordial but socially constructed and variable have not been reconciled. The Census Bureau may let parents and mixed-race people choose their race, but it still must force them to choose only one race at a time because of legal and political requirements.

The irony of the situation is that the more successfully a truly equal pluralist society is implemented on a political and social level, the more the existence of the groups themselves is undermined by the contact that leads to high intermarriage rates. The increasing intermarriage rates reported here are the result of the success of American pluralism. Intermarriages occur because people from different racial and ethnic groups go to school together, work together, and live side by side as equals. This is a new situation for the vast majority of Americans. Before the 1960s civil rights revolution and the 1965 immigration reform, many of these groups were systematically excluded from the mainstream.

Yet the very laws that opened the doors of these schools, workplaces, and neighborhoods to all Americans have required us to count our minorities. The Voting Rights Act may have opened the doors of government to black representatives by ensuring black participation in elections, but it also required the government to count how many black people live in each congressional district. The law left up to the census takers the task of defining "black people." In turn, the census takers leave that decision up to each individual, but within limits. As a growing number of people claim that they are both black and white, the census is forced to put them in only one category. In ensuring the protection or betterment of these minority groups, the government runs the danger of reifying them, by not allowing new groups to grow, by not allowing individuals the freedom to choose for themselves, or by keeping alive empty categories.

Intermarriage rates of these minority groups vary, as do immigration rates. For most census-defined groups in the United States—Chinese, Japanese, Filipino, Asian Indian, etc.—the levels of intermarriage are appreciably higher than for black-white couples, and the levels of identity shifting among children are also higher. Black-white marriages are still relatively rare and are not likely to reach very high levels anytime in the near future. A recent social survey reported that one in five whites still believes interracial marriage should be outlawed, and a majority of whites, 66 percent, said they would oppose a close relative's marrying a black.[29] Identity choices also are still very limited. In the 1980s when I interviewed whites of mixed ethnic ancestries about how they chose to identify themselves, they spoke about choosing to identify with one of their ancestries with ease and no worry about society at large imposing choices on them. Identity for them was largely a matter of personal choice.[30] This is not true for minority group members in our society who still face discrimination and prejudice when they are identified as a member of a minority group. We have not yet reached a postethnic America, but we are facing a situation where growing numbers of Americans no longer fit the categories we currently use to define Americans. There still is a definite need for legal protection for groups in our society, and to have that legal protection, we have to have a system for defining boundaries between groups. However, we have to be much more aware of how permeable those boundaries are and how much more permeable they will be as we become more successful in our endeavor to reach that equality.

Notes

1. See, for example, Richard Alba, *Ethnic Identity: The Transformation of White America* (New Haven, Conn.: Yale University Press, 1990); Mary C. Waters, *Ethnic Options: Choosing Identities in America* (Berkeley: University of California Press, 1990); and William L. Yancey, Eugene P. Ericksen, and Richard N. Juliani, "Emergent Ethnicity: A Review and Reformulation," *American Sociological Review* 41 (June 1976): 391–403.

2. On the historical development and impact of the one drop rule, see Virginia Dominguez, *White by Definition: Social Classification in Creole Louisiana* (New Brunswick, N.J.: Rutgers University Press, 1986); F. James Davis, *Who Is Black?: One Nation's Definition* (University Park: Pennsylvania State University Press, 1991); and Paul Spickard, *Mixed Blood: Intermarriage and Ethnic Identity in Twentieth-Century America* (Madison: University of Wisconsin Press, 1989). On the lack of regulation of mixed-ancestry people, see Waters, *Ethnic Options;* Alba, *Ethnic Identity;* Stanley Lieberson and Mary C. Waters, *From Many Strands: Ethnic and Racial Groups in Contemporary America* (New York: Russell Sage Foundation, 1988); and Herbert Gans, "Symbolic Ethnicity: The Future of Ethnic Groups and Culture in America," *Ethnic and Racial Studies* 2 (January 1979): 1–20.

3. David A. Hollinger, "Postethnic America," herein.

4. Stanley Lieberson, "Unhyphenated Whites in the United States," *Ethnic and Racial Studies* 8 (January 1986): 159–80.

5. Milton Gordon, "Models of Pluralism," *Annals of the American Academy of Political and Social Science* 454 (1981), 178–88.

6. Spickard, *Mixed Blood;* Davis, *Who Is Black?* Dominguez, *White by Definition.*

7. John Ogbu, *Minority Education and Caste: The American System in Cross-Cultural Perspective* (New York: Academic, 1978).

8. Deanna L. Pagnini and S. Philip Morgan, "Intermarriage and Social Distance among U.S. Immigrants at the Turn of the Century," *American Journal of Sociology* 96 (September 1990): 405–32; Lieberson and Waters, *From Many Strands.*

9. Matthew Snipp, *American Indians: The First of This Land* (New York: Russell Sage Foundation, 1989), 33–34.

10. For an overview of intermarriage research, see David Heer, "Intermarriage," in *The Harvard Encyclopedia of American Ethnic Groups*, ed. Stephen Thernstrom (Cambridge, Mass.: Harvard University Press, 1980), 513–21.

11. Gary Sandefur and Trudy McKinnell, "American Indian Intermarriage," *Social Science Research* 15 (December 1986): 348.

12. Akemi Kikumura and Harry L. Kitano, "Interracial Marriage: A Picture of the Japanese Americans," *Journal of Social Issues* 29, no. 2 (1973): 67–81.

13. Douglas T. Gurak and Joseph P. Fitzpatrick, "Intermarriage among Hispanic Ethnic Groups in New York City," *American Journal of Sociology* 87 (January 1982): 921–34.

14. Lieberson and Waters, *From Many Strands*, 171.

15. M. Belinda Tucker and Claudia Mitchell-Kernan, "New Trends in Black American Interracial Marriage: The Social Structural Context," *Journal of Marriage and the Family* 52 (February 1990): 209–18.

16. Claudette Bennett and J. Gregory Robinson, "Racial Classification Issues concerning Children in Mixed Race Households" (Paper presented at the annual winter meeting of the American Statistical Association, Fort Lauderdale, Fla., January 4, 1993).

17. Tucker and Mitchell-Kernan, "New Trends in Black American Marriage," 209.

18. Office of Management and Budget, "Race and Ethnic Standards for Federal Agencies and Administrative Reporting," Statistical Directive No. 15, *Federal Register* 43 (May 4, 1978): 19269–70.

19. "Death Rates for Minority Infants Were Underestimated, Study Says," *New York Times*, January 7, 1992.

20. Robert A. Hahn, "Differential Classification of Race on U.S. Infant Birth and Death Certificates: An Examination of Two Hypotheses" (Paper presented at the annual winter meeting of American Statistical Association, Fort Lauderdale, Fla., January 4, 1993).

21. Lieberson and Waters, *From Many Strands*; Alba, *Ethnic Identity*; Waters, *Ethnic Options*.

22. William A. Henry, "Beyond the Melting Pot," *Time Magazine*, April 9, 1990, 28.

23. Karl Eschbach, "Shifting Boundaries: Regional Variation in Patterns of Identification as American Indian" (Ph.D. diss., Harvard University, 1992); Nampeo R. McKenney and Arthur R. Cresce, "Measurement of Ethnicity in the United States: Experiences of the U.S. Census Bureau" (Paper presented at the Joint Canada–United States Conference on the Measurement of Ethnicity, Ottawa, Canada, April 1–3, 1992).

24. Michael Hout, "The Shamrock Explosion" (Paper presented at the meetings of the American Sociological Association, Cincinnati, August 24–27, 1991).

25. *USA Today*, December 11, 1992.

26. McKenney and Cresce, "Measurement of Ethnicity in the United States."

27. Hollinger, "Postethnic America," herein. See Werner Sollors, *Beyond Ethnicity: Consent and Descent in American Culture* (New York: Oxford University Press,

1986), for the distinction he makes in American use of consent and descent in determining identities.

28. This analysis is part of a larger collaborative research project with William Alonso on the implications of mixed-race children's identities for the future ethnic and racial composition of the United States. See William Alonso and Mary C. Waters, "The Future Composition of the American Population: An Illustrative Projection" (Paper presented at the annual winter meeting of the American Statistical Association, Fort Lauderdale, Fla., January 4, 1993).

29. "As Black-White Marriages Increase: Couples Still Face the Scorn of Many," *New York Times,* December 2, 1991.

30. Waters, *Ethnic Options,* particularly 16–51.

3   Postethnic America

David A. Hollinger

If Alex Haley had carried out on his father's side the genealogical inquiry reported in *Roots,* he would have experienced his great moment of self-knowledge in Ireland, not Gambia. This observation was made by Ishmael Reed in the course of a symposium entitled "Is Ethnicity Obsolete?"[1] Haley's choice of roots and Reed's comment on it together constitute an emblem for three points this essay addresses. The United States is endowed with a *nonethnic* ideology of the nation. It is possessed by a predominantly *ethnic* history. It may be now squandering an opportunity to create for itself a *postethnic* future in which affiliation on the basis of shared descent would be voluntary rather than prescribed.

The national ideology is "nonethnic" by virtue of the universalist commitment—proclaimed in the prevailing constitutional and political discourse—to provide the benefits of citizenship irrespective of any ascribed or asserted ancestral affiliations. This commitment lies behind our sense that Haley had a real choice, one that was truly his to make: individual Americans are to be as free as possible from the consequences of social distinctions visited upon them by others. Yet the decision Haley made was driven by a history predominantly "ethnic" in the extent to which each American's individual destiny has been determined by ancestrally derived distinctions flagged, at one time or another, by such labels as Negro, Jewish, Indian, Caucasian, Hispanic, Oriental, Irish, Italian, Chinese, Polish, white, black, Latino, Euro-American, Native American, Chicano, and African American.[2] That any person now classified as "black" or "African American" might see his or her own life as more the product of African roots—however small or large a percentage of one's actual genealogy—than of European roots reflects this history.

Hence "Haley's choice" comes close to being the "Hobson's choice" of genealogy in America. Haley could choose to identify with Africa, accepting, in effect, the categories of the white oppressors who had determined that the tiniest fraction of African ancestry would confer one identity and erase another, or Haley could choose to identify with Ireland, denying, in effect, his solidarity with the people who shared his social destiny and appearing to wish he were white. The nature of this "choice" is illuminated by an experience reported by Reed, who shares Haley's combination of African and Irish ancestry and who has flirted with the other option in the structured dilemma I am calling "Haley's Choice": Reed mentioned his "Irish-American heritage" to a "Professor of Celtic Studies at Dartmouth," who "laughed."[3]

A "postethnic" America is one in which someone of Reed's color could comment casually about his Irish heritage without our finding it a joke. A postethnic America would offer Haley a choice more real than the one Hobson offered visitors to his livery. But the notion of postethnicity entails more than this. To clarify this ideal and to explore its prospects in the context of the nation's nonethnic ideology and its ethnic history are the chief concerns of this essay.[4]

Any such enterprise must begin by underscoring the inequalities that have dominated the historical record and by recognizing that these inequalities now lend credibility to claims made on behalf of communities defined by descent. Not every citizen's fortune has been influenced to the same degree or in the same direction by America's notorious failure to act on its universalist aspirations. Being classified as Euro-American, white, or Caucasian has rarely been a basis for being denied adequate employment, housing, education, or protection from violence. One response to the patently unequal consequences of ethnoracial distinctions has been to invoke and sharpen the nation's official, Enlightenment-derived commitment to protect all its citizens from any negative consequences of ethnoracial distinctions. What this commitment means has been contested, of course, from the day a committee of the Second Continental Congress deleted from the Declaration of Independence Thomas Jefferson's denunciation of slavery right down to the most recent decisions of the Supreme Court concerning the limits of affirmative action. The commitment is plain enough, however, to make obvious the gap between the theory and the practice of American nationality.[5] Indeed, the magnitude and persistence of this gap have inspired a second, very different response: the applying of pressure from the gap's other side, its ethnic side.

This alternative strategy for closing the gap asks public authorities to facilitate and actively support affiliation on the basis of ancestry. By promoting the development of communities defined by descent, one might reasonably hope for more equal treatment of every descendant of every "tribe." After all, the results produced by the long-preferred method of gap-closing—the invoking and sharpening of the nonethnic ideological tradition—remain disappointing even to most people who believe progress has been substantial. Hence the nonethnic character of the ideological tradition can be construed as part of the problem rather than part of the solution. That tradition treats as irrelevant to citizenship the very distinctions that, in this view, need to be asserted, reinforced, and celebrated.[6] This feeling that equality interests demand for America a future even more ethnic than its past is reflected in much of what is said in the name of "multiculturalism."

Yet multiculturalism sometimes functions as a shibboleth behind which are concealed a range of initiatives often not in agreement about just how much ethnoracial particularism is wise. The debate over multiculturalism is often scripted as a two-sided confrontation, but it has generated a number of distinctions, refinements, and possibilities that get missed when participants characterize each other as separatists or as defenders of Eurocentric domination and when they construct the issue as a choice between similarity or difference, wholeness or fragmentation, assimilation or dissimilation, monism or pluralism.[7] No doubt these terms describe fairly some participants in this debate and some of the doctrines advanced, but not all. A convenient example of a perspective not encompassed by these familiar dichotomies is an essay by the historian Gary B. Nash.

Nash defends multiculturalism, which in the context of American historical studies he takes to be an emphasis on cultural diversity, an elimination of ethnocentrism, and the "integration of the histories of both genders and people of all classes and racial or ethnic groups."[8] Indeed, Nash is not only the author of scholarly works that manifest these ideals but also the principal author of the widely discussed series of textbooks recently adopted by most public school districts in California, explicitly designed with these multicultural goals in mind.[9] Yet Nash is resoundingly critical of the Afrocentrism that is sometimes counted as a version of multiculturalism, and he mocks the ethnocentric reasoning by which our schools might be asked to design "Sinocentrist," "Khmercentrist," and "Hispanocentrist" curricula and to ignore the needs of "mixed-race children in a society where . . . interracial marriage is at an all-time high." Nash defends the idea of "common ground" routinely invoked by critics of multiculturalism. "If multiculturalism is to get beyond a promiscuous pluralism that gives everything equal weight and adopts complete moral relativism," says Nash in words that might have come from Diane Ravitch, Arthur M. Schlesinger Jr., or even William Bennett, "it must reach some agreement on what is at the core of American culture."[10]

Moreover, Nash is forthright in telling us what we should take as that "core": the democratic values "clearly stated in the nation's "founding documents." These old principles "are a precious heritage," endowing with the same rights all "individuals" of "whatever group attachments." Nash thus invokes the nonethnic ideological tradition, identifies himself with one of this tradition's greatest defenders, Gunnar Myrdal, and points to that tradition's helpful role in "virtually every social and political struggle carried out by women, religious minorities, labor, and people of color." Scorning the varieties of particularism that encourage young people to identify only with antecedents of their own ethnoracial category, Nash insists that "Harriet Tubman and Ida B. Wells should inspire all students, not simply African American females," and he reminds us that W. E. B. Du Bois once "wed" a color-neutral "Truth" and sought to "live above the veil" of color by learning from Aristotle and Shakespeare. Nash several times invokes "cosmopolitanism," a concept that matches his ideas more comfortably than does the more ambiguous "multiculturalism" with which he, like so many other opponents of an Anglo-Protestant curriculum and public culture, finds himself saddled.[11]

Cosmopolitanism should be sorted out from several other persuasions and counter-persuasions that sometimes get confused in the multiculturalism debates. Part of the confusion derives from the fact that virtually no one defends monoculturalism, with the result that multiculturalism is deprived of an honest, natural opposite. Eurocentrism is often said to be the enemy, but this word is more an opprobrious epithet than a fair description of any but a few of the people who have expressed concerns about fragmentation and loss of pedagogic focus.[12] Many who do uphold European traditions insist that what makes these traditions worth defending is their decidedly multicultural character.[13] Hence the "opponents" of multiculturalism sometimes end up seeming to claim its banner for their own, apparently different programs.[14] Another alleged opposite of multiculturalism is universalism, but here the highly problematic claim that a given single culture is good enough for the entire globe is often conflated with more modest assertions that some truths and rights apply to every member of the species and that all the world's peoples share a destiny sufficiently common to demand mutual engagement and cooperation.[15] These assertions can be consistent with multiculturalism unless the latter is understood—as it sometimes is—as a mere multiplicity of ethnocentrisms. Universalism's suspicion of enclosures is shared by cosmopolitanism, which is defined by an additional element not essential to universalism itself: recognition, acceptance, and eager exploration of diversity. Cosmopolitanism urges each polity and each individual to absorb as much experience as it can while retaining its capacity to function as a unit. Although this ideal is attractive to many adherents of multiculturalism, multiculturalism's amorphousness obscures a crucial distinction between cosmopolitanism and "pluralism."[16]

Pluralism differs from cosmopolitanism in the degree to which it endows with privilege particular groups, especially the communities that are well established at whatever time the ideal of pluralism is invoked. While cosmopolitanism is willing to put the future of every culture at risk through the critical, sympathetic scrutiny of other cultures and is willing to contemplate the creation of new affiliations, pluralism is more concerned to protect and perpetuate particular existing cultures.[17] In its extreme form, this conservative element in pluralism takes the form of a bargain: "You keep the acids of your modernity out of my culture, and I'll keep the acids of mine away from yours." If cosmopolitanism is casual about community building and community maintenance and tends to seek voluntary affiliations of wide compass, pluralism promotes affiliations on the narrower grounds of shared history and is quicker to see reasons for drawing boundaries between communities. Cosmopolitanism is more oriented to the individual, whom it is likely to understand as a member of a number of different communities simultaneously, while pluralism is more oriented to the group and is likely to identify each individual with reference to a single primary community. Cosmopolitanism is more suspicious than is pluralism of the potential for conformist pressures within the communities celebrated by pluralists, while pluralism is more suspicious than is cosmopolitanism of the variousness and lack of apparent structure in the wider world celebrated by cosmopolitans. Arguments offered by universalists that certain interests are shared by many groups will get a longer hearing from cosmopolitans than from pluralists, who are more likely to see in such arguments the covert advancement of the interests of one particular group. Pluralism and cosmopolitanism have often been united in the common cause of promoting "tolerance" and "diversity," and thus both are strong ideological tributaries feeding the multiculturalism of our own time. But a tension between pluralist and cosmopolitan tendencies runs throughout the multiculturalist debate and is rarely acknowledged.

Cosmopolitanism is worth singling out because its renewal in the context of the debate over multiculturalism can yield what I call a "postethnic" perspective. A postethnic perspective is more historically specific than cosmopolitanism. *Post*ethnicity reacts against the nation's invidiously ethnic history, builds on the current generation's unprecedented appreciation of previously ignored cultures, and supports on the basis of revokable consent those affiliations by shared descent that were previously taken to be primordial. The great pluralist Horace Kallen thought he had made a knock-down argument for the primacy of ethnoracial identities when he observed that one thing no one can change is his or her grandfather, but a postethnic perspective challenges the right of one's grandfather or grandmother to determine primary identity. Let individuals affiliate or disaffiliate with others of shared or differing descent as they choose.[18] The postethnic ideal recognizes the need for affiliations that mediate between the individual and such gross entities as the state, the economy, and the species. If this need has been often slighted by universalists—for whom the species as a whole can be community enough—the reality of this need has led some pluralists to reify ethnoracial categories and to deny the contingent contextual character of the process of affiliation. Part of the "post" in postethnicity is the acceptance of the constructed character of "races" and "ethnic groups": a postethnic perspective is willing to "problematize"—as we say nowadays—identities that unreconstructed ethnocentrists preferred to take as given.[19]

The shifting socially constructed character of ethnoracial groups is apparent in the recent amalgamation of what were once a host of distinctive "ethnic identities" into "Euro-American," now widely seen alongside Asian American, African American, Latina/o, and Native American as one of the five basic demographic blocs that constitute the bulk of American society. American multiculturalism accomplished in short order a task that centuries of British imperial power could not complete: the making of the Irish indistinguishable from the English.[20] Jewish identity, too, receded in significance when all Americans of predominantly "European" stock were grouped together.[21] It is tempting to see the new system of classification as a quintuple melting pot, replacing Will Herberg's triple melting pot of Protestants, Catholics, and Jews, all of whom are now grouped together as "Euro-Americans."[22]

If the new American ethnoracial pentagon, or quintuple melting pot, serves to erase dramatically much of the cultural diversity within the Euro-American bloc, the very drama of this transformation is salutary in two respects. First, this drama is a reminder of the contingent contextual character of the entire process by which social identities are created, perpetuated, and altered. A New Hampshire resident of French-Canadian ethnicity may learn, by moving to Texas, that he or she is actually an "Anglo." Many European immigrants of the nineteenth century did not come to see themselves as significantly Italian or German until these identities were thrust upon them by the novel demographic conditions of the United States that rendered obsolete the local identities into which they had been acculturated in Sicily and Swabia. Distinctions between Protestants, Catholics, and Jews of European extraction were once taken as seriously as are the distinctions now made between Euro-Americans and Asian Americans. Most ironically, those from Arab countries and Iran are called not Asian Americans but "whites" or, by transfer, "Euro-American."

A second valuable consequence of the sudden transformation of a host of ethnic identities into "Euro-America" is the invitation this experience provides to recognize the comparable erasures of diversity that victimize people within the other four pseudo-primal categories. The tribal and linguistic distinctions among Native Americans have long been lost on many non-Indian observers. The purchase one gets on Koreans, Cambodians, Chinese, Vietnamese, and Japanese by calling them all "Asian Americans" (or, in the older usage, "Orientals") is obtained at the cost of diminishing the significance of the differences between these, and other, Americans of Asian extraction. The Hispanic, or Latina/o, bloc has more linguistic cohesion than does the Asian American or the Native American bloc, but it, too, can be broken down into subgroups defined, for example, by such points of origin as Puerto Rico, Cuba, Mexico, and El Salvador. The internal diversity of the African American bloc may be the least striking, as measured by some indicators, but nothing illustrates more tellingly the selective suppression of diversity and the socially constructed character of these ethnoracial blocs than the historic denial, by generations of empowered whites, that they share with black Americans a substantial pool of genes. As Barbara Fields has put it, we still have a convention "that considers a white woman capable of giving birth to a black child but denies that a black woman can give birth to a white child."[23] Hence, "Haley's Choice."

And it is choice, so highly valued by the postethnic perspective, that by its very limits within the new ethnoracial pentagon defines it. A Cambodian American does not have to remain so in the eyes of non–Asian Americans, but only with great difficulty can he or she cease to be an Asian American. So, too, with Japanese Americans or Chinese Americans (and, as might be asked by the Euro-American auto worker from Detroit who clubbed to death the Chinese American Vincent Chin, thinking him Japanese, "What's the difference, anyway?"). The same applies to the other blocs: Native Americans might care who is a Cherokee and who is a Kwakiutl, but outside that section of the pentagon, an Indian is an Indian. Some Euro-Americans might make a big deal of being Jewish, but from the viewpoint of many African Americans—returning an old favor—it is the whiteness of the whole lot of them that counts. And so on.

The lines between the five unequally inhabited sides of the ethnoracial pentagon mark the limits of individual movement, as set by an implicit informal concord among the most well-positioned of the people who practice identity politics in America today.[24] These several lines are not resistant in exactly the same degree to intermarriage and other types of border crossing and category mixing, but all are strong enough to function as "racial" as opposed to "ethnic" boundaries. Exactly where ethnicity ends and race begins has been much contested in our time, when zoologists and anthropologists have found so little scientific utility in the concept of race and when humanists and social scientists have found so much evidence for the socially constructed character of ethnicity, of race, and even of gender. What is shown by the prominence of what I am calling the ethnoracial pentagon, however, is that two kinds of lines are, in fact, being drawn and widely accepted, at least for now: fainter lines distinguish the "ethnicities" found within each of the five blocs, while bolder, thicker lines render these five blocs themselves into "races" or race equivalents.

Nowhere within the entire ethnoracial pentagon do individuals have more freedom to choose how much or how little emphasis to place on their "ethnicity"—speaking now about the identities conferred by the "faint" lines noted above—than within the Euro-American "race," or, as I would prefer to say, bloc. The ease with which Euro-Americans can affirm or ignore their ethnic identity as Italians, Norwegians, Irish, etc., has often been noted by sociologists and was convincingly documented by Mary C. Waters in *Ethnic Options: Choosing Identities in America.* Many white, middle-class Americans of third- or fourth-generation immigrant descent get a great deal of satisfaction out of their ethnic affiliations, which, in the current cultural and political environment, cost them little.[25] Waters found that these "white ethnics" tended to shy away from aspects of communal life that imposed obligations and intruded on their privacy and individuality, but they affirmed what Herbert Gans calls "symbolic ethnicity": a subjective "feeling" of identity rather than the socially substantive ethnicity entailed by involvement in a concrete community with organizations, mutual commitments, and some elements of constraint.[26]

Although Waters found abundant evidence for the voluntary character of the ethnicity affirmed by middle-class whites, she also encountered among these manifestly voluntary ethnics the persistence of the notion that ethnicity is a primordial, biological status. Waters's subjects' denial of the voluntary character of their own ethnic identities rendered them, in turn, insensitive to the involuntary character of the ethnoracial identities of nonwhites: they see a formal "equivalence between the African-American and, say, Polish-American heritages," while often denying the depth and durability of the racism that has largely constructed and persistently bedeviled African Americans. Waters's book is intended, in part, to liberate whites from these blindnesses, which inhibit extending to all Americans the freedom now experienced by middle-class whites to affiliate and disaffiliate at will. When Waters argues for such a consummation—a time when "all Americans" are equally "free to exercise their 'ethnic option'"—she upholds the ideal I am calling postethnic.[27] In such a consummation, the vividly etched lines that define the ethnoracial pentagon would be fainter, more like the lines internal to each of the five segments. An "ethnic" America, in contrast, would be what we have already had, only more so: the lines now vivid would be underscored, and the lines now faint would become bolder. Some programs expressed in the name of multiculturalism—those deriving more from pluralism than from cosmopolitanism—proceed in this contrary, "ethnic" direction.

It would be a mistake to ask the ideal of postethnicity to do more than serve as a distinctive frame within which can take place argument and contention over the nature of American nationality and over more specific issues in social policy. It is a frankly idealistic frame, embodying the hope that the United States can be more than an empire serving as a site for a variety of diasporas and projects in colonization and conquest. The ideal is not a blueprint or a set of concrete programs. Its generality is not, however, a reason to doubt its utility. The notion of multiculturalism is considerably less specific, yet the work we have been asking this concept to do in our national discussion of ourselves testifies to our need for sweeping concepts. We cannot do without them. When we try, someone else's sweeping concept comes into the discourse and fills the relevant space.

Among the resources available to support the ideal of postethnicity is the tradition of cosmopolitanism as found in modern American intellectual history. "It is not because of diversity that we are in trouble," nor should our goal be to "cancel" or even to "conceal" our "differences" in the interests of "uniformity," wrote one figure in this tradition, the editor of a collection entitled *Unity and Difference in American Life.* "The problem is to get along with these differences," which should be welcomed in this "endlessly varied" universe filled with "all kinds of differences" displayed in many "groups" and many "communities."[28] The book is from 1947, and the voice is that of the Columbia University sociologist Robert M. MacIver. As a theorist of diversity, MacIver is not superior to most of the participants in our multiculturalist debate, but his voice, if heard at today's symposia, would be conventionally harmonious on many points. Examples of those articulating the antiprovincial strain of cultural criticism cited more widely than MacIver include Randolph Bourne, John Dewey, Walter Lippmann, Margaret Mead, Ruth Benedict, and Lionel Trilling, but the literature in which they are cited is a decidedly monographic one, informing little of the popular debate over multiculturalism.[29]

It would not do to insist that these intellectuals solved effectively the problems that we struggle with today,[30] nor would it do to deny that nearly all of us would find provincial and sexist the specific range of ideas they took up in a spirit of cosmopolitanism. Yet the vitality of a tradition of cosmopolitan aspiration among a substantial minority of Euro-American intellectuals is worth emphasizing at this multiculturalist moment, when the imperative to confront and renounce the racism and ethnocentrism within the Euro-American bloc threatens to erase from the history of that bloc the antiracist and anti-ethnocentric voices raised from within it. If historical representation inevitably entails the selective silencing and perpetuating of specific voices from the inventory of the accessible past— as we are now reminded at every turn by our analysts of discourse as a form of power—it is in the interests of a potentially postethnic future to keep within our hearing the cosmopolitan voices that opposed some of the same evils now being fought and that rendered the academic culture of the midcentury decades a terrain more contested than some of our current savants find it convenient to recall. Some multiculturalist programs for academic reform justify themselves by means of a slash-and-burn rendition of the intellectual and academic history of the United States (and sometimes of Europe), according to which even the relatively recent past partook of a virtually monolithic culture of Anglo-conformist domination that remained mystified and concealed until courageously exposed by the present generation of keynote speakers and deans of humanities. But the American academy's critical tradition offers contemporary egalitarians more aid than some of them have noticed; "not everybody," as the distinguished classicist Frank M. Snowden Jr. has put the point cogently, "is a racist."[31]

There remain all too many racists, of course, but revulsion at racism is now sufficiently strong in our society to render the ideal of postethnicity worth discussing. Even the failure of the "Rodney King jurors" to convict the Los Angeles police officers of criminal assault should not distract us, as Orlando Patterson and Chris Winthrop have wisely cautioned, from recognizing long-term indicators that "the vestigially prejudiced majority may be changing."[32] In an age when community closure on the basis of shared descent is being sought in so many parts of the globe, the relatively open, contingent, negotiated character of American nationality renders the United States a world-historical project more conducive than are most nationalist endeavors to the development of postethnicity. Yet the idea of a postethnic America is a challenge to be met rather than a description of a reality already achieved. The latter misrepresentation is tempting when one contemplates the range and intensity of ethnic violence in Balkan Europe, the Caucasus, East Africa, India, and many other locales throughout the world. But a misrepresentation it truly would be, and one comparable to a misrepresentation against which this essay warned at the start: the confusion of the nation's actual condition—its persistently ethnic history—with its nonethnic ideology.

The democratic-egalitarian core of that old ideology remains vital to the vision of America I am calling postethnic. The potential of democratic-egalitarian ideals to serve as a common ground for persons of diverse descent will be diminished to the extent that these ideals become "ethnicized," which is the effect of defining them as "Eurocentric" in an era when people are encouraged in many quarters to line up their culture with their genes. The routes by which "democracy" and "equality" have traveled to reach the modern United States have been overwhelmingly Anglo-American and Western European, but that need not mean that Euro-Americans of today have a greater claim on these ideals than does anyone else. Americans within the other four ethnoracial blocs need not feel the slightest pressure to reserve their enthusiasm for democratic-egalitarian ideals until such time as evidence is produced that their own ancestral group experienced libertarian moments no less portentous than the Putney Debates of the New Model Army.

The jealous particularisms that fear "common ground" as a field for covert Euro-American domination are not, however, what most immediately threatens progress toward a postethnic America. Critics of "the Balkanization of America" who focus their complaints on the educational and political programs of ethnoracial "separatists" would do well to concentrate, instead, on the rigidification of the class structure.

Economic opportunities have been vital to the process by which the once-bold lines dividing the various Euro-American ethnic groups from one another have become relatively faint, but today's poor and unskilled are offered fewer and smaller opportunities for advancement than were their comparably positioned predecessors. People outside the Euro-American bloc who enter the American social system with strong skills and relatively high-class position often flourish, even in the current political economy. Many of these individuals—as recent immigration from Korea, Taiwan, and Vietnam demonstrates especially well—respond very positively indeed to the public culture of the United States and in their behavior approximate the classic pattern of a certain amount of "enclaving" and a certain amount of "assimilation." If all citizens of the United States had a reasonable hope of attaining the standard of living associated with "the middle class," the prospects for a postethnic America at this point in history—when so many energies are deployed against racism—would be encouraging. But the opportunity of the United States to create for itself a postethnic future may well be squandered through its own refusal to address the needs of its poor and unskilled citizens of all ethnoracial blocs.

Notes

This essay was first published in *Contention* 2 (Fall 1992): 79–96, and appears here, with slight editorial modifications, by permission of the author.

1. Ishmael Reed, "America's 'Black Only' Ethnicity," in *The Invention of Ethnicity*, ed. Werner Sollors (New York: Oxford University Press, 1989), 227, commenting on Alex Haley, *Roots: The Saga of an American Family* (New York: Dell, 1976). Reed does not take the position that ethnicity is obsolete; on the contrary, he argues (229) that "ethnicity will never become obsolete" in the United States so long as "public attitudes" tend to type as "black" anyone with the slightest apparent African ancestry and to associate with "Black America" many problems common to the society as a whole.

2. I confine this list to labels understood to be neutral or honorific. But the ethnoracial map of American society owes much to a dynamic of contempt, including the colloquial, hate-speech epithets that correspond to these socially accepted labels.

3. Reed, "America's 'Black Only' Ethnicity," 229.

4. This essay elaborates on my argument in "How Wide the Circle of the We? American Intellectuals and the Problem of the Ethnos since World War Two," *American Historical Review* 98 (April 1993): 317–37. There I sketch the movement from species-centered to ethnos-centered discourse in American thought during the last several decades and outline a "postethnic perspective" on epistemic, moral, and political communities. The concept of postethnic became known to me through the writings of Werner Sollors.

5. In speaking of American nationality, I do not mean that virtually everyone was a liberal egalitarian "in theory" and only choked when it came time to put the theory "into practice." The "theory" itself was often contested by people who preferred more narrowly communitarian and ethnoracially homogeneous visions of nationality. Regarding efforts to move the theory of American citizenship in "ethnic" directions, see Rogers M. Smith, "The 'American Creed' and American Identity: The Limits of Liberal Citizenship in the United States," *Western Political Quarterly* 41 (June 1988): 225–51.

6. The nonethnic national ideology is sometimes said to suppress "difference" in the interest of "sameness," but this misses the real issues: What kind of difference? What kind of sameness? And for what purpose might a difference be suppressed? No one now says that ancestral differences should be considered in deciding which citizens vote, but our refusal to consider such differences is certainly an example of the suppression of difference.

7. Defenders of multiculturalism have complained with reason that critics have lumped together a range of distinctive ideas, but their next step is all too often to sweep all critics of multiculturalism into a single reactionary, establishmentarian group. A striking example of this is Evan Carton, "The Self Besieged: American Identity on Campus and in the Gulf," *Tikkun* 4 (July/August 1991): 40–47, which characterizes as "Operation Campus Storm" criticisms of multiculturalism and attacks on "political correctness" published in *Time, Newsweek,* the *New Republic,* and *Atlantic.* Carton links these to "Operation Desert Storm" in the Gulf and treats as a fair emblem for this George Will's praise for Lynne Cheney as our "secretary of domestic defense." For a sharply contrasting mode of response, see Louis Menand, "Illiberalisms," *New Yorker,* May 20, 1991, 101–7, in which Menand dares to acknowledge—amid a scorching and effective critique of Dinesh D'Souza's *Illiberal Education* (New York: Free Press, 1991)—that some of what is said in the name of multiculturalism is pretty silly and implies that we should not shrink from saying so for fear of being linked with the Far Right.

8. Gary B. Nash, "The Great Multicultural Debate," *Contention* 2 (Fall 1992): 11.

9. See the three books, for different grade levels, by Beverley J. Armento, Gary B. Nash, Christopher L. Salter, and Karen K. Wixson, all published by Houghton Mifflin in 1991: *From Sea to Shining Sea, America Will Be,* and *A More Perfect Union.* Based on a selective reading of these books, I believe they do fulfill the goals of multiculturalism as Nash defines it. These books devote extensive and sympathetic attention

to a great variety of American ethnoracial groups and interpret the major episodes in the history of British North America and the United States in terms that are refreshingly consistent with the antiracist scholarship of professional historians during the past generation.

10. Nash, "Great Multicultural Debate," 22, 23. Diane Ravitch, "In the Multicultural Trenches," *Contention* 2 (Fall 1992): 29–36, distinguishes between Afrocentrism and multiculturalism as sharply as does Nash and pleads for the recognition of commonalities amid easily distinguished cultural diversities. See also Diane Ravitch, "Multiculturalism," *American Scholar* 59 (Summer 1990): 337–54; and Arthur M. Schlesinger Jr., *The Disuniting of America: Reflections on a Multicultural Society* (New York: W. W. Norton, 1992). I do not mean to slight the differences between Nash, on the one hand, and Ravitch and Schlesinger, on the other. Nash is more deeply critical of the interpretations of American history and culture that prevailed before the multicultural enthusiasms of recent years and is more insistent that ways be found to articulate and appreciate the variety of culture traditions that have gone into the making of the contemporary United States. Yet their writings confirm that some of multiculturalism's defenders and critics are backing into one another as they recoil from the ethnocentrism of either the European or the African variety.

11. Nash, "Great Multicultural Debate," 23, 24, 25. Nash's intervention in the multicultural debate can be compared with that of another historian, Elizabeth Fox-Genovese, "Between Individualism and Fragmentation: American Culture and the New Literary Studies of Race and Gender," *American Quarterly* 42 (March 1990): 7–34. See also Bruce Robbins, "Othering in the Academy: Professionalism and Multiculturalism," *Social Research* 58 (Summer 1991): 355–72, which makes a vigorous and discerning defense of "cosmopolitanism," an "unfashionable term that needs defending" (358–59). Robbins also vindicates democratic values as the desired "common project" (372).

12. The term *Eurocentric* may be fair, however, as applied to Lewis S. Feuer, who identifies "disease and massacre" as the "principal offerings" of "Central African culture" and attacks multiculturalism as "a secession from Western Civilization," comparable to that carried out by the Christian anti-intellectual sects that burned the library in ancient Alexandria. See Feuer, "From Pluralism to Multiculturalism," *Society* 29 (November/December 1991): 19–22.

13. For an agitated example of this insistence, see Reed Way Dasenbrock, "The Multicultural West," *Dissent* 38 (Fall 1991): 550–55. Dasenbrock does not, however, disparage the study of non-European cultures; he argues (553) that "multiculturalism is simply the standard human condition" and that it applies to Europe and the United States as a matter of course and endows both with much of the value they have.

14. Diane Ravitch comes out foursquare for multiculturalism in her "In the Multicultural Trenches."

15. A vivid example of a universalist pronouncement in American discourse is the great courtroom speech of Eugene Victor Debs: "So long as there is a lower class, I am in it; so long as there is a criminal element, I am of it; so long as there is a soul in prison, I am not free." These proclamations of extensive fraternity contrast with all prescriptions to look after "one's own kind."

16. I have tried to distinguish "cosmopolitanism" from "pluralism" in my *In the American Province: Studies in the History and Historiography of Ideas* (Bloomington: Indiana University Press, 1985), 57, using Randolph Bourne as an exemplar of the former and Horace Kallen as an exemplar of the latter.

17. A rich literature on pluralism exists that is little used in the multiculturalism debate. Especially important is John Higham, "Ethnic Pluralism in Modern American Thought," in Higham's *Send These to Me: Immigrants in American Life*, 2d ed. (Baltimore, Md.: Johns Hopkins University Press, 1984), 198–232. A helpful overview is Olivier Zunz, "The Genesis of American Pluralism," *Tocqueville Review* 9 (1988): 201–19. See also Werner Sollors, "A Critique of Pure Pluralism," in *Reconstructing American Literary History*, ed. Sacvan Bercovitch (Cambridge, Mass.: Harvard University Press, 1986), 250–79, with its provocative interpretation of Horace Kallen, the most prominent theorist of "cultural pluralism" in the United States.

18. The partial reconfiguration of the discourse over "race" and "ethnicity" into the terms "descent" and "consent" has been a contribution of Werner Sollors, *Beyond Ethnicity: Consent and Descent in American Culture* (New York: Oxford University Press, 1986).

19. A recognition that ethnoracial groups are constructed in contingent circumstances and shift their boundaries according to context is a major theme in recent scholarship. Alexander Nehamas, "A Touch of the Poet," *Raritan* 10 (Summer 1990): 113, summarizes the implications of this scholarship in a recent challenge to Richard Rorty: "When the very idea of one's ethnos is being put everywhere into question how can one be 'ethnocentric'?"

20. This point is made by the journalist Bob Callahan in a clever account of a decision by the California Arts Council concerning who was and was not a "minority." See Callahan, "The European Immigrant Response," in *Invention of Ethnicity*, ed. Sollors, 232.

21. "So much for the distinctiveness that has enlivened our souls for three millennia," complains Arnold Eisen on behalf of Jews, "and, again recently, led to the destruction of our bodies." Eisen, "University Truths," *Tikkun* 6 (July/August 1991): 55. But compare Walter P. Zenner, "Jewishness in America: Ascription and Choice," in *Ethnicity and Race in the U.S.A.: Toward the Twenty-First Century*, ed. Richard D. Alba (New York: Routledge, 1988), 117–33, which addresses the diminished distinctness of the Jewish population within the Euro-American block, regardless of what perspective may be brought to the issue by members of other blocks.

22. Will Herberg, *Protestant-Catholic-Jew: An Essay in American Religious Sociology* (Garden City, N.Y.: Doubleday, 1955).

23. Barbara J. Fields, "Ideology and Race in American History," in *Region, Race and Reconstruction: Essays in Honor of C. Vann Woodward*, ed. J. Morgan Kousser and James M. McPherson (New York: Oxford University Press, 1982), 149.

24. Although this ethnoracial pentagon is now in vogue, it is not the only demographic map being advanced. One prominent competitor centers on "people of color," which implies a bipolar construction. In this view, white and nonwhite are the two relevant categories, and all distinctions between the various "colored" peoples are less significant than their being nonwhite. The greater acceptance of the ethnoracial pentagon is indicated by the frequency with which one is asked to identify

oneself in terms of this pentagon on application forms, health-care questionnaires, and other forms.

25. Mary C. Waters, *Ethnic Options: Choosing Identities in America* (Berkeley: University of California Press, 1990), 147. See also Richard D. Alba, "The Twilight of Ethnicity among Americans of European Ancestry: The Case of the Italians," in *Ethnicity and Race,* ed. Alba, 134–58.

26. Herbert Gans, "Symbolic Ethnicity in America," *Ethnic and Racial Studies* 2 (January 1979): 1–20, especially 9.

27. Waters, *Ethnic Options,* 157–58, 167, 164.

28. R. M. MacIver, "What We All Can Do," in *Unity and Difference in American Life,* ed. R. M. MacIver (New York: Columbia University Press, 1947), 152–53. This volume is an interesting document in the history of American discourse about unity and difference. See, for example, the essays by Lawrence K. Frank (33–40), E. Franklin Frazier (43–59), and Clyde R. Miller (107–18).

29. Examples of this literature include Terry A. Cooney, *The Rise of the New York Intellectuals: Partisan Review and Its Circle, 1934–1945* (Madison: University of Wisconsin Press, 1986); Thomas Bender, *New York Intellect* (New York: Alfred A. Knopf, 1987); Thomas Bender, "Lionel Trilling and American Culture," *American Quarterly* 42 (June 1990): 324–47; Richard Handler, "Boasian Anthropology and the Critique of American Culture," *American Quarterly* 42 (June 1990): 252–73; Leslie J. Vaughan, "Cosmopolitanism, Ethnicity, and American Identity: Randolph Bourne's 'TransNational America,'" *Journal of American Studies* 25 (December 1991): 443–59; and Susanne Klingenstein, *Jews in the American Academy, 1900–1940: The Dynamics of Intellectual Assimilation* (New Haven, Conn.: Yale University Press, 1991).

30. One feature of this earlier discourse that seems significant in today's context is the struggle of Jewish intellectuals to work out an orientation toward Jewish identity consistent with their identity as Americans and as cosmopolitans.

31. Quoted in Molly Myerowitz Levine, "The Use and Abuse of *Black Athena*," *American Historical Review* 97 (April 1992): 440.

32. Orlando Patterson and Chris Winthrop, "White Poor, Black Poor," *New York Times,* May 3, 1992.

4   The Multiculturalism Debate as Cultural Text

Werner Sollors

According to many accounts that are familiar from the press, a debate is going on in the world of American higher education. It is a debate that concerns educational contents, forms of instruction, and the changing composition of the student and faculty bodies; and it revolves around such terms as *the canon* and *political correctness* and such policies as affirmative action. There is said to be a conflict between a "traditional," "conservative" emphasis on keeping established values of liberal arts education and a "radical," "ethnic," and "feminist" demand for such changes as the "diversification" of faculty and of reading lists. The word that has most galvanized these discussions is *multiculturalism.* It is a word that seems omnipresent now but has been part of debates in the United States for only a short time. It seems to have come into use in the wake of reactions, on the one hand, to the traditionalist assertions by Allan Bloom and William J. Bennett or, somewhat differently, E. D. Hirsch and, on the other, to the vehement public debate about a modification in the Stanford core curriculum, a substitution in one of eight tracks that permitted the inclusion of non-Western literature in a great books course.

Most instances of the word that surveys and library data bases have indexed do come from the past few years; the frequency intensified in

1990, especially in the worlds of education and journalism, and may have reached its peak by 1991. *Multiculturalism* as an -ism word apparently originated in discussions about Africa,[1] Australia, and Canada. As a key term of the official Canadian government policy introduced by Pierre Trudeau on October 8, 1971, multiculturalism included various features, such as giving "grants to ethnic organizations to help them preserve their culture," with an annual budget that increased from $1.5 million in 1971 to $10 million in 1973, and the appointment of a cabinet minister, Dr. Stanley Haidasz, "whose exclusive responsibility was multiculturalism."[2] John Porter's essay "Ethnic Pluralism in Canada" may have helped transport the new "-ism" into the context of U.S. academics. This contribution to the widely read *Ethnicity* of 1975 contains a section entitled "Multiculturalism within a Bilingual Framework," in which Porter outlines Trudeau's policy.[3]

Multiculturalism came into wider use in the United States only in the late 1980s. Of course, there are probably many earlier isolated instances, such as Edward Haskell's *Lance: A Novel about Multicultural Men* (1941),[4] whose hero is, as the *New York Herald Tribune* reviewer noted, "polyglot, bi-national, tied to no patriotic loyalties but ardently a servant of science and of social science particularly" who feels happy only with people who "are 'multicultural' like himself."[5] The reviewer put the term in quotation marks here, and she assessed the book as a "fervent sermon against nationalism, national prejudice and behavior in favor of a 'multicultural' way of life and a new social outlook more suited to the present era of rapid transport and shifting populations." Haskell was the son of Swiss-American missionaries and grew up in the United States, Turkey, Greece, Bulgaria, and Switzerland before going to Oberlin, Columbia, and Harvard and becoming an activist aiding political prisoners and an investigator of political trials. As the dust jacket tells the reader, Haskell regarded his novel "not only as the statement of a problem, but also its partial theoretical solution." His mouthpiece, Major Campbell, states at a dramatic point in the novel, "Men in all climes and all times live by the narrow little things they know. . . . Their contact has been with one language, one faith, and one nation. They are unicultural. . . . But we, being children of the great age of transportation and communication, have contacts with *many* languages, *many* faiths, and *many* nations. We are *multi*cultural." Haskell's characters, whose life stories transcend the confines of individual nation-states, of one language, or of a single religion, may be representative harbingers of what has happened in the world at a much larger scale since World War II. Haskell anticipated the anxieties that

multiculturalism could unleash in readers accustomed only to the unicultural model of the nation-state, readers who might suspect Haskell's
"multicultural men" of disloyalty and lack of patriotism. Thus he also lets
Campbell stress the similarities between multiculturalists and unicultur-
alists: "Multicultural people . . . are just like unicultural people. They develop faith and loyalty and patriotism too: faith in science, loyalty to world
organization, and patriotism for mankind."[6]
    Edward Haskell's 1941 novel introduced the word *multicultural* to
describe the pioneering quality of a few exceptional men. Before the wider
dissemination of *multiculturalism,* the issues with which the word has
become associated were usually debated under such terms as *cultural pluralism,* introduced by Horace Kallen in 1924,[7] or *ethnicity,* a 1941 coinage
by W. Lloyd Warner that slowly replaced the older, compromised word
race.[8]
    Now that it exists lexically, what does the word *multiculturalism* mean?
Definitions are not always easy to come by, and they differ widely. In 1990,
for example, the Ford Foundation gave nineteen grants to universities "to
broaden cultural and intellectual diversity in American higher education,"
reflecting the "rapid demographic changes under way in American society"; yet the Ford Foundation spokesman refused to provide a definition,
giving the reason that "the Foundation does not define multiculturalism."[9]
    Critical definitions resemble reactions that the "new ethnicity" received
in the 1970s. Michael Walzer and Richard Bernstein call it "the new tribalism."[10] Isaiah Berlin speaks of "the return of the *Volksgeist.*"[11] Yet the
proponents Ted Gordon and Wahneema Lubiano distance multiculturalism expressly from ethnicity—as well as from "Western culture"—when
they write: "Multiculturalism is not a tourist's eye view of 'ethnicity,' nor
is it a paean to the American mythology defining this nation as a collection of diverse and plural groups living happily together and united by
their knowledge of, and proper respect for, something called 'Western
culture.'"[12] According to Arthur Schlesinger Jr.'s book *The Disuniting of
America,* multiculturalism is quite unlike, and much more sinister than,
cultural pluralism, for "instead of referring as it should to all cultures,
[multiculturalism] has come to refer only to non-Western, nonwhite
cultures. The former president of the Modern Language Association even
wonders why 'we cannot be students of Western culture and multiculturalism at the same time'"—as if they were opposites.[13] Lewis Feuer also
distinguishes between multiculturalism and cultural pluralism when he
asks, "Why was 'multiculturalism' chosen to replace the already existing

expression 'cultural pluralism?' The answer is a simple one. 'Cultural pluralism' was invented by supporters of liberal democracy who had a strong faith in American civilization."[14] By contrast, Mortimer Adler, the senior defender of the "Great Books" concept, writes, "Multiculturalism is cultural pluralism," but he advocates a "*restricted* cultural pluralism."[15] According to the Afrocentrist Molefi Kete Asante, "Either you support multiculturalism in American education, or you support the maintenance of white supremacy."[16]

Roger Kimball, whose book *Tenured Radicals* sharply criticizes *multiculturalism,* [17] calls the word "an omnibus term for the new academic orthodoxy" that "has provided common cause and something of a common vocabulary for a profession otherwise riven by an allegiance to competing radicalisms."[18] The term *multiculturalism* is sufficiently ambiguous to contain different and indeed incompatible programs and ideas. Paul Berman, the editor of an anthology of essays entitled *Debating P.C.,* concludes, "No three people agree about the meaning of central terms like . . . 'multiculturalism'. . . . Every participant carries around his own definitions, the way that on certain American streets every person packs his own gun. . . . The debate is unintelligible. But it is noisy!"[19] Larry Yarbrough finds that the debate "may seem as interminable as some faculty meetings."[20] By now a sense of fatigue is palpable in the "interminable" debate.

If the battle is indeed one between "traditionalists" and "radicals," then the image that multiculturalism evokes as a promise for a better future is particularly important. In the interest of a utopian vision, Henry Giroux, for example, advocates a pedagogy "which refuses to reconcile higher education with inequality."[21] Such rhetoric of hope is certainly present in the discussion. Less strongly pronounced is what Karl Mannheim saw as a feature of utopias, that is, that they function as "wish-images which take on revolutionary functions."[22] One of the essays that comes closest to such wish-images is Ishmael Reed's "America: The Multinational Society," which has as its motto a clipping from the *New York Times:* "At the annual Lower East Side Jewish festival yesterday, a Chinese woman ate a pizza slice in front of Ty Thuan Duc's Vietnamese grocery store. Beside her a Spanish-speaking family patronized a cart with two signs: 'Italian Ices' and 'Kosher by Rabbi Alper.' And after the pastrami ran out, everybody ate knishes."[23] Reed's essay continues in the same vein: "On the day before Memorial Day, 1983, a poet called me to describe a city he had just visited. He said that one section included mosques, built by the Islamic people who dwelled there. Attending his reading, he said, were large numbers of Hispanic people, forty thousand of whom lived in the same city. He was not talking about a fabled city located in some mysterious region of the world. The city he'd visited was Detroit."[24]

This strategy of making the familiar strange and of presenting the American experience as an increasingly syncretistic give-and-take multiculturalism is, of course, a well-known feature from the traditions of melting pot and pluralist rhetoric; it is also worth remembering that Reed's essay was written before *multiculturalism* had become such a central term. Yet the exciting research that has been undertaken by scholars who have explored such polyethnically interactive features of American culture has not been drawn on much for multicultural utopianism. Berndt Ostendorf, for example, has investigated and theorized the Creolization of American culture.[25] Donald Weber has worked on the subtle ways in which ethnic difference made itself felt in such national television series as *The Goldbergs;* he cites, for example, a character who said, "America I love you. If I didn't hear an accent every day I'd think I was in a foreign country."[26] Christopher Newton studied the linguistic mix in the Italo-American commedia dell'arte tradition. The play *Iammo a Connailanda* (Let's Go to Coney Island), for example, contains such lines as "Ai brecche iu fesse" and a comment on the ridiculous notion that in America *femmine* are called "uomini" (women).[27] The absence or weakness of such visions is illustrated by the fact that Cornel West has to make the following plea in the multiculturalism debate: "If you're Afro-American and you're a victim of the rule of capital, and a European Jewish figure who was born in the Catholic Rhineland and grew up as a Lutheran, by the name of Karl Marx, provides certain analytical tools, then you go there."[28] Utopian vision seems in decline at this moment in history, and, even when critics articulate a hopeful model, they may add disastrous qualifiers—as does Isaiah Berlin, who develops a concept of non-hegemonic pluralism only to conclude "that at the end of the twentieth century, there is little historical evidence for the realizability of such a vision."[29] John Higham rightly mentions that the question of whether multiculturalism should present divergence or convergence is rarely addressed in the debate,[30] which is often looking backward to various ethnic histories and rarely looking forward to a polyethnic future. Perhaps one of the last areas for utopian thinking is the belief that multiculturalism will increase the self-esteem and hence the performance of some students,[31] a belief that is also seriously questioned in the literature.[32]

What we are more likely to find in the debate about multiculturalism than wish-images of future interactions of many cultures and languages are demographic projections according to which in fifty years half of all U.S. citizens will be nonwhite. Such journalistic statistical estimates, Stephan Thernstrom argues, simply project high birthrates of rural populations into the future. There is, however, reason to expect birthrates to decline in cultural environments where children signal high costs rather than wealth. Thernstrom also points out that such visions of the coming "minority majority" resemble the American "race suicide" predictions in the face of the fertile South and eastern European immigrants a century ago. He cites one worrier from the past who "calculated that after 200 years 1,000 Harvard men would have left only 50 descendants, while 1,000 Romanian immigrants would have produced 100,000." Yet whereas then such predictions were made in order to argue for immigration restrictions, the current projections "are trotted out as evidence of the need for bigger and better social programs. Don't try to keep Genghis Khan out of the country; just make sure his kids are enrolled in Head Start," Thernstrom comments.[33]

Nonetheless, the 1990 census figures show a significant increase in "minority populations," from approximately 20 percent in 1980 to nearly 25 percent of the total population (i.e., from one in five to one in four). In a total resident population of nearly 250 million, there are now an estimated:

- 30 million blacks (12.0 percent of the total and a 13.2 percent increase over 1980);
- 22.4 million Hispanics (9.0 percent of the total and a 53.0 percent increase over 1980) (they may be "nonwhite" or "white");[34]
- 7.3 million Asians (3.0 percent of the total and an astounding increase of 107.8 percent over 1980); and
- 2 million American Indians (0.8 percent of the total and a 37.9 percent increase over 1980).[35]

According to official census figures from 1980 to 1990, 8.6 million immigrants came to the United States (though according to the New York Times, May 31, 1992, the total legal immigration was only 7,338,062). While this figure is nearly as high as the previous maximum for the period from 1900 to 1910 (nearly 8.8 million), one has to remember that the total population in 1910 was 92 million (as opposed to nearly 250 million in 1990).[36] Similarly, the number of foreign-born was 13.3 million in 1910 (⅐ of the total populace then), but 19.7 million in 1990 (only ⅟₁₃ of the total now).[37]

Demographic predictions may not make much of a utopia, but the discussion of the changing composition of the United States and of higher education in this country certainly is a factor that has animated the debate. Yet, as several observers have also pointed out, such statistics do not translate into an increase in cultural activities. Not all ethnic groups are interested in multiculturalism, and many of the new immigrants have shown restraint in their endorsement of multicultural education.[38] Gerald Early suggests three reasons why the rhetoric of demography is not convincing in supporting claims of a growing diversity: first, there is no increased interest in foreign languages; second, the multicultural reform efforts seem directed at the present rather than the future; and, third, there is no indication that power relations would be changing as well.[39]

Whatever may explain the thinness of utopianism (or its substitution by demographic prophecy) in the debate on multiculturalism, there certainly is no paucity of ideological energy that makes itself felt in commodification and exporting, ethnicization and identity politics, top-down approach and compromise strategy. No matter what one's definition or position on the subject, multiculturalism may be an excellent marketing device. Benetton set the tone for multicultural commercials, and the academy, too, has moved closer than ever to the marketplace in the context of multiculturalism. Upon closer inspection, some battles turn out to involve such earthshaking issues as the choice between two widely marketed literary anthologies for classroom use. Michael Bérubé has noted the (by no means rare) mutual endorsements of two prominent cultural conservatives: "Allan Bloom (apparently thinking that Kimball is working on a major motion picture) heads Kimball's front cover with the line, 'All persons serious about education should see it.' With uncanny symmetry, Bloom and Kimball now occupy the front covers of each other's books, but Kimball's salute to Bloom is more rigorous: 'An unparalleled reflection on today's intellectual climate. . . . That rarest of documents, a genuinely profound book.'"[40] An advertisement for Schlesinger's book *The Disuniting of America* in the *New York Times Book Review* cites an equally enthusiastic Roger Kimball: "*Trenchant* . . . One of the most devastating and articulate attacks on multiculturalism yet to appear."[41]

Schlesinger's book has certainly been marketed in unusual ways. It was widely cited in the press at a time when it was not yet available in bookstores, but only by mail order from Whittle Direct Books in Knoxville, Tennessee. Having sent my check for $11.95, I was surprised to receive the book by return mail via Federal Express. Opening it, I was even more surprised to find a hardback book that was interrupted by nine double-paged color ads for Federal Express which counted in the pagination of the 98-page book and which had such pertinent slogans as "We didn't start an air express service. We started a revolution" and "We know our way around like the natives. Because we *are* the natives"—in Japanese and English translation.[42]

The debate itself may be a commodity, too. This is certainly true for the recycled articles that are hectically marketed in widely disseminated mass market paperback collections, as the back cover of Paul Berman's collection *Debating P.C.* demonstrates:

> ### WHITE MALE EUROCENTRISM . . . OR AN ESSENTIAL CULTURAL HERITAGE?
>
> The debate . . . is the most important discussion in American education today and has grown into a major national controversy raging on the covers of our top magazines and news shows. This provocative anthology gives voice to the top thinkers of our time.
>
> A LAUREL TRADE PAPERBACK DELL PUBLISHING

The public debates themselves, on college campuses, radio, and television, are at least partly also forms of "orchestrated" marketing devices. Marketing may even bridge political differences: "Dinesh D'Souza, the 30-year-old former Reagan White House policy analyst whose book [*Illiberal Education*] graced the best-seller list for three months last year" was inspired by his lecture agent to invite his intellectual opponent Stanley Fish to join him "in a series of one-to-one debates." They "put themselves on the market—for a fee of $10,000 per debate. On five occasions in the last year the two men appeared before packed houses on college campuses to engage in orchestrated verbal fisticuffs. 'He debates issues very energetically and passionately, but without bitterness,' says D'Souza. 'As a result, we can have a knockdown, drag-out debate and still have a drink afterward.'"[43] The title of Adam Begley's *New York Times Magazine* essay, "Souped-Up Scholar," from which this information was culled, also suggests stylish commodification. The essay opens, for example, with a photo montage by Burk Uzzle of Stanley Fish, the spines of some of his books, and the front of a red sports car.

Multiculturalism may be offered and propagated politically as America's new trademark, now that the end of the cold war has made democracy and an electoral system so much more widespread. The question "Is Japan open enough to multiculturalism to justify an academic association meeting there" or the notion that American multiculturalism can be (or ought to be) a model for a world torn by nationalisms is occasionally voiced. The American Federation of Teachers Union president Albert Shanker, for example, quoted the Czech leader of the Civic Forum, Jan Urban, as saying, "'Do you realize that every country in Europe—Czechoslovakia, Yugoslavia, Bulgaria, Romania—is looking at this great miracle, which is the U.S. We cannot understand how different people can live together for hundreds of years and think of themselves as one. We are trying to understand how to emulate you so we can remain unified and not return to the racism, pogroms and wars of the past.'"[44] It is, of course, the consensus model of multiculturalism that is being advocated for export.

Multiculturalism may reduce participants to self-interested articulators of predictable points; it may inhibit not only cross-ethnic critique but also intraethnic critique among creative writers as well as critics and scholars. Many discussions are turned into autobiographies. As Elizabeth Fox-Genovese writes, "At the core of the multicultural agenda lies a commitment to education—and, indeed, culture itself—as primarily the quest for an acceptable autobiography."[45] Such autobiographic forms may look more like talk shows, Oprah Winfrey confessions that are quickly followed by the next one, and the autobiography itself is often a list of generalized items and clichés. Individuals seem to fall into categories carved out by "corporate pluralism"[46] and feel obliged to assert and express themselves through ethnic identity. Thus the talk about diversity may actually assert a shared frame; there are few unpredictable divisions, only the familiar groupings on grounds of race, gender, and sexual orientation (not *politics,* which is a theme that a new student Right may be beginning to claim, and not *class,* though it is often invoked by name).

Such identity politics is intellectually flabby. The term *identity* in connection with *ethnic,* which may go back only to Erik Erikson,[47] is omnipresent today. A sense of belonging to a race, ethnic group, or gender is generally permitted, at times even encouraged, to "hypercathect" itself upon all other social categories to which an individual may also belong— a phenomenon George Devereux has analyzed in the extreme case of fascism.[48] Multiculturalism as an educational policy is based on *very* soft social science and has been criticized for its weak anthropological foundations—for example, in blurring the distinctions between culture and race[49]—and for its poor philosophical underpinnings.[50]

Racial incidents and instances of interethnic hostility (as well as of sexual harassment) have increased in the past few years.[51] The notion of ethnos has certainly been reinstated in the process; as Higham points out, ethnic mobilization tends to spread rapidly.[52] Ethnicization also is likely to direct discussions to ethnic origins rather than to a possible polyethnic future—which may be a reason why there seems to be more ideology than utopia in the debate. Humor is at risk, as many jokes are now con sidered "insensitive." A new flurry of cultural production generates an often shrill debate focusing on the dividing line between permissible "free speech" and what is now called "hate speech," to be banned from college campuses. The areas in which conflicts erupt have undoubtedly prolifer-ated in the past ten years, and the boards and committees deciding disci-plinary matters are busier than ever.

Critiques of these aspects of multiculturalism are on the rise. David Hollinger compellingly articulates the need to construct a new, "posteth-nic" universalism that is informed—but not stymied—by the particularist challenges:[53] "A postethnic perspective recognizes the psychological val-ue and political function of groups of affiliation, but it resists a rigidifi-cation of exactly those ascribed distinctions between persons that vari-ous universalists and cosmopolitans have so long sought to diminish."[54] In a similar vein, Kwame Anthony Appiah argues, "The task is not to re-place one ethnocentrism with many or to reject old ideals of truth and impartiality as intrinsically biased. Rather, it is to recognize that those ideals have yet to be fully lived up to in our scholarship, that the bias has derived not from scholars who took Western standards (which often turn out to be everybody's standards) of truth for granted but from those who did not take them seriously enough."[55] In the last part of his 1993 *On Human Diversity*, Tzvetan Todorov similarly argues for a position of moderation and considers untenable the opinion that universalism is *necessarily* ethnocentric. He reminds readers that today ethnocentrism is not the only or even the most important perversion of universalism. One only has to think of relativism and scientism. For him the key question is how we can fend off the dangers of perverted universalism *and of rel-ativism*.[56] The Australian anthropologist Marie de Lepervanche consid-ered the possibility as early as 1980 "that where racist behavior and ide-ologies were convenient to ruling class interests one hundred years ago, the apparent opposite—the promotion of ethnicity—performs a similar role today."[57] In that sense, the distinction between "conservatives" and "radicals" may, in fact, be one between two interest groups. One does not have to agree with Robert Hughes's general harangue to appreciate his point that in cultural matters "we can hardly claim to have a left and a right anymore. Instead we have something more akin to two puritan sects, one masquerading as conservative, the other posing as revolutionary but using academic complaint as a way of evading engagement in the real world."[58] Instead, Hughes portrays one possible background of the mul-ticulturalism debate as the arrival of a new elite: "though élites are never going to go away, the composition of those élites is not necessarily static.

The future of American ones, in a globalized economy without a cold war, will rest with people who can think and act with informed grace across ethnic, cultural, linguistic lines."[59] Robert Christopher's book *Crashing the Gates,* tellingly subtitled *The De-WASPing of America's Power Elite,* gives a vivid account of the dramatic changes the United States has undergone and expresses the author's belief that a new American ruling class has emerged "in which with each year that passes ethnicity becomes less and less of a touchstone, and the distinctions between 'them' and 'us' become more and more blurred."[60] He views America as "far more inclusionary than most contemporary Americans assume."[61] Christopher explicitly includes black Americans in this vision, and his book opens with a chapter significantly entitled "Room at the Top."

The push for multicultural changes, in such a view, comes not necessarily from the populace but from the top; and what is sometimes noteworthy is a "top down" approach in multicultural education, too. Thus the chair of the Institute for Educational Management, Arthur Levine, gives the following advice to administrators in a pro-multiculturalist, yet conservative-sounding magazine: "Vigorous support must come from the top. Avoid politicization. The effort must be faculty-driven. . . . Try to avoid a top-down emphasis, but offer support (moral and fiscal)."[62]

Multiculturalism may be attractive to governments and agencies because it is cheap. As Louis Menand writes, "Changing the curriculum is the cheapest social program ever devised."[63] It is certainly much cheaper than a full social security, medicare, and unemployment insurance system in a society that is also increasingly polarized by class. From 1977 to 1989—the period of the rise of multiculturalism—pretax income of the rich grew sharply:

In the top 1 percent it grew by 77 percent, to an average annual income of $559,800;

in the top fifth by 29 percent, to $109,400;

in the second fifth by 9 percent, to $47,900;

the income of the third fifth grew by only 4 percent, to $32,700;

that of the fourth fifth sank by 1 percent, to $20,100;

and annual income in the bottom fifth declined by 9 percent, to $8,400.[64]

This shift is all the more dramatic since all efforts by other statisticians to deflect from its essentials have failed,[65] and since philanthropic efforts also declined very dramatically in the Reagan and Bush years.[66]

Multiculturalism may be less expensive than social equalization, but it is by no means "free." While the idea of multiculturalism is often ar-

ticulated as if it were phrased against the controlling powers of the status quo, it is, in fact, endorsed by many presidents of major universities
and by the Rockefeller and Ford foundations, whereas the Olin, Mobil,
Earhart, Smith-Robertson, Sarah Scaife, and Bradley foundations support
the "conservatives." (The debate may thus also be a battle of foundations.)
Many institutions have assigned large amounts of money to offices, foundations, fellowships, and so forth through which efforts are channeled.
Neil Rudenstine, the president of Harvard University, for example, declared that nothing is higher on his priority list than diversifying the faculty.[67] A special 1992 issue of *Change* magazine devoted to multiculturalism, which was sponsored by a grant from the Ford Foundation, listed
some rather startling statistics, according to which more than a third of
all colleges in the United States have a multicultural requirement; more
than a third offer black, Hispanic, Native American, or Asian American
studies courses; more than half have increased departmental multicultural
course offerings; half have multicultural advising programs; 60 percent
offer recruitment and retention programs for multicultural faculty; more
than 40 percent offer faculty development programs focusing on multicultural issues; and more than a third have multicultural institutes or
centers.[68] Arthur Levine and Jeanette Cureton conclude, "The sheer quan-
tity of multicultural activity . . . belies the belief that the traditional curriculum has been largely impermeable to, or has simply marginalized,
diversity. . . . multiculturalism today touches in varying degrees a majority of the nation's colleges and universities."[69] It may thus constitute a
firmly launched, but segmental and top-heavy experience rather than
promise a utopian vision for a whole society.

John Porter argued twenty years ago that for the United States and
Canada the dilemma is between mobility and ethnicity: "on the one hand
if they value and emphasize ethnicity, mobility and opportunity are en-
dangered, on the other hand if they emphasize mobility and opportunity, it will be at the cost of submerging cultural identity."[70] Here multiculturalism could work as a compromise. By simultaneously emphasizing
ethnicity and visibly incorporating representatives of the most important
ethnic groups into elites without having to make changes in the social
structure, multiculturalism might combine a stress on ethnicity with a
symbolic demonstration of mobility. The two lines come together most
plausibly in the biographical format of widely circulating success stories
of previously excluded Americans, such as Colin Powell and Clarence
Thomas.

A persistent paradox in the debate about multiculturalism is that the assertion of diversity is expressed in a rather homogeneous fashion, since only a limited arsenal of formal strategies and a recurrent set of motifs and themes are employed. It is thus tempting to take the debate as if it were a text and review some of its formal and thematic characteristics. Formally, many contributions to the discussion have generic affinities with the *jeremiad* (Schlesinger, Bloom, Kimball); they tend to be critical or vituperative as Puritan sermons once were, yet they end on a note of hope and promise. This affinity is recognized and thematized in the debate itself: Fish, for example, refers to D'Souza and Kimball as "our modern Jeremiahs."[71] The nature of the debate may be responsible for a smaller formal feature that recurs with some frequency: the Whitmanian *catalog* of ingredients that proponents or opponents tend to ascribe to multiculturalism. Kimball, for example, having observed a Modern Language Association meeting, listed the following items he regards as "substitutes" for literature: "Marxism, feminism, what we might call homosexuality, 'cultural studies,' ethnic studies, and any number of indeterminate mixtures of the above leavened with dollops of deconstructivist or poststructuralist theory—in other words, multiculturalism *de luxe.*"[72] The recurrence of such cataloging has also been noted in the debate. Henry Louis Gates Jr. speaks ironically of the "trinity" of race, class, and gender.[73] Barbara Ehrenreich writes, "Too often [multiculturalism] . . . leads to the notion of politics as a list. Political 'theory' becomes a list of all the groups, issues, and concerns that you must remember to check off lest you offend somebody with no larger perspective connecting them. But a list does not define a political outlook."[74]

The smallest defining formal unit of the debate is probably the *anecdote.* With its cultural origins in such champions of anecdotal writing as Franklin and Emerson, its master in the debate on multiculturalism is undoubtedly D'Souza, whose anecdotes of incidents on campuses are often retold, varied, and corrected by other readers. The issues that led to Thernstrom's decision to discontinue offering a course called "The Peopling of America" have been told and retold in so many fashions since D'Souza highlighted his version of the story that printed interpretations are beginning to reach the indeterminacy threshold. Even when there is agreement about (or only one printed source of) an anecdote, interpretations in the context of race and gender may veer in different directions since the assessment of human motives can be difficult at this moment. Shelby Steele, a black opponent of affirmative action, stylizes some episodes in such a way as to show the outline of a world in which race may matter less. He frames a scene in a California supermarket as follows:

> When we [he is speaking of blacks here] first meet, we experience a trapped feeling, as if we had walked into a cage of racial expectations that would rob us of our individuality by reducing us to an exclusively racial dimension. We are a threat, at first, to one another's uniqueness. I have seen the same well-dressed black woman in the supermarket for more than a year now. We do not speak, and we usually pretend not to see each other. But, when we turn a corner suddenly and find ourselves staring squarely into each other's eyes, her face freezes and she moves on. I believe she is insisting that both of us be more than black—that we interact only when we have a reason other than the mere fact of our race. Her chilliness enforces a priority I agree with—individuality over group identity.[75]

Yet, as one reviewer pointed out, this woman may actually be miles ahead of Steele in the struggle for individuality. She, too, might not be thinking of race at all and only find him to be not likable enough individually to thaw her chilliness. She might also have recognized him and be showing her disapproval of his widely publicized political views by snubbing him. It is good to remember that much of the debate rests on the plausibility of anecdotes that no one can possibly verify completely. This again strengthens the autobiographical format of the debate.

A variant of the anecdote—which at least purports to be based on facts—is the *fable,* or parable, which derives its point or moral from an admittedly hypothetical scenario. John Searle used such a "counterfactual situation" to review the assumptions of the "traditionalists" and the identity politics of the multicultural challengers:

> Suppose it was discovered by an amazing piece of historical research that the works commonly attributed to Plato and Aristotle were not written by Greek males, but by two Chinese women who were cast ashore on the coast of Attica when a Chinese junk shipwrecked off the Piraeus in the late fifth century B.C. What difference would this make to our assessment of the works of Plato and Aristotle. From the traditionalist point of view, none whatever. It would just be an interesting historical fact. From the challengers' point of view, I think it would make a tremendous difference. Ms. Plato and Ms. Aristotle would now acquire a new authenticity as genuine representatives of a previously underrepresented minority, and the most appropriate faculty to teach their works would be then Chinese women.[76]

Searle uses this fable to drive home the following moral: "Implicit in the traditional assumptions . . . is the view that the faculty member does not have to exemplify the texts that he or she teaches. They assume that the works of Marx can be taught by someone who is not a Marxist, just as Aquinas can be taught by someone who is not a Catholic, and Plato by someone who is not a Platonist. But the challengers assume, for example, that women's studies should be taught by feminist women, Chicano studies by Chicanos committed to a certain set of values, etc."[77]

On the borderline between formal and thematic features is a repeated syllable in the present discussion. Whereas a *Rhyming Dictionary* from 1936 lists only ten words rhyming with "-centric,"[78] our own age is so much richer for poets who want to rhyme words ending with -centric and -centrism. The fashion may actually be going back to William Graham Sumner's coinage of *ethnocentrism* in 1906. For Sumner, *ethnocentrism* is "the technical name for [a] view of things in which one's own group is the center of everything, and all others are scaled and rated with reference to it. . . . ethnocentrism leads a people to exaggerate and intensify everything in their own folkways which is peculiar and which differentiates them from others. It therefore strengthens the folkways."[79] Now -*centric* is attached to many words that have become familiar, from *Afrocentric* to *Eurocentric.* Jean Devisse uses the less familiar *Mediterraneocentrism.*[80] The catalog has been further enriched by *Amerocentric* or *Americentric.* Thus Diane Ravitch writes, "American education, if it is centered on anything, is centered on itself. It is 'Americentric.' Most American students . . . know very little about Europe, and even less about the rest of the world . . . . When the Berlin Wall was opened in the fall of 1989, journalists discovered that most American teenagers had no idea what it was, nor why its opening was such a big deal. Nonetheless, Eurocentrism provides a better target than Americentrism."[81]

Some recurrent thematic elements in the multiculturalism debate also deserve attention. There is, for example, a decided preference for the term *discontents,* often an allusion to Freud's *Unbehagen an der Kultur.*[82] We find panels and essays on "multiculturalism and its discontents"; the word is used even when one might think that others might fit better. Thus Catharine Stimpson writes, "Obviously, our multiculturalism has many antagonistic discontents. . . . Even though multiculturalism has . . . discontents, it is a great, defining feature of our historical moment."[83] Interestingly, recent critics of the multiculturalism debate, such as Ostendorf and Marshall Sahlins, have been drawn to Freud's work for the expression "narcissism of minor differences," which Freud applied to the "phenomenon that it is precisely communities with adjoining territories, and related to each other in other ways as well, who are engaged in con-

stant feuds and ridiculing each other—like the Spaniards and the Portuguese, for instance, the North Germans and the South Germans, the English and Scotch, and so on."[84]

According to Sahlins, Freud was concerned about Balkanization when
he spoke of this particular narcissism;[85] and Balkanization is another
thematic cluster that traverses the multiculturalism debate. Steele feels
that as "racial, ethnic, and gender differences become forms of sovereign-
ty, campuses become balkanized."[86] D'Souza's opinion of the new university politics (characterized by affirmative action) is summed up in this
way: "I think this is a formula for racial division, for Balkanization, and
ultimately for racial hostility."[87] Itabari Njeri writes, "Schlesinger and
other critics see [multiculturalism] as a kind of tribalism, a dangerous
balkanization of American society."[88] Todd Gitlin finds in "group narcissism" "a perfect recipe for a home-grown Yugoslavia."[89]

There is also a widespread desire to explore the semantic possibilities
of a word like *canon* through repeated punning. Thus we read of "loose
canons" (Todd Gitlin, Adam Yarmolinsky, and Henry Louis Gates Jr.);
canons of the past simply become "canon-fodder" of the present (Irving
Louis Horowitz); and there is talk of firing the canon (Bryan Wolf).[90]

Probably no phrase is used as much in the multiculturalism debate as
E pluribus unum—out of many one. It has been connected with the discussion of American diversity for some time, for example, in Arthur
Mann's 1979 book *The One and the Many*. Schlesinger's book *The Disuniting of America* contains a long meditation on this theme: "The national
ideal had once been *e pluribus unum*. Are we now to belittle *unum* and
glorify *pluribus?* Will the center hold? Or will the melting pot yield to the
Tower of Babel? . . . The question poses itself: how to restore the balance
between *unum* and *pluribus?*"[91] Yet Schlesinger has no monopoly on
wordplay with *e pluribus unum*. Ravitch gave her essay on "Multiculturalism" the subtitle "E Pluribus Plures."[92] "More pluribus, more unum,"
a *New York Times* editorial of June 23, 1991, followed suit. "*E pluribus
what?*" the *American Studies Newsletter* (September 1991) asked as a lead-
in to a special section. "E Pluribus nihil," Midge Decter answered in *Commentary* in September 1991, followed by Stanley Schmidt's editorial "E
pluribus zero" in *Analog Science Fiction and Fact* in April 1992. Or the
other way around: "Ex uno, plus," as a 1991 *National Review* editorial put
it. In this company, the title of one of Albert Shanker's ad-columns in the
New York Times on February 23, 1992, sounds modest since it only adds a
question mark and asks, "E Pluribus Unum?"

Given the large circulation that the phrase *e pluribus unum* enjoys in
multiculturalism, it is regrettable that its origins have been largely neglect-

ed. To my knowledge, no participant in the current debate on multiculturalism—with the exception of the internationally pitched *American
Studies Newsletter*—has paid attention to the source of this saying, which
appears on coins and is immortalized on the back of each dollar bill, reproducing the Great Seal of the United States. The motto was, as Kenneth
Silverman writes, part of the original proposal for the seal that a committee (which included Benjamin Franklin, Thomas Jefferson, Thomas Paine,
and John Adams) had made on August 20, 1776. In 1782 Congress adopted a design by William Barton, who "made the central image of the seal
a large eagle displaying a reduced shield of thirteen stripes on its chest.
In its talons the eagle would grip an olive branch and a bundle of arrows.
In its beak would be a scroll reading *e pluribus unum*. Above the eagle
would hover a cloud shrouding a constellation of thirteen stars."[93] The
"one" was clearly meant to signify the confederation, the "many" its united thirteen colonies; but how and where did the founders find this neat
Latin phrase? The most plausible source is the title page of the popular
London *Gentleman's Magazine,* where *e pluribus unum* promised "a variety of literary texts" under one cover.[94] A poem of 1734 explained, "To
your motto most true, for our monthly inspection / You mix various rich
sweets in *one* fragrant collection."[95] The epigraph had been copied from
the *Gentleman's Journal or the Monthly Miscellany,* originally edited by the
Huguenot refugee Pierre Antoine Motteux from 1691 to 1694.[96]

Ultimately, the phrase goes back to Horace's *Epistle to Florus* (circa 20
B.C.) or to the poem *Moretum,* ascribed to Virgil. Horace's exhortative
epistle asks at the end, "Do you grow gentler and better, as old age draws
near. What good does it do you to pluck out *a single one of many* thorns?
If you know not how to live aright make way for those who do."[97] Horace provided the motto for the *Spectator* of August 20, 1711, but Horace
meant "one selected from many," not "one composed of many."[98]

The *Moretum* (Ploughman's Lunch) is a short poem about the farmer
(perhaps ex-slave) Simulus who, with some help from the African woman Scybale, prepares a meal, a dumpling made of something resembling
pesto or, according to another reader, a salad.[99] Having added hard cheese,
salt, and herbs, and having mashed the garlic, he pounds everything:
"Round and round went his hand; gradually the original ingredients lost
their own properties and *one* colour emerged *from several,* not wholly
green, since the milky fragments held out, nor shining milk-white, being
variegated by all the herbs."[100]

"E pluribus unus," one source of *e pluribus unum,* comes from the same
metaphoric realm as do such alternatives to the melting pot as stew or
salad bowl, and an African woman is involved in it. Monroe Deutsch's

conclusion of 1929 deserves to be cited: "And so a Frenchman adapted and published on the title-page of a magazine issued in England a group of three Latin words which became the national motto of this composite people, the United States of America."[101] All the interest in "cultural studies" has not redirected academics toward this truly ironic story of origins of the noble motto, which had nothing to do with political federalism, let alone ethnic diversity. In this instance, the multiculturalism debate also continues to canonize a few words by Horace or Virgil.

Similar canonization processes take place with other snippets of "Western culture." Giroux, for example, writes in the course of his democratic critique of canons, "The liberal arts curriculum, composed of the 'best' that had been said or written, was intended, as Elizabeth Fox-Genovese has observed, 'to provide selected individuals with a collective history, culture, and epistemology so that they could run the world effectively.'"[102] The phrasing, "the best that has been said or written," is favored by many contributors to the multiculturalism debate and goes back, of course, to Matthew Arnold.

Here is D'Souza: "I'm in favor of a multicultural curriculum that emphasizes what Matthew Arnold called the best that has been thought and said."[103] Kimball thinks that Arnold "had looked to the preservation and transmission of the best that had been thought and written as a means of rescuing culture from anarchy in a democratic society."[104] Gertrude Himmelfarb also describes a better past, when "it was considered the function of the university to . . . liberate [students] intellectually and spiritually by exposing them, as the English poet Matthew Arnold put it, to 'the best which has been thought and said in the world.'"[105] Alexander Nehamas responds by calling attention to an inaccuracy in such uses of Arnold:

> Nostalgia has colored . . . Professor Himmelfarb's . . . recollection of Arnold, who actually wrote that the "business" of criticism is "to know the best that is known and thought in the world." . . . Himmelfarb's . . . replacement of Arnold's present-tense "is" by the perfect tense "has been" . . . allows her to appeal to Arnold's authority in order to insinuate, if not to argue outright, that the university's concern is with the past and that the present, at least in connection with the humanities, lies largely outside the scope of its function.[106]

Some advocates of multiculturalism have criticized conservative uses of Arnold more generally by declaring him irrelevant to democratic education or to the electronic age. Searle observes that what were once undisputed educational platitudes have now become contested, for example, the demand that students should, "in Matthew Arnold's overquoted words, 'know the best that is known and thought in the world.'"[107]

To my knowledge, the multicultural "left" has not yet claimed and defended Matthew Arnold against his "conservative" admirers who have appropriated him, yet a look at Arnold's "platitude" could actually be helpful at this moment. (Morris Dickstein has written a brief for Arnold's radicalism that I shall relate a little later.) In his essay "The Function of Criticism at the Present Time," first published in 1864, Arnold distinguishes a practical "English" tradition from a "French" world that cherishes ideas. He takes up the demand for critical "disinterestedness" (perhaps derived from Goethe's term "Uneigennützigkeit in *Dichtung und Wahrheit,* used to characterize Spinoza).[108] Criticism can show this

> by resolutely following the law of its own nature, which is to be a free play of the mind on all subjects which it touches. By steadily refusing to lend itself to any of those ulterior, political, practical considerations about ideas, which plenty of people will be sure to attach to them, which perhaps ought often to be attached to them, which in this country at any rate are certain to be attached to them quite sufficiently, but which criticism has really nothing to do with. Its business is, as I have said, simply to know the best that is known and thought in the world, and by in its turn making this known, to create a current of true and fresh ideas.[109]

Arnold repeats the famous phrase when he praises the *Revue des Deux Mondes* as an organ that—unlike the practical and partisan English journals—has chosen "for its main function to understand and utter the best that is known and thought in the world."[110] Baudelaire's *Fleurs du mal* had appeared in the *Revue* there a few years earlier. Arnold chastises the notion "that truth and culture themselves can be reached by the processes of this life," a notion advocated by critics who seem to proclaim, "We are all *terrae filii,* all Philistines together."[111] Encouraging a broader view, Arnold points out that "as England is not all the world, much of the best that is known and thought cannot be of English growth;"[112] hence, Arnold demands that the "English critic of literature must dwell much on foreign thought, and with particular heed on any part of it, which, while significant and fruitful in itself, is for any reason specially likely to escape him."[113]

When Arnold put the essay into his collection, he added a passage addressing the reader's possible complaint that his observations lacked practical use and were not enough devoted to "the current English literature of the day."[114] He responded, "I am sorry for it, for I am afraid I must disappoint these expectations. I am bound by my own definition of criticism: a disinterested endeavor to learn and propagate *the best that is known and thought in the world.* How much of current English literature comes into this 'best that is known and thought in the world?' Not very much, I fear; certainly less, at this moment, than of the current literature of France and Germany."[115] He concludes with his vision of a contemporary criticism that transcends national boundaries and "regards Europe as being, for intellectual purposes, one great confederation, bound to a joint action and working to a common result; and whose members have, for their proper outfit, a knowledge of Greek, Roman, and Eastern antiquity, and of one another."[116]

Arnold's "overquoted" phrase (overused perhaps even by Arnold himself) comes from a context that is not irrelevant to the multicultural discussions of today, since Arnold was concerned here not with a static canon of the past, as his conservative adherents claim at times, but with the open exploration of fresh ideas in a cosmopolitan spirit of disinterestedness that went beyond predictable *parti pris* positions and national boundaries. Hence he could be cited to strengthen calls for reading "the best that is known and thought in the world," with a stress on *world,* not just the works of one country or in one language.

Arnold used his expression several more times in *Culture and Anarchy,* drawn from lectures he had given in 1866 and 1867. Once he demands that we get to know "whether through reading, observing, or thinking, the best that can at present be known in the world."[117] Furthermore I should mention, in fairness to Gertrude Himmelfarb, that when Arnold added a preface for the book publication in 1869, he wrote, "The whole scope of the essay is to recommend culture as the great help out of our present difficulties; culture being a pursuit of our total perfection by means of getting to know, on all matters which most concern us, the best which has been thought and said in the world."[118] Yet, again, this does not make Arnold play a cultural past against the present. He explicates later in the preface, "If a man without books or reading, or reading nothing but his letters and the newspapers, gets nevertheless a fresh and free play of the best thoughts upon his stock notions and habits, he has got culture."[119] Moreover, when he uses the familiar phrasing again in the "Sweetness and Light" section of *Culture and Anarchy,* it is to express his view that it must be the aim of culture "to do away with classes; to make the best that has been thought and known in the world current everywhere." The great men of culture carry, "from one end of society to the other, the best knowledge, the best ideas of their time,"[120] with a distinct focus on the *contemporary* context.

It is noteworthy that for twentieth-century American Jewish intellectuals who moved into the humanities, Matthew Arnold was a central subject of interest. Horace M. Kallen, Ludwig Lewisohn, and Lionel Trilling chose Arnold as an important topic for their reflections.[121] Inspired by Trilling, Dickstein has articulated his own appreciation of Arnold, stressing Arnold's originality in demanding "relevance" in literary studies and the fact that Arnold's "canon" was "anti-canonical, existential."[122] Dickstein notes the irony (vividly illustrated by the multiculturalism debate) that Arnold's "attacks on English insularity . . . became the ground of a new traditionalism, the justification for a new insularity, not very different from the insularity he attacked."[123] He summarizes: "Mistaken for a conservative, Arnold belongs if anything to this great tradition of cultural radicalism which recoiled from the alliance between liberalism and 'progress,' and hence did much to establish the modern humanist critique of industrial society."[124] Contrasting Arnold with his present-day detractors who see in his striving for "disinterestedness" a "mask for specific social interests: white, male, and middle-class," Dickstein, whose most famous earlier book was a sympathetic account of the 1960s, points out that for Arnold, "disinterestedness" "was a social as well as literary goal—really a utopian ideal"[125]—of which we have found so little in the multiculturalism debate.

The Englishman who is most systematically invoked in current debates is George Orwell, as an exploration of "political correctness" suggests. In a letter to the *New York Times Book Review* in May 1992, Mark Kurlansky writes, "There was a time when I loved the phrase 'politically correct' as a wonderfully snide label for the safe conformism of the liberal establishment. But then it became a tedious cliché used to describe the tyranny of that same establishment, which tries to censor anyone who does not conform. Now we see another use. An idea can simply be dismissed by asserting that it is politically correct."[126] The term *politically correct*—PC for short—is pervasive in the multiculturalism debate. It was traced by Ruth Perry to 1970, to an essay by Toni Cade (who was yet to add Bambara to her name). Perry suspects that the term may come from Maoist rhetoric.[127] It is possible that the phrasing gained wider currency only in post–World War II critiques of totalitarianism.[128] Thus when the protagonist of Ralph Ellison's novel *Invisible Man* gets censored by the brotherhood and is questioned, Brother Tobitt sarcastically asks, "You mean he admits the *possibility* of being incorrect?"[129]

Though the term *politically correct* does not seem to appear in George Orwell's novel *Nineteen Eighty-Four,* its meaning might come from the ambience of this work. When Julia asks Winston Smith about his wife Katharine, for example, he answers:

> "She was—do you know the Newspeak word *goodthinkful?* Meaning naturally orthodox, incapable of thinking a bad thought?"
> "No, I didn't know the word, but I know the kind of person, right enough."[130]

In "The Principles of Newspeak," the appendix to the novel, Orwell states that "a Party member called upon to make a political or ethical judgment should be able to spray forth the correct opinions as automatically as a machine gun spraying forth bullets."[131] Even though Orwell said "goodthinkful" to characterize Winston's wife and legitimate his adultery, and though he placed the words *political* and *correct* in the same sentence without actually saying "politically correct," the multiculturalism debate is suffused with nothing more than allusions to Orwell—with whose works many intellectuals refamiliarized themselves in the year 1984.

First, there is the general sense of "newspeak" about all the new words that have emerged as a result of the desire to be more sensitive and gender neutral. Walter Goodman, for example, reviewed one of the many new and politically correct dictionaries that are now on the market under the title "Decreasing Our Word Power: The New Newspeak." In a similar vein, Robert Lerner and Stanley Rothman complained about "Newspeak, feminist-style" in *Commentary* in 1990.[132] If the conservatives call the liberals' pleas for more sensitive language "newspeak," the liberals retaliate in kind. "Hate speech" is the term generally used now to describe offensive or insensitive language. Orwell readers will recognize the echo of "Hate Week" and the "Hate Song" that people intone during this event.[133] Bérubé uses the word *doubleplusungood* to describe the media campaign against political correctness.[134] In Orwell it refers to pornography in *Pornosec* of the Ministry of Truth Records Department.[135] Paula Rothenberg writes, "But in the end, war is *not* peace, slavery is *not* freedom, and no matter what the N.A.S. [the conservative National Association of Scholars] may believe, ignorance is *not* strength." She is, of course, alluding to the inscriptions on the ministries in *Nineteen Eighty-Four.*[136]

The most frequently circulating Orwellian term may be *Thought Police,* used by the Right, center, and Left. George Will employs the term to denounce politically correct thinking at American universities; Michael Novak, writing on politically correct thinking at American universities, uses it in *Forbes* in 1990;[137] and journalists have used it again and again—in organs ranging from *Playboy* to *Reader's Digest*, in articles with such titles as "Campus Christians and the New Thought Police," "Thought Police on Campus," and "The Thought Police Get Tenure"—to describe the atmosphere of censorship in university life. Hughes argues against comparisons between McCarthyism and political correctness by pointing out that the "number of conservative academics fired by the lefty thought police . . . is zero."[138] Camille Paglia deplores women's studies programs and finds that they have "hatched the new thought police of political correctness."[139] Nat Hentoff cites Henry Louis Gates Jr.: "We must not succumb to the temptation to resurrect our own version of the thought police, who would determine who, and what, is 'black.'"[140] Patricia Williams distinguishes the "joy of multiculturalism" from "the oppression of groupthink and totalitarianism."[141]

The elusive nature of "truth" and "reality" has also been seen in terms of *Nineteen Eighty-Four*. Thus *Speaking for the Humanities* (a controversial pamphlet produced by the American Council for Learned Societies) stated, without giving evidence, "As the most powerful modern philosophies and theories have been demonstrating, claims of disinterest, objectivity, and universality are not to be trusted and themselves tend to reflect local historical conditions."[142] When Todorov reviewed and rightly criticized the pamphlet in the *New Republic*, he pointed out that it is "awkwardly reminiscent" of O'Brien's speech to Winston Smith in Orwell's *Nineteen Eighty-Four*: "You believe that reality is something objective, external, existing in its own right. . . . But I tell you, Winston, that reality is not external. Reality exists in the human mind and nowhere else." Todorov's review is—in the characteristic fashion of anecdote-retelling—cited by Kimball.[143] Searle supplements it with the remark that "according to the literary theorists influenced by Derrida, there is nothing beyond or outside texts. So O'Brien is supposed to have triumphed over Winston after all."[144] Searle argues that one cannot, within human linguistic practices, "intelligibly deny metaphysical realism, because the meaningfulness of our public utterances already presupposes an independently existing reality to which expressions in those utterances can refer."[145]

The context of Orwell's novel actually is slightly different from such uses, as it concerns a dialogue in the feared torture chamber 101 of the Ministry of Truth about the Party's right to history. O'Brien shows Winston a photograph of three one-time Party members that constitutes proof that they were later executed for trumped-up charges; then he destroys it in the memory hole:

"Ashes," he said. "Not even identifiable ashes. Dust. It does not exist. It never existed."

"But it did exist! It does exist! It exists in memory. I remember it. You remember it."

"I do not remember it," said O'Brien."[146]

In teaching Winston "doublethink," O'Brien forces him to recite the Party slogan about the past: "Who controls the past controls the future; who controls the present controls the past."[147] Then O'Brien lectures Winston, as he responds to the question of how one can control memory that is involuntary. It is from the following passage that some sentences were taken:

> "Only the disciplined mind can see reality, Winston. You believe that reality is something objective, external, existing in its own right. You also believe that the nature of reality is self-evident. When you delude yourself into thinking that you see something, you assume that everyone else sees the same thing as you. But I tell you, Winston, that reality is not external. Reality exists in the human mind, and nowhere else. Not in the individual mind, which can make mistakes, and in any case soon perishes; only in the mind of the Party, which is collective and immortal."[148]

Of course, Orwell may seem concerned just as much about individual resistance to collective power as about metaphysical realism, yet the reading that casts O'Brien as a protodeconstructionist interestingly suggests the totalitarian aspects of relativism that leaves all room for arbitration to pure power, as Erich Fromm stressed when he discussed the term *mobile truth*, then used to describe corporate America, in his 1961 afterward to the novel.[149] Rereading Orwell, one notices his strange misrepresentation of totalitarianism that one might expect would collide with multiculturalism. Orwell, for example, strongly stresses sexual freedom yet portrays Julia as generally uninterested in politics and as a rebel only "from the waist downwards,"[150] which makes the book a "sexist" text to today's readers. Indeed, Daphne Patai discussed Orwell's novel under the category "androcentrism" and focused on narrative comments that make women the embodiment of what we would now call political correctness: "It was always the women, and above all the young ones, who were the most bigoted adherents of the Party, the swallowers of slogans, the amateur spies and nosers-out of unorthodoxy."[151] Amazingly, racial (but not sexual) integration is ascribed to the realm of totalitarianism (which is strange if one remembers that *Nineteen Eighty-Four* depicts a conglomerate of communism and fascism). Thus Orwell writes, "In principle, membership . . . is not hereditary. Admission to either branch of the Party is by examination, taken at the age of sixteen. Nor is there any racial discrimination . . . Jews, Negroes, South Americans of pure Indian blood are to be found in the highest ranks of the Party."[152] This might give a reader the impression that fighting for racial integration might be fighting for the world of *Nineteen Eighty-Four,* for the Party, and for totalitarianism.

No matter how incompatible the issues of the multiculturalism debate and of Orwell's novel may be, the present debate is a form of "living Orwell." Like *multiculturalism, Orwell* has become a compromise term that can be used for contrary political purposes. In the United States, he has been taken up by radicals, liberals, neoconservatives, old conservatives, and the John Birch Society,[153] and he has been marketed successfully as a commodity. Orwell's two most famous novels sold 40 million copies worldwide, "more than any other pair of books by a serious *or popular* postwar author."[154] Thus Orwell is a white male English author whose canonical status (however recently acquired) all sides in the multiculturalism debate reinforce by taking general knowledge of his work for granted. John Rodden calls the posthumous adoption of "St. George" Orwell "Assimilation Through Canonization" and points out that "'Big Brother,' '1984,' 'doublethink,' 'Newspeak,' 'Orwellian,' and even 'Orwell' *are* obfuscatory language. . . . Whether hurled with intent to confuse or in ignorance of Orwell's life and work, they have become charged code words, easily manipulated to call up reflexively all sorts of (often widely exaggerated) associations with a police state."[155] This way, Rodden says, Orwell has become the Dr. Frankenstein of the twentieth century. Yet all sides in the multiculturalism debate find it useful to define themselves against totalitarianism, as represented by Orwell, in order to characterize their opponents.

Whether through Orwell or not, all factions in the multiculturalism debate evoke Hitler, National Socialism, and the Holocaust to make their points. Contemporary American students demonstrating for homosexual rights wear buttons imitating the pink triangles homosexuals were forced to wear in German concentration camps. In an instance in which Ishmael Reed uses the word *monocultural* (before *multiculturalism* had come into vogue), he asks whether Adolf Hitler was not "the archetypal monoculturalist who, in his pigheaded arrogance, believed that . . . one blood was so pure that it had to be protected from alien strains at all costs?"[156]

The general Orwellian atmosphere and such instances raise the question of how theories of group relations were affected by totalitarianism, especially by the Nazi extermination policies of the 1940s. Historians have for a long time emphasized the significance of totalitarianism and World War II for the development of integrationist policies in the United States. Richard Polenberg has described the discrediting of racialism that took place in American scholarship of the 1940s;[157] Philip Gleason has carefully traced the effect of the war years on such central terms of group relations as *identity, minorities,* and *pluralism;*[158] Arthur Mann noted that the assumptions of post–World War II cultural pluralism rested on the notion of a shared national culture;[159] and John Higham, in his survey of pluralistic thinking, formulated memorably the relationship between European totalitarianism and American pluralism: "If the enemy was totalitarian, America would have to be pluralistic."[160]

This connection may have been constitutive for the origins of multiculturalism. (Perhaps it is an inversion of this maxim that characterizes the cultural logic of this moment: If America is multicultural, then those Americans who question such ascriptions—or those countries that fail to follow this model—may be called totalitarian.) "The unique fact that characterizes America is that it is a multiculture society. Consider at random almost any community in the country. Its social structure reveals a variety of culture groups, which differ widely in pattern, enlisting more or less distinctive racial folkways, religious faiths, languages, Old-World or indigenous household practices, social mores, and economic class status."[161] This observation was made by Stewart Cole and Mildred Wiese Cole in a chapter entitled "Disunity among Americans," and the discussion proceeds to mention Crèvecoeur and Zangwill, distinguishing such concepts as "Anglo-Conformity," "Melting Pot," and "Pluralism"; yet the text is not from the multiculturalism debate but from the year 1954. It is one of the earliest, fully developed instances of the term *multiculture* that I have found, apart from Haskell's "multicultural" novel of 1941. Hence what is now being debated under the label *multiculturalism* may not be all that new.

Though many participants in the debate speak about the importance of history, the relatively short history of the concept of America as a multicultural society has largely remained ignored. I offer here only a brief consideration of some of the many works that appeared from the mid-1940s to the mid-1950s—roughly contemporary with Orwell's novel—to suggest the need for further investigations. I focus on the sociologists around the Columbia University sociologist Robert MacIver, on Robin Williams and the Social Science Research Council, and on the movement for "intercultural education" surrounding the Coles. Donald R. Young, the sociologist who helped propagate the term *minority* for American use,[162] articulated in MacIver's 1945 book, *Civilization and Group Relationships,* what was the goal of many studies of that moment:

> A practical program to reduce the social visibility of our minorities would reverse Hitler's measures to increase anti-Semitism in Germany. He increased awareness of the Jews and assured their identification by marking their clothing and their places of business, by designating special areas where they could live. He increased fear of the Jews by a constant stream of propaganda emphasizing their success and their wealth, asserting that they monopolized the professions, ran the government, held all the best jobs, and so threatened the welfare of all the rest of the population. His campaign was very effective in Germany and in a good part of Europe; its influence reached across the ocean to this country.[163]

Young's response to the Holocaust was to work for better group assimilation, since the Nazis had based their program on exaggerating difference. He discusses first how this would work with various immigrant groups and Indians and then proceeds to consider the case of African Americans:

> In the single case of the Negro, both numbers and visibility are such that awareness and fear are less easily decreased. But fear can be reduced by seeing to it that white people become familiar with the fact that Negroes can do and are doing everything that anyone else does. A campaign to make Negro activities of all kinds usual and matter-of-fact will both allay fears and reduce social visibility in spite of great numbers and biological visibility. *But* such a campaign must emphasize differences neither by stressing alleged special abilities and accomplishments, even though they are considered to be of high social value, such as dancing, musical, or dramatic talent, nor by needlessly overemphasizing mistreatment and conflict. The former unconsciously lends support to theories of race differences. The latter sharpens issues, increases visibility and fears, and can do little more than increase general awareness that there is a "Negro problem." We have too great a tendency, in our efforts to prove that there is no basis for discrimination, to stress the exceptional qualities and achievements of all minority groups instead of concentrating on making their participation in all the ordinary aspects of life so commonplace that it does not cause concern. The current campaign against anti-Semitism is wise in that it does not accentuate special Jewish contributions to modern civilization, does not needlessly publicize cases of discrimination, and does as little as possible to bring Jews to the attention of the nation as Jews.[164]

For Young, as for many social scientists of that time, things could not just be left to the wisdom of the populace; what was needed was a program, formulated in opposition to the Nazis: "The Nazis and the Fascists . . . had a racial goal for a purpose and they knew what had to be done to achieve it. It is incredible that we should help them do it simply because we can only state that the integration of democratic principles and intergroup behavior is our goal and vow to hold to it, when we should be actually blazing the trail by work on a planned program of practical accomplishments."[165] This is the emphatic ending of Young's essay of 1945. In his demand for a program and his suggestion that deemphasizing difference should be a constitutive part of it, he shared beliefs widely held by social scientists of that era.

Robert M. MacIver, an eminent Columbia University sociologist, similarly advocated, in 1945, a "line" of "social re-education" for Americans (the word *re-education* was certainly in the air elsewhere). His principle was "What we do for one [group], we are doing for all, we are doing for ourselves. The accent must not be on difference, because that is already our trouble."[166] MacIver was interested in finding a middle way between pluralism and assimilation. As Higham writes, MacIver "made a significant effort to give that middle way some conceptual coherence . . . [he] developed a fundamental distinction between culture and coercion."[167] MacIver wrote, "What we have to advance toward is the common rights of all groups, and we can help by showing how some are denied these common rights, and proceeding to indicate these rights in the name of all rather than in the name of any group."[168] He saw the danger of distorted ideas about groups because "they exaggerate the differences between the group that makes them and the group they are supposed to represent. They give the one group many virtues, and, of course, they give the other group many less favorable qualities. Thus they exaggerate the differences between groups, and, even more, they exaggerate the likeness within the single group."[169]

This sense of crisis in 1945 was also evident in the Social Science Research Council, which appointed the new Committee on Techniques for Reducing Group Hostility. The committee, under the direction of the sociologist Robin M. Williams Jr., produced a most interesting report in 1947, *The Reduction of Intergroup Tensions: A Survey of Research on Problems of Ethnic, Racial, and Religious Group Relations*, which cited numerous empirical studies that supported the MacIver group's approach.[170] Williams's findings led him to formulate a careful program toward positive changes in group relations that is particularly concerned about possible unintended side effects. His research findings and suggestions include the following:

> Simultaneous direct attack on every form of intergroup discrimination is likely to intensify the reaction it attempts to stop. Generally speaking, any policy which tends to make Jews as Jews more conspicuous, and particularly those Jews who are at the same time vulnerable symbols in other respects, would tend to be an invitation to anti-Semitic reaction. Thus, indiscriminate attack on every form of existent discrimination, regardless of anything but the immediate effectiveness of the means, is not likely to achieve the actual elimination of anti-Semitism, but on the contrary to intensify the reactions it attempts to stop [drawing on Talcott Parsons].

> [P]roblems of group conflict are usually most readily resolved by indirection than by frontal assault.

> Where strong prejudice is present in a group which is highly self-conscious, and strongly bound together, outside criticism of its prejudice is likely to be taken as an attack on the group; and *one* immediate effect is to strengthen the prejudice, which by virtue of the attack becomes a symbol of in-group membership and solidarity [citing northern criticism of the U.S. South as one example].

> Propaganda which appeals for minority rights on the basis of the group's achievements tends beyond a certain point to arouse insecurity-hostility in the dominant group by stressing group differences and competitive success.

> An effective propaganda approach in intergroup relations is that which emphasizes national symbols and common American achievements, sacrifices, destinies, etc., while unobtrusively indicating the common participation of minority group members.

> Hostility is reduced by arranging for reverse role-taking in public drama or ceremony (e.g., an anti-Negro person plays a realistic Negro role).

> The likelihood of conflict is reduced by education and propaganda emphases upon characteristics and values *common* to various groups rather than upon intergroup *differences*.[171]

Yet Williams is also alert to the problems inherent in such an approach and makes two important qualifications: "But there is danger that attitudes thus created may lead to expectation of greater similarity than later experience demonstrates, and this can lead to disillusionment and secondary reinforcement of hostility. A second qualification is that some persons holding to *a doctrine of cultural pluralism advocate awareness of*

*differences on the assumption that acceptance of differences comes only af-
ter a transitional period, which may involve temporary intensification of
hostilities.*"[172] Williams's paradigm is clearly designed to deemphasize
difference, yet he is open to the possible workings of a pluralistic program
too. The tradeoff is simply a hopefully "transitional" intensification of
hostilities that might lead to acceptance of differences. I return to this
point at the end.

Another way of reconciling the integrationist reactions to World War
II with more pluralism than was suggested in Young's essay came with
the concept of intercultural education, advocated by a group of educa-
tors and sociologists in the 1940s and 1950s. The Bureau for Intercultural
Education in New York published a series of monographs on such topics
as prejudice, race relations, and assimilation.

Cole and Cole's *Minorities and the American Promise: The Conflict of
Principle and Practice* is also characteristic of a balanced approach toward
the shortcomings and merits of both assimilationist and pluralist strategies. Looking today at this text from 1954 makes a good part of the current debate look like a slightly touched-up déjà vu. The Coles were the
authors of the sentence quoted earlier: "The unique fact that characterizes America is that it is a multiculture society." I have not found any recognition or mention of this even semantically interesting precursor text
in the literature on multiculturalism.

After a rejection of "Anglo-conformity," the Coles weigh the approaches of "melting pot" and "pluralism and tolerance" against each other.
They criticize the practice of assimilation for sacrificing the "significance
of ethnic differences," for overemphasizing "social likeness and cultural
solidarity of the people," and for often being "impracticable in human
relations."[173] Pluralism, however, "tends to border indecisively on the
shaky rim of intolerance" and tends to exaggerate "the social separate-
ness of peoples and the individuality of their subcultures."[174] Hence they
conclude, "A multiculture society needs a more comprehensive conception of democratic human relations."[175] In diagrams and discussions, they
search for principles of democratic human relations that combine the
advantages (and eschew the shortcomings) of both melting pot and pluralism. The Coles saw the need for, and the drawbacks of, thinking about
unity and diversity. Their book is also clearer than many contributions
to the current debate about what is at stake in stressing or in deemphasizing difference. Thus they describe their project of articulating an educational philosophy adequate for a "multiculture society" in ways that
differentiate "pluralism" from education for "dynamic democracy"

(which includes assimilation and shared values). Finally, they view American education in a global context and demand that students should learn not only to negotiate ethnic and American identities but also to be prepared as citizens of the world.

Things have changed so radically that neither a reasoned choice between pluralism and assimilation nor the hope for a synthesis of the two emerges at the present. A 1992 report entitled *Meeting the Challenges of Multicultural Education* seems representative in its overwhelming focus on teaching "cultural identity" and "racial or ethnic pride and self-esteem" as the mission of schooling.[176] Multiculturalism seems largely unaware of its precursors and has worked out its own rhetorical conventions and hopes.

How did we get from the 1950s to the present? Milton Gordon has offered an account that illuminates the transformation from liberal pluralism (giving no formal recognition to categories of people on the basis of race or ethnicity) to corporate pluralism, which recognizes ethnic entities.[177] More than the social sciences, it was probably black political language of the 1960s that changed things by redefining assimilation and melting pot as if they were associated with the Holocaust. This was suggested earlier in the reference to Young's promotion of ethnic assimilation in response to the Holocaust. The following longer remarks from Malcolm X's *Autobiography* signal the collapse of the assimilationist paradigm:

"Integration" is called "assimilation" if white ethnic groups alone are involved: it's fought against tooth and nail by those who want their heritage preserved. Look at how the Irish threw the English out of Ireland. The Irish knew the English would engulf them. Look at the French-Canadians, fanatically fighting to keep their identity.

In fact, history's most tragic result of a mixed, therefore diluted and weakened, ethnic identity has been experienced by a white ethnic group— the Jew in Germany.

He had made greater contributions to Germany than German themselves had. Jews had won over half of Germany's Nobel Prizes. Every culture in Germany was led by the Jew; he published the greatest newspaper. Jews were the greatest artists, the greatest poets, composers, stage directors.

But those Jews made a fatal mistake—assimilating.

From World War I to Hitler's rise, the Jews in Germany had been increasingly intermarrying.

Many changed their names and many took other religions. Their own Jewish religion, their own rich Jewish ethnic and cultural roots, they anesthetized and cut off . . . until they began thinking of themselves as "Germans."

And the next thing they knew, there was Hitler, rising to power from the beer halls—with his emotional "Aryan master race" theory. And right at hand for a scapegoat was the self-weakened, self-deluded "German" Jew. Most mysterious is how did those Jews—with all of their brilliant minds, with all of their power in every aspect of Germany's affairs—how did those Jews stand almost as if mesmerized, watching something which did not spring upon them overnight, but which was gradually developed—a monstrous plan for their own *murder*. The self-brainwashing had been so complete that not long after, in the gas chambers, a lot of them were still gasping, "It *can't* be true!" If Hitler *had* conquered the world, as he meant to—that is a shuddery thought for every Jew alive today. The Jew will never forget that lesson. Jewish intelligence eyes watch over every neo-Nazi organization. Right after the war, the Jews' Haganah mediating body stepped up the longtime negotiations with the British. But this time, the Stern gang was shooting the British.

And this time the British acquiesced and helped them to wrest Palestine away from the Arabs, the rightful owners, and then the Jews set up Israel, their own country—the one thing that every race of man in the world respects, and understands.[178]

For Malcolm X, in this passage at least,[179] "Jew" was a stand-in for "Negro" and "German" for "American."[180] The lesson of the Holocaust had become an opposition to racial integration, and militant Zionism was seen as the model for black Americans—the very opposite of Young's conclusions. Malcolm stands for many other cultural figures of the 1960s who have similarly opposed racial integration in the name of the Holocaust. One only needs to think of LeRoi Jones (later to become Amiri Baraka) who in the essay "What Does Nonviolence Mean?" draws the analogy between the situation of black Americans and the fate of German Jews under Hitler:

> The German Jews, at the time of Hitler's rise to power, were the most assimilated Jews in Europe. They believed, and with a great deal of emotional investment, that they were Germans. The middle-class German Jew, like the middle-class American Negro, had actually moved, in many instances, into the mainstream of the society, and wanted to believe as that mainstream did. Even when the anti-Jewish climate began to thicken and take on the heaviness of permanence, many middle-class Jews believed that it was only the poor Jews, who, perhaps rightly so, would suffer in such a climate.
>
> Like these unfortunate Jews the middle-class Negro has no real program of rebellion against the *status quo* in America, quite frankly, because he believes he is pretty well off. The blatant cultural assassination, the social

and economic exploitation of most Negroes in this society, does not really impress him. The middle-class Negro's goal, like the rest of the American middle class, is to be ignorant comfortably.[181]

The formulation "cultural assassination" in this context gives expression to the post-Holocaust parallel of genocide and racial assimilation that helps tilt the scale in favor of difference. Jones pursued a similar strategy in his poetry, and he did not always focus on African Americans. In his poem "Black Dada Nihilismus," he invokes the "ugly silent deaths of jews under / the surgeon's knife."[182] Having thus suggested the image of a Dr. Mengele and the inhuman medical experiments that accompanied the Holocaust, he continues in the same line: "To awake on / 69th street with money and a hip / nose."[183] Plastic surgery as the enactment of assimilation is thus put into the symbolic universe of genocide. Jones's "hip nose" may pun on "hypnosis," just as Malcolm had used the word "mesmerized"—and both would refer to "brainwashing"—to describe assimilation as a form of being taken possession of by a deadly alien force. In a universe in which assimilation—of blacks or Jews—becomes culturally linked to the Holocaust, the image of the melting pot could become as threatening as that of a gas chamber. Assimilation now could be viewed as if it were annihilation—and the careful weighing of pluralism and assimilation gave way to a strong assertion of difference, first in the "new ethnicity" of the 1970s and now in multiculturalism.

It seems quite disturbing that much of the multiculturalism debate reinvents—and reintroduces with less scholarly evidence—what has been discussed for nearly fifty years and has often led earlier scholars to recommendations that differ dramatically from the ones that are now being institutionalized, practiced, and simply taken for granted. Is it an expression of the postmodern moment that the debate is based on weak empirical analysis of the present and pits "radicals" without a utopian vision of the future against "conservatives" with no deep concern for the past they wish to preserve? That the endless debates about "the canon" are flanked by implicitly enacted canonizations of a Latin motto, Matthew Arnold, George Orwell, and a belated and displaced opposition to totalitarianism? Perhaps the pluralist's hope is well founded that intensification of hostilities may only be a temporary stage toward greater intergroup understanding. (This was mentioned by Robin Williams in an aside.) But what if it is not? What if the racist and sexist incidents that have been reported in the literature of multicultural anecdotes signal an increase in hostilities that are at least partly a reaction to the top-down enactment of multiculturalism itself? Is American university life going through a "transitional period" at the end of which mutual acceptance will be greater, or is it at an explosive crisis point, made all the more volatile by the far-reaching institutional support that is being extended to difference in a social system in which the classes are drifting further apart?

In the last few years, concerns about multiculturalism seem to have receded somewhat, while the term has become so omnipresent that Nathan Glazer's 1997 book *We Are All Multiculturalists Now* constitutes a perfect counterpiece to Edward Haskell's 1941 novel that introduced the word *multicultural* to describe the quality of a few exceptional men. Glazer's new endorsement of multiculturalism comes as the result of his recognition that it is the price the United States has to pay for having failed to integrate blacks. Against that historical backdrop, multiculturalism may be the next best thing to universalism, he argues—in fact, it may be the only way to go. Glazer cites approvingly the most detailed brief for multiculturalism published: Lawrence Levine's book *The Opening of the American Mind,* a 1996 response to the late Allan Bloom. In a lecture series of 1997 entitled "Achieving Our Country," Richard Rorty offered a much more cautious endorsement of the various movements that later became known under the slogan multiculturalism as having helped reduce the forms of social sadism (against women, against members of ethnic minorities, against homosexuals, against handicapped people, and so forth) that were still commonplace in American life of the 1950s, including the academic world. This is no small accomplishment. Yet Rorty also sees the danger that the international world of cultural politics has helped to eclipse the real issues of a growing social inequality in the United States and around the globe. There may now be many multicultural men and women who are completely disconnected from any proletariat anywhere, and multicultural internationalism may even serve as the marker that separates these intellectuals from people, instead making multiculturalists part of a global ruling class. How can new social movements be built, Rorty therefore asks, that would (as did precursors from the 1930s to the 1960s) attempt to fight the crimes of (social) selfishness with the same vigor that multiculturalists have focused on the crimes of sadism?

Notes

A slightly different version of this essay was published in German under the title "DE PLURIBUS UNA/E PLURIBUS UNUS. Matthew Arnold, George Orwell, Holocaust and Assimilation. Bemerkungen zur amerikanischen Multikulturalismusdebatte," in *Multikulturelle Gesellschaft: Modell Amerika,* ed. Berndt Ostendorf (Munich: Fink, 1994), 53–74. I am grateful for the many comments and suggestions I received from students and colleagues, especially those made by Daniel Aaron, Howard Adelman, Anthony Appiah, Sacvan Bercovitch, Nathan Glazer, Margaret Gullette, Lauren Gwin, John Higham, David Hollinger, Wendy Katkin, Stanley Lieberson, Jeffrey Melnick, Berndt Ostendorf, Maxine Senn-Yuen, Marc Shell, Windfried Siemerling, Brook Thomas, Stephen Toulmin, Adam Weisman, and Robin M. Williams Jr.

1. Audrey I. Richards, *The Multicultural States of East Africa* (Montreal and London: McGill–Queen's University Press, 1969), vii.

2. John Porter, "Ethnic Pluralism in Canada," in *Ethnicity: Theory and Experience*, ed. Nathan Glazer and Daniel P. Moynihan (Cambridge, Mass.: Harvard University Press, 1975), 287–88.

3. Ibid., 284–88.

4. Edward F. Haskell, *Lance: A Novel about Multicultural Men* (New York: John Day, 1941).

5. Iris Barry, "Melodrama, Tract, Good Story" [Review of Edward F. Haskell's *Lance*], *New York Herald Tribune Books*, July 12, 1941, 3.

6. Ibid.; Haskell, *Lance*, 320–21.

7. Horace M. Kallen, *Culture and Democracy in the United States: Studies in the Group Psychology of the American Peoples* (New York: Boni and Liveright, 1924).

8. W. Lloyd Warner and Paul S. Lunt, *The Social Life of a Modern Community*, vol. 1 (New Haven, Conn.: Yale University Press, 1941).

9. Itabari Njeri, "Multiculturalism," *Los Angeles Times*, January 13, 1991.

10. Michael Walzer, "The New Tribalism: Notes on a Difficult Problem," *Dissent* 39 (Spring 1992): 164–72; Richard Bernstein, "The Arts Catch Up with a Society in Disarray: America's 'New Tribalism' Is Producing a Climate of Cultural Combat," *New York Times*, September 2, 1990.

11. Quoted by Berndt Ostendorf, "The Costs of Multiculturalism" (Working Paper No. 50, John F. Kennedy-Institut für Nordamerikastudien, Freie Universität Berlin, 1992), 19.

12. Ted Gordon and Wahneema Lubiano, "The Statement of the Black Faculty Caucus," in *Debating P.C.: The Controversy over Political Correctness on College Campuses*, ed. Paul Berman (New York: Dell, 1992), 249.

13. Arthur M. Schlesinger Jr., *The Disuniting of America: Reflections on a Multicultural Society* (Knoxville, Tenn.: Whittle Direct Books, 1991), 40.

14. Louis S. Feuer, "From Pluralism to Multiculturalism," *Society* 29 (November/December 1991): 9.

15. Mortimer Adler, "Multiculturalism, Transculturalism, and the Great Books," in *Beyond P.C.: Towards a Politics of Understanding*, ed. Patricia Aufderheide (St. Paul, Minn.: Graywolf, 1992), 64.

16. Quoted in Amitai Etzioni, "Social Science as a Multicultural Canon," *Society* 29 (November/December 1991): 15.

17. Roger Kimball, *Tenured Radicals: How Politics Has Corrupted Our Higher Education* (New York: Harper and Row, 1990).

18. Roger Kimball, "The Periphery v. the Center: The MLA in Chicago," in *Debating P.C.*, ed. Berman, 64.

19. Paul Berman, "Introduction: The Debate and Its Origins," in *Debating P.C.,* ed. Berman, 6.

20. Larry Yarbrough, "Three Questions for the Multicultural Debate," *Change: The Magazine of Higher Learning* 24 (January/February 1992): 64.

21. Henry A. Giroux, "Liberal Arts Education and the Struggle for Public Life: Dreaming about Democracy," in *The Politics of Liberal Education,* ed. Daryl J. Gless and Barbara Hernstein Smith (Durham, N.C.: Duke University Press, 1992), 139.

22. Karl Mannheim, *Ideology and Utopia: An Introduction to the Sociology of Knowledge,* trans. Louis Wirth and Edward Shils (New York: Harcourt Brace, 1936), 193.

23. Ishmael Reed, "America: The Multinational Society," in *Graywolf Annual Five: Multicultural Literacy, "Opening the American Mind,"* ed. Rick Simonson and Scott Walker (St. Paul: Graywolf, 1988), 155.

24. Ibid.

25. Berndt Ostendorf, "Creoles and Creolization: Notes on the Multi-Cultural Origins of New Orleans Music," *Rivista di Studi Anglo-Americani* 5, no. 7 (1989): 289–302.

26. Donald Weber, "Gertrude Berg and the Goldbergs," in *The Other Fifties: Interrogating Mid-Century American Icons,* ed. Joel Forman (Urbana: University of Illinois Press, 1997), 144–67.

27. Christopher C. Newton, "Commedia at Coney Island," *Theatre Symposium,* vol. 1 (Tuscaloosa: University of Alabama Press, 1993), 104–15.

28. Cornel West, "Diverse New World," in *Debating P.C.,* ed. Berman, 330.

29. Quoted in Ostendorf, "Cost of Multiculturalism," 17.

30. John Higham, "Multiculturalism and Universalism: A History and Critique," *American Quarterly* 45 (June 1993): 212–13.

31. Gary D. Gottfredson, Saundra Murray Nettles, and Barbara McHugh, eds., *Meeting the Challenges of Multicultural Education: A Report from the Evaluation of Pittsburgh's Prospect Multicultural Education Center* (Baltimore. Md.: Johns Hopkins University Center for Social Organization of Schools, 1992), 4–9.

32. See, for example, Diane Ravitch, "Multiculturalism: E Pluribus Plures," in *Debating P.C.,* ed. Berman, 297.

33. Stephan Thernstrom, "The Minority Majority Will Never Come," *Wall Street Journal,* July 26, 1990.

34. See a discussion of this point in Stephen Thernstrom, "American Ethnic Statistics," in *Immigrants in Two Democracies: French and American Experience,* ed. Donald L. Horowitz and Gérard Noiriel (New York: New York University Press, 1992), 90–91.

35. Fred Barringer, "U.S. Minorities' Share of Melting Pot Soars," *International Herald Tribune,* March 12, 1991.

36. Felicity Barringer, "New Census Data Reveal Redistribution of Poverty," *New York Times,* May 29, 1992.

37. Ibid.

38. Nathan Glazer, "In Defense of Multiculturalism: Why the Sobol Commission Was Right," *New Republic,* September 2, 1991, 19; Gottfredson, Nettles, and McHugh, *Meeting the Challenges of Multicultural Education,* 8.

39. Gerald Early, "American Education and the Postmodern Impulse," *American Quarterly* 45 (June 1993): 220–23.

40. Michael Bérubé, "Public Image Limited: Political Correctness and the Media's Big Lie," in *Debating P.C.,* ed. Berman, 131.

41. *New York Times Book Review,* March 15, 1992, 20.

42. Schlesinger, *Disuniting of America,* 85, 75.

43. Adam Begley, "Souped-Up Scholar: Prof. Stanley Fish, Duke University's 'Politically Correct' Showman, Never Met a Debate He Didn't Like," *New York Times Magazine,* May 3, 1992, 50.

44. Albert Shanker, "E Pluribus Unum?" *New York Times,* February 23, 1992.

45. Elizabeth Fox-Genovese, "The Self-Interest of Multiculturalism," in *Beyond P.C.,* ed. Aufderheide, 231.

46. See Milton N. Gordon, "Toward a General Theory of Racial and Ethnic Group Relations," in *Ethnicity,* ed. Glazer and Moynihan, 106–10; and Milton M. Gordon, *The Scope of Sociology* (New York: New York University Press, 1988), 157–66.

47. See Philip Gleason, "Identifying Identity," in *Theories of Ethnicity: A Classical Reader,* ed. Werner Sollors (Basingstoke: Macmillan; New York: New York University Press, 1996), 460–87. In a 1926 B'nai Brith address, Sigmund Freud had opposed religious faith and national pride but described his sense of Jewishness as the result of unconscious elements and what he called "the secret familiarity of identical psychological construction" ("Heimlichkeit der gleichen inneren Konstruktion"). In *Childhood and Society* (1950), Erikson offered the term *identity* as a shortened English formula for Freud's notion. It was a formula that took.

48. George Devereux, "Ethnic Identity: Its Logical Foundations and Its Dysfunctions," in *Ethnic Identity: Cultural Continuities and Change,* ed. George De Vos and Lola Romanucci-Ross (1975; reprint, Chicago: University of Chicago Press, 1982), 66–68.

49. Richard J. Perry, "Why Do Multiculturalists Ignore Anthropologists?" *Chronicle of Higher Education,* March 4, 1992.

50. John R. Searle, "Is There a Crisis in American Higher Education?" (Lecture to the American Academy of Arts and Sciences, May 1992).

51. United States Commission on Civil Rights, *Civil Rights Issues Facing Asian Americans in the 1990s* (Washington, D.C.: United States Commission on Civil Rights, 1992); Richard de Silva, "The Race Crisis on Campus." *Harvard Crimson Commencement Issue,* June 4, 1992.

52. Higham, "Multiculturalism and Universalism," 195–219.

53. David A. Hollinger, "Postethnic America," herein.

54. David A. Hollinger, "How Wide the Circle of the 'We'? American Intellectuals and the Problem of the Ethnos since World War II," *American Historical Review* 98 (April 1993): 335–36.

55. Kwame Anthony Appiah, "Afterword: How Shall We Live as Many?" herein.

56. Tzvetan Todorov, *On Human Diversity: Nationalism, Racism, and Exoticism in French Thought,* trans. Catherine Porter (Cambridge, Mass.: Harvard University Press, 1993), 353–99.

57. Marie de Lepervanche, "From Race to Ethnicity," *Australian and New Zealand Journal of Sociology* 16 (March 1980): 34.

58. Robert Hughes, "The Fraying of America," *Time Magazine*, February 3, 1992, 46.

59. Ibid., 47.

60. Robert C. Christopher, *Crashing the Gates: The De-WASPing of America's Power Elite* (New York: Simon and Schuster, 1989), 283.

61. Ibid., 22

62. Arthur Levine, "A Time to Act," *Change: The Magazine of Higher Learning* 24 (January/February 1992): 5.

63. Louis Menand, "Illiberalisms," in *Beyond P.C.*, ed. Aufderheide, 233.

64. Sylvia Nasar, "Even Among the Well-Off, the Richest Get Richer," *New York Times*, March 5, 1992.

65. Sylvia Nasar, "However You Slice the Data the Richest Did Get Richer," *New York Times*, May 11, 1992.

66. Felicity Barringer, "Giving by the Rich Declines, on Average," *New York Times*, May 24, 1992.

67. Michele K. Collison, "Angry Protests over Diversity and Free Speech Mark Contentious Spring Semester at Harvard," *Chronicle of Higher Education*, May 6, 1992.

68. *Change: The Magazine of Higher Learning* 24 (January/February 1992): 4.

69. Arthur Levine and Jeanette Cureton, "The Quiet Revolution," in ibid., 29.

70. Porter, "Ethnic Pluralism in Canada," 294.

71. Quoted in Begley, "Souped-Up Scholar," 52.

72. Kimball, "Periphery v. the Center," 66.

73. Personal notes.

74. Barbara Ehrenreich, "The Challenge for the Left," in *Debating P.C.*, ed. Berman, 337.

75. Shelby Steele, *The Content of Our Character: A New Vision of Race in America* (1990; reprint, New York: Harper, 1991), 22–23.

76. Searle, "Is There a Crisis in American Higher Education?" 9.

77. Ibid.

78. Clement Wood, *The Complete Rhyming Dictionary and Poet's Craft Book* (Garden City: Doubleday, 1936).

79. William Graham Sumner, *Folkways: A Study of the Sociological Importance of Usages, Manners, and Morals* (1906; reprint, Boston: Ginn, 1940), 13.

80. Jean Devisse, in *The Image of the Black in Western Art: From the Early Christian Era to the "Age of Discover,"* vol. 2.1, series ed. Ladislas Bugner; trans. William Granger Ryan (n.p.: Menil Foundation; distributed by Harvard University Press, 1979), 249.

81. Ravitch, "Multiculturalism," 289.

82. Sigmund Freud, "Civilization and Its Discontents" (1930), *Standard Edition of Complete Psychological Works*, vol. 21, trans. James Strachey (London: Hogarth, 1961).

83. Catharine R. Stimpson, "The White Squares," *Change: The Magazine of Higher Education* 24 (January/February 1992): 77–78.

84. Freud, "Civilization and Its Discontents," 114. See also Sigmund Freud, "The Taboo of Virginity" (1918), in *Standard Edition of Complete Psychological Works*, trans.

James Strachey, vol. 11 (London: Hogarth, 1957), 199; and Sigmund Freud, "Group Psychology" (1921), in *Standard Edition of Complete Psychological Works*, trans. James Strachey, vol. 18 (London: Hogarth, 1955), 101.

85. Marshall Sahlins, "Goodbye to Tristes Tropes" (Paper presented at National Identity and Ethnic Diversity, Greater Philadelphia Philosophy Consortium, March 7, 1992).

86. Steele, *Content of Our Character*, 132.

87. Dinesh D'Souza and Robert MacNeil, "The Big Chill? Interview with Dinesh D'Souza," in *Debating P.C.*, ed. Berman, 35.

88. Njeri, "Multiculturalism."

89. Todd Gitlin, "On the Virtues of a Loose Canon," in *Beyond P.C.*, ed. Aufderheide, 190.

90. Todd Gitlin, "Toward a Loose Cannon," *Dissent* 37 (Spring 1990): 254; Adam Yarmolinsky, in *Change: The Magazine of Higher Learning* 24 (January–February 1991); Henry Louis Gates Jr., *Loose Canons: Notes on the Cultural Wars* (New York: Oxford University Press, 1992); Irving Louis Horowitz, "The New Nihilism," *Society* 9 (November–December 1991): 27; Bryan Wolf, "Firing the Canon," *American Literary History* 3 (Winter 1991): 707–52.

91. Schlesinger, *Disuniting of America*, 280.

92. Ravitch, "Multiculturalism."

93. Kenneth Silverman, *A Cultural History of the American Revolution* (New York: Crowell, 1976), 417.

94. Ibid., 658.

95. Monroe Deutsch, "E Pluribus Unum," *Classical Journal* 18 (1922–23): 392

96. Ibid.

97. Horace, Epistles II, in *Satires, Epistles and Ars Poetica*, trans. by H. Rushton Fairclough (Cambridge, Mass.: Harvard University Press, 1956), 211–13. Fairclough translated from "Lenior et melior fis accedente senecta? Quid te exempta iuvat spinis *de pluribus una*. vivere se recte nescis, decede peritis" (emphasis added).

98. Deutsch, "E Pluribus Unum," 391.

99. Edward Kennard Rand, *The Magical Art of Virgil* (Cambridge, Mass.: Harvard University Press, 1963), 59–60.

100. E. J. Kenney, ed., *The Ploughman's Lunch Moretum: A Poem Ascribed to Virgil* (Bristol: Bristol Classical Press, 1984), 8–9. Kenney translated from "it manus in gyrum: paulatim singula uires deperdunt proprias, color est *e pluribus unus*, nec totus uiridis, quia lactea frusta repugnant, nec de lacte nitens, quia tot uariatur ab herbis" (emphasis added).

101. Deutsch, "E Pluribus Unum," 406.

102. Giroux, "Liberal Arts Education and the Struggle for Public Life," 131.

103. D'Souza and MacNeil, "The Big Chill?" 31.

104. Quoted in Bérubé, "Public Image Limited," 134.

105. Quoted in Alexander Nehamas, "Serious Watching," in *Politics of Liberal Education*, ed. Gless and Smith, 163.

106. Ibid., 163–64.

107. John Searle, "The Storm over the University," in *Debating P.C.*, ed. Berman, 88.

108. Matthew Arnold, "The Function of Criticism at the Present Time" (1864), in *Lectures and Essays in Criticism*, ed. R. H. Super (Ann Arbor: University of Michigan Press, 1962), 477.

109. Ibid., 270.

110. Ibid.

111. Ibid., 276.

112. Ibid., 282.

113. Ibid., 282–83.

114. Ibid., 283.

115. Ibid., 284 (emphasis added).

116. Ibid.

117. Matthew Arnold, *Culture and Anarchy: With Friendship's Garland and Some Literary Essays*, ed. R. H. Super (Ann Arbor: University of Michigan Press, 1965), 191.

118. Ibid., 233.

119. Ibid., 529.

120. Ibid., 113.

121. See Horace M. Kallen, *Judaism at Bay: Essays toward the Adjustment of Judaism to Modernity* (New York: Bloch, 1932), 8–9; Susanne Klingenstein, *Jews in the American Academy, 1900–1940* (New Haven, Conn.: Yale University Press, 1991), 43–45, 161–78.

122. Morris Dickstein, *Double Agent: The Critic and Society* (New York: Oxford University Press, 1992), 12.

123. Ibid., 15.

124. Ibid., 16.

125. Ibid., 17.

126. Mark Kurlansky, letter to *New York Times Book Review,* May 31, 1992, 46.

127. Ruth Perry, "A Short History of the Term *Politically Correct,*" in *Beyond P.C.,* ed. Aufderheide, 72–73.

128. Natalie Wexler has pointed out in "Goes Back to 1793," letter to the editor, *New York Times,* December 15, 1993, that the term was used once in 1793 by Supreme Court Justice James Wilson in *Chisholm v. Alabama* in what may be an isolated occurrence: "Is a toast asked? 'The *United States,*' instead of the 'People of the *United States,*' is the toast given. This is not politically correct."

129. Ralph Ellison, *Invisible Man* (1952; New York: Vintage Books, 1972), 453.

130. George Orwell, *Nineteen Eighty-Four* (New York: Harcourt Brace, 1949), 133. All Orwell quotes are from this first American edition.

131. Ibid., 311.

132. Walter Goodman, "Decreasing Our Word Power: The New Newspeak," *New York Times Book Review,* January 27, 1991, 14; Robert Lerner and Stanley Rothman, "Newspeak, Feminist Style," *Commentary* 89 (April 1990): 54.

133. Orwell, *Nineteen Eighty-Four,* 149.

134. Bérubé, "Public Image Limited," 139. See Orwell *Nineteen Eighty-Four,* 45, for the occurrence of *doubleplusungood* in the novel.

135. Orwell, *Nineteen Eighty-Four,* 52.

136. Paula Rothenberg, "Critics of Attempts to Democratize the Curriculum Are

Waging a Campaign to Misrepresent the Work of Responsible Professors," in *Debating P.C.*, ed. Berman, 268; Orwell, *Nineteen Eighty-Four,* 5.

137. George Will, "Radical English," in *Beyond P.C.,* ed. Aufderheide, 112; Michael Novak, "The New Ethnicity," *Center Magazine* 7 (July/August 1974): 18–25.

138. Hughes, "Fraying of America," 146.

139. Camille Paglia, "The Nursery-School Campus: The Corrupting of the Humanities in the US," *Times Literary Supplement,* May 22, 1992, 19.

140. Nat Hentoff, "Black Counterpoint," *Village Voice,* October 15, 1991, 27.

141. Patricia Williams, "Defending the Gains," in *Beyond P.C.,* ed. Aufderheide, 197.

142. Quoted in Searle, "Storm over the University," 110.

143. Quoted in ibid., 111.

144. Ibid., 113.

145. Ibid.

146. Orwell, *Nineteen Eighty-Four,* 250–51.

147. Ibid., 251.

148. Ibid.

149. Erich Fromm, Afterword to George Orwell, *1984* (1949; reprint, New York: Signet, 1961), 263–64.

150. Orwell, *Nineteen Eight-Four,* 128.

151. Daphne Patai, *The Orwell Mystique: A Study in Male Ideology* (Amherst: University of Massachusetts Press, 1984), 241; Orwell, *Nineteen Eight-Four,* 12.

152. Orwell, *Nineteen Eight-Four,* 210.

153. John Rodden, *The Politics of Literary Reputation: The Making and Claiming of "St. George" Orwell* (New York: Oxford University Press, 1989), 26–27.

154. Ibid., 16.

155. Ibid., 30, 37.

156. Reed, "America," 157–58.

157. Richard Polenberg, *One Nation Divisible: Class, Race, and Ethnicity in the United States since 1938* (New York: Viking, 1980), 70.

158. Philip Gleason, *Speaking of Diversity: Language and Ethnicity in Twentieth-Century America* (Baltimore, Md.: Johns Hopkins University Press, 1992), 153–228.

159. Arthur Mann, *The One and the Many: Reflections on the American Identity* (Chicago: University of Chicago Press, 1979), 142–43.

160. John Higham, *Send These to Me: Jews and Other Immigrants in Urban America* (New York: Atheneum, 1975), 220.

161. Stewart G. Cole and Mildred Wiese Cole, *Minorities and the American Promise: The Conflict of Principle and Practice,* Bureau for Intercultural Education Publication Series, No. 10 (New York: Harper and Brothers, 1954), 3.

162. Gleason, *Speaking of Diversity,* 93–94.

163. Donald R. Young, "Democracy and Group Relations," in *Civilization and Group Relations,* ed. Robert MacIver (New York: Institute for Religious Studies, 1945), 157.

164. Ibid., 158–59.

165. Ibid., 159.

166. Robert M. MacIver, "The Ordering of a Multigroup Society," in *Civilization and Group Relations*, ed. MacIver, 164.

167. Higham, *Send These to Me*, 221.

168. MacIver, "Ordering of a Multigroup Society," 165.

169. Ibid., 167.

170. Robin M. Williams Jr., *The Reduction of Intergroup Tensions: A Survey of Research on Problems of Ethnic, Racial, and Religious Group Relations*, Social Science Research Council Bulletin 57 (New York: Social Science Research Council, 1947), 63. Compare Higham, *Send These to Me*, 218n.

171. Williams, *Reduction of Intergroup Tensions*, 63 ("Simultaneous direct attack," "[P]roblems of group conflict," "Where strong prejudice is present,"), 67 ("Propaganda which appeals," "An effective propaganda approach"), 72 ("Hostility is reduced"), 64 ("The likelihood of conflict").

172. Ibid., 64 (emphasis added).

173. Cole and Cole, *Minorities and the American Promise*, 152.

174. Ibid., 153.

175. Ibid.

176. Gottfredson, Nettles, and McHugh, *Meeting the Challenges of Multicultural Education*, 8.

177. Gordon, *Scope of Sociology*, 140–68.

178. Malcolm X, with the assistance of Alex Haley, *The Autobiography of Malcolm X* (1965; reprint, New York: Grove, 1966), 277–78.

179. But compare ibid., 372–73.

180. Explicitly in ibid., 341.

181. LeRoi Jones, "What Does Nonviolence Mean?" in his *Home: Social Essays* (New York: William Morrow, 1966), 149–50.

182. LeRoi Jones, *The Dead Lecturer: Poems* (New York: Grove, 1964), 61–62.

183. Ibid., 62.

5 Pluralism, Protestantism, and Prosperity: Crèvecoeur's American Farmer and the Foundations of American Pluralism

Ned Landsman

There are many ways to view American pluralism. One is as a specific philosophy of group relations that emerged during the twentieth century in response to nativist and assimilationist ideologies prevalent in American culture. That philosophical pluralism is the subject of several other essays in this collection. It had its roots in a deeper cultural pluralism that has been, for better or for worse, an integral part of the American identity from the beginning of the nation and even earlier: the belief in America as a society that accepts and, in one manner or another, incorporates and encourages diverse customs and expressions of people with various origins, nationalities, and faiths.

The validity of that identity as a pluralistic nation has been at the heart of much contemporary debate. To most participants, the principal issues have revolved around two issues that the term *pluralism* has come to imply: the application of pluralism, especially to those members whose identities are normally distinguished by labels pertaining to what is usually called "ethnicity" and to "race"; and the desirability of incorporation—not only into the society but also into a common culture.[1] For the most part, both sides in those debates have shared the assumptions that, even if the privileges of pluralism have not been extended in full measure to all of the nation's inhabitants (which they obviously have not), its reach has increased over time to incorporate a greater number of people and peoples and that in theory it could and should be extended into a universal principle to encompass all of the many groups living within the boundaries of the nation.

Whether that incorporation will occur, only time will tell. An examination of the origins of American pluralism suggests the need to look more closely at some of our assumptions about its functions and its meanings. The concept of pluralism as it emerged in the United States was the product of a particular kind of society at a distinct historical moment. In important respects, the language of pluralism from its first expression and the conception of group identity upon which it rested were integrally linked to the values and circumstances of a colonial settler society in an age of religious conflict and Enlightenment and were formulated in a manner suitable to the needs of Protestants and settlers. In short, American pluralism from the outset was particular rather than universal in its purposes and justifications; it served not only to include but also to exclude. All of that suggests that if Americans truly aspire to implement a broader kind pluralism designed to accommodate all of the nation's inhabitants, they may need to rethink some of its conceptual foundations.

* * *

An obvious place to begin the discussion is with what was perhaps the first and certainly one of the most influential voices in the canon of American pluralism, that of the self-styled "American Farmer," the French-born J. Hector St. John de Crèvecoeur, who settled in the colony and then state of New York during the era of the American Revolution and whose *Letters* of 1782 posed the famous question, "What is an American?"[2] Crèvecoeur's answer has been among the most often quoted passages in the historical literature, both for its early role in the creation of American letters and for its insights into the relationship between pluralism, democratization, and the American character. Yet for all the attention it has received, neither Crèvecoeur's basic assumptions about the nature of group relations in America nor the context within which they emerged has been fully explored. Both provide substantial insights into the historical foundations of American pluralism.

Let us attend to the Farmer's words. "What, then, is the American, this new man?" he asked.

> He is either an European, or the descendant of an European; hence the strange mixture of blood, which you will find in no other country. I could

point out to you a family whose grandfather was an Englishman, whose wife was Dutch, whose son married a French woman, and whose present four sons have now wives of four different nations. He is an American, who leaving behind him all his ancient prejudices and manners, receives new ones from the new mode of life he has embraced, the new government he obeys, and the new rank he holds. . . . Here individuals of all nations are melted into a new race of men.[3]

I will postpone consideration of what may seem the most striking phrase to a contemporary academic audience, that of the American as new *man*, and address the part that has stood out over the years: the American as a composite figure, "melted" from all nations and forming a "new race." That the passage anticipated the metaphor of the melting pot in both concept and language is obvious enough and has been noticed earlier. In the twentieth century, we have come to view pluralism and the melting pot as opposing perspectives—the one emphasizing the expression of difference, the other its removal through assimilation—but to Crèvecoeur they were not. The letter managed to incorporate both sets of images. Thus while the Farmer waxed eloquent about the development of a bold new American character, he also referred to the ease with which people of diverse backgrounds and faiths coexisted in America, under "indulgent laws" that left all free to follow their own ways and think for themselves.

In fact, the one implied the other in the Farmer's formulation; the acceptance of diversity in America was made possible by the very considerable core of values that Americans shared or came to share. European immigrants, upon arriving in America, did not have to abandon their Old World beliefs and customs, but they did have to adjust their way of relating to them. The German Lutheran, the Quaker, and even the Scots seceder—the strictest of all denominations, according to Crèvecoeur—all lived peaceably as neighbors, not because they all believed the same thing or worshipped in the same way but because as Americans all of them had reconceived the significance of their disagreements and the place of worship in their lives. Crèvecoeur's term for that was religious "indifference," which he considered among the principal effects of moving to America. "Indifference," to the Farmer, did not imply the lack of interest in religion but rather meant a diminished attachment to any particular manner of practicing it. The broader idea—that tolerating specific differences was predicated on the existence of underlying commonalities, including some common and markedly controlled ways of experiencing and expressing difference—suggests an important aspect of American pluralism.

The key to Crèvecoeur's ability to link pluralism with assimilation was a redefinition of religious life that derived from the Enlightenment and, before that, from the Protestant Reformation. The redefinition began with the Protestant claim to locate religion in the consciousness and the conscience of the individual. That would result in a considerable narrowing of the realm of religion in public life, allowing for the establishment of sharp distinctions between the essentials of religion and what were labeled "things indifferent" or between private faith personally held and the manner of its public expression. By the eighteenth century, a broad range of Protestant groups, although differing from one another in the content of their faiths, would come to share some basic attitudes toward belief in general. Most Protestants would privilege private faith over mere ritual or "ceremony," scriptural "truth" over speculative "opinion"—in John Locke's famous phrase—and, as the result of the lessened attachment to outward forms, moral and civic duty over ecclesiastical allegiance.[4]

The assumption behind all of this was that despite the differences in superficial religious matters, one could establish a common core of Protestantism at the level of personal faith, a critical idea at a time when conflict between Catholic and Protestant powers still loomed large in Europe and America. One of the goals was to forge a degree of unity among the diverse Protestant groups under a form of toleration that can be labeled Protestant pluralism. The logical outcome would be the American denominational structure, which included an array of essentially parallel and voluntary religious organizations that differed in their specific creeds and practices but agreed on the primacy of the internal experience of religion and the subordination of the denomination to the needs of both the individual and the civil order.[5]

Toleration, defined in this manner, was based on a distinctly Protestant conception of the place of religion in civil life. That it effectively excluded a Catholic population, which included among its beliefs the existence of a single, divinely instituted church under the ecclesiastical hierarchy in Rome that possessed transnational authority, was of little concern in the predominantly Protestant societies of Britain and the United States. Even during Crèvecoeur's day, prejudice against Catholics combined with the fear of the expansionist policies of Europe's Catholic powers to produce such anti-Catholic episodes as the anti-Catholic Gordon riots in Britain and the blatantly anti-Catholic rhetoric of American opposition to the Quebec Act, which had granted civil and religious liberties to the largely Catholic inhabitants of that province just before the American Revolution.[6] Yet those incidents reflected more than simple prejudice; they were also the result of the unwillingness of Catholics to reduce themselves to the position of being simply one more denomination in an ecumenical Protestant secular state.

By the end of the eighteenth century, the original reasons for excluding Catholics from toleration had substantially receded. Beginning with the U.S. Constitution, Catholics were increasingly brought under the protection of toleration and a broader religious liberty. Yet the relationship between Roman Catholics and the civil authority remained sufficiently problematic in American pluralism that they resisted secular public education in the United States and the essentially Protestant conception of public responsibility, which have continued into the twentieth century. If Catholics are no longer excluded from public office, Catholic officeholders are left with the occasional dilemma of reconciling their participation in a public realm that posits as its highest value the autonomy of the individual conscience with their religious commitment to following, also as a matter of conscience, the ethical positions of the church.[7]

* * *

Crèvecoeur took on the persona of a farmer, and not just any farmer but a farmer in Pennsylvania, which was not his real home but was the most diverse, tolerant, and prosperous family farming region (as opposed to plantation region) in North America. It was an area that inhabitants and promoters regularly called the "best poor man's country in the world." Tolerance and prosperity were not unrelated. To prospective emigrants from Europe, Pennsylvania signified a land of tolerance and opportunity. Moreover, Americans during the age of the Enlightenment frequently cited Pennsylvania as the prime example of the supposed positive effect of religious liberty on public prosperity. In Pennsylvania, we can therefore locate the emergence of the American pattern of pluralism and the particular conditions within which it developed.

There are two distinct reasons for associating Pennsylvania with pluralism. One was the legacy of William Penn and the Quakers, who extended the individualist implications of Protestantism much further in the direction of tolerance and spiritual autonomy than did most other groups. In establishing Pennsylvania as a Quaker homeland, Penn did not restrict the settlement to Friends but recruited a variety of Protestant sectaries from across northern Europe. Liberty of conscience, at least for Protestants, was embedded in all of the colony's early constitutions.[8]

More than just the Quaker legacy was at work in Pennsylvania, however. If that colony represented the most tolerant and heterogeneous of the American settlements, both diversity and the acceptance of diversity could be found in considerable measure throughout the Mid-Atlantic region. Moreover, they were increasingly prevalent throughout British colonial society. Crèvecoeur recognized that, and he and nearly every writer after him explained those developments by referring to the high level of economic opportunity that existed in the region and in America at large. The prevalence of opportunity led to an ethic of individual achievement and personal autonomy—the values we associate with classical liberalism—without respect to origin, rank, or belief.[9] One important result was that from the beginning, American pluralism rooted free expression more in the rights of individuals than in the privileges of groups.

Pennsylvania and the rest of the Middle Atlantic developed their leading characteristics at a particular moment in the history of the American colonization. Settled principally during the last quarter of the seventeenth century, later than most of their neighbors, the Middle Atlantic colonies developed during a period of expansion, differentiation, and consolidation in the colonial world. Earlier in the century, mainland North America had contained separate European settlements of New Englanders, New Netherlanders, New French, New Swedes, New Spanish, and New Scots. By 1675 these had been reduced to three sets of colonies, under the dominions of England, Spain, and France, with England controlling most of the northern Atlantic seaboard. European Protestants who traveled to the New World thereafter would mingle almost exclusively in English and, after the Union of 1707, British colonies.

As the number of European claims to mainland North America diminished, the character of the immigrant population became even more diverse. Britain's colonies, which had been predominantly English in origin, came to include substantial numbers of Scots, Irish, Dutch, German-speakers, and Huguenots. The majority of Pennsylvania's settler population was non-English by birth, and English natives made up an ever-decreasing proportion of the population of the whole Mid-Atlantic region.[10] American pluralism, then, emerged in concert with diverse European religious and national groups under the dominion of a single imperial nation.

This was not the whole picture. Even more dramatic than the diversification of the population of European immigrants was the growing presence of African slaves. During the first three-quarters of a century of English colonization of mainland North America, Africans played only a minor role, but that would change rapidly toward the end of the seventeenth century. Over the next century, more than 1.5 million slaves were sent to British America, making Africans by far the largest group of immigrants during the eighteenth century.[11]

Only a small portion of that migration went to Pennsylvania, and only a minority to the mainland colonies at all. More than 80 percent of all slaves imported into British America went to the Caribbean, where they worked on the sugar plantations of the British West Indies. Yet their impact on the Mid-Atlantic region was great nonetheless, for what was most distinctive about the region, and what made it attractive to emigrants from the European continent, was the unusual profitability of its family farms. To an unprecedented degree, European farmers could reasonably expect to travel to the New World, take up farms, and produce not just a subsistence but a comfortable surplus for themselves and their families. The most important market for that surplus was in the plantation colonies. For three-quarters of a century, much of Pennsylvania's surplus production found its way to ready markets in the British West Indies, where it helped feed the expanding slave population. New York, with its Dutch roots, offered the additional export route to the Dutch West Indies, which maintained commercial connections with the slave societies of Spanish and Portuguese America. Although Pennsylvania would remain primarily a colony of and for Europeans, the foundation of its reputation as a "poor man's country" depended to no small degree on the profits of the plantation colonies.[12]

Pennsylvania and the British mainland colonies thus represented a very particular kind of society, with a special and relatively privileged place within the colonial world. Despite the growing dominance of African slaves in the eighteenth-century migration, most of the mainland provinces remained colonies by and for Europeans, who would serve the empire at the same time they served themselves. They were settler societies, societies where the immigrant population displaced and replaced the native inhabitants. The principal need of such societies was population, or, more precisely, a loyal and productive population, to develop the land and defend their claims against those of rival European powers and natives. Historically, the need for settlers has imposed on such societies a special kind of settler pluralism, one that has often relied on a sharp distinction between those considered potential contributors to the welfare of the society and those who were not.[13]

None of this was planned by Pennsylvanians, of course. Most emigrants went there to improve on what were often meager opportunities for themselves and their families; they certainly did not set out to deny them to others. Nonetheless, from the beginning, pluralism and prosperity were inseparable in Pennsylvania, and prosperity was intertwined with the profits of the plantation system. Moreover, the liberal focus of Pennsylvania pluralism, which emphasized opportunity for immigrants and individuals, was consistent with a generally unreflective attitude about the conditions of others. That attitude was rather nicely captured by Crèvecoeur's Farmer, who proudly cited as a sign of his prosperity the general health and contentment of his "Negroes," without expressly considering their role in that prosperity.[14]

Like many of his fellow Pennsylvanians, the Farmer was not without sympathy for the slaves. Crèvecoeur devoted considerable attention in the *Letters* to lauding the ways of the Quakers, who were the first American group to speak out against slaveholding, which was eventually banned by the Philadelphia Yearly Meeting in 1776. The Friends were also among the few Americans to work actively to improve the condition of freed blacks in American society, an effort the Farmer himself emulated.[15] The treatment of slaves in the plantation colonies provided a clear ironic note in Crèvecoeur's treatment of American liberty. After caustically describing the "horrors of slavery" in his letter on Charlestown as examples of "crimes of the most heinous nature," he contrasted the "joy, festivity, and happiness in Charles Town" with the "scenes of misery" that "overspread the country" on the plantations.[16]

That Crèvecoeur resorted to irony in his treatment of slavery suggests the depth of the problem and the difficulty of resolving it within the framework of Pennsylvania pluralism. Even Quakers required nearly a century in the New World to decide officially that the denial of personal liberty to their slaves outweighed the economic and religious liberty that slave labor helped provide to the settlers. Few Americans other than the Friends devoted much effort to incorporating freed slaves into American society in Pennsylvania or elsewhere. The Farmer's antipathy toward slavery was directed more at the brutality of the system than at its exclusiveness. While he bitterly denounced southern slaveholding, he found slavery in Pennsylvania and the North much less objectionable. There, he wrote, slaves enjoyed as much liberty as their masters to eat, marry, and raise families. "In short," he declared, "they participate in many of the benefits of our society without being obliged to bear any of its burthens," a sentiment that few slaves were likely to have shared.[17] Pluralism as it evolved in Pennsylvania thus reflected the concerns not of humanity in general but of those participating in a particular kind of social mission.

Pennsylvania pluralism as expressed by the Farmer reflected the particular needs of a settler society. Consider, for example, the Farmer's description of a tour through his neighborhood. To the right, he wrote, "lives a Catholic, who prays to God as he has been taught and believes in transubstantiation; he works and raises wheat, he has a large family of children, all hale and robust; his belief, his prayers, offend nobody." Farther along lived a German Lutheran, "who addresses himself to the same God . . . agreeably to the modes he has been educated in, and believes in consubstantiation; he also works in his fields, embellishes the earth, clears swamps, etc. . . . ." Next to him lived a Scots seceder, "the most enthusiastic of all sectaries; his zeal is hot and fiery. . . . He likewise raises good crops, his house is handsomely painted, his orchard is one of the fairest in the neighborhood. How does it concern the welfare of the country, or of the province at large, what this man's religious sentiments are, or really whether he has any at all? He is a good farmer, he is a sober, peaceable good citizen."[18]

The implication, of course, is that the fact that the seceder was a good farmer did concern the welfare of the country, whereas his religious principles did not. Here the Farmer echoed John Locke's famous *Letter on Toleration*, perhaps the classical statement of the Enlightenment view of the relationship between religion and the civil polity, in which he had declared that "no man should be deprived of his earthly goods on account of religion."[19] The Farmer continued, "If they are peaceable subjects and are industrious, what is it to their neighbors how and in what manner they think fit to address their prayers to the Supreme Being?"[20]

In one respect, the Farmer went even further than Locke. To the American, toleration was justified not only because the settlers were peaceable, as Locke had argued, but also because they were industrious, "which to me who am but a farmer is the criterion of everything."[21] He had in mind industriousness of a very particular kind: industriousness that led to development, especially the development of the land. The Scots seceder's presence in Pennsylvania was justified not by an abstract right to live unmolested in the enjoyment of his position but by the positive good he did for the settlement in his improvement of the land and the flourishing condition of his house, his orchard, and his crops. Indeed, the Farmer attributed his very rights to his possession and improvement of the land.[22]

In linking pluralism to prosperity and development, Crèvecoeur assumed an immigration model of economic development in America: the land would be improved by those who came here. Bernard Bailyn confirmed the accuracy of such a picture of the development of the early American frontier, demonstrating the importance of immigrant families to its settlement and improvement. By Crèvecoeur's day, their importance was commonly assumed.[23] Still, equating immigration with development and with the very rationale for toleration placed significant constraints on the reach of American pluralism.

One of the most important of those constraints appeared in the Farmer's conception of groups and group identities. Early in the letter "What is an American?" he described Americans as a new race, melted down from "all nations"; they were "a mixture of English, Scots, Irish, French, Dutch, Germans, and Swedes." All of these, of course, were from northern Europe, and the Farmer's depiction of a new "race" prefigured later conceptualizations of the Anglo-Saxon and white races, if only inadvertently.[24] More important, the Farmer's portrayal of nationality itself was intrinsically European and may have been even more limiting.

The Farmer approached nationality from a perspective that combined Enlightenment concepts with American conditions. Its first characteristic was what might be called heritage—"national genius," in the Farmer's words—a collection of attributes deriving from one's national background. Those heritages were all distinct. They could be described and evaluated; in typical Enlightenment fashion, they could even be measured and quantified. "Out of twelve families of emigrants of each country," the Farmer projected, "generally seven Scots would succeed, nine Germans, and four Irish. The Scotch are frugal and laborious. . . . The Irish do not prosper so well; they love to drink and to quarrel; they are litigious and soon take to the gun."[25] Underlying the last comment were Enlightenment ideas about the progress of human society from savagery to civility and the inferiority of hunting societies to their agricultural and commercial successors.[26] It also conformed to the Farmer's general valuing of industriousness above all other character traits. If industriousness varied from one national group to another, the "national genius" of every one provided at least a measure of character and industry useful to settlers in a developing society.

Two points about the Farmer's discussion of heritages deserve further attention. Although the categories he employed were not precisely racial, he did link heritage rather rigidly to ancestry, reflecting a way of thinking about nationality that would long dominate American discussions. One's character derived not from divine providence or personal volition but from descent. It was a part of one's inheritance, an asset, passed down from parent to child in an unbroken line, much in the manner of the

Farmer's farm, which he had received from his father and was destined for his son after him. In that respect, the Farmer's view of ancestry conformed to the pattern of family life James Henretta has labeled the "lineal family," which emphasized the succession of sons to family farms.[27] The language of nationality that resulted linked it to male descent in a manner that would long be reflected in connecting ethnicity with surnames. Such a view implicitly privileged the heritages of those of traceable, or presumably traceable, lineages over those of less well-documented or less well-defined backgrounds—those lacking in what the Farmer meant by nationality.

The commitment to the idea of an unbroken ancestry created some rather anomalous results. For all of the Farmer's lauding of the mixing of people in America, his portrayal left no room for truly mixed peoples. Thus he described a family where one grandfather was English and his wife Dutch, their son married a French woman, and the four grandsons had wives of four different nations. When they intermarried, they became something else: the American, a new race. There was no middle ground, no mixed nationality, and no room for choice.[28]

A second important point about heritages was suggested in the long story of Andrew the Hebridean, the Scottish Islander who settled in Pennsylvania and achieved success through industry, determination, and the support of patrons pleased with his honesty and work ethic. Andrew's Scottish heritage certainly contributed to his taste for work, but that was not the only important thing about his ethnic background. All of Andrew's determination would have done little for him had he not found patrons to sponsor him. The other critical point about his ethnicity was therefore the entry it provided into a network of other settlers who were from his country. They would sponsor new immigrants upon arrival, provide temporary employment, and lend money and assistance to help find and establish a farm or other endeavor. Nationality chiefly benefited those groups that had established sufficient resources and connections to contribute to their mutual advancement.[29]

The Farmer's language associated nationality with particular groups in other ways as well. To the title question, "What is the American?" he stated that Americans had a "strange mixture of blood, which you will find in no other country," another assertion that Americans have continued to make about themselves ever since. But how, exactly, was the blood of the Americans so uniquely mixed? The Farmer again failed to notice the circumstances of his fellow Americans of African descent, who in the course of a century and a half of enslavement had certainly become at least as intermixed in custom, language, and origin as those Crèvecoeur called "Americans," who were all of European descent. That they were not considered of mixed nationality or heritage was true only in the very particular manner in which the Farmer used those terms.

Nor were the European nations from which the "Americans" derived as wholly unmixed as the Farmer implies. Certainly the Netherlands was a grand conglomerate of peoples, including Dutch-speakers from several provinces, German-speakers, Huguenots, and other French-speakers, among other peoples. Great Britain itself housed natives of England, Scotland, Wales, and Ireland, as well as significant clusters of French Huguenots and others.[30] To make diversity into a uniquely American experience, the Farmer had to separate their ancestors into altogether distinct peoples before he could proceed to assimilate them. In that sense, the celebration of the plural traditions in America was also a celebration of American uniqueness.

Yet if the Farmer insisted on the distinctness of those national groups, he did not consider them as altogether different. They were rather like denominations, exhibiting a diversity of character and expression but also underlying commonalities and parallel structures. They were directly traceable to known ancestries, and all had identifiable and continuous traditions. Moreover, those traditions served essentially the same functions for each. To Crèvecoeur, what was important were those elements of character that contributed to industriousness, which all of the European peoples he cited evidenced to some degree. The rest was mere custom or ceremony, to which he attached little real significance; indeed, like religious inheritances, these national "prejudices" would be swept away and extinguished in the American environment.[31] The result was that for all the celebration of heritages, they appeared rather transient and shallow.

The link between industry and ancestry would prove to be an important expansive force in eighteenth- and nineteenth-century America. The combined emphases on lineal inheritance and the development of the land in settler pluralism were probably sufficient to ensure a continuous geographical expansion among colonials and preclude any peaceful solution to the frontier problem. Although William Penn and some of his Quaker successors made real efforts to avoid military confrontation with their Indian neighbors and Crèvecoeur's Farmer expressed real admiration for many Indian ways, those sentiments were consistently overcome by the forces of expansion in Pennsylvania and throughout America. In the end, there was little room in settler society to accommodate native populations, whose very presence signified limits on settlement and development.[32] In general, settler pluralism promoted the fortunes of those whose presence fit most easily into the European settlement project.

By the middle of the nineteenth century, settler pluralism would combine with an extreme racialism to produce bizarre and seemingly incongruous depictions of unified Anglo-Saxon and white races that would be associated with white supremacy and manifest destiny. The myth of Anglo-Saxonism as it emerged in America managed to affirm simultaneously the virtues of pluralism and the fiction of national purity, since the principal Protestant groups that had intermixed in the United States would all be portrayed as varieties of an Anglo-Saxon race that was reunited into an improved American breed. In its most rabid manifestations, at the time of the Mexican War, promoters of manifest destiny would project the inevitable ascendancy of Anglo-Saxons over a "mongrel" race of Mexicans, whose European "blood" had been corrupted rather than improved through intermixing with an inferior racial stock, and whose heritage of industriousness had consequently been replaced by idleness. The images employed at the time were both militaristic and strikingly male; even some who denied the necessity of military conquest assumed the eventual displacement of Mexicans through a process of natural selection. In one version, Mexican females would uplift their race by breeding with Anglo-Saxon males, as it was assumed they would surely prefer to do. The new race would thus extend itself across the continent. The principle of lineal succession could therefore become a tool of ethnic and racial domination. Such images give a very particular meaning to Crèvecoeur's idea of Americans as a new race of men.[33]

* * *

There were alternatives to the version of pluralism expressed by the Farmer among some of the national groups that lived in Pennsylvania and the Mid-Atlantic region. Several of those groups attached considerably greater significance to ethnic association and group identity than he allowed. Those attachments were often less shallow and transient, less lineal and territorial—in that sense, less male—and more distinctive and flexible than he described. Those identities tended to be less purely ascriptive and more voluntary and inclusive, with community networks extended through both female and male lines. Those groups created their own forms of ethnic pluralism, which facilitated the establishment of significant and broadly based ethnic communities in America.

One such group was the "Dutch" colony that began as New Netherland and persisted in colonial New Jersey and New York. From the begin-

ning, the New World "Dutch" were not really a national group at all. New
Netherland was intended more as a commercial outpost than a territorial settlement, and from the beginning it was settled by a diverse mixture
of French-speaking Walloons from southern Netherlands, German-
speakers, Flemish, Dutch-speakers from Utrecht and from the North, Huguenots, English, Scots, and others, creating a still more heterogeneous
offshoot of the diverse confederation that was the Netherlands in the seventeenth century. The English conquest of 1664 changed the political
dominion and opened the way for an eventual new wave of settlement
in New York, without necessarily making it much more heterogeneous
than it had been or radically altering the economic objectives of the resident population.[34]

Over the course of the next century, the "Dutch" both divided and drew
together. For the wealthiest and best connected among the Dutch merchant elite, especially in New York City, the English conquest was a time
of opportunity, which was best pursued by accepting English rule and
English ways and participating in the emerging British colonial world. For
the majority of poorer inhabitants, however, especially for those living
outside of New York City, Anglicization had less to offer. Instead, those
inhabitants practiced their own form of ethnic pluralism, assembling
diverse elements into unified "Dutch" communities that had not existed
earlier. The Dutch Reformed church assumed an important role as a cultural institution, especially for female members, including those who had
married outside the ethnic community, even as it lost some of its wealthier
members to the Anglican church. The Dutch language was adopted even
by some whose New Netherland ancestors had spoken other tongues.
Moreover, through a system of partible inheritance that guaranteed the
rights of wives and daughters as well as sons, both inheritance and attachment to the community passed through female as well as male lines. The
Dutch enclaves in New Jersey and New York thus remained more stable
territorially than the expansive settlements of many of their English-
speaking neighbors. The "Dutch" of New York remained an identifiable
community into the nineteenth century.[35]

The Scots community in the Mid-Atlantic did not persist quite as long
as the Dutch, but it shared a number of characteristics. Spanning the New
Jersey corridor linking New York and Philadelphia, the Scots settlement
was oriented to commerce from the beginning. Like the Dutch colony, it
was heterogeneous, including among its members not only natives of
Scotland but also others of northern Irish, southern Irish, northern English, and Huguenot origin. The Scots community was diverse in religion

as well, incorporating Anglicans, Presbyterians, Quakers, members of various radical Presbyterian sects, and a few Catholics.[36]

Over half a century, these various groups gradually coalesced into a common community, sharing trade networks and, increasingly, participation in a unified Scottish Presbyterian church. The community added new members, not only through immigration but also through intermarriage with others. Spouses and children were welcomed into the Scottish church and community, which was extended through both the male and female lines. As a trading community with its own tradition of partible inheritance, Scots in America drew on their experience as a geographically mobile people to create a network of interlocking settlements. Instead of privileging territorial development, those Scots settlers who did move to available lands at some distance from their original homes almost invariably retained commercial, cultural, and familial ties to the Scottish neighborhoods.

Only rarely did the experiences of these groups affect the discussion of pluralism as it evolved in early America, which continued to project notions of descent much purer than that which most Americans actually possessed. Rather, Americans in general would continue to depict ethnicity as the unmixed and involuntary product of ancestry rather than the result of a succession of flexible and voluntary choices of allegiance, and to view heritage as a form of property allowing entry into one of the various subgroups that constituted the wider community of Americans.[37]

That occurred partly because since Crèvecoeur's day ethnicities have been evaluated principally for their ability to contribute to American settlement and development. They provide a foundation for personal character, which has been valued especially for industriousness and diligence. Moreover, where they have offered mutual support—to one's fellow nationals in the manner of Andrew the Hebridean—the privileges and connections granted have almost uniformly been characterized as social assets; only rarely have they been condemned as discriminatory. In practice, ethnicities serve both functions, as the often exclusive character of ethnic neighborhoods and social institutions makes clear. That the language of American pluralism has chosen only to celebrate them may derive from the perception of their essential contribution to the settlement model of developing the land and the economy of a settler society.

At the same time, as was implied by Crèvecoeur, pluralism has also tended to minimize the distinctiveness of ethnic groups. The celebration of heritages has often emphasized precisely those elements of cultural backgrounds that have been least distinctive—their contribution to development—and those most amenable to the needs of settler society. The rest has been viewed as mere ceremony. If recent generations of ethnics have taken more positive views of those other elements as well, they have still been likely to laud them primarily for their contributions to industriousness and development. Particular group customs are still largely confined to a rather narrow place in cultural life; they are not supposed to challenge the general pursuit of economic goals.[38]

From its earliest stages, then, American pluralism was not a universal concept but was limited by the imperatives of settler society in an age of plantations, colonization, and religious wars. It was formulated in a manner compatible with the need to recruit a settler population loyal to Protestantism, the state, and the developmental needs of settler society. It was designed to maximize economic opportunities for a settler population of increasingly diverse origins.

"Settlers," in what was never an empty or "virgin land," were defined not simply by who they were but also by who they were not: neither those inhabitants who previously occupied the land, nor those whose labor on the plantations provided the necessary underpinnings for settler pluralism. At best, the society has tolerated those whose faiths have placed them at odds with the prevailing gospel of development. Constructed in that fashion, American pluralism has allowed for the integration of an increasing number of diverse groups into the race of Americans. At the same time, it has rendered problematic the relationship between that society and those whose involvement in the projects of settlement and development have been more ambiguous, if not hostile.

Lest this seem an unduly pessimistic view of American pluralism, we should of course note that its parameters have always been qualified by its inception during the Enlightenment, an era strongly committed to the idea of a universal human nature and to general laws. American pluralism was codified in fundamental law, from the Fundamental Constitutions and Frames of Government of Pennsylvania to the nation's founding documents, in arrestingly universal language. The pronouncement by slaveholders of the natural equality of men still puzzles us today. It is not difficult to demonstrate that the founders of the nation did not fill out their system of statutory law with the universal content that their constitutional language seemed to imply. Yet the very use of that language has allowed subsequent generations, if only intermittently, to succeed in extending the range of those included as American beyond what the founders intended or—at least occasionally—beyond what the original construction of ethnicity in America would seem to permit.

Notes

1. I take the latter to be the principal issue implied by the debate over the terms *pluralism* and *multiculturalism,* although I doubt that all of the participants in that debate would agree on any single definition of the issue. By such a standard, even the boldest advocates of a "core" culture could be considered pluralists of a sort, provided that the core is not restricted to the contributions of a single group and that the culture grant some social space to the expression of limited cultural differences.

2. For a recent biography, see Gay Wilson Allen and Roger Asselineau, *St. John de Crèvecoeur: The Life of an American Farmer* (New York: Viking, 1987). Some recent literary discussions have considered the question of how much Crèvecoeur shared the optimism of his fictional author, and how far he should be distanced from the Farmer; the context and assumptions underlying the Farmer's optimistic pluralism remains relevant nonetheless. See especially Norman S. Grabo, "Crèvecoeur's American: Beginning the World Anew," *William and Mary Quarterly,* 3d ser., 48 (April 1991): 159–72.

3. St. John de Crèvecoeur, *Letters from an American Farmer and Sketches of Eighteenth-Century America,* ed. Albert E. Stone (New York: Penguin Books, 1981), 69–70. All quotes from Crèvecoeur are from Letter III, "What Is an American?" 66–105, unless otherwise noted. I have substituted "either" for "neither" in the first line to conform to the 1793 Philadelphia edition, which makes a good deal more sense than the phrase as cited by Stone.

4. John Locke's *A Letter Concerning Toleration: Humbly Submitted, &c* (1689; reprint, Indianapolis: Hackett, 1983) is probably the most influential and often-cited work on toleration.

5. The classical discussion of denominations is Sidney Mead, "Denominationalism: The Shape of Protestantism in America," *Church History* 23 (December 1954): 291–320. In the nineteenth century, many Protestant denominations would join together in forging a united evangelical front committed to the propagation of a Protestant faith characterized by personal religious experience and the enlistment of the state in the promotion of an evangelical moral order. For a somewhat different use of the term *Protestant pluralism* in relation to colonial New York, see Richard W. Pointer, *Protestant Pluralism and the New York Experience: A Study of Eighteenth-Century Religious Diversity* (Bloomington: Indiana University Press, 1988).

6. On the relationship between anti-Catholic sentiment and pro-American positions in Britain, see John Sainsbury, *Disaffected Patriots: London Supporters of Revolutionary America, 1769–1782* (Kingston, Ont.: McGill–Queens' University Press, 1987); and Robert Kent Donovan, "The Popular Party of the Church of Scotland and the American Revolution," in *Scotland and America in the Age of the Enlightenment,* ed. Richard B. Sher and Jeffrey B. Smitten (Princeton, N.J.: Princeton University Press, 1990), 81–99.

7. As late as 1960, Americans still debated an argument that dated from the Reformation, whether a Roman Catholic could be safely trusted to head a secular state without subsuming the interests of that state under the interests of the Catholic church. Although that issue has faded in recent years, it has been replaced by anoth-

er that represents the other side of the same question: whether public officials could follow the dictates of their own consciences, as Protestant liberty suggests, and still remain good Catholics.

8. The most comprehensive treatment of the topic is J. William Frost, *A Perfect Freedom: Religious Liberty in Pennsylvania* (New York: Cambridge University Press, 1990). See also Sally Schwartz, *"A Mixed Multitude": The Struggle for Toleration in Colonial Pennsylvania* (New York: New York University Press, 1987).

9. On the emergence of the liberal ethic in Pennsylvania, see James T. Lemon, *The Best Poor Man's Country: A Geographical Study of Early Southeastern Pennsylvania* (Baltimore, Md.: Johns Hopkins University Press, 1972).

10. For a recent general introduction to colonial immigration, see Bernard Bailyn, *The Peopling of British North America: An Introduction* (New York: Alfred A. Knopf, 1986); on immigration to Pennsylvania, see Marianne S. Wokeck, "German and Irish Immigration to Colonial Philadelphia," *Proceedings of the American Philosophical Society* 133 (1989): 128–43.

For contrasting views of the national origins of the population of the Middle Atlantic colonies, see Ellen McDonald and Forrest McDonald, "The Ethnic Origins of the American People, 1790," *William and Mary Quarterly,* 3d ser., 37 (April 1980): 179–99; Thomas L. Purvis, "The European Ancestry of the United States Population, 1790," *William and Mary Quarterly,* 3d ser., 41 (January 1984): 85–101; and the discussions in the same journal, 41 (January 1984): 102–35, and 41 (October 1984): 680–83.

11. The classic work is Philip D. Curtin, *The Atlantic Slave Trade: A Census* (Madison: University of Wisconsin Press, 1969). For recent demographic surveys, see Jim Potter, "Demographic Development and Family Structure," and Richard S. Dunn, "Servants and Slaves: The Recruitment and Employment of Labor," both in *Colonial British America: Essays in the New History of the Early Modern Era,* ed. Jack P. Greene and J. R. Pole (Baltimore, Md.: Johns Hopkins University Press, 1984), 123–56 and 157–94; and John J. McCusker and Russell R. Menard, *The Economy of British America, 1607–1789: Needs and Opportunities for Study* (Chapel Hill: University of North Carolina Press, 1985), chapter 10.

12. McCusker and Menard, *Economy of British America,* 191–94. For an excellent discussion of the relationship between slavery and particular American ideas of liberty, see Edmund S. Morgan, *American Slavery, American Freedom: The Ordeal of Colonial Virginia* (New York: W. W. Norton, 1975).

13. Compare this situation with that described in George Frederickson, *White Supremacy: A Comparative Study in American and South African History* (New York: Oxford University Press, 1981), chapter 3.

14. Crèvecoeur, *Letters from an American Farmer,* 53.

15. See especially Jean R. Soderlund, *Quakers and Slavery: A Divided Spirit* (Princeton, N.J.: Princeton University Press, 1985); and Gary B. Nash and Jean R. Soderlund, *Freedom by Degrees: Emancipation in Pennsylvania and Its Aftermath* (New York: Oxford University Press, 1991).

16. Crèvecoeur, *Letters from an American Farmer,* 166–79.

17. Ibid., 171. See also Nash and Soderlund, *Freedom by Degrees.*

18. Crèvecoeur, *Letters from an American Farmer*, 74–75.

19. Locke, *Letter on Toleration*, 113.

20. Crèvecoeur, *Letters from an American Farmer*, 75.

21. Ibid.

22. Ibid., 54.

23. Bernard Bailyn, *Voyagers to the West: A Passage in the Peopling of America on the Eve of the Revolution* (New York: Alfred A. Knopf, 1986). A similar assumption pervaded Benjamin Franklin's "Information to Those Who Would Remove to America," in *Writings* (New York: Library of America, 1987), 975–83, which appeared within a few years of the *Letters from an American Farmer*. There Franklin suggested that immigrant tradesmen should anticipate using their skills only to acquire a stake, which they could use to invest in a farm. That Franklin for most of his career was unreflective about the opportunities afforded Pennsylvania's slave population is argued in Nash and Soderlund, *Freedom by Degrees*, ix–xiv.

24. On the white and Anglo-Saxon races, see the discussion by Matthew Jacobson in this volume.

25. Crèvecoeur, *Letters from an American Farmer*, 85. For the interest in quantification among Enlightened Americans, see Patricia Cline Cohen, *A Calculating People: The Spread of Numeracy in Early America* (Chicago: University of Chicago Press, 1982).

26. See Ronald L. Meek, *Social Science and the Ignoble Savage* (Cambridge: Cambridge University Press, 1979).

27. James Henretta, "Families and Farms: Mentalité in Pre-Industrial America," *William and Mary Quarterly*, 3d ser., 35 (January 1978): 3–32; Crèvecoeur, *Letters from an American Farmer*, 52–54.

28. That such a view of ethnicity would enter public discussion in America is suggested by the later development of the term *ethnics* to refer to all immigrant communities, or at least all of European national heritage. Such communities have been assumed to be parallel structures, differing principally in the area of custom but serving similar functions in most important areas of life.

29. Gary B. Nash, *Forging Freedom: The Formation of Philadelphia's Black Community, 1720–1840* (Cambridge, Mass.: Harvard University Press, 1988), details major efforts in Philadelphia's free black community to provide assistance to its members. The role of immigrant networks has been discussed many times. See the recent summaries by Charles Tilly, "Transplanted Networks," and Eva Morawska, "The Sociology and Historiography of Immigration," both in *Immigration Reconsidered: History, Sociology, and Politics*, ed. Virginia Yans-McLaughlin (New York: Oxford University Press, 1990), 79–95 and 187–238, especially 84–86 and 194–96.

30. On diversity in the Netherlands, see Oliver A. Rink, *Holland on the Hudson: An Economic and Social History of Dutch New York* (Ithaca, N.Y.: Cornell University Press, 1986), chapter 6.

31. Crèvecoeur, *Letters from an American Farmer*, 83.

32. On the eventual failure of Quaker Indian policy, see especially Francis Jennings, *The Ambiguous Iroquois Empire: The Covenant Chain Confederation of Indian Tribes with English Colonies* (New York: W. W. Norton, 1984), 248, 254–74; and Daniel K.

Richter, "Onas and the Long Knives: Pennsylvania-Indian Relations, 1783–1791" (Paper presented to the Philadelphia Center for Early American Studies, March 27, 1992).

33. Reginald Horsman, *Race and Manifest Destiny: The Origins of American Racial Anglo-Saxonism* (Cambridge, Mass.: Harvard University Press, 1981), provides a relentless account of some of the truly harrowing details of the worst of this rhetoric (see especially 233ff.). That rhetoric exemplifies some of the contradictions inherent in the marriage between pluralism and an emphasis on unmixed lineages. For other materials on the gendered quality of Crèvecoeur's pluralism, see Werner Sollors, *Beyond Ethnicity: Consent and Descent in American Culture* (New York: Oxford University Press, 1986), 75–81.

34. Rink, *Holland on the Hudson*; Joyce D. Goodfriend, "The Social Dimensions of Congregational Life in Colonial New York City," *William and Mary Quarterly*, 3d ser., 46 (April 1989): 252–78; David Cohen, "How Dutch Were the Dutch of New Netherland?" *New York History* 62 (January 1981): 43–60.

35. See especially Joyce D. Goodfriend, *Before the Melting Pot: Society and Culture in Colonial New York City, 1664–1730* (Princeton, N.J.: Princeton University Press, 1992); David E. Narrett, *Inheritance and Family Life in Colonial New York City* (Ithaca, N.Y.: Cornell University Press 1992); Randall H. Balmer, *A Perfect Babel of Confusion: Dutch Religion and English Culture in the Middle Colonies* (New York: Oxford University Press, 1989); and Donna Merwick, *Possessing Albany, 1630–1710* (New York: Cambridge University Press, 1990).

A. G. Roeber, "'The Origin of Whatever Is Not English among Us': The Dutch-Speaking and the German-Speaking Peoples of Colonial British America," *Strangers within the Realm: Cultural Margins of the First British Empire*, ed. Bernard Bailyn and Philip D. Morgan (Chapel Hill: University of North Carolina Press, 1991), 220–83, emphasizes the "thinness" of Dutch high culture in America and what he considers the rapid Anglicization of Dutch life, in contrast to a longer-lived and more visible German culture. Given the significantly earlier arrival of the "Dutch" in the Mid-Atlantic and the persistence—or rather the creation and establishment—of a domestic Dutch-American culture organized around church, family, and female association throughout the eighteenth century, as Roeber himself describes, the vibrancy of that culture may be the more significant fact.

36. Ned C. Landsman, *Scotland and Its First American Colony, 1680–1760* (Princeton, N.J.: Princeton University Press, 1985), especially chapter 5. Some markedly different ethnic experiences in the Mid-Atlantic are discussed in Roeber, "'Origin of Whatever Is Not English among Us'"; A. G. Roeber, *Palatines, Liberty, and Property: German Lutherans in Colonial British America* (Baltimore, Md.: Johns Hopkins University Press, 1993); and Jon Butler, *The Huguenots in America: A Refugee People in New World Society* (Cambridge, Mass.: Harvard University Press, 1983).

37. See the essays by Stanley N. Katz and Mary C. Waters in this volume.

38. That has had positive ramifications as well. The celebration of ethnic heritages as contributing to development has allowed for a reconciliation between Protestant and Catholic groups in the United States and has restricted the roles of religion in economic life.

6   Pluralism and Hierarchy: "Whiz Kids," "The Chinese Question," and Relations of Power in New York City

John Kuo Wei Tchen

Many political analysts fear that the recent emphasis on the distinctive histories and experiences of particular ethnic and racial groups has been leading to the "Balkanization" of the U.S. polity. They insist the *unum* has been lost in the emphasis on the diversity of the *pluribus*.[1] By posing the *unum* as paramount, such pundits have formulated a "winner-take-all" discourse. What has been glossed over in these often alarmist debates has been a more careful examination of the theory and practice of the notion of America as a pluralist nation. How has the ideal of *E pluribus unum* actually been played out historically? Rather than give in to the caricature that this nation can only be mainly one or the other, we might do better to ask what the historical relationship between the many and the one has been.

This essay uses the peculiarities of the Chinese experience in New York City as a case study to explore the mythos and experience of Gotham[2] as a "center of difference."[3] By examining how "the Chinese question" was formulated by liberal Manhattanites in the post-Reconstruction period and how Chinese New Yorkers are represented after the civil rights movement, we can shed light on how the all-purpose usage of the term *pluralism* has obscured the actual nature of the racialized and ethnicized hierarchy in the

United States.[4] From such a critique, we can begin to build a far more precise and democratic pluralist analysis and practice.

* * *

Sometime after New Year and before the first winter thaw, I have regularly taken great pleasure in unfolding the *New York Times* to see a photo showing how many Asian American students are among the semifinalists and finalists of the Westinghouse Science Talent Search. Having been born and reared in the Midwest and quite weary of being praised for how well I speak English, I continue to delight when the media acknowledges those of Asian heritage who are being touted as American successes. Yet as I have followed press coverage and public discussion of these students, I have become increasingly concerned about the dissonance between their actual achievements and how those achievements have been construed—declaring Asian Americans a "model minority" despite compelling evidence defying overgeneralization.

The 1988 *New York Times* coverage of this annual event offers a clear example of this phenomenon. The front-page headline "Science Whizzes Abound in a School and a City" was punctuated by a striking photograph of the eleven semifinalists from Benjamin Cardozo High School, all of whom were of one Asian ethnicity or another. Jane Perlez's accompanying article highlighted New York City's preeminence in the competition and sought to explain Cardozo's particular dominance. Despite all the Asian faces in the photograph, the article judiciously underplayed the fact that all eleven semifinalists were Asian. The school's principal was quoted as saying that the Asian sweep was "a fluke," pointing out that in the previous year just four of the nine semifinalists from Cardozo were Asian. The reporter then noted the recent eight-year increase in the proportion of Asian students at the school, from 2.9 percent to 24.7 percent, and the school's location in "a stable enclave with many single family homes" in the Borough of Queens.[5] The psychology project of one of the students, Mina Choi, was then given extensive coverage. Although Choi's paper examined teachers' perceptions of European American, African American, and Asian American students, only the Asian part of the study was discussed in the *Times* article. A fascinating media debate ensued. But first, more on Choi's study.

Choi's Westinghouse paper was called "Analysis of Teacher Perceptions of Students with Respect to Student Race and Gender—Queens New York City High Schools." Choi showed eighty teachers an array of twenty-eight photographs of male and female European American, African American, and Asian American students—with and without eyeglasses—and then asked them to rate each picture according to the following categories: physical ability, English language ability, math/science ability, social science ability, and motivation level. Overall, Choi's statistics showed that these high school teachers considered European American students to be the most well-rounded, in that their scores fluctuated less, a claim many college admissions officers also believed; that Asian American students were believed to be best in math and science and were highly motivated; and finally, that African Americans were considered best in sports. Choi concluded that for each of these perceptual patterns "the high expectation feedback that students receive from their teachers might push them a little further than if teachers had a low expectation of them."[6]

Choi's nuanced and carefully worded study is significant for at least two reasons. First, she added a third group to the still-dominant social science paradigm of the United States as a biracial society primarily defined in terms of blacks and whites. This triracial or multiracial perspective allows for a far more dynamic interpretation of American society.[7] Indeed, making sense of this triracial hierarchy became the heart of the subsequent media coverage. Second, Choi's study clearly demonstrates the impact of teacher perceptions. Teachers' racialized expectations about their students need to be factored into any analysis of students' abilities to perform or not perform. Choi commented that "some teachers expected Asians to do better in math than other students. There was even a rumor that one teacher could be counted on to give Asians higher grades than non-Asians."[8] Conversely, low expectations of black students "might be part of the reason that there is a large black drop-out rate in the New York City educational system."[9]

Oddly, the ensuing debate had little to do with the actual students at Cardozo. In a lengthy Op-Ed response published in the *New York Times* entitled "Why Do Asian Pupils Win Those Prizes?" Stephen G. Graubard, the editor of *Daedalus*, argued for the larger significance and complexity of the question of "why certain children 'succeed' and why others fail." Even while pleading for a fuller understanding, however, Graubard latched onto Perlez's rather parenthetical comment about stable, single-family neighborhoods and made it the primary cause of Asian student success. Then, in the spirit of social welfare planning, he speculated about what might be done for all those hundreds of thousands of children who did not live in such stable environs. While arguing for greater understanding of what made these Cardozo students "successful," Graubard assumed that stable single-family neighborhoods provided the prerequisites for success. Reference to Choi's paper was made third-hand, citing the *New York Times* article; her work was used out of context to substantiate his own "nurture" position.[10]

A few weeks later, two letters appeared in the *New York Times*. The first was titled "The New Protestant Ethic Is the Asian Ethic." The lead letter was from a professor of psychology who vehemently rejected Graubard's position faulting "the defects of the system." The psychologist attributed high cultural esteem for intellectual accomplishment and education as the reason for Asian children's success. Steady hard work, where the individual child is "held responsible for shortcomings," is the essence of the Asian version of the Protestant work ethic, a quality the psychologist felt had to be restored to all levels of American society. This opinion was echoed virtually verbatim in *U.S. News and World Report*'s coverage of the Westinghouse competition. The reporter's conclusion regarding "What Puts the Whiz in the Whiz Kids" was simple and formulaic: family values, immigrant hope, and hard work.[11]

The second *New York Times* letter, entitled "Parents Not the Answer," was written by one of the Cardozo semifinalists on behalf of all of the other students. Critical of judgments made in the print and electronic media, as well as other "expert" pronouncements, the letter made several key points: (1) too much emphasis was placed on the Cardozo semifinalists' all being Asian; (2) the theories offered to explain such Asian performance had little to do with the winners' actual motivations; and (3) such "labeling" could easily lead to stereotyping, "which in its most extreme form is the root of prejudice, a disease that can never be solved by science." Instead of giving credence to any single causal theory, the letter insisted that the influences and motivations were quite varied. The parental role was said to range from apathy to intense involvement. Moreover, parental pressure to enter the competition was not a primary motivational factor. Instead, each student entered "to meet the expectations of our school and teachers, and because we, on our own, decided to." The collective letter of these students essentially confirmed Choi's findings of the powerful interactional role teachers' expectations played in their intellectual growth and success.[12] Despite the highly articulate letter from the young adults at Cardozo, journalists, scholars, and other "experts" have dominated mainstream public discourse. The representation of these promising Queens high school students had little to do with their actual lives and experiences; a larger politics has been at work. This formulation of Asian student success turned a complex phenomenon into a simplistic and historical representation of the unchanging nature of Asian cultures.[13] Such formulations have a long history in American public discussion.

* * *

New York City has long been extolled as a primary site of pluralist ideology and practice in the United States. Those of us who have lived in or frequented this metropolis know that this mythos is omnipresent and pervades daily life as much as political and intellectual discourse, even if the term rarely is used consistently or defined clearly. The lead-in to the local evening news, the background scenes of Woody Allen's films, and all sorts of ads invariably flash scenes of Harlem, Chinatown, subway riders, gentrified brownstones, bodegas, delis, salumerias, and, of course, the Statue of Liberty.

When incidents of gross intolerance erupt in some sector of our urban landscape—whether it be the vigilantism of Howard Beach or the boycott on Flatbush Avenue, gay-bashing on Christopher Street, or the Crown Heights riots—the authoritative civic powers argue that such heinous and narrow-minded acts are but temporary lapses of good judgment. Indeed, such neighborhoods are often represented by the city's liberal establishment as backwaters of unenlightened prejudice—places populated by "ignorant" blue-collar Italians, or "idle" blacks, or wayward, heavy-metal/hip-hop-loving youth—and not indicative of what New York City is truly about.[14]

Scholarship on "the Chinese question" has tended to reinforce this mythos. Mary Roberts Coolidge's 1909 classic study entitled *Chinese Immigration* set forth what has become the accepted interpretation explaining the passage of the 1882 Chinese Exclusion Act. Central to her analysis was the strategic role played by the largely Irish-led, California-based working-class movement in the ultimate passage of national exclusionary immigration laws. In contrast, there has been no examination of those who stood on the "pro-Chinese" side of the national debate. Indeed, in the absence of any critical discussion, northeasterners and bourgeois gentry nationwide have been represented in Coolidge's analysis as tolerant, progressive groups that believed in American pluralist ideals.[15] Has this mythos been practiced in Gotham? If so, how has it operated?

Historical scholarship has located three emblematically New York traditions of pluralism. First, there was the formation of the late-eighteenth-century policy of Protestant pluralism. Grounded in the European Enlightenment's belief in human reason and Locke's writings on religious toleration, this pluralistic vision manifested itself in the Anglo-American conviction that "truth" would not suffer amidst a variety of religious views[16] and that "reasonable men" would conduct equally reasonable dialogue that would demonstrate the innate superiority of Protestant values and ideals.[17] Progress defined by capitalist economic moderniza- tion has undergirded this faith in Protestant superiority.[18] Conversion to this spirit of cultural and technological advance became a prerequisite to Anglo-Americanism.[19]

A second tradition of New York pluralism has been traced to the com- mercial cultural marketplace of the post-universal, white-male-suffrage nineteenth century in the expansive but rudely democratic culture of the stage, dime museum, and print media. In taking note of this odd and very American hybrid of Adam Smith and blackface minstrelsy, we become well aware of the simultaneously contested and exclusive nature of such a culture.[20] Finally, social historians have delineated a legacy of democratic movements involving mechanics, trade unions, and coalitions, which gained substance with the General Trades Union (GTU) of the 1830s. The GTU was able to develop a centralized, disciplined organization while resolving the issue of representing diverse individual unions from a va- riety of trades.[21]

In this era following the civil rights movement, it is useful to explore how these three traditions have operated in relation to the formulation of "the Chinese question" in the nineteenth century. These various tra- ditions have long influenced the way New Yorkers have viewed Asian Americans. The cultural productions of three preeminent New Yorkers of the late nineteenth century will serve to demonstrate some of the lim- its of this pluralist faith when confronting the powerful hierarchies of race, ethnicity, and class.[22] Thomas Nast and Joseph Keppler, arguably two of the most important political artists of the nineteenth century, both sup- ported the Chinese right to immigrate to the United States, but their "sup- port" bears careful scrutiny. Edward Harrigan, the major New York play- wright and actor writing for the emergent Five Points Irish, presented still more ambivalent working-class representations of Chinese New Yorkers.

Thomas Nast arrived in New York with his family from Germany in the 1840s. The elder Nast was a "Forty-Eighter" who saw the United States as a beacon of secular, liberal, Protestant, and romantic nationalist en- lightenment. The city's tradition of Protestant pluralism enabled Ger- mans, unlike Chinese immigrants, to partake quickly of the cultural, eco- nomic, and political life of the city. With the help of a German American network of supporters, Nast landed his first assignment with *Harper's*

Weekly, the major national newspaper of the Victorian era, and with the advent of the Civil War, Nast became the nation's foremost political artist. His most important and influential work—spanning the 1860s through the 1870s—rose with the victory of the North and declined with the failure of Reconstruction.[23]

In this context, we can begin to approach Nast's drawings of "the Chinese question." "Uncle Sam's Thanksgiving Dinner," drawn in 1869, expresses Nast's radical republican iconoclasm (see figure 6.1). At a huge family table with a centerpiece celebrating "self government" and "universal suffrage," Uncle Sam carves a turkey in front of a welcoming painting of Castle Garden, which had by 1869 been turned into New York's immigration depot. The figure of Columbia is flanked by those of an African American family and a Chinese man with his son and inappropriately Japanese-garbed wife. The nations and races of the world are represented at the table, with the portraits of Presidents George Washington, Abraham Lincoln, and Ulysses S. Grant looking down from on high. "Come one come all" and "free and equal," written on the bottom corners, further underscore Nast's proto-pluralist vision.

Nast's unambiguous use of his noble "John Confucius" character consistently argued for appreciating China as a global trading partner and according equal rights for Chinese Americans.[24] In his 1868 drawing "The Youngest Introducing the Oldest," Columbia plays the role of a good hostess and presents a dignified and princely robed Chinese, surrounded by crates (representing the perceived material wealth of the East), to European heads of state. "Brothers and Sisters," says "America," "I am happy to present to you the Oldest member of the Family, who deserves our better acquaintance."[25] John Confucius was cast within the eighteenth-century romantic Enlightenment view of China—the China of chinoiserie, cherished luxury goods, such public works projects as the Grand Canal, the civil service, and, of course, the sage Confucius. In this representation, Chinese merchants were honest, hard-working, rational, and fair-minded, qualities that neatly fit New York Protestants' self-image.

The most important "Chinese question" drawings came in a series of eight full-page cartoons from 1871 to 1880, when anti-Chinese feelings in California were bursting onto the national scene and would ultimately lead to legalized exclusion. These drawings clearly articulated Nast's radical Republican and reform sensibilities: Irish and other immigrant rabble unfairly scapegoated nonnormative racial groups, politicians were corrupted by catering to the popular vote, and anti-Chinese agitation was jeopardizing important diplomatic and trade relations with China. "The

Figure 6.1. Thomas Nast, "Uncle Sam's Thanksgiving Dinner," *Harper's Weekly*,
November 20, 1869.

Chinese Question," one of Thomas Nast's most powerful "pro-Chinese"
drawings, depicts Columbia center stage defending a huddled, over-
whelmed Chinese American man (see figure 6.2). She looks fiercely at a
male crowd of armed rioters and shouts "Hands off, Gentlemen! America means fair play for all men." The rioters' faces are threatening and
animal-like, with deep-set, beady eyes and menacing scowls. The leader
is typical of Nast's anti-Irish caricatures: he holds a rock in one hand, a
raised club in the other. The rioters are depicted as having just torched a
"colored" orphanage—an event that actually took place during the New
York City draft riots—and are now ready to get John Confucius.[26]
     Nast did not have much of an American tradition of political art on
which to draw, but he was very much influenced by British conventions.
Columbia's facial features exemplified prevailing Anglo-American ideals of perfect beauty and strength of character. Conversely, Nast's crowds
and racial groups were generally drawn with little individual distinctiveness. Nast adapted uncritically, even wholesale, the conventional British
caricature of the Irish as a lowly and thuggish racial group. His unkempt
Irish were drawn with simian features: square-jawed, low foreheads, and

Figure 6.2. Thomas Nast, "The Chinese Question," *Harper's Weekly,* February 18, 1871.

up-turned noses. Columbia was always represented as a principled individual seeking justice, whereas the Irish were mainly portrayed as an undifferentiated mob. The two representations were interdependent, their
respective characteristics a critical foil each to the other. This racialization of British-Irish cultural and religious differences was prototypical.

The art historian Mary Cowling has demonstrated the powerful influence that the nineteenth-century sciences of phrenology and physiognomy had on the visual arts. Serious artists understood their role in nationalist high culture to capture the true nature and personality of the
person being drawn. Even among the largely light-complected British,
skin color was insinuated into class differences. The lower classes and Celts
were depicted as linked to the colored races. John Beddoe invented his
Index of Nigrescence to measure the degree of darkness among the various races of Britain. Of course, the darkest proved to be the "Africanoid"
type of Irish that occasionally overlapped with the "Mongoloid" type of
Celt. One British anthropologist posited that it was the Irish intermarriage with this "Mongoloid" element from Iberia that produced "the lazy,
rollicking, merry Irishman of the caricaturist." As Lewis Perry Curtis has
pointed out, in an England influenced by Darwinian ideas, the Celts were
the apes and the Normans the angels.[27]

In the United States, Nast carried on the Anglo-American caricature
of the degenerate, low-class Irish Catholic but had the additional challenge of representing other racial groups living in the United States. The
population of the United States was far more diverse. The domestic hierarchy was first and foremost racialized between slave and free, white and
nonwhite, and then class-determined. Nast's Protestant-bound radical
Republicanism essentially transplanted the visual language of Anglo-
American antipathy for the Irish and then folded in Indians, Chinese, and
African Americans. Nast's profession of equal rights and universal suffrage communicated one set of ideas, while his drawings, which followed
uncritically the Anglo-American representational tradition of racial types,
set forth a somewhat different message. His Reconstruction iconoclasm
led him to state that all men should have suffrage and equal rights. If
brutish Irish could have the right to immigrate and the vote, then why
not the Chinese? His seeming sympathy for the Chinese had purposes of
his own.

Nast's representational system, essentially conservative and imperialist, belied his professed egalitarian ideals: the figure of Columbia, the
Americanized version of the Saxon-aristocratic ideal, represented an essentially British pinnacle of racial purity and enlightenment, while the

Irish and Chinese were relegated to racialized biological types. His overall message proclaimed that all the races in the United States should be able to vote, but Nast's drawings of people communicated that "equal rights" was not to be equated with the essential equality of all people. Just as capitalists should have the right to use Chinese labor to sustain their positions in society, so should Chinese laborers have the right to sell their labor for the most menial jobs this country offered.

In the 1880s, his fellow German-American artist Joseph Keppler, the founder of *Puck*, eclipsed Nast's popularity. Though he was a defender of the Chinese right to immigrate to the United States, Keppler's 1880 drawing "The Chinese Invasion" illustrates the changing representation of the Chinese (see figure 6.3). This three-color centerfold illustration was essentially anti-Irish and only nominally pro-Chinese. The "Chinese Wave," in carnivalesque fashion, displaces the Irish, not only taking their jobs but also beating them up. Keppler depicts a volunteer Chinese fire company, intended ultimately to wash the city clean of Mayor John Kelley, the successor to "Boss" Tweed, and the corruption of the Irish Democrats (see figure 6.4).[28]

Keppler's Chinese appear to be drawn with the same underlying physiognomic assumptions as Nast's. However, in significant contrast to the drawings of his predecessor, Keppler's central image employs a marked-

Figure 6.3. Joseph Keppler, "The Chinese Invasion," *Puck*, March 12, 1880.

Figure 6.4. Detail of "The Chinese Invasion."

ly negative image. As the ship *California* sinks, hordes of rats jump off and swim toward Manhattan Island. Halfway there, the rats turn into the heads of Chinese men and their tails are transformed into queues.[29]

In this drawing Keppler conveys an ambivalent, even contradictory message. On the one hand, he is clearly standing for the rights of Chinese to be in the United States for legal, economic, and humanitarian reasons. On the other hand, he fully and unquestioningly endorses associating Chinese with rats. With such an equation, Keppler reinforces the notion that Chinese came in hordes, quickly overpopulating the already crowded tenements of the Lower East Side. This shift from Nast's defenseless John Confucius to Keppler's more aggressive rats is a telling sign of the changing nature of "pro-Chinese" support, leading to the 1882 Chinese Exclusion Act. Race, physiognomy, and character were becoming so deeply intertwined in late-Victorian thought that the view of the Chinese as people to be admired or accepted as equals became less possible, even on Manhattan Isle, the land of "Liberty and Justice."

Keppler's iconoclasm expressed a far more empiricist faith in a modern rationalism. His 1883 drawing the "Universal Church of the Future" showed European American men, women, and children at the altar of geography, astronomy, and chemistry. The portraits of Paine, Spinoza, Darwin, and Copernicus hung on the walls, with the legends "Knowledge Is Power" and "Know Thyself" inscribed on the ceiling. "Highbrow" rationalism steadily guided the path to the future. Where Nast used the stark good and evil ethics of melodrama, Keppler used the light-hearted, top-sy-turvy world of the carnival to make his points. Where Nast believed in moral absolutes and correctness, Keppler advocated a social faith in scientific knowledge.[30]

Both caricaturists drew Chinese and Irish with racialized traits of prognathous heads and animal-like jaws. Their Chinese were drawn with high cheekbones and chimpanzeelike mouths, while their Irish were depicted in the classic Anglo-American fashion, with square-jawed, large-nostriled, gorillalike faces.[31] In this sense, Nast's and Keppler's shared physiognomic-infused principles of drawing people far outweighed their generational and political differences.[32] From the vantage of Anglo-Saxon conceits, both racial types were seen as subhuman and developmentally backward.

Although Keppler claimed he was in favor of Chinese immigration, his highly coded representation of Chinese and Irish tended to make both groups the object of ridicule and scorn. In a sense, Keppler argued for Chinese rights through the backdoor. His highly successful and lucrative humor rested on a clear worldview and an equally clear sense of how his view related to that of his audience. Essentially he used his drawing skills to argue satirically: if the Irish, who were inherently so degenerate, could be immigrants and citizens, then should the comparably degenerate race of Chinese not also have the same status?

Keppler's audience clearly enjoyed these comical "others" burlesquing before their eyes. Their sense of self was largely male, Anglo-Saxon, and genteel; and the knowledge to which they subscribed was the ethnological science of the races. They were comfortable in their seats and equally secure in the knowledge that they were superior to these comical figures. Keppler's success and genius lay in appealing to the ethnocentric sensibilities of this particular audience. He drew on the tradition of Protestant pluralism, but in contrast to the older Nast he was also conversant with the crass, more raucous, commercial pluralism of the variety-hall stage, in which every group was equally fair game.

However contradictory Nast's and Keppler's images of Chinese were, they were far less hostile than those of Irish-American artists, such as the playwright Edward Harrigan. In various efforts to improve their lot, aspiring Irish writers and performers took advantage of opportunities available to them in the expanding commercial culture. The publishing industry was already well established by the Protestant elite; however, new venues for popular expression were open for Irish involvement. The Bowery, with its accessible forms of entertainment, in contrast to the far more "proper" Broadway venues, was a dynamic marketplace for mechanics, self-styled "Bowery Boys," and newly arrived immigrants.[33]

Edward Harrigan has been often called the "American Dickens"; Harrigan and his partner, Tony Hart, were known as the "American Gilbert and Sullivan." After leaving minstrelsy for variety theater in 1873, Harrigan wrote a series of plays that portrayed, for the basically male theater-going audience of the Bowery, everyday ethnic life in the Lower East Side. In contrast to the gross Irish caricatures of minstrelsy, Harrigan developed Irish portraits of depth and range. While he still borrowed from the long-established stereotypes of Hibernian laziness, brawling, and drinking, his Irish characters represented a far greater range of personalities. One of his main characters, Dan Mulligan, was a positive and realistic figure with whom his Irish audiences could identify. As Robert Toll has pointed out, Harrigan's audiences both laughed at and laughed with his Irish.[34] In effect, Harrigan broke through the Anglo-Protestant-dominated representational hierarchy of ethnic and racial groups by injecting a positive Irish image into the commercial theater. The Irish, through Harrigan's writing and performances, were in effect made normative.[35]

Among his stock characters were stereotypic Chinese and African Americans. In 1879, Harrigan introduced his primary Chinese figure in *Mulligan Guard Chowder,* one of the series of plays revolving around the popular Dan Mulligan character. Hog-Eye, Harrigan's main comic antagonist to Dan Mulligan, was portrayed as a lustful, pidgin-English-speaking laundry man with a penchant for stealing clothing. In the Sixth Ward, a district that Anglo- and German-Protestants considered filled with "heathens" of all types, Hog-Eye was the heathen's heathen. Harrigan drew on the well-known presence of Chinese-Irish couples and families in the Lower East Side and played out scenes pitting his oddball Chinese against his dignified, if sometimes flawed, Irish heroes and heroines. The caricature's exaggeratedly made-up appearance—complete with skullcap and queue—his bumbling yet predictable desire to lure Irish women into smoking opium, his inability to compete honestly with Irish washerwomen, and his childlike speech were all presented with great comic effect to Harrigan's white male audiences.[36] Harrigan's work, drawing on an immigrant, working-class perception of pluralism that contrasted with the earlier elite representation set forth by Keppler and Nast, served to distinguish among groups in a decidedly different way, setting off an emerging pan-Christian, pan-European, and decidedly male identity against all the various "colored" others.

The Irish working class played a pivotal role in broadening popular definitions of what it meant to be an American. One could be Catholic, one could be Celtic, and one could be a loyal American citizen. Yet the price they paid for inclusion was their advocating the exclusion of others. Irish on the Pacific Coast led the demonizing racialization of Chinese as unassimilable "coolie" laborers incapable of acting as free, rational individuals who could own their own labor and act on their own behalf. In New York, the Irish competed directly with freed slaves and vented their most virulent anger toward them. The racialization of Chinese was part and parcel of the same relational dynamics. To move up the hierarchy, more lowly racial others had to be constructed. In this context, Ned Harrigan's writings and performances take on great political significance. Given the preestablished racial hierarchy, Irish humanization could most easily be gained by African and Chinese dehumanization. Anglo-American Protestants were still on top, but in New York, Irish did not have to be on the bottom.[37]

Contrary to Mary Coolidge's "California thesis," the nation's first racially exclusive immigration policies were soon to be sanctioned by Atlantic Coast public opinion as well. The three traditions of pluralism in New York City were forged on the anvil of struggle among those groups that were present in enough numbers to create paying audiences, generate votes, and support their own artists and intellectuals. Significantly, the tradition of Protestant pluralism could manage to support the image of elite Chinese, such as Nast's John Confucius. Most important, these interests could win a loophole in the Chinese Exclusion Act, allowing scholars, students, diplomats, and merchants—deemed to be counterparts of Protestant businesspeople—to continue immigrating to the United States. Yet even if we were to conclude that New York City favored more liberal policies than did the Pacific Coast, as all post-Coolidge analyses have done, we would need to take into account the conceptual limits posed by both the commercial and working-class traditions of pluralism.

* * *

Since the 1943 repeal of the heinous Chinese Exclusion Act and the reform of the racially restrictive immigration laws in 1965, it has been generally believed that Chinese, among other Asian Americans, are now free to be included among "We the People." Yet to this day a hierarchical racialized pattern persists. Although expressive styles and specifics may have changed with the times, the underlying power dynamics have undergone little real change. A look at the depiction of Asians in the United States in recent years raises the question of how much real change there has been.

Thomas Nast would not have much to quibble with in the *New York Times* coverage of the "whiz kids." In 1986, for example, Fox Butterfield, one of the paper's senior and most influential reporters, wrote the cover story for the Sunday educational supplement. In the article, entitled "Why Asian Student's Excel," Butterfield intoned the predictable litany of keys to upward mobility: Asians students work harder, they try to meet the expectations of their families, they come from cultures that value education and self-improvement, they come from the "cream of the societies" in which they originate, and maybe it's in their genes. These various theories were cited in a hodgepodge manner and all lumped under the theory of the "human capital" these students possessed. Of the sixteen experts cited in the article, only two Asian American specialists were quoted, and no expert was presented as being critical of the "model minority" thesis.[38]

Yet the thesis has been criticized quite extensively by many Asian American scholars for overemphasizing roughly formulated cultural explanations, while virtually ignoring actual people, communities, and sociohistorical contexts.[39] Social and educational policy analysts, such as Kwang Chung Kim, W. M. Hurh, Amado Cabezas, and Morrison Wong, have persuasively challenged the use of family income as the sole indicator of economic success. Since Asian immigrant families tend to live together in large, multigenerational groups that pool together a number of incomes, generalizations based on aggregate incomes are terribly misleading. In fact, the individual income rates for Asian Americans have been significantly below those of comparably educated European Americans.[40] Furthermore, the lumping together of various Asian ethnic groups as a monolithic model minority makes the argument even less coherent. Hence, Americans from India, which despite images of pervasive poverty has the largest middle class in the world, do not share the Confucian ethic of East Asian elite cultures. A strong cultural sense of family, which exists in most non-Protestant capitalist cultures, does not explain why Latinos and Italian Americans remain heavily blue collar in the United States. Asian immigrants' strong faith in formal education cannot simply be explained by some pan-Asian culture. Without some grounding in larger realities, these explanations ring false.

As early as 1958, Harold Isaacs was able to document a cyclical pattern of public perceptions of China and India, tied to the vagaries of U.S. foreign policies. The sustained image of Chinese as a "yellow peril" was reversed only with the repeal of the Chinese Exclusion Act in 1943, when the United States joined China in the fight against Japanese aggression. Outright exclusion of Chinese "laborers" was then replaced with a quota of 105 per year. Thereafter, Chinese Americans have been portrayed as accommodating, thrifty, and uncomplaining model citizens. Clearly, both extremes had little to do with lived reality but instead embodied the way in which everyday Americans thought about, and related to, Asian Americans and policies toward Asian governments.[41]

The effective repeal of racially based immigration laws was not actually accomplished until 1965; it was brought about largely by the civil rights movement. Since the Korean War, the United States has sought to import highly educated and professional people to shore up personnel shortages. The 1965 immigration reform law and subsequent amendments to immigration statutes gave preference to highly trained Asians. This policy directly affected both the number and type of Asian immigrants, who subsequently were touted as "successes." Moreover, educational policy researchers have found that one reason why Asian students have tended to do well in math and the sciences is that they have been trained in much better educational systems in their nations of origin. These systems emphasize group problem solving and offer substantially more support for teacher preparation and shared curricular approaches than does the American system.[42]

Clearly, the elite consensus that Asians represent a "model minority" has less to do with actual experience than with larger public policy debates about race and social responsibility.[43] Yet if the cultural emphasis does not bear much analytical weight, it is quite consistent with the nature of the Protestant pluralist tradition. If the biologized images of Thomas Nast have been replaced with racialized cultural representations, their function is still a projection of the needs of American elite groups. Just as the 1882 representations exempted elite Chinese, so do modern images privilege their role in Asian American communities. Just as Nast's John Confucius was partly intended as a criticism of the behavior of working-class Irish, so do contemporary images of Asians implicitly criticize the behaviors of other minorities that do not conform to the dominant culture.

This model minority discourse has critical implications for the way Americans view less successful Asian American groups. This is illustrated in press coverage of Chinese poverty and crime in a two-part series on Chinatown written in 1991 for the *New Yorker* by Gwen Kinkead. Just when the New York Chinese American community has made breakthroughs in claiming the right to speak for its own experience, commercial publishers have rushed to cash in on this nascent market.[44] On the basis of a book proposal and her *New Yorker* credentials and despite her lack of previous research or writing on Chinese or Asian Americans, HarperCollins gave Kinkead a six-figure advance. The publisher projected sales of 25,000 books in hardcover and even more in paper.[45] This perceived salability manufactured an "expert."

Kinkead's voice is that of a self-appointed and sympathetic interlocutor speaking on behalf of those "invisible" new immigrants who "lead lives segregated from the rest of America." She establishes her own identity to readers as being a bit like a waif or victim. "For months, I roamed the streets, trying to find people who would talk to me." Although she spoke no Chinese and was a total stranger to the community, she seemed dismayed that "for a long time, no new immigrants would speak to me."[46]

In her articles Kinkead takes readers over the threshold, "inside" this "foreign" yet touristically familiar neighborhood, offering her version of Chinatown life. We meet many individuals who authenticate various parts of her story. Her thesis, for example, that "being interviewed or expressing one's individuality in any way is generally frowned upon, because it means committing the cardinal sin in Asian cultures: 'losing face'" is supported by quotes from two very successful businessmen who talk about jealousy and how "Americans like to show off. The Chinese don't. We think: 'stay low key so we will have the least obstacles to success.'" In the process the East Asian concept of losing face (which has to do with family duties and proper behavior) is misconstrued as an all-purpose "cardinal sin," explaining why Chinese do not seem, at least to Kinkead, to be voicing their opinions or distinguishing themselves in public. The same paragraph concludes with a statement about Chinese superstitions and how "prominence invites supernatural evil."[47] Kinkead's portrait is 180 degrees from the "model minority" stereotype that views Chinese as scientifically oriented and by inference extremely rational—at least, calibrated by the way westerners regard science. As such, it bears a good qualitative resemblance to the difference between Nast's and Keppler's attitudes.

Where Keppler's visual iconography showed rats jumping off a ship and becoming Chinese men, Kinkead redeploys the old rodent image. In a metaphoric passage, Kinkead describes peering into the window of an old noodle factory on Mott Street lit by "one bare bulb" with "noodles boxed and stacked on the wooden floor. . . . As I stared into the old-fashioned shop, unchanged since the nineteen-thirties—a giant rat ran across the floor to the storage racks. It paused there, sneaked ahead carefully until only its tail, slender and quivering, was visible, and then, in a flash, slid between the boxes."[48] Kinkead proceeds to discuss the terrible living and working conditions of the most exploited of the poor and illegal immigrants.

Of the two hundred pages of a book purportedly about all of the present-day realities of Chinatown, over one-third is devoted to the Chinese underworld and its supposed Machiavellian control over the entire community. Kinkead attributes to that mafia a history of continuous and unchallenged power: "The tongs are even stronger now than they were fifty years ago and are doing their best to keep Chinatown isolated." The author ignores the longstanding pattern of the succession of ethnic groups living and working in the same rundown tenements and profit-driven factories by focusing on a single overriding explanation for community degradation. The tongs "overwhelm the community, influencing every aspect of its life—business, politics, journalism, tourism. Their members sponsor crimes that terrorize and cow the community."[49] While Kinkead has pointed out some of the very serious problems facing the community—and provides a representation that many in the community are loath to show to the larger public—the author unknowingly and uncritically repackages some of the most simplistic and xenophobic caricatures of Chinatown and Chinese people in New York's past.

With a progressivist intent similar to that expressed by Keppler's nominal plea for tolerance, Kinkead "favors" Chinese and Chinese immigration. She writes with the conviction that this is a community that should be understood from the point of view of insiders, but she also perpetuates time-worn stereotypes of Chinatown as a monolithic, isolated, "closed" society whose values are diametrically opposed to those of the West. What starts out as a human portrait showing the difficulties of new immigrants quickly regresses into a representation of Chinatown under the totalitarian rule of Fu Manchu–like mafia bosses.

Kinkead ends her article series and book as she began. Framing her construction of New York Chinatown are dramatic scenes from her ersatz journey, comparable to those in Joseph Conrad's *Heart of Darkness*— "The rear tenement, its windows broken or blackened with soot, its front door gone, looks uninhabited. . . . The stairway is nearly blocked with trash. . . . I climb the stairs. . . . I knock. A frail old man appears. He greets me quizzically. He has lived in Chinatown for sixty years, he says [in English?], and has never spoken to a white person."[50] We are left with the feeling of pity.

Similar attitudes surrounded media coverage of the 1993 tragedy of the *Golden Venture*—a freighter carrying Fujianese émigrés seeking their fortunes in the United States. On June 6, 1993, a decrepit freighter originating from the South China Sea via Kenya ran aground off Rockaway Beach in Queens, New York, while trying to drop off some 276 immigrants who were attempting to enter the United States illegally. At least eight people died trying to come ashore. Journalists soon revealed that many of these individuals had contracted themselves to traffickers in human labor to be smuggled into the United States for $10,000–$40,000. Traffickers were also reported to have threatened uncooperative workers with harm to their families.

In sharp contrast to Gwen Kinkead's representation of social dynamics in Chinatown, many community activists entered into the fray—both to help the individual victims and to educate the larger public about the longstanding and systemic abuses that such smuggling operations had been perpetrating. Joann Lum, for example, the program director of the Chinese Staff and Workers Association, was quoted as speaking of this activity as a modern-day slave version of the trade. In the following weeks, New York newspapers generally used this term, echoed by the lawyers, scholars, and activists directly involved in coming to the aid of the now-detained immigrants.[51]

Ironically, community activists fighting to improve the conditions of immigrants have been caught in the tyranny of the very language that was long used to exclude Chinese workers in the United States.[52] The nineteenth-century debates identifying Chinese male laborers with slavery and "coolie labor" were the main justifications for the passage of the 1882 Chinese Exclusion Act. In the period immediately following the Civil War, Chinese laborers were actively recruited to the South as contract laborers to replace the "freed" African Americans. Organized labor quickly mobilized across the nation to protest what it considered the unfair competition of this "semi-slave" labor force. As promulgated by the anti-Chinese labor orator Denis Kearney and the playwright Edward Harrigan, Chinese were represented racially as a generic category of nonwhite heathens with nonrepublican beliefs. The important distinctions between actual slave labor, indentured labor, contract labor, and wage labor were not made. Hence, all Chinese workers—including the great majority who were noncontract workers—were excluded from entry into the United States until the effective repeal of racially based laws in 1965.[53]

This longstanding discourse linking Chinese laborers to "cheap" or "slave" labor has once again been evoked by these horrible events. Indeed, despite the tremendous sympathy that was elicited by media coverage of the plight of individuals involved, one major aftereffect of the disaster was a renewed cycle of general anti-immigrant labor hostility and scapegoating in the New York City area and elsewhere. Immediately following the great flourish of media coverage of the *Golden Venture,* public opinion polls tracked a marked increase in anti-immigrant feelings, with many favoring renewed immigration restrictions. One Chinese family in the largely working-class community of East Brunswick, New Jersey, received a letter labeling Chinese people as "illegals and slave traders" and threatening to get rid of local Chinese one month after the Fourth of July. The letter was signed by "the ping pong exterminators."[54] Such incidents have been common in the New York area during the past several years.

Indeed, the most blatant acts of aggression against Asians consistently appear to erupt in blue-collar neighborhoods. The anti–South Asian violence perpetrated by a Hoboken group calling themselves the Dot-Busters, the tens of thousands of xenophobic anti-Asian boycott flyers distributed in the Italian blue-collar neighborhood of Bensonhurst, Brooklyn, and the sporadic boycotts of Korean greengrocers in African American neighborhoods all need to be understood within this racialized, anti-immigrant discourse. These expressions of racial hostility and violence developed against a backdrop of a stagnant urban economy that has lost hundreds of thousands of jobs over the past decades, many in light manufacturing and related blue-collar industries.[55]

The larger problems of the regional and national economy have tended to be perceived as embodied by the immigrants who appear most "new" and different, according to working-class New Yorkers' racialized worldview. Consequently, although a New York City Planning Department study has shown that Ecuadoreans, Polish, and Italians form the largest undocumented populations in the city and that undocumented Chinese were not even among the top ten groups, Chinese and other Asians have become convenient public targets of class-rooted frustration and hatred.[56]

Despite the very real gains Chinese have made in the New York City labor movement, Chinese, along with other Asian workers, continue to be racialized in the longstanding discourse of "cheap" and "slave" labor. This racialization is often expressed in terms of unassimilable foreignness. Asians cannot be Americans in this view. Therefore, when dramatic incidents occur that involve the exploitation of Chinese American workers, the labor movement has not rallied around its fellow laborers. Instead, the historical reflex has been movements to reimpose immigration restrictions based on exploiting longstanding representations of unbridgeable, racialized differences.

Protestant-defined pluralism has also had inherent contradictions that can be located in the hierarchy in which privilege and power have been configured. In this stratified view of differential power segmented by such factors as class, racialization, or religion, U.S. history has repeatedly demonstrated that one group has been favored at the same time that groups defined as "others" have been disparaged. Here I fully agree with Richard Williams's analysis of the fundamental importance of the free white–enslaved black dyad. Since the codification of slavery in the Virginia slave laws of 1664, African males have been defined as the lowest and most enslaved and Anglo-Saxon Protestant males as the highest and freest Americans.[57] As New York traders and merchants actively participated in the commerce of slavery, all three forms of pluralism were framed by these unjust social relations.

"The Chinese question" and "whiz kids" need to be understood within this tragic black-white divide. During periods that have been considered favorable and unfavorable alike, Chinese and other Asians in the United States have generally been cast in an instrumentally useful, yet effectively limited, middle position between European Americans and African Americans.[58] In the nineteenth and early twentieth centuries, Chinese were defined as biologically in the middle. Now Chinese Americans are defined as economically and culturally in the middle. Regardless of the differences that actually exist, the basic power dynamics have effectively determined the manner of representation. In the post-Reconstruction era, ideals for reconfiguring racialized human relations in the United States were beaten back. In the post–civil rights era, ideals for reconfiguring racialized human relations in the United States are under attack once again.

The major difference between then and now, and this is a significant shift, is the post-1968 elimination of racially defined immigration laws, which has enabled Asians to enter the United States in unprecedented numbers. Chinese and other Asians now have an increasing impact on the social, political, and cultural life of the nation. While Protestant pluralism, with all its contradictory openness and exclusivity, still holds sway, it is increasingly possible for Asians to make both commercial and working-class cultures far more inclusive than they have been. The protests over the production of Cameron MacKintosh's *Miss Saigon*, for example, can be understood in this light.[59] The influx of Asians into various working-class occupations and activist coalitions has had and will continue to have a pluralizing impact on how we understand what it means to be "Made in America." With greater numbers of consumers in the marketplace,

Chinese and other Asian Americans now have the chance that Irish such as Edward Harrigan enjoyed over one hundred years ago—to represent themselves with a fuller range of qualities than the one-dimensional stereotypes that still dominate the commercial and political culture of the United States. Yet, as was true with Harrigan, this newly acquired power of self-representation is still proscribed within a basic polarity: "good" Chinese who behave like old-fashioned Protestant capitalists are acceptable, whereas "bad" Chinese who behave like "slaves" should be banned.

Clearly, inclusion in Gotham's public discourse only marks the beginning of the contest for status and resources. In this conservative era in which the "savage inequalities" of racialized and ethnicized class relations have become dramatically worse, I hardly need add that the fundamental, intrinsic conflicts of hierarchical pluralism still remain dangerously far from any intelligent public discussion, let alone intelligent plan for resolution.[60] Yet the basic question remains: can the *unum* be formulated without a racialized, hierarchic *pluribus?*

Notes

I would like to thank Tom Bender, William Taylor, Judy Susman, Roger Sanjek, Wendy Katkin, and Ned Landsman, who have commented on earlier versions and various parts of this essay. Much appreciation also goes to Mina Choi for her important study, Lori Kitazono for making it into an Asian/American Center Working Paper, and Bertram Linder for his very useful insights.

1. Two influential books represent the basic critiques that have been aired: Allan Bloom, *The Closing of the American Mind* (New York: Simon and Schuster, 1987); and Arthur M. Schlesinger Jr., *The Disuniting of America: Reflections on a Multicultural Society* (New York: W. W. Norton, 1992).

2. Originally Gotham was a village outside of Nottingham, England, in which the residents were said to be quite foolish. *Webster's Third New International Dictionary of English Language, Unabridged* (Springfield, Mass: Merriam-Webster, 1981).

3. Tom Bender, "New York as a Center of 'Difference,'" *Dissent* 34 (Fall 1987): 1–7.

4. This study has benefited greatly from Richard Williams's trilateral analysis of hierarchic racial segmentation among blacks, Irish, and elite whites. Richard Williams, *Hierarchical Structures and Social Value: The Creation of Black and Irish Identities in the United States* (Cambridge: Cambridge University Press, 1990), 1–23.

5. Jane Perlez, "School Basks in Spotlight of Contest," *New York Times*, January 14, 1988. The front-page photograph was by Sara Krulwich.

6. Mina Choi, "Race, Gender, and Eyeglasses: Teacher Perceptions of Asian, Black, and White Students" (Asian/American Center Working Paper, Asian/American Center, Queens College, 1989), 18. On the perceptions of college admission officers, see Dana Y. Takagi, *The Retreat from Race: Asian-American Admissions and Racial Politics* (New Brunswick, N.J.: Rutgers University Press, 1992).

7. Asians, Latinos/as, and Native Americans are rarely factored into race relations models as independent players outside of a black and white dynamic. This tendency automatically hampers our ability to understand the heavily Chicano/a Southwest, localities that are largely populated by Native Americans, and the growing Asian presence in universities nationwide, as well as in the cities of Chicago, Los Angeles, San Francisco, and New York.

8. Choi, "Race, Gender, and Eyeglasses," 3.

9. Ibid., 18.

10. Stephen G. Graubard, "Why Do Asian Pupils Win Those Prizes?" *New York Times,* January 29, 1988.

11. Edith Neimark, "The New Protestant Ethic Is the Asian Ethic," Letters to the Editor, *New York Times,* February 12, 1988; Lew Lord and Nancy Linnon, "What Put the Whiz in the Whiz Kids?" *U.S. News and World Report,* March 14, 1988, 48–58.

12. Irene Eng, "Parents Not the Answer," Letters to the Editor, *New York Times,* February 12, 1988. An unpublished letter written to the *New York Times* by the Cardozo High School principal also refuted many of the assumptions and conclusions Graubard made. Private correspondence to Asian/American Center, Queens College, from Bertram L. Linder, September 7, 1989.

13. For the foundational analysis about the Occident's construction of the "Orient," see Edward Said, *Orientalism* (New York: Pantheon Books, 1978).

14. The African American and African Caribbean boycott of the Red Apple green-grocer in Brooklyn, New York, has been covered extensively by New York City and national media; however, the largely Italian American boycott of Asian stories in the Bensonhurst section of Brooklyn has not been widely covered. See Rita Giordano, "Anti-Asian Fliers' Origin a Mystery," *New York Newsday,* November 4, 1987. The Council of Business and Concerned Homeowners of Bensonhurst issued a single-spaced, double-sided legal length flyer, "Urgent Message to All Bensonhurst Home Owners and Residents!!!" advising them to boycott all Chinese and Korean-owned businesses because their neighborhood had been targeted "for a *complete takeover* within 5 years" (underlined in original flyer).

15. Mary Roberts Coolidge, *Chinese Immigration* (New York: Henry Holt, 1909). By focusing on the most virulent enemies of the Chinese in California, important studies by Alexander Saxton and Gwendolyn Mink on the California labor movement have also effectively served to reinforce this emphasis on working-class racism, a racism that Herbert Hill has argued was nationwide. Alexander Saxton, *The Indispensable Enemy: Labor and the Anti-Chinese Movement in California* (Berkeley: University of California Press, 1971); Gwendolyn Mink, *Old Labor and New Immigrants in American Political Development: Union, Party, and State, 1875–1920* (Ithaca, N.Y.: Cornell University Press, 1986); Herbert Hill, "Anti-Oriental Agitation and the Rise of Working-Class Racism," *Trans-Action: Social Science and Modern Society* 10 (January/February 1979): 43–54. For a fuller discussion of these issues, see John Kuo Wei Tchen, "New York before Chinatown: Orientalism, Identity Formation, and Political Culture in the American Metropolis, 1784–1882" (Ph.D. diss., New York University, 1992).

16. Bender, "New York as a Center of 'Difference,'" 1.

17. Richard W. Pointer, *Protestant Pluralism and the New York Experience: A Study of Eighteenth-Century Religious Diversity* (Bloomington: Indiana University Press, 1988), 86–88.

18. Max Weber, *The Protestant Ethic and the Spirit of Capitalism,* trans. Talcott Parsons (London: G. Allen and Unwin, 1931).

19. The top-down allocation standards of the New York State Council on the Arts (NYSCA) and the caretaker ethos of the Municipal Arts Society exemplify the modern-day legacy of this highly secularized Protestant pluralist tradition. Both organizations are committed to a paternalistic benevolence in which a cosmopolitan gentry elite advocates sharing its moral guardianship with as many people as possible so long as the economic pie can expand. Such has been the case with NYSCA's "New Audiences" initiative of the 1980s. See C. Gerald Fraser, "Aid to 'New Audiences' Is Challenged," *New York Times,* March 4, 1989; and Paul Goldberger's review of the Municipal Art Society's exhibition *Kid City,* "New York Strikes a Pose for Its Heirs," *New York Times,* March 17, 1995.

20. See, for example, William R. Taylor, *In Pursuit of Gotham: The Commerce and Culture of New York City* (New York: Oxford University Press, 1992); Robert W. Snyder, *The Voice of the City: Vaudeville and Popular Culture in New York* (New York: Oxford University Press, 1989); and Kenneth Cmiel, *Democratic Eloquence: The Fight over Popular Speech in Nineteenth-Century America* (New York: William Morrow, 1990). For a contemporary critique, see Ella Shohat and Robert Stam, *Unthinking Eurocentrism and the Media* (New York: Routledge, 1994). Today the visual urban internationalist pluralism of MTV and Philip Morris's underwriting of multicultural exhibitions at "major" cultural institutions are direct descendants of this commercial tradition.

21. See, for example, Sean Wilentz, *Chants Democratic: New York City and the Rise of the American Working Class, 1788–1850* (New York: Oxford University Press, 1984); Christine Stansell, *City of Women: Sex and Class in New York, 1789–1860* (New York: Alfred A. Knopf, 1986); and Howard B. Rock, *Artisans of the New Republic: The Tradesmen of New York City in the Age of Jefferson* (New York: New York University Press, 1979).

22. Williams, *Hierarchical Structures and Social Value,* 24–34, 131–47.

23. Morton Keller, *The Art and Politics of Thomas Nast* (New York: Oxford University Press, 1977), 6, 8–9, 11–38, 39–45. The American taste for political art was first whetted by the patriotic enthusiasms stirred by the War of 1812. This early political art celebrated the rise of American nationalism and mused on the foibles of party politicians. The figures of Columbia, representing Protestant-inflected freedom, civilization, and enlightenment, and Uncle Sam (also known as Brother Jonathan) first appeared at this time. The Civil War became the next great thematic vehicle for the next generation of graphic artists.

24. Nast does not use the name "John Confucius" for this man until March 8, 1879, but the drawing of the man is essentially the same. See *Harper's Weekly,* July 18, 1868, and March 8, 1879. The "John Confucius" representation was probably modeled after one of the two Chinese ambassadors, "Chih-Tajin or "Sun-Tajin," who had come to the United States with Anson Burlingame a month earlier. A woodcut based on a

photograph by Mathew Brady was published in June 1868. The hat with feather tassels, mustaches, and high cheek bones were incorporated into Nast's drawing "The Chinese Embassy," *Harper's Weekly,* June 13, 1868. For a similar print of the same grouping, see also "Chinese Embassy to Foreign Powers," a steel engraving print by Johnson, Fry and Co. of New York City (Wong Ching Foo Collection, Museum of Chinese in the Americas, New York City).

25. Thomas Nast, "The Youngest Introducing the Oldest," *Harper's Weekly,* November 20, 1886, 250. Anson Burlingame, having completed his travail as the negotiator of the treaty bearing his name, sits behind the mustached Chinese ambassador. The pope, depicted as aghast at the sight, peeks fearfully at the Chinese dignitary from behind a pillar.

26. The eight cartoons were "The Chinese Question," *Harper's Weekly,* February 18, 1871; "'Every Dog' (No Distinction of Color) 'Has His Day,'" ibid., February 8, 1879; "The Civilization of Blaine," ibid., March 8, 1879; "A Matter of Taste," ibid., March 15, 1879; "'Protecting White Labor,'" ibid., March 22, 1879; "'The Nigger Must Go,' or 'The Chinese Must Go,'" ibid., September 13, 1879; "Political Capital and Compound Interest," ibid., January 31, 1880; and "The Ides of March," ibid., March 20, 1880. These same unruly mobs reappear in three of the other full-page drawings as representing the "Solid South," the "Sand Lots" of San Francisco, and "Hoodlum Alley."

27. Mary Cowling, *Artist as Anthropologist : The Representation of Type and Character in Victorian Art* (Cambridge: Cambridge University Press, 1989), 119, 94, 124–25, 125–29 (quote on 129), 186; Lewis Perry Curtis, *Apes and Angels: The Irishman in Victorian Caricature* (Washington D.C.: Smithsonian Institution Press, 1971).

28. Mayor Kelley appears in Joseph Keppler, "King or Clown—Which?," *Puck,* August 13, 1879, cited in Richard Samuel West, *Satire on Stone: The Political Cartoons of Joseph Keppler* (Urbana: University of Illinois Press, 1988), 162.

29. Puck's anti-Irish, antiworker, and pro-Chinese immigration stand was repeated in Keppler's "Uncle Sam's Lodging House," *Puck,* June 7, 1882, and in F. Graetz's "The Anti-Chinese Wall," *Puck,* March 1882.

30. West, *Satire on Stone,* 118, 128; Keller, *Art and Politics of Thomas Nast,* 243–47.

31. West, *Satire on Stone,* 5–8, 28–29, 64; Curtis, *Apes and Angels,* 7–11, 20, 21, 91, 98–104.

32. West, *Satire on Stone,* 5–8, 28–29, 64; Curtis, *Apes and Angels,* 7–11, 20, 21, 91, 98–104.

33. Stansell, *City of Women,* 89–101. For a fuller discussion of the relations and representation of Irish and Chinese in New York, see John Kuo Wei Tchen, "Quimbo Appo's Fear of Fenians: Chinese-Irish-Anglo Relations in New York City," in *The Irish in New York,* ed. Ronald Bayor and Timothy Meagher (Baltimore, Md.: Johns Hopkins University Press, 1996), 125–52.

34. Robert C. Toll, *Blacking Up: The Minstrel Show in Nineteenth-Century America* (New York: Oxford University Press, 1974), 177.

35. Richard Moody, *Ned Harrigan: From Corlear's Hook to Herald Square* (Chicago: Nelson-Hall, 1980), 5, 170; Toll, *Blacking Up,* 177–79.

36. For two examples, see scene 7 of *The Mulligan Silver Wedding* (1881), Harrigan manuscripts, Rare Books Room, New York Public Library, Box 18, no. 47; and

act 2 of *The O'Reagans* (1886), Harrigan manuscripts, Rare Books Room, New York Public Library, Box 20, no. 53.

37. For a fuller discussion of "slave" versus "coolie" versus "free" labor, see Tchen, "New York before Chinatown," 281–326. See also Jacobson's essay in this volume.

38. Fox Butterfield, "Why Asian Students Excel: Asians Are Going to the Head of the Class," Education Life Section, *New York Times,* August 3, 1986. For earlier variations of this same argument, see "Success Story of One Minority Group in the U.S.," *U.S. News and World Report,* December 26, 1966, 73–76. For a more updated version of the same basic argument, see Eva Pomice, "The Ties That Bind and Enrich," *U.S. News and World Report,* April 25, 1988, 42–46. See also Dinesh D'Souza, *Illiberal Education: The Politics of Race and Sex on Campus* (New York: Free Press, 1991); and Thomas Sowell, *Ethnic America* (New York: Basic Books, 1981).

39. Two standard general histories of Asian Americans, for example, devote extensive sections of their concluding chapters to a critique of the "model minority" thesis: Roger Daniels, *Asian America: Chinese and Japanese in the United States since 1850* (Seattle: University of Washington Press, 1988), 317–21; and Ronald Takaki, *Strangers from a Different Shore: A History of Asian Americans* (Boston: Little, Brown, 1989), 474–84.

40. Amado Cabezas, "The Asian American Today as an Economic Success Model" (Paper presented at "Break the Silence: A Conference on Anti-Asian Violence," Berkeley, 1986); Kwang Chung Kim and W. M. Huh, "Korean Americans and the 'Success' Image—A Critique," *Amerasia Journal* 10 (Fall/Winter 1983): 3–21, cited in Keith Osajima, "Asian Americans as the Model Minority: An Analysis of the Popular Press Image in the 1960s and 1980s," in *Reflections on Shattered Windows: Promises and Prospects for Asian American Studies,* ed. Gary Y. Okihiro, Shirley Hune, Arthur A. Hansen, and John M. Liu (Pullman: Washington State University Press, 1988), 165–74.

41. Harold R. Isaacs, *Scratches on Our Minds: American Images of China and India* (New York: Harper and Row, 1962); Gil Loescher and John A. Scanlan, *Calculated Kindness: Refugees and America's Half-Open Door, 1945–Present* (New York: Free Press, 1986); Michael H. Hunt, *Ideology and U.S. Foreign Policy* (New Haven, Conn.: Yale University Press, 1987).

42. Harold W. Stevenson and James W. Stigler, *The Learning Gap* (New York: Summit Books, 1992).

43. Takagi, *Retreat from Race.*

44. The founding of the Museum of Chinese in the Americas in 1980 (originally the New York Chinatown History Project) and the publications of Peter Kwong's two books, *Chinatown, N.Y.: Labor and Politics, 1930–1950* (New York: Monthly Review, 1979) and *The New Chinatown* (New York: Hill and Wang, 1987), have greatly increased the general public's awareness of the history and issues of New York's Chinatown.

45. All information about Kinkead's contract with HarperCollins and promotional information is from an informed source who wishes to remain anonymous.

46. Gwen Kinkead, "Chinatown 1," *New Yorker,* June 10, 1991, 45, 46.

47. Ibid., 48. The essays were subsequently expanded and published in Gwen Kinkead, *Chinatown: Portrait of a Closed Society* (New York: HarperCollins, 1992), 9.

48. Kinkead, "Chinatown 1," 64; Kinkead, *Chinatown,* 17.

49. Gwen Kinkead, "Chinatown 2," *New Yorker,* June 17, 1991, 64; Kinkead, *Chinatown,* 70.

50. Kinkead, *Chinatown,* 203–4. It is useful to compare such journalistic "outsider" representations with John Alpert's far more insightful documentary *Chinatown* (Downtown Community Television, New York, 1973). For a discussion of Joseph Conrad and his journey discovering his "other," see Marianna Torgovnik, *Gone Primitive* (Chicago: University of Chicago Press, 1990), 145–47, 154–56.

51. Lum cited in Peg Tyre, "A Soft Spoken, Polite Merchant of Slaves," *New York Newsday,* June 9, 1993. For examples of newspapers using the term, see Carol Agus, "Slavery Pays Freedom's Cost," *New York Newsday,* June 13, 1993; and "Free 13 Chinese 'Slaves' in Sunset Park Basement," *Park Slope Paper,* June 11–17, 1993. For earlier usage, see T. J. English, "Slaving Away: Chinese Illegals Oppressed at Home, Exploited Here," *Village Voice,* February 5, 1991.

52. Renqiu Yu, *To Save China, to Save Ourselves: The Chinese Hand Laundry Alliance of New York* (Philadelphia: Temple University Press, 1992), 156–64; Kwong, *Chinatown, N.Y.,* 83–91; R. Takashi Yanagida, "The AAFEE Story: Asian Americans for Equal Employment," *Bridge Magazine,* February 1975, 47–51. See also Xiaolan Bao, "Holding Up Half the Sky: A History of Women Garment Workers in New York's Chinatown, 1948–1991" (Ph.D. diss., New York University, 1991); and Sucheta Mazumdar's forthcoming collection of essays on the New York garment trades written in collaboration with the Museum of Chinese in the Americas. Recent years have signaled a sea change in Chinese and Asian American involvement in the trade union movement.

53. Tchen, "New York before Chinatown," 299–326.

54. Seth Mydans, "Poll Finds Tide of Immigration Brings Hostility," *New York Times,* June 27, 1993; Tim Weiner, "On These Shores, Immigrants Find a New Wave of Hostility," *New York Times,* June 13, 1993; Robert D. McFadden, "Immigration Hurting City, New Yorkers Say in Survey," *New York Times,* October 18, 1993; "Chinese Family Gets Threatening Letter," *New York Times,* July 7, 1993 (quotes).

55. Every four years the incumbent mayor of New York City is blamed for the job losses incurred during his tenure. In 1989, challenger David Dinkins blamed Mayor Ed Koch for 450,000 jobs lost from 1985–89, and in 1994, challenger Rudolf Giuliani blamed Mayor David Dinkins for losing 350,000 jobs. This penchant for the personalization of blame for larger problems is directly related to the racialization of blame.

56. Deborah Sontag, "Study Sees Illegal Aliens in New Light," *New York Times,* September 2, 1993.

57. Williams, *Hierarchical Structures and Social Value,* 1–14.

58. In this sense, Chinese Americans as a "model minority" is comparable with Irish Americans' becoming "white." See Williams, *Hierarchical Structures and Social Value,* 131–47. See also David R. Roediger, *The Wages of Whiteness: Race and the Making of the American Working Class* (London: Verso, 1991), 133–63.

59. For a sampling of the debates generated around the opening of *Miss Saigon,* see Mervyn Rothstein, "Union Bars White in Asian Role; Broadway May Lose 'Miss Saigon,'" *New York Times,* August 8, 1990; Mervyn Rothstein, "Producer Cancels 'Miss Saigon'; 140 Members Challenge Equity," *New York Times,* August 9, 1990; Frank Rich,

"Jonathan Pryce, 'Miss Saigon' and Equity's Decision," *New York Times,* August 10, 1990; Alex Witchel, "British Star Talks of Racial Harmony and Disillusionment with Equity," *New York Times,* August 11, 1990; and Ellen Holly, "Why the Furor over 'Miss Saigon' Won't Fade," *New York Times,* August 26, 1990.

60. Jonathan Kozol, *Savage Inequalities: Children in America's Schools* (New York: Crown, 1991). For one view on the revival of class divisions and warfare, see A. M. Rosenthal, "American Class Struggle," *New York Times,* March 21, 1995. Two very accessible books analyzing the globalization of the U.S. economy are Jeremy Brecher and Tim Costello, *Global Village or Global Pillage: Economic Reconstruction from the Bottom Up* (Boston: South End, 1994); and Nancy Folbre, *The New Field Guide to the U.S. Economy* (New York: New Press, 1996).

7 Malevolent Assimilation: Immigrants and the Question of American Empire

Matthew Frye Jacobson

In March of 1899, weeks after fighting had broken out between American soldiers in Manila and the insurgents who had taken up arms for Philippine independence, a Polish American journalist in Milwaukee commented, "For us Poles, this war is not necessarily pleasant. Traditionally we stand on the side of the oppressed; since we have repeatedly taken up arms in defense of our independence, we naturally sympathize with all other peoples struggling for independence—even if they be half-savage Malays."[1] Michael Kruszka's sympathy with all the world's oppressed and his ambivalent "even if" regarding the rights of people of color embody a vital dynamic of American political culture in the age of massive immigration and a dawning American empire. The particular sensibilities of immigrant groups broadened the stream of American political discourse; in this instance, conquered Poland's bitter history informed a critique of American imperial conquest. Yet it is in part through the alchemy of *inter*national relations that nations crystallize and cohere internally as, in Benedict Anderson's words, "imagined communities."[2] It is no small matter that hundreds of thousands of white European immigrants were defining their relationship to America and "Americanness" at the very moment that the United States was pursuing highly racialized policies in such places as Hawaii, Cuba, Puerto Rico, the Philippines, Samoa, and China. When it came to weighing the claims of the United States against the political aspirations of colonized peoples, race began to rival even the lessons of Old World history in salience, as Kruszka's comments illustrate.

Nor was Kruszka alone in his ambivalence. In December of 1898, before guerrilla war had broken out at Manila, Humphrey Desmond, the Irish editor of the *Catholic Citizen,* had likewise written "Why We Don't Want the Philippines." Two points in particular revealed the tension that he shared with Kruszka concerning the politics of nation and the politics of race. He rejected annexation "because it is playing England's game in the Orient" and also "because it means that American citizenship is to be diluted by Malay citizenship, and that America's democracy is to stand the trial of working itself out among inferior people."[3] Like Kruszka, Desmond expressed both an empathy with the potential victims of "England's game" of imperial politics and a racialist contempt for those same victims.

The vexing question of overseas expansion was not new, to be sure. Well before the war with Spain, various islands in the Caribbean and the Pacific had been the focus of much interest and speculation in the United States. Decades of American business practice were distilled, for instance, in Secretary of State James Blaine's 1891 identification of Cuba, Puerto Rico, and Hawaii as "three places that are of value enough to be taken."[4] The imperialism question gained particular force in the months following Admiral Dewey's victory over the Spanish fleet. Over the course of the summer of 1898, cries of "Cuba Libre!" gradually gave way to debate over America's newly discovered "responsibilities" and the ultimate disposition of Spain's colonies. In ousting Spain, had the United States not rightfully won control of Cuba, Puerto Rico, and the Philippines?

The debate over American imperialism further intensified in the fall of 1898, as it became clear that Spain's cession of the Philippines to the United States would be one stipulation of the peace treaty between the two countries. The Treaty of Paris, providing for U.S. control of the islands, provoked a heated public debate and a vigorous fight in the Senate over ratification.[5] Discussion reached its starkest polarities in February 1899, when fighting broke out between Filipino nationalists and American soldiers in the outskirts of Manila. The imperialism question now hinged on competing allegations of the Filipinos' savage ingratitude, on the one hand, and the McKinley administration's brutal grandeur, on the other.

For immigrants, the Philippine question was especially divisive and often bitter. When Father McKinnon, chaplain of the First California Volunteer Regiment, lectured in favor of expansion on the grounds that the Filipino leader Emilio Aguinaldo was another "Nero" and that his followers were incapable of "understanding what freedom means," he was heckled for making "the English argument." "Why shouldn't they be free?" one member of his New York audience challenged, before being escorted from the hall.[6] Likewise, letters to the editor of the *Yiddishes Tageblatt* expressed worry over the militarism necessarily involved in expansion. "We see from enslaved Russia that a great army impoverishes the people," argued one writer. Another warned that the United States would become a great military power "like France"—a charged analogy in the emotional days of the Dreyfus affair. Yet another argued that it is impossible to "beat freedom into someone's head with cannons and rifles" in any case. The editor, for his part, held that the Filipinos were merely "half wild men about whom every barbaric action can be believed." Besides, he wrote, "it is . . . a sickness to hate the country where one has rescued oneself from Russia"; he took every occasion roundly to denounce "the Aguinaldos in the United States."[7]

This essay will examine the complex position of Irish, Polish, and Jewish immigrant nationalists in the United States as their adopted country embarked on its imperial adventure at the turn of the century. Old World nationalism—popularized in a myriad of immigrant cultural forms—outfitted immigrants with a unique lens on the events of 1898 and 1899. For many, Old World analogies lent salience and meaning to the principles of Cuban and Philippine independence, but the politics of race, in some instances, countervailed these "natural" nationalist empathies. The racial rhetoric of American empire prompted some immigrants to recast their sympathies, dismiss the Filipino rebels as inherently "other," and embrace the (Euro-) American "civilizing mission" in the Pacific as their own.

Turn-of-the-century imperialism was crucial in the complex *domestic* process by which European immigrants came to see themselves—and came to be seen—as "Americans." If immigrant discussion of the Philippine question demonstrated the ability of immigrants, as outsiders, to reject their adopted country's "manifest" and grandiose destiny, it also hinted at the capacity of imperialism to transform outsiders into insiders on the basis of race. The imperial moment of 1899 suggests a close connection between the political process by which European nationals became "Americans" and the cultural process by which the nineteenth century's white "racial" groups—"Slavs," "Celts," and "Hebrews"—became the twentieth century's "Caucasians." The vigorous debates over the Philippine question thus highlight both the national and the racial dimensions of "identificational assimilation," as immigrants sought to define their relationship to a political idea called "America" and to an imagined community of "Americans."[8]

The Politics of Nation

Among the meager bundles that many immigrants brought ashore with them in the New World was a deep and enduring interest in the fate of the communities they had left behind. Nationalisms in the Old World had emerged from the injuries of British imperial power in Ireland; the political partition of Poland by Russia, Prussia, and Austria; and the rising tides of European anti-Semitism. The movements for redress that took hold in each case engendered considerable attention and sympathy on the part of emigrants who had resettled in North America in the mid- to late nineteenth century. Out-migration from these regions took place against a backdrop of deep social and political crisis, and the migrants' own harsh experiences were particularly well suited to nationalist interpretation. Disproportionately touched by their nations' troubles, these antagonized and now transplanted communities were also powerfully drawn to arguments for social, economic, and political redress through national liberation. The establishment of an independent Irish, Polish, or Jewish state promised to relieve precisely the woes and the injustices that the emigrants had fled in the first place. For the emigrants themselves, the idioms of nationalism offered consolation that the family and friends whom they had left behind (often in dire, even cataclysmic, circumstances) had not merely been abandoned. For political leaders in Europe, meanwhile, the growing assemblies of exiles abroad were both living symbols of national catastrophe and natural allies in the struggle to alleviate that catastrophe. In the fine phrase of Michael Davitt, Irish America was to be "the avenging wolfhound" of Irish nationalism.[9]

Immigrants founded a variety of organizations on American soil to raise money for these national causes, to train immigrant men for future wars of liberation, and to win the sympathies of an American government whose influence in international affairs was steadily growing. These included revolutionary groups, such as the Clan na Gael; groups that preached liberation through religious devotion, such as the Polish Roman Catholic Union; working-class groups, such as the Knights of Zion; genteel groups, such as the Friendly Sons of St. Patrick; women's groups, such as the Polish Women's Alliance; and staunchly masculinist groups, such as the Gaelic Athletic Association and some branches of the Polish Falcons.[10]

More than this, however, nationalism fully infused immigrant cultures. As the labor leader Elizabeth Gurley Flynn recalled, "The awareness of being Irish came to us as small children, through plaintive song and heroic story. . . . As children we drew in a burning hatred of British rule with our mother's milk."[11] As Flynn describes it, nationalism pervaded the ordinary rhythms of everyday life—in bedtime stories about Irish martyrs or in her father's Anglophobic curses. (He "never said 'England' without adding 'damn her!'" she recalled.)[12]

A range of cultural forms recapitulated and reinforced the language and logic of nationalism among an immigrant public far broader than the tightest cadres of Clan na Gael or Polish National Alliance devotees.[13] Nationalism infused popular religion, in such figures as Poland's Holy Virgin of Czestochowa, whose works were believed to include the miraculous defense of Poland against the invading Swedes, or St. Patrick, whose status as a defender of both faith and nation inspired such homilies as "For an Irishman to Forget Patrick Is to Become Recreant to Every Duty, God and Country, Kith and Kin, Honor and Manhood." Jewish nationalism borrowed heavily from religious narratives of national chosenness, national calamity, and the national promise summed up in the Passover pledge, "Next year in Jerusalem." Although many religious leaders denounced secular nationalism, the mythologies and icons of these three religions lent themselves to a politicized understanding of "nationality" or "peoplehood."

Nationalism also punctuated the secular calendar in commemorations of various national rebellions and the births and deaths of national heroes. Most common in the Irish and Polish communities, these festivals were typically fraught with insurrectionary promise. They included patriotic speeches, quasi-military displays, such prescriptive addresses as "To Polish Mothers—On Raising Sons as Heroes," and such anthems as "They Exiled Me from the Fatherland" or "Poland Has Not Yet Perished as Long as We Are Living."

The myths of nationalism informed immigrant vernacular theater and literary life. Popular plays, produced in Catholic parish halls across the country, re-created such pivotal moments as the Polish uprising of 1863 or the martyrdom of Robert Emmet, while the flourishing Yiddish theater boasted such potboilers as *The Destruction of Israel* and *Lovers of Zion*.

Immigrant newspapers likewise addressed their readers not simply as Americans-in-the-making but as members of transnational diasporas with enduring obligations to their suffering nation. Teofila Samolinska, known as the mother of Polish nationalism in America, once predicted that *Orzēl Polski* would "lead the emigrants to armed action" with the "magnificent thought" of victory inscribed on its standard.[14]

As an impulse toward armed action, nationalism may have remained but a dim spark among the immigrants in America, but as a sensibility, as a common idiom of cultural expression, as a latent outlook, nationalism was pervasive and widely nourished. The immediacy and the tone of street-level nationalism were perhaps best conveyed by one immigrant who told a WPA interviewer years later, "I was born in east Galicia, under the reign of mean Austrians."[15]

It was in the context of their own experience with "mean rulers," as it were, that many immigrants interpreted and debated contemporary affairs. When the possibility of Hawaiian annexation was under discussion in 1897, for instance, Patrick Ford of the *Irish World* argued that to adopt such a policy would be "to copy the worst precedents set by the British and other nation-destroying empires."[16] When China became the object of imperial rivalry among the Western powers, *Kuryer Polski* announced flatly, "What is happening in China is what happened in Poland a hundred years ago."[17]

Similarly, in the spring of 1898, as the villainy of Spain, the plight of the Cuban *reconcentrados,* and the possibility of U.S. intervention began to dominate American discussion both in print and on the popular pavements, these Old World nationalisms translated quickly into New World polemics. When some had objected to intervention in Cuba on the grounds that the Cubans were "[merely] mongrel negroes, Indians, and Spaniards, savage and disorderly," Stefan Barszczewski answered that Poles were bound to fight for the *principle* of liberty in every known instance—regardless of the specifics of race or clime.[18] The outbreak of war was not simply an opportunity for immigrant men to "prove" their loyalty to their adopted country. Rather, the Cuban cause drew its meaning and its righteousness from each group's own national struggle. "The Jews in Russia are . . . just like the Cubans," one Yiddish editor wrote: "The May Laws [in Russia] proclaimed this sort of tyranny, and Ignatiev discovered it even before [Spain's] General Weyler."[19]

Immigrant fraternal organizations passed resolutions supporting Cuba in the familiar idioms of Irish, Polish, or Jewish nationalism. The Irish American press denounced the Spaniards in Cuba as "Iberian Orange-men" (a reference to pro-British sectarians in Ulster), while the Yiddish press routinely vilified Spain as "the inquisition country." St. Patrick's Day celebrations included rousing speeches on Cuban history. Ethnic regiments mustered in duty, amid much waving of Old World flags and singing of Old World anthems; and editorials and popular plays depicted the Cuban war as a military rehearsal for the immigrants' own inevitable wars of liberation.[20]

As early as 1897, the Polish National Alliance had donated money to the Cuban insurgents, proclaiming that "if the Polish nation wants to be free, it must work for the freedom of others." A characteristic resolution read, "Ourselves exiles, who have felt the hand and the hostile knout of oppressors, whose hearts ever fill with bitterness at the sight of the oppression of our brothers . . . from the depth of our souls we send out a voice of sympathy . . . to the brave sons of Cuba, who, like the Polish heroes of yore, sacrifice their blood, property, and life for Cuban liberty. . . ."[21] These sentiments were echoed by the women's auxiliary of the Ancient Order of Hibernians, among others, which hoped that England might learn a lesson from colonial Spain's defeat.[22]

Old World analogy characterized the massive displays of enthusiasm for the war among immigrant men who established military units across the country under the names of such insurrectionists as Napper Tandy, Robert Emmet, Tadeusz Kosciuszko, and the Maccabees. "We are Poles to a man," wrote one private in the Kosciuszko Guard, "and if not for the commands in English, we could be marching on the Moscovite, like a Polish army. . . ."[23] Later, after early victories over Spain in the Philippines, one Irish volunteer wrote home that he and his comrades wanted to stop in Ireland on the way home and free the Irish.[24] For communities whose political aspirations surfaced in such homilies as "On Raising Sons as Heroes," this was a noble moment. Polish women had indeed "suckled avengers at their breasts," as one writer put it in a play called *Cuba Libre!*[25]

The energy and the depth of feeling attached to the liberation of Cuba, so thoroughly grounded in each group's own national history, point to the dilemma that some would feel when the United States began to entertain schemes for annexing the liberated territories. "Uncle, why do the Americans call their war with Spain a 'war of liberation?'" a child asked in an editorial sketch in the *Abend blatt*. The father's answer: "Because the war has liberated the American people from many illusions regarding their economic and political masters; because it has liberated Spain from her colonies; and because it has liberated Cuba from every hope of independence."[26] This particular writer was but one of many who saw liberation *from* independence as the gist of his adopted country's policy in the former Spanish colonies.

Immigrant dissent was resounding, and sentiments toward the Filipinos often bore the same liberatory stamp as the earlier solidarity with Cuba's revolutionaries. The hallmark of immigrant anti-imperialism was an undying insistence on the broad principle of national rights, whose emotive, logical, and polemic energy derived from the narrower specifics of Old World history. When the question arose about how the United States would learn to rule Spain's newly "freed" colonies, Ben Efrim likened American militarism to that of the Russian czars, who, "with several tens of thousands" of soldiers at hand, "can rule without learning how."[27] The *Pilot,* an Irish nationalist paper in Boston, counseled Irish American volunteers to leave the ranks of the U.S. military as soon as possible. "The American soldier who enlisted for the freeing of Cuba did not enlist for the enslaving of the Philippines," James Jeffrey Roche insisted.[28] At least one Irish soldier who had fought to free the Philippines from Spain now refused to support an "unjust U.S. policy now that Philippine liberation had been achieved"; and the *Irish World* reported with some satisfaction that, despite huge bonuses being offered by the army, the reenlistment rate among American volunteers in the Philippines was a slim 7 percent.[29]

The parallels were evidently as deeply felt as they were sharply drawn. In an agonized, page-one editorial during the early weeks of fighting in Manila, Stefan Barszczewski took up the question of the Polish National Alliance's official position on American imperialism. By charter, he acknowledged, *Zgoda* was to avoid mixing in America's partisan politics and was to concentrate purely on Polish nationalist politics, but American imperialism *was* ultimately an issue of Polish nationalist portent, he concluded. Not as a Republican, Democrat, Populist, or Socialist but as a Pole, he wrote, he could not remain indifferent to those "new currents" in American politics that might lead "the United States along a completely new path, completely change the relationships of all the states of the world, and influence the fate of the Polish cause." Barszczewski conceded that some might regard America's ascendance to world power as a potential benefit to Poland, but, he concluded, as Poles, "we do not agree with the trend of a politics of conquest, which has appeared on American ground."[30]

This concern for Filipino rights united Barszczewski with Kazimierz Neuman, his crosstown rival in the religionist Polish Roman Catholic

Union. In assessing the stakes in the 1900 presidential election, for instance, Neuman asserted, "First and foremost is the matter of the Filipinos, the Puerto Ricans and other 'conquered' nations. What does that have to do with us? Oh, it concerns us enormously. . . ." "Poles, as Poles," he echoed, "knowing what bondage to an alien country means, drawn to the United States by the liberty and equality of *all* peoples," must condemn a politics based on bondage rather than free citizenship. The Filipinos "demand, and have a right to demand, that their liberty is honored"; America's "beautiful sounding phrases" regarding Spanish tyranny and Cuban independence would come to nothing if William McKinley were merely to throw a new yoke over the necks of the liberated colonies.[31]

More vociferous still was the Irish activist Patrick Ford: "Today the Filipinos are treated in their own country by their would-be foreign masters the same way the Irish were treated by the English in 1798. Like the Irish, [the Filipinos] see their religion insulted and their most sacred rights infringed on by insolent foreigners, who are trying to steal their country from them. They would be deserving of contempt if they did not resist to the last the 'benevolent assimilation' William McKinley would force upon them."[32] Under the banner "That Benevolent Assimilation," the *Irish World* reported that torture was among the techniques American soldiers had employed to discover the locations of Filipino arms caches. The soldiers in the Philippines looked on the water cure as "a huge joke," confessed one American. "A little over a hundred years ago," commented Ford, "similar 'huge jokes' were perpetrated in Ireland by British soldiers. . . . Your 'Anglo-Saxon' has on more than one occasion shown himself an adept [*sic*] at such jokes."[33] Hence American General Chafee became "the Cromwell of the Philippines" in the popular Irish press; and, indeed, it seems to have been their commitment to armed resistance that earned the Filipinos such nicknames as "the O'Hoolys" and "the smoked Irish" among Irish American soldiers who were serving there.[34]

Just as the cause of the Cuban *reconcentrados* had resonated with the nationalist strains embodied in such stories as "The Pikemen of '98" or in the public rituals commemorating the Polish uprisings, just as the pageantry surrounding the immigrant regiments evoked a nationalist mythology of Maccabeean or Fenian heroics, so the struggle in the Philippines evoked visions of the nationalist defeats and the civil oppressions endured in the Old World. While the American trade union movement worried over the impact of so-called coolie labor in the case of Philippine annexation, while many socialists dismissed Filipino resistance as irrelevant in the face of the mechanistic forces of maturing capitalism, and while mugwump reformers and southern Democrats fretted over the havoc imperialism might wreak not on the Philippines but on America's republican institutions, immigrant nationalists forged a critique of imperial conduct from the vantage of the conquered and insisted on the national right to self-determination. In the wake of the election of 1900, seen by many as a referendum on empire, the *Irish World* declared in a headline banner, "England's Candidates Triumphed," adding in a subhead, "Pronounce It a Defeat for the Irish."[35]

The Politics of Race

In a proclamation on the Philippines in late 1898, President McKinley had asserted that "the mission of the United States is one of benevolent assimilation, substituting the mild sway of justice for arbitrary rule."[36] McKinley's policy and the terms of its articulation held wildly complex resonances for immigrants. On the one hand, the bitter histories of Anglicization, Russification, and Kulturkampf—histories kept current by the legends and icons of immigrant popular culture—promoted an ironic interpretation of "benevolent assimilation" as "malevolent." Indeed, was McKinley's policy not "arbitrary rule" after all? The dominion of "Anglo-Saxondom" abroad, moreover, mirrored a fierce Anglo-supremacism at home: "assimilating" the Philippines to superior Anglo-Saxon culture was not without its implications for America's non-Anglo-Saxon residents.

On the other hand, perceptions of race could also mitigate immigrant discussion of Filipino rights. Overt racialism surfaced in periodic references to the archipelago's "savage" or "half-savage" population in the *Yiddishes Tageblatt,* the *Abend blatt,* and even such typically sympathetic journals as *Zgoda* and the *Pilot.* "'The Philippine vote' will become an important, possibly a decisive, factor in a national election," warned the *Pilot.* "Dost like the picture?"[37] Others, such as Michael Kruszka of *Kuryer Polski,* fully endorsed the mission of "civilizing" the Filipinos. "The partition of Poland brought the Poles slavery," he asserted, "[but] the taking of the Philippines will bring the Filipinos freedom."[38]

While some immigrant writers were quick to identify the Philippine situation as a conflict between "white" and "nonwhite" worlds, others saw the matter much less starkly. "Those miserable foreigners in Manila, Cuba, Porto [*sic*] Rico or wherever you please," commented one sardonic writer in the *Pilot,* "if they are not ready to accept and adopt every 'Yankee notion' offered them, are manifestly unfit for self-government, and our equally manifest duty and destiny is to pitchfork our institutions down their throats, or, failing that, to govern them ourselves in the good old time-honored 'Anglo-Saxon' way."[39] As the writer's bitter reference to the "'Anglo-Saxon' way" suggests, the map of immigrant sympathies was complicated by a late nineteenth-century racial taxonomy, which, in this context, nuanced the opposition between "white" America and the "non-white" Pacific islands. It was not just that dearly held principles of national rights and popular Euro-American conceptions of racial hierarchy cross-cut one another in the instance of Philippine conquest; rather, the peri-od's conventional articulation of "race" in and of itself offered Irish, Polish, and Jewish immigrants several possible avenues of self-identifi-cation and suggested several different ways of positioning themselves in relation to McKinley and the "Anglo-Saxons," on the one hand, and Aguinaldo and the "Malays," on the other. To the extent that the Philip-pine war was cast in popular discussion not only as a war of white against nonwhite or of civilization against savagery but also of Anglo-Saxon against non-Anglo-Saxon, these immigrants could summon alternate logics to locate their interests on either side of the conflict.

The ambiguity derived from the slippage between two distinct but coexisting terms of racial identification in turn-of-the-century America: "white" and "Anglo-Saxon." On the one hand, immigrants from all three European groups were considered (and considered themselves) "white"— a crucial distinction under the terms of the naturalization law of 1790, which limited naturalized citizenship to free "white" immigrants. By American law and by less formal conventions of social consensus, immi-grants from Ireland and eastern Europe were "white," belonging to a community of "whites" imagined in opposition to other communities of "nonwhites."

The salience of this racial conception was reflected not only in the rights bestowed on European immigrants in the United States but also in the terms of their own identifications of "self" and "other" in a variety of contexts. The California Irish of the 1870s, for instance, had felt sufficient footing as members of the "white" community to spearhead an anti-Chinese movement without fear of its lapsing into more generalized ag-itation against the foreign-born.[40] Similarly, in his memoir of the Indian wars, *Warpath and Bivouac* (1890), the Irish nationalist John Finerty drew the line between "whites" and the "aborigines" of North America in the sharpest, most virulent terms possible. "The Sioux must be descendants of Cain," he wrote, "and are veritable children of the devil. The rest are a very little behind them, except in point of personal appearance and daring, in which the Sioux excel nearly all other Indians. Most of them are greedy, greasy, gassy, lazy, and knavish."[41] Conversely, James Jeffrey Roche invoked the same categories of "white" and "other" to decry exactly this kind of virulence. In Roche's poem "The White Wolf's Cry," the indictment of white supremacist thought is cast as a *self*-indictment: "We are the Chosen People—whatever we do is right— / Feared as men fear the leper, whose skin like our own is white!"[42]

Yet in both nineteenth-century science and popular understanding, the "white" community comprised many sharply distinguishable races. The categories "Celt," "Slav," "Hebrew," and "Anglo-Saxon" represented an order of difference far beyond what is now attached to the notions of "ethnicity." The perceived chasm among them was indicated by the simianized caricatures of Irish immigrants that appeared in the popular press, by political debate over the "natural" propensities of various peoples for adaptation to American institutions, by phrenological tracts on the European races, and by the concerns of biologically minded nativists that the high birthrate of "the inferior European races" threatened to alter the character of the United States. It was within this framework of racial difference that, in a survey of the Irish countryside, an English observer could remark, "To see white chimpanzees is dreadful."[43]

The term *race* was highly unstable and was applied with a staggering imprecision. It could connote a social difference whose basis was biological, historical, political, psychological, physiological, linguistic, or some combination of these, depending on the speaker and the moment. What did remain stable, however, was the degree of difference that the term was understood to describe. As the racial theorist Alfred Schultz put it in his early twentieth-century tract, *Race or Mongrel?* "The principle that all men are created equal is . . . a little declamatory phrase, and only one objection can be raised against it, that it does not contain one iota of truth."[44] Through a variety of vivid analogies, Shultz endeavored to make the point that what are now widely regarded as cultural differences were not a matter of culture at all but a matter of *stock:* "The opinion is advanced that the public schools change the children of all races into Americans. Put a Scandinavian, a German, and a Magyar boy in at one end, and they will come out Americans at the other end. Which is like saying, let a pointer, a setter, and a pug enter one end of a tunnel and they will come out three greyhounds at the other end."[45]

Significantly, it was not only from the "Anglo-Saxon" side of the racial divide that "Celt," "Slav," and "Hebrew" were held up as coherent and meaningful categories. Asked whether Judaism was a race or a religion,

Emma Lazarus maintained emphatically that *"it is both,"* and she went on to congratulate the Jews on having "adapted ourselves to the practical requirements of American life without ever losing the fire of our Oriental blood. . . ."[46] In his popular Yiddish novella *Yekl* (1896), Abraham Cahan offers a conceit of immutable, unassimilable *Yiddishkayt*—Jewishness—rooted in biology and ever betrayed by the Jew's "Semitic" features. Well into the twentieth century the poet Morris Winchevsky, Cahan's colleague at the *Forverts,* could write of the "historical physiognomy" and "facial distinctiveness" of nations. "I believe in complete faith," he wrote of Jewish identity, "that even if the melting down of other races were to be wished, such a national suicide would be simply impossible for us. The Jewish race is simply stronger by far than the others—and while the other side of the contest would sink into the concoction, the Jew would not."[47]

Likewise, the Polish nationalist leader Agaton Giller described the German colonization of western Poland as a contest between the Teuton and the Slav in which Germany hoped to "distort the Polish-national face of our land" with "Teutonic features."[48] Despite an overall social profile that reflected their earlier arrival and higher level of acculturation in the United States, the Irish, too, remained racially distinct in the eyes of many. John Brennan's novel of Irish republicanism, *Erin Mor,* described assimilation as a cultural veneer overlaying a stubborn biological difference: "it was only *by the physiognomy, or the color of their countenances,* that one was enabled to distinguish between the children of the Irish exiles and those of the wealthiest Americans."[49] In response to the rampant Anglo-Saxonist agitation for an American alliance with England, an Irish poet in the spring of 1898 likewise struck the chord of immutable racial difference. "Alliance? Never!" he announced to the Anglo-Saxon, "you are not of the self same race / Nor blood of the self same clan. . . ."[50]

While immigrant writers tended to accept the basic categories of differentiation among the white races, many grew increasingly uncomfortable with the arguments advanced from the Anglo-Saxon side of the divide. The ascendant definition of the United States as an "Anglo-Saxon" nation held ominous portents for the social position of non-Anglo-Saxons in the domestic sphere and for the nation's conduct in the international sphere. Leading politicians, reformers, and Protestant clergy on both sides of the Atlantic began to speak of a "natural" harmony of interests between the two leading Anglo-Saxon nations and of a "patriotism of race," by which all Americans should be favorably disposed to Great Britain. One likely result of America's entrance in European power struggles, according to Chauncy Depew, would be "the union of the

Anglo-Saxon race." Similarly, a Protestant minister in Brooklyn hailed England as "bone of our bone, flesh of our flesh," while a Boston preacher trumpeted Anglo-Saxondom as "the one great race to whom God has given the endowment to civilize the world. . . ." The United States and England, by these lights, were "destined by the Most High to rule this earth. . . ."[51]

Political Anglo-Saxonism met with a powerful and manifold resistance on the part of immigrants. A frequently enunciated objection to Anglo-American entente was the racial logic that lay behind it. The remarkable elasticity of the category "Anglo-Saxon" as applied to the United States rendered it an easy target for ridicule. Finley Peter Dunne jested that when the worldwide alliance of Anglo-Saxons is completed (including "the Ancient Ordher iv Anglo-Saxon Hibernyans," "the Pollacky Benevolent Society," and the "Benny Brith," among others), it will be hard going for "th' eight or nine people in th' wurruld that has th' misfortune iv not bein' brought up Anglo-Saxons." In the same vein, Roche quipped that the name of the dowager empress of China, Tsi An, was "evidently a corruption of Betsy Ann. Thus does the onward march of Anglo-Saxonism wend its westward way." Those who were foremost in condemning "hyphenated Americanism," he later jabbed, were "always perfectly willing to call us all 'Anglo-Saxons' with the hyphen in full view."[52]

At the heart of such parody was a deadly serious question: "Who is America?" Among the 75 million "Anglo-Saxons" in the country, immigrant writers routinely pointed out, were "about 20,000,000 of Irish blood, nearly as many of German, 7,000,000 of African, and at least a dozen million of French, Italian, Polish, Scandinavian, Spanish, Portuguese, etc. . . . No wonder that the Anglo-Saxon race is so powerful."[53] New York's '98 Centenary Committee passed a resolution denouncing Anglo-Saxonism as "an insult to the intelligence of the American people, not one in twenty of whom is, or ever was 'Anglo-Saxon.'" In an editorial piece that is striking in the light of more recent curricular debates, the Irish World questioned the Anglo-dominance of public education, which taught "each rising generation of Irish, German, French, Scandinavian, Polish, Italian, and other children that they were the descendants of a class of commercial marauders in England styling themselves the great 'Anglo-Saxon race.'"[54]

Significantly, again, while immigrant writers may have dismissed Anglo-Saxonism as a "solemn and persistently asseverated piece of nonsense" or "an ethnological lie,"[55] they did not reject either the fundamental racial distinction between "Anglo-Saxon" and "other" or the level of perceived difference such racial distinctions represented. Most accepted the fundamental categories and challenged only the Anglo-Saxonists' imprecise application of the racial scheme and the presumption of Anglo-Saxon supremacy. Thus, under the banner "Two Race Elements That Should Unite," activists could call for a political alliance of Irish and French Canadian immigrants because "in the veins of both flows the Celtic blood," and they could complain that "the great currents of Teutonic and Celtic blood flowing through the veins of the nation count for nothing" in the current climate of rampant Anglo-Saxonism.[56] Roche could counter the Anglo-Saxonist denunciation of the highly prolific "lower races" and their biological impact on the nation without altering that argument's fundamental premise. "Let the Anglo-Saxon call the roll of his relations," he wrote with some satisfaction, "and confess, with shame, that a grand race like that of the Puritan and pilgrim is vanishing. . . . The fittest will always survive, when they care to do so."[57] These writers thus identified the contest between Saxon and Celt in precisely the terms of the staunchest Anglo-Saxonists.

As the United States stepped onto the stage of international politics at the century's end, racialist assumptions of fundamental difference, of Anglo-Saxon greatness, and of the nation's racial "duty" to the "lower races" served as a mainspring for public discussion of policy. As early as 1885, enthralled by a vision of the religio-racial destiny of "our country," the evangelist Josiah Strong had predicted that the world was to "enter upon a new stage of its history—*the final competition of races for which the Anglo-Saxon is being schooled.* If I do not read amiss," he had ventured, "this powerful race will move down upon Mexico, down upon Central and South America, out upon the islands of the sea, over upon Africa and beyond."[58]

Similar conceptions of the racial order of world politics guided the debate over the Philippine question. William Howard Taft, for instance, allowed that the Filipinos would need 150 years of American tutelage to develop "Anglo-Saxon political principles and skills." Theodore Roosevelt concurred, doubting that independence alone could transform the "pirates and headhunters" of the Philippines into "a dark-hued New England town meeting." For Roosevelt, moreover, military adventure and ultimate control of the Philippines was as necessary for the Anglo-Saxon as it was for the Malay: imperialism was but one manifestation of that "masterful instinct which alone can make a race great."[59] No one was as unbridled in his enthusiasm for racial conquest as Indiana's Senator Albert Beveridge. In a gloss of American history fully Whitmanesque in its sweep and energy (and, indeed, in its capacity for global absorption), Beveridge celebrated "the Anglo-Saxon impulse," whose "watchword [in Thomas Jefferson's time] and whose watchword throughout the world today is 'Forward!'"[60]

The framing of trans-Pacific expansion as a meeting of the "white" and "nonwhite" worlds thus coexisted with its alternate definition as a contest between "Anglo-Saxons" and their pitiable "inferiors." By the terms of this latter definition, the interests of Celts, Slavs, and Hebrews by no means rested unquestionably with the United States. When, upon reviewing the American troops in the Philippines, Beveridge lauded "these thoroughbred soldiers from the plantations of the South, [and] from the plains and valleys and farms of the West," he was distinguishing the "Saxon type" not only from the "Malay" enemy but from the non-Saxon types of the United States as well. "The fine line is everywhere," he wrote, reflecting the (typically exclusionary) aesthetic of male beauty that so often accompanies militarist nationalism: "The nose is straight, the mouth is sensitive and delicate. There are very few bulldog jaws. There is, instead, the steel-trap jaw of the lion. The whole face and figure is the face and figure of the thoroughbred fighter, who has always been the fine-featured, delicate-nostriled, thin-eared, and generally clean-cut featured man."[61]

One rejoinder to this racialized view of American military imperatives and successes was to publicize the fact that some conspicuous Americans in the war were actually Celtic—members of "the fighting race."[62] "The American is neither Anglo-Saxon nor Celt, nor German, nor French, nor anything else individually," commented the *Pilot;* whatever successes the country enjoyed were due to its diversity, not to "Anglo-Saxon" pluck.[63]

More common, however, were direct challenges to the righteousness of "Anglo-Saxon principle." "Either it is or is not a good and desirable thing for the United States to join with England and 'rule the world,' as the clap-trap phrase goes, on 'Anglo-Saxon principles,'" wrote Roche, "but it is surely a better thing to obey the eleventh commandment and mind our own business, leaving the ruling of the world to its Ruler."[64] Elsewhere, in a fit of Celtic despair, Roche lamented the interventionist policies of the United States in Samoa and especially the participation of Irish Americans in the ranks of the U.S. military there. "The superior 'Anglo-Saxon'. . . will let the foolish 'foreigner' do the work," he remarked, "while he . . . 'sits on the fence and does the heavy work of supervising.' That is what Anglo-Saxon civilization means the world over, and we are not sure that it is anything other than [what] the 'inferior races' who submit to it deserve."[65]

Responses to the crosscurrents of national and racial politics varied a great deal within each of these immigrant groups. Robert Ellis Thompson could heartily reject Anglo-American entente but then let slip his inherent Eurocentrism: "it is sixty years too late for this talk of an identity of either blood or interest between the two countries. America is a great composite nation, in which all *European* nationalities are represented. . . ."[66] Letters to the editor of the *Yiddishes Tageblatt* ran roughly half and half on the Philippine question. While some denounced the islands' "half-savage revolutionaries" and despaired of ever bringing order to this "savage country of mulattoes," others felt that the United States should not enslave those who were "beautiful and right before God." Still others agreed with the administration that the Filipinos were not ready for self-government: the Filipino rebel was "like a sick child who will not take the medicine the doctor prescribed."[67]

Despite the considerable range of opinion, however, a few broad patterns are discernible. Given the emotive power that the very word *Anglo-Saxon* held for the Irish, commentators in this group were particularly inclined to dwell on the language of Anglo-Saxonism and on the relationship among English empire, Anglo-American rapprochement, and McKinley's "large policies" in the Pacific. Though less obsessed with notions of specifically *Anglo*-supremacism and their rebuttal, Poles still generally shared with the Irish a certain bitterness on questions of racial supremacy as expressed in the language of comparative "civilization." Both groups had long been objects of a rhetoric of "barbarism" and "civilization" in their homelands. The phrase "unfit for self-government" had long been applied to describe the necessity of English rule in Ireland, such as when Matthew Arnold depicted the Celts as "undisciplinable, anarchical, and turbulent of nature." In a similar vein, Bismarck had urged the Poles of the Prussian territories to participate in "the benefits of civilization offered to you by the Prussian state." The salience of this model of racial supremacy and political tutelage was reflected in 1899, a few weeks into the Philippine war, when, during one of their many political observances, the Poles of Milwaukee denounced "the arrogant pretention of German chauvinism" and its "civilizing mission" among the Slavs.[68]

Irish and Polish writers were particularly energetic in their critiques of the reigning notions of civilization that came into play as the United States sought hegemony in the Pacific. In *The Sorrows of Sap'ed* (1904), a novel of the "Orient," for example, James Jeffrey Roche parodied the pretensions of beneficent uplift. When a ship is sighted off the coast of his fictional Asian land, a wave of terror overtakes the villagers as word spreads of its identity: "'I fear me much it is the *Helping Hand*. She has been cruising in these waters of late, after her performances in the China seas, and I have little hope but that her mission is civilizing.'" Everyone is much relieved to discover that the ship is only a pirate ship and that it is on no such (hostile) civilizing mission after all. ("'You will do well another time,'" remarks the indignant pirate captain, "'to think twice ere you make rash judgments about a ship which has done you no injury—as yet.'" But, he has to admit, "'Maybe the mistake was natural. . . .'")[69]

The Polish press, too, routinely featured this kind of satire. *Straż* pointed out the much-publicized abuses and frauds in the U.S. military as "a good example of civilization for the Filipinos," and the journal printed its own satiric ballad, "Oh, Civilization Is with Us!" which offered a catalogue of the inglorious features of American civilization—Kentucky lynch-law, the persecution of Mormons in Utah, the fleecing of the poor by bankers, the gunning down of workers who "driven by poverty went on strike." The poem ends with a bitter comment on race as the justification for domination of the Philippines:

> Oh, civilization is with us,
> And those Tagalogs are savages!
> You don't believe it? You can doubt it?!
> They look dark, like a shoe.[70]

Dziennik Chicagoski raised similar objections in an editorial entitled "The Americans as Culture-Bearers." The editor's deliberate use of *kulturtraeger*, a German word, evoked the history of German "culture-bearing" policies in Poland, in which legal proscriptions on the Polish language, Polish culture, and Polish Catholicism had gone hand-in-hand with the confiscation of Polish lands. A piece on Aguinaldo's protest against the establishment of English as the "official" language of the Philippines carried similar symbolic freight from the de-Polonizing era of Bismarck's Kulturkampf. The journal further questioned the logic by which the United States seemed willing to kill half the Filipino population to "lift" the other half out of "barbarism." In Manila, as in Poland, violence and victimization seemed among the chief "blessings of civilization."[71]

Jewish immigrants, by contrast, related very differently to the underlying question of "civilization" and "savagery." Traditions of anti-Semitism had generated a range of negative images and had branded the Jews in a variety of ways, but the charge of savagery was not prominent among them. On the contrary, when Jews were despised, it was most often for a kind of *over*-civilization. They were seen as shrewd manipulators, Europe's (and now America's) scheming intermediaries and usurers, and their alleged crimes were more often conceived to be crimes of intellect and cunning, not of violence or brutishness. Shylock, in short, was no "barbarian."[72]

Jewish commentators did occasionally question the premise of America's "civilizing" mission in the Philippines. The *Abend blatt* noted with some irony that "Aguinaldo, whom the Americans represent in the shape of a murderous and ridiculous savage . . . wrote two long letters to General Otis about human rights and international jurisprudence";[73] and a *Naye Tzayt* essay entitled "Are the Filipinos Savage?" dismantled the noblesse oblige at the heart of much expansionist polemic. At the time Spain took the Philippines under Philip II, the *Naye Tzayt* piece explained, "in Manila rifles, swords, bayonets, and spears were already being made (what better sign do you need of civilization?)."[74]

Jewish observers, however, were generally far more detached than their Irish and Polish counterparts on this question of political tutelage. The disinclination of Jews to identify with the Filipinos as unjustly maligned "inferiors" was reflected, on the Right, by a wholehearted endorsement of the "civilizing" aspects of American expansion. The *Yiddishes Tageblatt* editorial staff drew an ingenious biblical analogy to equate McKinley's policy of imperial conquest with Mosaic liberation. The Filipinos, in this configuration, played the Levites to McKinley's Moses:[75] Moses himself had to "fight with swords against those he freed from Egypt because they did not understand his plan and the path along which he led them. . . ." Likewise, Aguinaldo and his followers were "so savage and confused by their freedom that they do not recognize their liberators and their friends." The transition to true freedom, explained the journal, "works like the emergence from a dark cellar into a bright, light place where the sun warms and shines. It dazzles the eyes and raises a clamor in the head and causes one to mistake a friend for an enemy."[76] If the Filipinos of this representation were implicitly perfectible, they nonetheless had a long, long way to go in relation to their "civilized" counterparts: "the savage people there are like babies who break the bottle which nourishes them."[77]

On the Yiddish Left, meanwhile, two very different lines of political argument reflected a similar distancing from the plight of the Filipinos. Inasmuch as the archipelago was to serve as the U.S. stepping-stone to the commerce of China, the Philippine question reignited American labor's fear of the "yellow peril" (*geler shrek*)—imported "coolie labor" from Asia.

Writers in the Yiddish socialist journals characteristically regarded imperialism as a tragedy for the American worker, but they had relatively little concern for Philippine independence and the protection of Filipino rights. What will happen, one writer in the *Abend blatt* wanted to know, "when the American capitalists import the Filipinos to America as scabs?"[78] For white workers, "protected" for the moment by the Chinese Exclusion Act, "what will Exclusion help if the Philippine islands become 'ours' and through them 'we' 'open China'?" Like the white workers of the 1870s who had agitated against Chinese immigration, the Yiddish Left in 1899 tended to look upon Filipinos not as fellow proletarians but as potential tools of capital in America's ongoing class struggle.[79]

A second argument, rooted in a cool logic of the evolutionary stages of civilization and the developmental stages of capitalism, wrote off the Filipino peasantry as necessary casualties to the "natural" progression of industrialization. As Karl Kautsky had framed the issue, the taking of the Philippines and the opening of China were both inevitable and good. "Each step forward that capitalism makes in Asia," he asserted, "means a step forward toward socialism in Europe and America." Benjamin Feygenbaum of the Socialist Labor party therefore concluded, "It is not our place to join hands with either the expansionists or the anti-expansionists in the struggle either for or against colonial rule." There was little to be done on the behalf of the Filipinos until they had become a true, industrialized proletariat.[80]

Across the Yiddish political spectrum from right to left, then, was an implicit consensus on racial hierarchy that limited expressions of empathy with the Asians who had become the objects of American imperialism. While the *Yiddishes Tageblatt* endorsed the scientific principle that the world's diverse races all "stem from one father,"[81] most Yiddish comment departed from the empathy (albeit ambivalent) that characterized Irish and Polish writings of solidarity with the "Malay" rebels. The *Abend blatt,* for instance, described one Philippine tribe as "very dirty and savage" and declared that many among the Filipino population "remain in the same state of savagery [*wildkayt*] in which the Spaniards found them. . . ."[82]

Significantly, as it became clear that the war in the Philippines was to be more than a mere skirmish—that the "savages" could hold their own against the "civilized" United States—the editor of the *Yiddishes Tageblatt* did not question his own assumptions about "savages" but instead *re-racialized* the Filipinos to bring their image into line with known racialist "truths." "In the appearance of his face and the skeleton of his head," the editor now announced with certainty, "Aguinaldo looks like a European rather than a Filipino Asiatic. He is not tall, but he can pass for a handsome man even in a civilized country."[83]

As the *Yiddishes Tageblatt*'s nimble revision of Aguinaldo into a European suggests, consistency was not necessarily among the hobgoblins that plagued political commentary on the Philippines. The immigrant presses differed little from the mainstream, English-language press in this respect; this was, after all, a time when Theodore Roosevelt could boast that he had not a drop of English blood and yet fully partake of the glories of triumphant Anglo-Saxondom.

It should be emphasized that the broad generalizations sketched out above were not without their instances of contradiction. Yiddish commentators were on occasion as sympathetic to the Filipinos as their Polish or Irish counterparts were. Industrial evolutionism notwithstanding, for example, Feygenbaum could cite certain traditions of collectivity in Asian culture and suggest that the proto-socialist "savage" had a thing or two to teach the "civilized" Yankee individualist.[84] Nonetheless, the generally sympathetic Polish papers could describe the "polynesian race" as "distinguished by extreme ugliness of body and by savagery." Like the *Yiddishes Tageblatt, Zgoda* associated Filipino political skill with "European blood."[85]

Despite such inconsistencies and the overall diversity of opinion, however, it is clear that immigrant allegiances in this conflict between the imperial United States and the insurgent Philippines were largely mapped out on the terrain of race and racialism. For Irish, Polish, and Jewish immigrants alike, the imperialism debate took place within the fluid boundaries of two distinct but coexisting cultural systems of race: as Celts, Slavs, and Hebrews in an era of rampant Anglo-Saxonism, they could look askance at America's "civilizing mission" or even sense themselves among the problem populations subject to "benevolent assimilation"; but as white Europeans living in an environment where white supremacy and European centrality were among the founding assumptions of so much public discussion, these immigrants could distance themselves from the Filipinos and adopt America's mission in the Pacific as their own. As one letter to the editor of the *Yiddishes Tageblatt* asserted, betraying at once a hierarchical view of racial diversity and an exclusive view of the United States as a nation of white Europeans, "The United States, which was able to educate the Indian and the Negro, will also be able to educate the Filipino."[86]

There is, then, a two-fold malevolence lurking behind McKinley's gentle rhetoric of "benevolent assimilation." Viewing world affairs from a perspective derived from their own nationalist attachments to the Old World, many immigrants identified McKinley's policy in the Philippines as malevolent in its imperialist designs and its disregard for the political ideal of "the consent of the governed." At the same time, however, there was a second, decidedly malevolent cultural undercurrent of that policy, by which other immigrants became assimilated to notions of American belonging through a process of racial reinscription. Michael Kruszka, for instance, whose professed sympathy for all the world's oppressed opened this essay, later decided that these "half-savage Malays" had "nothing to lose" by the "protection" of the United States. In defense of this position he explained, "In regard to civilization, the Polish nation stands higher beyond comparison than the Filipinos. . . ."[87] Like the initial campaign for Cuban liberation, the Philippine crisis resonated with the liberationist strains of immigrant culture. Far more than the Cuban cause, however, the Philippine crisis tested the strengths and limits of New and Old World political identifications, bringing the two into logical collision. That such immigrant commentators as Patrick Ford, James Jeffrey Roche, Stefan Barszczewski, and Ben Efrim were among the most vociferous, consistent, and empathetic protesters on behalf of Filipino rights is testimony to the salience of Old World nationalist aspirations in assessing New World political conduct. That race emerged as the dominant motif by which others resolved this tension suggests the extent to which, for European immigrants, becoming American depended on becoming "Caucasian."

Notes

The author wishes to thank Harvard University Press for permission to use material from *Special Sorrows: The Diasporic Imagination of Irish, Polish, and Jewish Immigrants in the United States* (1995).

1. *Kuryer Polski,* March 27, 1899, 2.

2. Benedict Anderson, *Imagined Communities: Reflections on the Origin and Spread of Nationalism* (London: Verso, 1983).

3. *Catholic Citizen,* December 10, 1898, 4.

4. Walter LaFeber, *The New Empire: An Interpretation of American Expansion, 1860–1898* (Ithaca, N.Y.: Cornell University Press, 1963), 110, 203–9 (quote on 110).

5. E. Berkeley Tompkins, *Anti-Imperialism in the United States: The Great Debate* (Philadelphia: University of Pennsylvania Press, 1970), 161–82; Charles Campbell, *The Transformation of American Foreign Relations, 1865–1900* (New York: Harper and Row, 1976), 302–8; Daniel Schirmer, *Republic or Empire: American Resistance to the Philippine War* (Cambridge, Mass.: Schenkman, 1972), 105–20.

6. V. Edmund McDevitt, *The First California's Chaplain* (Fresno: Academy Library

Guild, 1956), 142, 146; *New York Herald,* October 30, 1899, 7; *New York Times,* October 10, 1899, 3.

7. *Yiddishes Tageblatt,* January 24, 1899, 7 ("We see from enslaved Russia"); January 19, 1899, 7 ("like France" and "beat freedom"); May 10, 1898, 1 ("half wild men"); February 12, 1899, 4 ("sickness to hate"); May 12, 1899, 4 ("Aguinaldos in the United States"); May 19, 1899, 4 ("Aguinaldos in the United States").

8. On the concept of identificational assimilation, see especially Milton Gordon, *Assimilation in American Life: The Role of Race, Religion, and National Origins* (New York: Oxford University Press, 1964), 71.

9. Cited in Lawrence J. McCaffrey, *The Irish Diaspora in America* (Washington, D.C.: Catholic University of America Press, 1976), 130. This theme is most fully developed in Kerby Miller, *Emigrants and Exiles: Ireland and the Irish Exodus to North America* (New York: Oxford University Press, 1985).

10. For general discussions of immigrant nationalism and its organizational expression in this period, see Thomas Brown, *Irish American Nationalism, 1870–1890* (Philadelphia: Lippincott, 1966); Marnin Feinstein, *American Zionism, 1884–1904* (New York: Herzl, 1965); Michael Funchion, *Chicago's Irish Nationalists, 1881–1890* (New York: Arno, 1978); Victor Greene, *For God and Country: The Rise of Polish and Lithuanian Ethnic Consciousness in America, 1860–1910* (Madison: University of Wisconsin Press, 1975); Lawrence McCaffrey, ed., *Irish Nationalism and the American Contribution* (New York: Arno, 1976); Kerby Miller, *Emigrants and Exiles;* Melvin Urofsky, *American Zionism from Herzl to the Holocaust* (Garden City, N.Y.: Anchor, 1975); and Joseph Wytrwal, *America's Polish Heritage: A Social History of Poles in America* (Detroit: Endurance, 1961).

11. Elizabeth Gurley Flynn, *The Rebel Girl: An Autobiography* (New York: International, 1955), 23.

12. Ibid.

13. This brief discussion of immigrant popular cultures is adapted from Matthew Frye Jacobson, *Special Sorrows: The Diasporic Imagination of Irish, Polish, and Jewish Immigrants in the United States* (Cambridge, Mass.: Harvard University Press, 1995), chapters 2 and 3.

14. Quoted in Arthur Leonard Waldo, *Teofila Samolinska: Matka Zwiazku Narodowego Polskiego w Ameryce* (Chicago: author, 1980), 20.

15. David Stephen Cohen, ed., *America the Dream of My Life: Selections from the Federal Writers' Project's New Jersey Ethnic Survey* (New Brunswick, N.J.: Rutgers University Press, 1990), 83 (quote), 106.

16. "The first feeling in the British editorial mind" when the proposal surfaced, he jabbed, "must have been one of extreme surprise that there had been something annexable not already annexed by Great Britain." *Irish World,* June 26, 1897, 4, 5. On Ford's anti-imperialism, see also James Paul Rodechko, *Patrick Ford and His Search for America: A Case Study in Irish-American Journalism, 1870–1913* (New York: Arno, 1976), 177–79.

17. *Kuryer Polski,* September 7, 1898, 2.

18. *Zgoda,* April 7, 1898, 4. The charge against the Cubans in the original was that they were "mieszanina murzynów, indjan, i hiszpanow, dzika i bezładna."

19. *Yiddishes Tageblatt,* April 12, 1898, 4. See also Moses Rischin, ed., *Grandma Never Lived in America: The New Journalism of Abraham Cahan* (Bloomington: Indiana University Press, 1985), 3–35.

20. Jacobson, *Special Sorrows,* chapter 4.

21. Stanisław Osada, *Historia Zwiazku Narodowego Poskiego i Rozwoj Ruchu Narodowego Polskiego w Ameryce* (Chicago: Zgoda, 1905), 467.

22. *Irish World,* June 18, 1898, 8.

23. *Zgoda,* July 14, 1898, 1.

24. *Pilot,* February 11, 1899, 4.

25. Stefan Barszczewski, *Cuba Libre!* (Chicago: n.p., 1899), 20–21.

26. *Abend blatt,* March 6, 1899, 2.

27. Ibid., February 25, 1899, 2.

28. *Pilot,* October 1, 1898, 4.

29. Quoted in David Emmons, *The Butte Irish: Class and Ethnicity in an American Mining Town, 1875–1925* (Urbana: University of Illinois Press, 1989), 331; *Irish World,* April 22, 1899, 10.

30. *Zgoda,* February 23, 1899, 1.

31. *Dziennik Chicagoski,* November 3, 1900, 4; January 6, 1899, 1; January 11, 1899, 2.

32. *Irish World,* June 23, 1900, 4.

33. Ibid.

34. John Bowe, *With the Thirteenth Minnesota* (Minneapolis: Farnham, 1905), 94, 133–34. Some links were forged between immigrant dissenters and the emerging New England Anti-Imperialist League, particularly among the politically established Irish of the Northeast. The *Pilot* initially described the league in a headline as "An Important Movement to Save the Republic," and, as David Noel Doyle observes, Irish Americans directly active in the league included "a fair cross-section of the Irish American elite at the time"—ranging from such conservative Democrats as Bourke Cockran and Patrick Collins to the erstwhile radical Patrick Ford. Ethnic rallies in affiliation with the league included a New England Clan na Gael affair and a Cooper Union rally, described in the *Abend blatt* under the banner "Three Cheers for Aguinaldo." *Dziennik Chicagoski* and *Kuryer Polski* occasionally covered or reprinted anti-imperialist speeches by Senator Hoar or William Jennings Bryan. David Noel Doyle, *Irish Americans, Native Rights, and National Empires* (New York: Arno, 1976), 268–69; Tompkins, *Anti-Imperialism in the United States,* 127–28. See also Carl I. Meyerhuber, "U.S. Imperialism and Ethnic Journalism: The New Manifest Destiny as Reflected in Boston's Irish-American Press, 1890–1900," *Eire/Ireland* 9, no. 4 (1974): 4, 22, 27 and passim.

35. *Irish World,* November 17, 1900, 1.

36. Stuart Creighton Miller, *"Benevolent Assimilation": The American Conquest of the Philippines, 1899–1903* (New Haven, Conn.: Yale University Press, 1982), frontispiece (quote), 52.

37. *Pilot,* November 19, 1898, 4. See also *Yiddishes Tageblatt,* May 10, 1898, 1; *Zgoda,* August 25, 1898, 4; and *Abend blatt,* May 7, 1898, 2; July 21, 1898, 2.

38. *Kuryer Polski,* June 9, 1899, 2.

39. *Pilot,* July 30, 1898, 4.

40. Dale Knobel, *Paddy and the Republic: Ethnicity and Nationality in Antebellum America* (Middletown, Conn.: Wesleyan University Press, 1986), 179.

41. John Finerty, *Warpath and Bivouac: Or, the Conquest of the Sioux* (1890; reprint, Norman: University of Oklahoma Press, 1961), 70. Later, in a discussion of the American-Canadian frontier, Finerty rather ingeniously blurred the demonologies of nationalism and racialism, describing John Bull and Sitting Bull as "cousins" who "hobnobbed comfortably" (263).

42. James Jeffrey Roche, *The V-A-S-E and other Bric-a-Brac* (Boston: Richard G. Badger, 1900), 59–60. When the *Boston Evening Record* remarked that "the 'brown man,' be he American Negro, Filipino, dervish or Chinese, is going to the wall with a velocity that is appalling . . . yet what has he done?" Roche responded caustically, "Hasn't he done enough to deserve extermination, in being born black, yellow, or brown?" *Pilot,* July 1, 1899, 4.

43. Quoted in F. S. L. Lyons, *Culture and Anarchy in Ireland* (New York: Oxford University Press, 1979), 12. See also Alfred P. Schultz, *Race or Mongrel?* (Boston: L. C. Page, 1908), 276; Thomas Dyer, *Theodore Roosevelt and the Idea of Race* (Baton Rouge: Louisiana State University Press, 1980), 143–67; Robert Singerman, "The Jew as Racial Alien: The Genetic Component of American Anti-Semitism," in *Anti-Semitism in American History,* ed. David A. Gerber (Urbana: University of Illinois Press, 1987), 103–28; Matthew Frye Jacobson, *Becoming Caucasian: The Vicissitude of Whiteness in American Politics and Culture* (Cambridge, Mass.: Harvard University Press, 1998); and James Barrett and David Roediger, "In between Peoples: Race, Nationality, and the New Immigrant Working Class," *Journal of American Ethnic History* (Spring 1998).

44. Schultz, *Race or Mongrel?* 259. Even Schultz's favorable comments on the various races hinge on this notion of biological difference: "Why do the Jews succeed?" he asked. "Because they deserve to succeed. They belong to a great race, and they kept and do keep that race pure" (43).

45. Ibid., 261.

46. Emma Lazarus, *An Epistle to the Hebrews* (1900; reprint, New York: Jewish Historical Society, 1987), 9, 20.

47. Morris Winchevsky, "Mayn natsionale ani-mamin," *Gezamlte verk,* vol. 7 (New York: Frayhayt Publishing Association, 1927), 221, 222.

48. Quoted in Osada, *Historia Zwiazku Narodowego Polskiego i Rozwoj Ruchu Narodowego Polskiego w Ameryce,* 101.

49. John Brennan, *Erin Mor: The Story of Irish Republicanism* (San Francisco: P. M. Diers, 1892), 35, 263 (emphasis added); Theodore Allen, *The Invention of the White Race: Racial Oppression and Social Control* (London: Verso, 1994).

50. *Irish World,* May 7, 1898, 1.

51. Quoted in ibid., May 21, 1898, 1. On the racial dimensions of turn-of-the-century diplomacy, see especially Stuart Anderson, *Race and Rapprochement: Anglo-Saxonism and Anglo-American Relations, 1895–1904* (Rutherford, N.J.: Fairleigh Dickinson University Press, 1981). Anglo-Saxonism often merged with (or fell under the rubric of) a second body of racialist thought, "Teutonism." See especially Reginald Horsman, *Race and Manifest Destiny: The Origins of American Racial Anglo-Saxonism* (Cam-

bridge, Mass.: Harvard University Press, 1981), 27–29, 62–77 passim. In the political rhetoric of the 1890s, however, "Anglo-Saxon" was the dominant classification.

52. Finley Peter Dunne, "On the Anglo-Saxon," in *Mr. Dooley in Peace and in War* (Boston: Small, Maynard, 1899), 56; *Pilot,* October 22, 1898, 4; July 8, 1899, 4.

53. *Pilot,* February 12, 1898, 4.

54. *Irish World,* May 28, 1898, 1; June 11, 1898, 2. For a sample of the effectiveness of the educational system in creating "Anglos," see Ludwig Lewisohn, *Up Stream* (New York: Modern Library, 1926), 89–119. Under the influence of Milton, Hazlitt, Coleridge, and others, the Jewish American Lewisohn was transformed into "a Pan-Angle of the purist type" (98).

55. *Pilot,* January 29, 1898, 1; *Irish World,* July 9, 1898, 1.

56. *Irish World,* February 26, 1898, 4; April 23, 1898, 4.

57. *Pilot,* February 4, 1899, 4.

58. Quoted in Richard Hofstadter, *Social Darwinism in American Thought, 1860–1915* (Philadelphia: University of Pennsylvania Press, 1944), 154. See also LaFeber, *New Empire,* 72–80.

59. Stuart Creighton Miller, *"Benevolent Assimilation,"* 132; Dyer, *Theodore Roosevelt and the Idea of Race,* 140, 141. For the breadth of racial consensus among white imperialists and anti-imperialists, see especially Christopher Lasch, "The Anti-Imperialist as Racist," in *American Imperialism and Anti-Imperialism,* ed. Thomas G. Paterson (New York: Crowell, 1973), 110–17; and Richard E. Welch Jr., "Twelve Anti-Imperialists and Imperialists Compared: Racism and Economic Expansion," ibid., 118–25.

60. Albert Beveridge, "The March of the Flag," in *An American Primer,* ed. Daniel J. Boorstin (New York: Mentor, 1966), 647.

61. Quoted in Richard E. Welch Jr., *Response to Imperialism: The United States and the Philippine-American War, 1899–1902* (Chapel Hill: University of North Carolina Press, 1979), 101.

62. *Catholic Citizen,* May 13, 1899, 1; September 2, 1899, 6. The *Pilot* ran a regular feature on the Irish soldiers called "The Fighting Race in the Present War."

63. *Pilot,* May 21, 1898, 4.

64. Ibid., June 25, 1898, 4.

65. Ibid., April 22, 1899, 4. The astonishing willingness of the oppressed to serve in the causes of the oppressor was a running theme in Roche's writing. In this connection, the Irish themselves were the objects of his sharpest invective. On the unfolding crisis in the Transvaal, for instance, he wrote, "There are Irishmen, God forgive them! serving today in the ranks of England against the Boers; . . . no true Irishman wishes to honor them with a monument, though all will rejoice when they qualify for it by dying as soon as possible." Ibid., November 18, 1899, 4.

66. *Irish World,* April 2, 1898, 5 (emphasis added).

67. *Yiddishes Tageblatt,* January 19, 1899, 7; January 20, 1899, 7; January 24, 1899, 7.

68. Matthew Arnold quoted in Lyons, *Culture and Anarchy in Ireland,* 5, 11; Bismarck quoted in Norman Davies, *God's Playground: A History of Poland,* vol. 2 (New York: Columbia University Press, 1982), 124–26; Milwaukee Poles quoted in *Kuryer Polski,* March 7, 1899, 2.

69. James Jeffrey Roche, *The Sorrows of Sap'ed: A Problem Story of the East* (New York: Harper and Bros., 1904), 42 (first quote), 47 (second quote), 48 (third quote).

70. *Straż*, April 13, 1900, 1; February 10, 1900, 2.

71. *Dziennik Chicagoski*, April 7, 1899, 2 (*kulturtraeger*); April 10, 1899, 1 (Aguinaldo's protest); April 20, 1899, 2 (violence). The piece on the violence involved in extending the "blessings of civilization" credited an article in the *Chicago Chronicle*.

72. David A. Gerber, "Cutting Out Shylock: Elite Anti-Semitism and the Quest for Moral Order in the Mid-Nineteenth-Century American Marketplace," in *Anti-Semitism in American History*, ed. Gerber, 201–32; John Higham, *Send These to Me: Immigrants in Urban America* (Baltimore, Md.: Johns Hopkins University Press, 1984), 95–116; John Higham, *Strangers in the Land: Patterns of American Nationalism, 1865–1925* (New Brunswick, N.J.: Rutgers University Press, 1955): 92–94.

73. *Abend blatt*, February 21, 1899, 4. "Business is business," commented another *Abend blatt* editorial, "that is the morality of capitalism. That is the civilization which we are going with holy enthusiasm to spread among the savages" (February 9, 1899, 4). Yet another piece identified a southern lynch mob with the banner "Savage Barbarians" (December 7, 1899, 1).

74. *Naye Tzayt*, May, 1899, 2.

75. Numbers 16.

76. *Yiddishes Tageblatt*, January 8, 1899, 4 (description of Aguinaldo and his followers); February 6, 1899, 4 (emergence from dark cellar).

77. Ibid., February 23, 1899, 4.

78. *Abend blatt*, November 15, 1898, 4.

79. *Naye Tzayt*, March 1899, 8–9; April 1899, 1–7 (quote on 3). On the nativist strains in the anti-imperialist arguments of American labor, see, for instance, Welch, *Response to Imperialism*, 84–88. On labor and the earlier movement for Chinese exclusion, see Alexander Saxton, *The Indispensable Enemy: Labor and the Anti-Chinese Movement in California* (Berkeley: University of California Press, 1971).

80. For Feygenbaum's most extended treatment of the subject (and his gloss of Karl Kautsky), see "Enderungen in Amerike durkh di eroberung fun di filipinen," *Naye Tzayt*, March 1899, 1–9; April 1899, 6–7 (Kautsky quote on 6); *Abend blatt*, February 6, 1899, 4 (Feygenbaum quote); Patrick Goode, ed., *Karl Kautsky: Selected Political Writings* (London: Macmillan, 1983), 74–96, especially 89–92.

81. *Yiddishes Tageblatt*, January 17, 1898, 5; January 18, 1898, 5.

82. *Abend blatt*, May 7, 1898, 2; July 21, 1898, 2.

83. *Yiddishes Tageblatt*, May 10, 1898, 1; March 6, 1899, 4.

84. *Abend blatt*, February 16, 1899, 4. Philip Krantz, too, if often given to the language of "savagery," was particularly respectful in his portraits of José Marti and Aguinaldo as political thinkers and actors. See *Naye Tzayt*, June, 1898, 7–8, 11–13; March, 1899, 43–45; and *Abend blatt*, February 8, 1899, 1.

85. *Dziennik Chicagoski*, January 23, 1899, 2 ("ugliness of body"); *Zgoda*, May 5, 1898, 4 ("European blood"). Indeed, although *Zgoda* was far more sympathetic to the Filipino cause, the journal's racial commentary followed a trajectory similar to *Yiddishes Tageblatt*'s. Early on Aguinaldo was identified as "an only superficially civilized Tagal" and a "savage dictator." *Zgoda*, August 25, 1898, 4. Once the struggle for inde-

pendence had begun, however, the journal cited a report by one general, who estimated that the Filipinos "stand far higher than Cubans in point of education." King's assessment, noted the editor, may give pause "to those impassioned adherents of empire who see in the Filipinos only savage, bloodthirsty mutineers." *Zgoda*, June 29, 1899, 8.

86. *Yiddishes Tageblatt,* January 16, 1899, 4.

87. *Kuryer Polski,* March 27, 1899, 2; May 2, 1899, 2.

8 From Jim Crow Racism to Laissez-Faire Racism: The Transformation of Racial Attitudes

Lawrence D. Bobo and Ryan A. Smith

The Swedish economist and social reformer Gunnar Myrdal arrived in the United States on September 10, 1938. He had come at the request of the Carnegie Corporation, which had commissioned him to head a comprehensive study of the status of African Americans. Among his first undertakings was a tour of the American South. This journey brought the energetic Swede face-to-face with Jim Crow segregation and discrimination against blacks. It also impressed on him the backwardness of the southern economy and the extreme poverty of most people in the region, especially but not only blacks. The journey convinced Myrdal of the importance of his mission for the nation as a whole.[1] With these stark images of a caste society and economic underdevelopment foremost in his mind, Myrdal and a distinguished staff and team of research collaborators began the research for *An American Dilemma: The Negro Problem and American Democracy.*[2]

The book was two impressive volumes. Throughout most of its pages, *An American Dilemma* provided a detailed account of discrimination against blacks in every domain of American life, debunked claims of innate black inferiority, and examined in detail black institutions (e.g., the church and political organizations). *An American Dilemma* provided the most comprehensive and shocking portrayal of the status of blacks ever assembled. Yet the legacy of Myrdal was not, in the main, the conditions he documented. Myrdal's legacy is to be found in the interpretive context in which he set "the Negro problem in American democracy."

Myrdal's analysis declared that above all else the race problem was a moral dilemma. He suggested that the United States, more than any other industrial society, possessed an explicit and popularly understood political culture that extolled the values of freedom, individual rights, democracy, equality, and justice. The status and treatment accorded African Americans by their fellow white citizens, however, stood in sharp contrast to what Myrdal viewed as the national religion or, more fittingly, the "American Creed."

Most white Americans, in his judgment, faced an "ever-raging conflict" between their general values, as expressed in the American creed, and their specific attitudes and behaviors toward blacks. The "American dilemma" was the inherent moral discomfort white Americans experienced in their relation to blacks.

An American Dilemma decisively reshaped how educated and liberal whites, especially those in the North, understood the race problem in American society. It is difficult to overestimate the impact of the book in this regard. According to the historian David Southern, "Myrdal's book played a significant role in changing the thought patterns and feelings of a people. For twenty years the Swede's authority was such that liberals simply cited him and confidently moved on."[3] Myrdal's biographer, Walter Jackson, wrote that *An American Dilemma* "established a liberal orthodoxy on black-white relations and remained the most important study on race issues until the middle 1960s."[4]

Indeed, Myrdal's work was a genuine cultural input to the coalescence of what has been called America's Second Reconstruction. The Second Reconstruction was a short but critical era from roughly the late 1950s to the mid-1960s, when the U.S. Supreme Court, the Congress, and the White House appeared to act in unison to protect the basic citizenship rights of black Americans.[5] The reach of Myrdal's influence is perhaps most clearly seen in explicit reference to *An American Dilemma* in the landmark 1954 *Brown v. Board of Education* ruling—the still controversial footnote 11—and the subsequent denunciation of Myrdal by southern defenders of segregation and other extreme right-wing groups.[6]

His influence had been seen earlier. The report of President Truman's Committee on Civil Rights, *To Secure These Rights,*[7] adopted Myrdal's theme of the contradiction between democratic values and the conditions of blacks. Truman's committee also borrowed one other notion from Myrdal, namely, his faith that American social values would win out over the customs, interests, and prejudices that had to that point combined to subjugate blacks in the postslavery American South.

From Optimism to Pessimism

Myrdal had been optimistic about the course future events would take. He anticipated positive change because the nation had much to gain from modernizing the southern economy; because levels of education were rising, particularly for blacks, who were increasingly migrating to urban and northern areas; and because changes had been induced by the wartime mobilization. The core, deeply rooted commitment to the American creed, along with these other inducements and opportunities, prompted him to adopt the optimistic assessment that the American dilemma would be resolved in favor of equality and integration.

Yet generating optimism about the course of black-white relations is perhaps harder now than at any other point in the post–World War II period. To be sure, a quarter of a century ago the Kerner Commission warned us: "Our nation is moving toward two societies, one black, one white, separate and unequal."[8] In the wake of the Simi Valley police brutality verdict and the rebellions in Los Angeles in 1992, even these words seem pallid and inadequate to capture the enormous gulf in perception, social standing, and identity that apparently still separates black and white Americans from one another. Myrdal's optimism now seems too naive. It is perhaps fitting then that Andrew Hacker's more recent book, *Two Nations: Black and White, Separate, Hostile, Unequal,* updates and provides an even bleaker assessment of race relations in the United States than the Kerner Commission did.[9]

At bottom, Hacker's point is that white-dominated society and institutions have never intended full inclusion for blacks and do not now show any real inclination toward bringing it about. An equally bleak depiction of race relations was offered in *Faces at the Bottom of the Well: The Permanence of Racism,* by Derrick Bell, a black legal scholar.[10] For Bell, each wave of racial change, reform, and apparent progress, in the end, merely reconstitutes black subordination on a new plane. The underlying racial hierarchy in the United States has not fundamentally changed. Although the Kerner Commission shared Hacker's and Bell's belief that white racism was the central cause of the oppressive conditions in which black Americans lived, it stressed that the rift between black and white could be reduced through "new attitudes, new understanding, and above all, new will" to address the racial divisions in the United States. Much of the recent scholarship and dialogue on race doubts the potential for genuine transformation of the type once envisioned by Myrdal and, to a degree, even the Kerner Commission.

The purpose of this essay is to assess whether these new attitudes have emerged or show any sign of emerging. Have racial attitudes genuinely improved, and are there grounds for optimism? Or is Hacker's prophecy that the United States faces "a huge racial chasm . . . and there are few signs that the coming century will see it closed" the more accurate forecast?[11] Although many positive changes in racial attitudes have taken place, we believe that racism is the core problem affecting black-white relations and that it remains a disfiguring scar on the American body politic.

We characterize and explain the changing racial attitudes of white Americans as a shift from Jim Crow racism to laissez-faire racism. We review patterns of change in racial attitudes as documented in major social surveys, evaluate several explanations of these changes, and then propose our own account. This account explores at some length key sociological works on the civil rights movement and its accomplishments. We do so because it is necessary to ground our argument firmly in a detailed understanding of the pivotal changes in social structure that opened the door for a shift from Jim Crow racism to laissez-faire racism. We then rely on Herbert Blumer's theory of "prejudice as a sense of group position" to link the attitudinal record of change to the record of social and political change.[12]

From Jim Crow Racism to Laissez-Faire Racism

Along with Howard Schuman and Charlotte Steeh, Lawrence Bobo, the senior author of this essay, wrote a book assessing broad patterns of change in American racial attitudes.[13] Writing in 1985, we concluded that whites' attitudes toward blacks had undergone a dramatic positive transformation. A key aim of this essay is to delimit the scope and meaning of that transformation more precisely. Specifically, we suggest that in the post–World War II period the predominant pattern of racial attitudes among white Americans has shifted from Jim Crow racism to a modern-day laissez-faire racism. We have witnessed the virtual disappearance of overt bigotry, demands for strict segregation, advocacy of governmentally enforced discrimination, and adherence to the belief that blacks are the categorical intellectual inferiors of whites. Yet Jim Crow racism has not been replaced by an embracing and democratic vision of the common human- ity, worth, dignity, and equal membership of blacks in the polity. Instead, the tenacious institutionalized disadvantages and inequalities created by the long slavery and Jim Crow eras are now popularly accepted and con- doned under a modern free-market or laissez-faire racist ideology.

Laissez-faire racism blames blacks themselves for the black-white gap in socioeconomic standing and actively resists meaningful efforts to ame- liorate America's racist social conditions and institutions. These racial at- titudes continue to justify and explain the prevailing system of racial dom- ination, even while a core element of racist ideology in the United States has changed. Jim Crow racism was premised on notions of black biolog- ical inferiority; laissez-faire racism is based on notions of black cultural inferiority. Both serve to encourage whites' comfort with and acceptance of persistent racial inequality, discrimination, and exploitation.

It is important to differentiate our ideas about laissez-faire racism from the concept of symbolic racism. Symbolic racism is a theory of modern prejudice proposed by David Sears and his colleagues.[14] It maintains that a new form of politically potent antiblack prejudice emerged after the civil rights era. The waning of "old-fashioned racism," which involved overt derogation of blacks as inferior to whites and explicit insistence on ra- cial segregation, opened the door to newer, more subtle antiblack senti- ments. These new sentiments fused deeply rooted antiblack feelings, typ- ically learned early in life, with long-standing American values, such as the Protestant work ethic. When blacks demand integration or such pol- icies as affirmative action, under this theory, many whites react with op- position based on this attitude. The symbolic racist resents blacks' de- mands and views them as unfair impositions on a just and good society that warrant rejection.

At no point, even in the most extensive theoretical statements offered after more than a decade and a half of research,[15] do the symbolic racism researchers attempt an explanation of why "old-fashioned racism" went into decline or why "modern racism" assumes the specific form and con- tent it does. This significant omission in theoretical development is, how- ever, a virtual necessity of the logic of the theory. To wit, this model of prej- udice expressly denies that there is any material social basis to the formation of antiblack attitudes outside of processes of socialization and the opera- tion of routine cognitive and emotional psychological processes.

Our proposition about the emergence of laissez-faire racism, while sharing with symbolic racism a concern with central strands of the modern racial attitudes of white Americans, nevertheless differs in three critical ways from symbolic racism. First, as we develop below, our theory of laissez-faire racism is explicitly based on a historical analysis of the changing economics and politics of race in the United States. We argue that Jim Crow racist ideology reflected the economic and political needs, as well the prevailing cultural trends, of a specific historical epoch (the post–Civil War American South) and set of historical actors (principally the old southern planter elite). As the economic and political power of this group waned, as cultural trends changed, and as the power resources of the black community developed, Jim Crow social structures and ultimately Jim Crow ideology were defeated. Left in its place was the new laissez-faire racism. Laissez-faire racism legitimates persistent black oppression in the United States but in a fashion appropriate to a modern, nationwide, industrial free-labor economy and polity. We view the labels Jim Crow racism and laissez-faire racism as more specific and historically accurate than the vague expressions "old-fashioned racism" and "modern racism" used in the symbolic racism literature.

Second, the theory of laissez-faire racism is expressly rooted in a sociological theory of prejudice. We elaborate on Blumer's classic statement on prejudice as a sense of group position.[16] It places a subjective, interactively and socially created, and historically emergent set of ideas about appropriate status relations between groups at the center of any analysis of racial attitudes. The framework takes seriously the imperatives deriving from the institutionalized structural conditions of social life and from the process of human interaction, subjectivity, and interpretation that lend meaning to social conditions and thereby come to guide behavior.

Third, the theory of symbolic racism focuses principally on the individual and several specific attitudes that individuals may or may not hold. The theory of laissez-faire racism, as we develop it here, focuses principally on predominant social patterns. These patterns are an aggregation of individual views, to be sure. Yet our main concern is not with variation in the attitudes of individuals but with the common or general pattern of thoughts, feelings, and beliefs about blacks. In that sense, we seek to characterize the current historical epoch, not simply or mainly to explain the distribution and effects of the attitudes of individuals.

If the nature and causes of this transformation from the once dominant ideology of Jim Crow racism to the currently dominant ideology of laissez-faire racism fit the data we discuss below, then Hacker's and Bell's pessimism may be solidly grounded. Neither the decline of Jim Crow racism nor the emergence of laissez-faire racism can be attributed to the goodwill of the American people or to the gradual ascendancy of the American creed of freedom, equality, justice, and democracy.[17] On the contrary, both of these epochal ideologies appear to involve support for specific forms of racial domination. These forms of domination each fit the different economic and political conditions of their eras.

Why Call it Racism?

For those who may doubt that the United States, which is legally committed to an antidiscrimination policy, still is a racially dominative society, we review a few facts.[18] First, the black-white gap in socioeconomic status remains enormous. Black adults remain two-and-one-half times as likely as whites to be unemployed. Strikingly, this gap exists at virtually every level of the educational distribution.[19] If one casts a broader net to ask about "underemployment"—those who have fallen out of the labor force entirely, are unable to find full-time work, or are working full-time at below poverty-level wages—then the black-white ratio in major urban areas has over the past two decades risen from the customary 2 to 1 disparity to very nearly 5 to 1.[20] Conservative estimates show that young, well-educated blacks who match whites in work experience and other characteristics still earn 11 percent less annually.[21] Studies continue to document direct labor market discrimination at both low-skill, entry-level positions[22] and more highly skilled positions.[23] A growing number of studies indicate that even highly skilled and accomplished black managers encounter "glass ceilings" in corporate America,[24] prompting one set of analysts to suggest that blacks will never be fully admitted to the power elite.[25]

Judged against differences in wealth, however, the huge black-white gaps in labor-force status and earnings seem absolutely paltry.[26] The average differences in wealth show black households lagging behind white ones by nearly twelve to one. For every one dollar of wealth in white households, black households have less than ten cents. In 1984 the median level of wealth held by black households was around $3,000; for white households the figure was $39,000. Indeed, white households with incomes of between $7,500 and $15,000 have "higher mean net worth and net financial assets than black households making $45,000 to $60,000."[27] Whites near the bottom of the white income distribution have more wealth than blacks near the top of the black income distribution.

Wealth is in many ways a better indicator of likely quality of life than earnings are. When we pose a few hypothetical questions, the reasons for this claim become clear. If we envision an "average" black family with about $3,000 in wealth and an average white family with about $39,000 in wealth we might then ask: which of these families is best equipped to send a child to college for four years? Which of these families could best survive a four-month period of unemployment? Which of these families could pay for costly medical treatment? Which of these families can attempt to start a business of its own? Indeed, which of these families might be able to do all of these things, and which one might be unable to do any? The gaping disparity in accumulated wealth is the real inequality in standard of living produced by three hundred plus years of systematic and pervasive racial discrimination.

Second, blacks are far and away the group from which whites maintain the greatest social distance.[28] The demographers Douglas Massey and Nancy Denton concluded that it makes sense to describe the black condition as "hypersegregation." Blacks are the only group, based on 1980 census data for large metropolitan areas, to rank as "hypersegregated" on four or more measures, and this was true for sixteen areas covering nearly a quarter of all blacks.[29] Housing audit studies continue to show high levels of direct racial discrimination in the housing market.[30] Middle-class blacks have enormous difficulty translating their economic gains into residential mobility, which has been a critical pathway to assimilation into the economic and social mainstream for other groups. Residential segregation has social consequences. As we all know, neighborhoods vary in services, school quality, safety, and levels of exposure to a variety of unwanted social conditions.[31]

Third, the value this society places on black life appears to be in steady decline. This is seen in how blacks and black life are treated by the criminal justice system as well as in overall figures in life expectancy. A 1990 study showed that fully 42 percent of black males between the ages of eighteen and twenty-four in the nation's capital are in jail, on probation, or have warrants out for their arrest. Blacks are seven times more likely than whites to die as victims of homicide. Blacks who kill whites are more severely punished than whites who kill blacks.[32] When blacks kill whites, prosecutors are forty times more likely to request the death penalty than when blacks kill other blacks. Such profound differences prompted retiring Supreme Court justice Harry Blackmun to publicly repudiate the death penalty.

Looking beyond violent crime and the criminal justice system, black life expectancy at birth declined for four years in a row between 1985 and 1989, although this was a period of modest but continuing increase in life expectancy for whites. Most stunning, the decline in 1988 reached such a level that it brought down the overall national average. Yet our national leadership conveyed no sense of real emergency about this shocking set of social statistics.

We could go on, but the severity of the disparities and the extent to which they cut across class lines in the black community are sufficiently clear to establish a strong prima facie case for maintaining that the United States society still has a system of racial domination.

The Attitudinal Record

In assessing whether there are any grounds for optimism about racial attitudes, we rely on data derived from sample surveys, especially national surveys, of Americans concerning their views on race and race relations. A word about the validity of such data is in order. Many observers doubt that people will honestly discuss their racial attitudes with an anonymous interviewer. Some contend that even if survey questions were answered accurately, the answers necessarily provide a superficial view of complex human thoughts and emotions and often have only a tenuous connection to behavior and other social outcomes.[33]

Evidence of "duplicity" in surveys takes several forms. White respondents have often been found to give more liberal responses to black interviewers than to white interviewers. Electoral contests that pit a black against a white candidate have on several occasions posed a serious problem for pollsters. There is little doubt that some "socially desirable" responses are given in surveys. At the same time, however, there is considerable evidence of complexity, nuance, and, in some instances, fairly overt racism in the attitudes expressed in response to survey questions.

Do racial attitudes, even if measured with reasonable accuracy, influence individual behavior? A number of the most glaring failures to find a connection between attitudes and behavior—most notably R. T. La-Piere's classic 1934 study[34]—have involved interracial settings.[35] Assuming that attitudes are accurately measured, there is good reason to believe that they will affect patterns of behavior,[36] even in the area of race relations.[37] Since the strength of the association between attitudes and behavior varies with situational and individual factors, however, attitudes must be regarded as but one input to behavior, not the overwhelming determinant of behavior.

Accumulating evidence also suggests that attitudes influence both interpersonal and larger political behaviors. For example, explicitly antiblack attitudes played an important role in determining support for California's historic Proposition 13.[38] Negative racial attitudes also played a part in people's willingness to join in collective action against the use of school busing for desegregation.[39] An increasing number of analysts and scholars are convinced that racial attitudes now play a central role in American political identities and behavior,[40] including voting in national elections. In sum, an individual's attitudes and beliefs about race have important effects on interpersonal behaviors and a range of political choices and actions.

Are attitudes measured in surveys superficial indicators? Perhaps so. Trend studies may be particularly subject to this charge since they are typically unable to probe the emotional tonality of beliefs, the frames of reference and assumptions that underlie individuals' attitudes, and the behavioral inclinations that flow from them. However, no other approach can assess in an empirically verifiable and replicable way how representative samples of a population think, feel, and believe. Nor can any other method trace as systematically how those thoughts, beliefs, and feelings have changed over time. Large-scale surveys are thus one important lens on how and why attitudes on race take the patterns they do.

Patterns of Change in Racial Attitudes

The longest trend data from national sample surveys may be found for racial attitude questions that deal with matters of racial principles, the implementation of those principles, and social distance preferences. Principle questions ask whether American society should be integrated or segregated and whether individuals should be treated equally, without regard to race. Such questions do not raise issues of the practical steps that might be necessary to accomplish greater integration or to ensure equal treatment. Implementation questions ask what actions, usually by government, especially the federal government, ought to be taken to bring about integration, to prevent discrimination, and to achieve greater equality. Social distance questions ask about the individual's willingness to personally enter hypothetical contact settings in schools or neighborhoods that vary from virtually all white to heavily black.[41]

Transformation of Principles

Questions on racial principles provide the most consistent evidence on how the attitudes of white Americans toward blacks have changed. From crucial baseline surveys conducted in 1942, trends for most racial principle questions show whites increasingly support the principles of racial integration and equality. Whereas a solid majority, 68 percent, of white Americans in 1942 favored segregated schools, only 7 percent took such a position in 1985 (see figure 8.1). Similarly, 55 percent of whites surveyed in 1944 thought whites should receive preference over blacks in access to jobs, compared with only 3 percent who offered such an opinion as long ago as 1972. Indeed, so few people were willing to endorse the discriminatory response to this question on the principle of race-based labor market discrimination that it was dropped from national surveys after 1972. On both these issues, then, majority endorsement of the principles of segregation and discrimination have given way to overwhelming majority support for integration and equal treatment.

This pattern of movement away from support for Jim Crow toward apparent support for racial egalitarianism holds with equal force for those questions dealing with issues of residential integration, access to public transportation and public accommodations, choice among qualified candidates for political office, and even interracial marriage. It is important to note, however, that the high levels of support seen for the principles of school integration and equal access to jobs (both better than 90 percent) do not exist for all questions on racial principles. Despite improve-

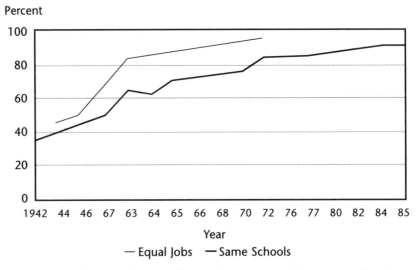

Figure 8.1. Trends in Racial Principle Questions among Whites, 1942–85. (Based on data in Howard Schuman, Charlotte Steeh, and Lawrence Bobo, *Racial Attitudes in America: Trends and Interpretations* [Cambridge, Mass.: Harvard University Press, 1985], 74–75.)

ment from extraordinarily low levels of support in the 1950s and 1960s, survey data continue to show substantial levels of white discomfort with the prospect of interracial dating and marriage, for instance.

Opinions among whites have never been uniform or monolithic. Both historical[42] and sociological research[43] has pointed to lines of cleavage and debate in whites' thinking about the proper place of African Americans. The survey-based literature has shown that views on issues of racial principle vary greatly according to region of the country, level of education, age or generation, and ideological factors. As might be expected, opinions in the South more lopsidedly favored segregation and discrimination at the time baseline surveys were conducted than was true outside the South. Patterns of change, except for a period of unusually rapid change in the South, have usually been parallel, though. The highly educated also typically express greater support for principles of racial equality and integration. Indeed, one can envision a tiered reaction to issues of racial justice. At the more progressive and liberal end are college-educated whites who live outside the South. At the bottom are southern whites with the least amount of schooling.[44] Age plays a part as well. Younger people usually express more racial tolerance than older people do. Differences in socialization during more tolerant time periods and in average levels of education across generations help account for this pattern.[45]

There has been a sweeping transformation of attitudes about the rules that should guide black-white interaction in the more public and impersonal spheres of social life. Those living outside the South, the well-educated, and younger people led the way on these changes. However, change has usually taken place in all categories of people. Schuman, Steeh, and Bobo characterized this change as a fundamental transformation of social norms regarding race. Robert Blauner's in-depth interviews with blacks and whites over nearly three decades led him to a very similar conclusion: "The belief in a right to dignity and fair treatment is now so widespread and deeply rooted, so self-evident that people of all colors would vigorously resist any effort to reinstate formalized discrimination. This consensus may be the most profound legacy of black militancy, one that has brought a truly radical transformation in relations between the races."[46] In short, a tremendous progressive trend has been evident in white racial attitudes where the broad issues of integration, equality, and discrimination are concerned.

Those who believe that America is making progress toward resolving the "American dilemma" point to this evidence as proof that Americans have taken a decisive turn against racism. As Richard G. Niemi, John

Mueller, and Tom W. Smith argued, "Without ignoring real signs of en-during racism, it is still fair to conclude that America has been success-fully struggling to resolve its Dilemma and that equality has been gain-ing ascendancy over racism."[47] If anyone doubts the validity of this transformation, it is noteworthy that even former Klansman David Duke felt compelled to assert that he was no longer a bigot and had shed parts of his past during his failed bid to become governor of Louisiana. Whether his claim is true is less important than the fact that Duke had to take such a public position. Some ideas—support for segregation, open discrimi-nation, and claims that blacks are inherently inferior to whites—have fallen into deep public disrepute. Surveys have documented the speed, social location, and breadth of this transformation.

Resistance to Policy Change

If trends in support of progressive racial principles are the optimistic side of the story of the transformation of racial attitudes, the patterns for implementation questions are the pessimistic side of the story. It should be noted that efforts to assess how Americans feel about government ef-forts to bring about greater integration and equality or to prevent discrim-ination really do not arise as sustained matters of inquiry in surveys un-til the 1960s. To an important degree, issues of the role of government in bringing about racial change could not emerge until sufficient change involving the basic principles had actually occurred.

There are sharp differences between support for racial principles and support for policy implementation. This is not surprising insofar as prin-ciples, viewed in isolation, need not conflict with other principles, inter-ests, or needs that often arise in more concrete situations. However, the gaps between principle and implementation are large and consistent in race relations. In 1964, for example, surveys showed that 64 percent of whites nationwide supported the principle of integrated schooling; how-ever, only 38 percent thought that the federal government had a role to play in bringing about greater integration (see figure 8.2). The gap had actually grown larger by 1986, when 93 percent supported the principle, but only 26 percent endorsed government efforts to bring about school integration. We return to this point later.

Similar patterns emerge in the areas of jobs and housing. Support for the principle of equal access to jobs stood at 97 percent in 1972. Support for federal efforts to prevent job discrimination, however, had reached only 39 percent. Likewise in 1976, 88 percent supported the principle that blacks have the right to live wherever they can afford, yet only 35 percent

Percent

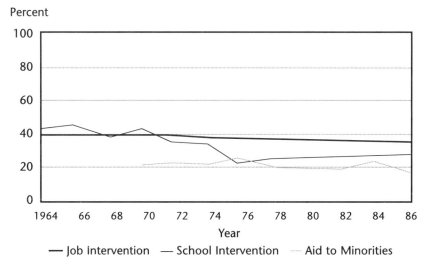

— Job Intervention   — School Intervention   ⋯ Aid to Minorities

Figure 8.2. Trends in Implementation Questions among Whites, 1964–86. (Based on data in Howard Schuman, Charlotte Steeh, and Lawrence Bobo, *Racial Attitudes in America: Trends and Interpretations* [Cambridge, Mass.: Harvard University Press, 1985], 88–89.)

said they would vote in favor of a law requiring homeowners to sell without regard to race.

There are not only sharp differences in absolute levels of support when moving from principle to implementation but also differences in trends. Most striking, there is a clear divergence of trends in the area of school integration. During the 1972 to 1986 time period, when support for the principle of integrated schooling rose from 84 percent to 93 percent, support for government efforts to bring about integration fell from 35 percent to 26 percent. It should be noted that this decline is restricted almost entirely to those living outside the South. This trend reverses the tier-tolerance effect described earlier. By 1978 there was virtually no difference between college-educated whites outside the South and southern whites who had not completed high school when it came to supporting federal efforts to help bring about school integration. To put it colloquially, Bubba and William F. Buckley increasingly found themselves in agreement on this issue.

Two complexities are worthy of note. First, a couple of implementation issues do show positive trends. The most clear-cut case involves a question on whether the government has a role to play in assuring blacks fair access to hotels and public accommodations. This may be the only instance where parallel questions on principle and implementation show parallel positive change. A somewhat similar pattern is found for the principle of residential integration and support for an open or fair housing law. However, even as recently as 1988 barely 50 percent of white Americans endorsed a law that would forbid racial discrimination in the sale or rental of housing.

It should be borne in mind that antiblack animus is not the only source of opposition to government involvement in bringing about progressive racial change. Howard Schuman and Lawrence Bobo have shown that whites are equally likely to oppose open housing laws whether the group in question is black, Japanese American, or another minority.[48] There appears to be an important element of objection to government coercion in this domain that influences attitudes. At the same time, however, Schuman and Bobo also found that whites express a desire for greater distance from blacks than they do from other groups.

Second, opposition to implementation is widespread and is not substantially affected by the usual socioeconomic characteristics of respondents, including education, region, and age. Weak to nonexistent effects of education and age in particular suggest that we are unlikely to see much change in the future.

Unfortunately, comparatively few survey trend questions speak directly to affirmative action policies. Many different questions have been asked beginning in the mid-1970s. Affirmative action is a much maligned and misunderstood concept. Affirmative actions can range from advertising and special recruitment efforts to preferential treatment requiring quotas. Support for affirmative action varies dramatically, depending on exactly which type of policy is proposed.[49] Policies that mainly aim to increase the human capital attributes of blacks are comparatively popular.[50] Policies that lean in the direction of achieving equal outcomes, as powerfully symbolized by the term *quotas,* elicit overwhelming opposition among whites.

Theories of the Change

Cohort vs. Individual Change

If we think in descriptive rather than explanatory terms, the progressive trend in racial attitudes can be traced to one of two sources. First, part of the rise in racial liberalism on matters of principle can be credited to what demographers call cohort replacement effects. As older, less tolerant individuals die and are replaced by younger, more tolerant individuals, a progressive trend results. Second, part of the progressive trend can be traced to individual change. People who once advocated segregation and discrimination might undergo soul-searching and a change of heart, coming instead to see the case for integration and equality. This process also helped produce the progressive trend in support for racial principles.

Research suggests that the process of change is itself changing. During the 1950s and 1960s, there is evidence that both a large measure of individual change and cohort replacement effects contributed to positive attitude change. During the 1970s, individual attitude change and cohort replacement effects shifted to a less balanced mixture of the two. In addition, the distance between younger cohorts and their predecessors began to narrow (the size of the cohort effect decreased), strongly suggesting that the engines of change were cooling off. Work by Glenn Firebaugh and Kenneth E. Davis shows that the mixture of cohort replacement effects and individual change is increasingly issue-specific and region-specific.[51] On the issue of racial intermarriage, for example, there was no evidence of individual-level change between 1974 and 1984. Furthermore, most of the change seen in the South in the post-1974 period was attributable to cohort replacement effects. Whatever the mix of forces that propelled the progressive movement in whites' attitudes on issues of racial principles appears to be grinding to a halt, especially in the South.

Despite these patterns, there is no evidence of a broad backlash in racial attitudes. Many have expressed special concern that young adults, those who underwent critical socializing experiences during the Reagan-Bush years, are the source of a racial backlash. Work by Charlotte Steeh and Howard Schuman indicates no distinctive pattern of backward movement among younger adults; indeed, they continue to be a bit more liberal than their immediate predecessors.[52] What evidence there is of retreat is quite issue-specific; most whites, regardless of age, have become less supportive of policies that imply racial preference.

These cohort studies are valuable, but they are also limited. None of these analyses of cohort replacement or individual change as sources of the sweeping increase in support for racial equality and integration is explanatory. They provide merely statistical decompositions of trends, not substantive explanation of the roots of change. For that we must turn elsewhere.

Myrdal's Hypothesis

One possibility, of course, is Myrdal's guilt hypothesis. He proposed that the discomfort and guilt created by the ever-raging conflict in the white American would increasingly be resolved in favor of racial equality. Any number of direct efforts to test Myrdal's hypothesis have failed to support it, however. Even in the 1940s and 1950s, few whites felt that blacks were unfairly treated.[53] Those who acknowledged differences in treatment were quick to offer justifications for it.[54] Even more recent efforts to create sophisticated tests of Myrdal's ideas produced no support for the hypothesis.[55] The empirical research literature also provides no support for it.

Rejecting Myrdal's guilt hypothesis does not mean embracing the position that whites' racial attitudes generally reflect undifferentiated hostility toward blacks. An argument closely related to Myrdal's formulation can be called the "ambivalence hypothesis." Irwin Katz, Joyce Wackenhut, and R. Glen Hass have proposed that whites' racial attitudes are profoundly ambivalent, mixing both aversive and sympathetic tendencies.[56] Which one of these inclinations predominates in thinking is a function, in their argument, of other contextual factors. Using college student subjects in experimental settings, Katz and his colleagues have shown that contextual cues validating individualism, hard work, and self-reliance will incline whites to focus on blacks' shortcomings in these areas. Contextual cues that reinforce egalitarianism and humanitarianism will elicit more sympathetic responses to blacks. The ambivalence theory, however, fails to specify the likely predominant tenor of responses or how these ambivalent feelings are likely to play out in concrete social settings. More important, the ambivalence hypothesis does not explain the persistent and considerable opposition to a broad range of policies aimed at substantially improving the conditions of blacks.

Decline of Biological Racism

A second substantive explanation of the larger progressive trend is that key beliefs in the case for segregation and discrimination suffered a direct cultural assault and quickly eroded. Surveys showed that popular acceptance of the belief that blacks were less intelligent than whites went into rapid decline in the post–World War II period. In 1942, 53 percent of white Americans nationwide expressed the opinion that blacks were less intelligent than whites. By 1946, this percentage had declined to 43 percent—a 10 percent drop in only four years. By 1956, fully 80 percent of whites nationwide rejected the idea that blacks were less intelligent.

What seemed the bedrock belief in the case for a racially segregated and discriminatory social order had undergone a precipitous drop in acceptance. It is therefore not surprising that support for segregation and discrimination in schools, in housing, and the like would also gradually go into decline. The fight against racism, the considerable contribution of blacks in the war effort during the 1940s, and the continued trend in academe away from accepting notions of biologically given racial groupings all may have contributed to this process.[57]

Yet this explanation seems lacking. It begs the question of why popular acceptance of biological racism, an attitude in its own right, went into decline. What is more, there are strong grounds to believe that negative stereotypes of blacks remain widespread. A major national survey carried out in 1990 used a set of questions intended to measure social stereotypes. Respondents used bipolar scales to rate traits. Members of each of several social groups were rated as to whether they tended to be rich or poor, hard working or lazy, intelligent or unintelligent, and so on. The format of the questions did not force respondents to merely accept or reject a simplistic statement.

White Americans rated blacks, Hispanics, and Asians as less intelligent, more violence prone, lazier, less patriotic, and more likely to prefer living off welfare than whites were. Whites typically placed Asian Americans lower than whites but substantially ahead of blacks and Hispanics. Not only were whites rated more favorably than were people of color, but on four of the five personality traits examined, many whites rated the majority of blacks and Hispanics as possessing negative qualities, whereas a majority of whites were rated as possessing positive qualities.[58]

As figure 8.3 shows, some 56 percent of whites rated blacks as less intelligent than whites (two-and-a-half times the rate suggested by older,

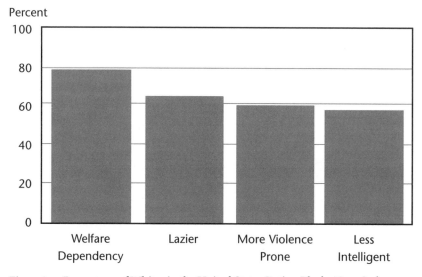

Figure 8.3. Percentage of Whites in the United States Rating Blacks Negatively, 1990. (Based on data in James A. Davis and Tom W. Smith, *The General Social Survey: Cumulative Codebook and Data File* [Chicago: National Opinion Reserach Center and University of Chicago, 1990].)

Percent

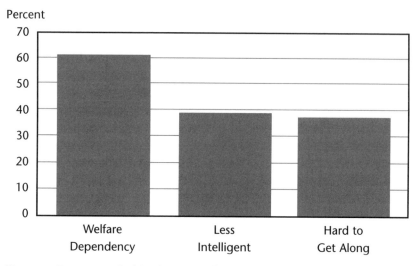

Figure 8.4. Percentage of Whites in Los Angeles County Rating Blacks Negatively, 1992. (Based on data in Lawrence Bobo, Camille L. Zubrinsky, and Melvin L. Oliver, "Public Opinion before and after a Spring of Discontent," in *The Los Angeles Riots: Lessons for the Urban Future,* ed. Mark Baldassare [Boulder, Colo.: Westview, 1994], 118.)

closed-ended format survey items). Fully 78 percent rated blacks as more likely to prefer living off welfare than whites were. Largely similar patterns—though not so extreme—were found in a more recent survey in the Los Angeles County area, as shown in figure 8.4.[59]

Whatever else one might say about the progressive trend in racial attitudes, it has not brought an end to negative stereotyping of blacks. Instead, the character or extremity of stereotyping has changed. What were once viewed as categorical differences based in biology now appear to be seen as differences in degree or tendency.[60] Furthermore, these differences in degree appear to be understood as having largely cultural roots, not biological roots.[61] We therefore do not accept the view of declining negative stereotypes about blacks as a crucial source of the broader shift in views on segregation, discrimination, and the principle of equal treatment.

African Americans appear to occupy the bottom rung of the American "rank order of discrimination." If the degree of social distance that members of other groups wish to maintain from members of a specific out-group provides any guide, blacks may be the most systematically avoided group in the United States. Data from the 1992 Los Angeles County Social Survey showed that feelings of social distance were greatest when nonblacks were asked to react to blacks. These are particularly telling results since they are based on data involving large samples of white, Hispanic, and Asian respondents. Figures 8.5 and 8.6 present, respectively, the average level of objection to residential integration and to interracial marriage across all groups toward a specific target group. That is, all nonblack respondents were asked to react to blacks, all nonwhite respondents were asked to react to whites, and so on. The exact percentage of expressed opposition to social contact is not the critical issue here, since that is highly dependent on the exact wording of the question. What seems more telling is the unambiguously greater average level of hostility to contact with blacks among nonblacks than occurs in reference to any other group.

Basic Roots of the Shift

If these other explanations, including Myrdal's guilt hypothesis, are unacceptable, what accounts for the momentous changes that occurred in whites' racial attitudes? We believe that structural changes in the American economy and polity that reduced the importance of the Jim Crow system of exploited black agricultural labor to the overall economy lie at

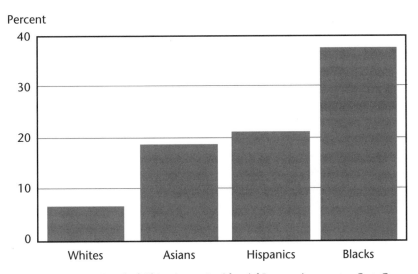

Figure 8.5. Average Level of Objection to Residential Integration among Out-Group Members, Los Angeles County, 1992. (Based on data in Lawrence Bobo, Camille L. Zubrinsky, and Melvin L. Oliver, "Public Opinion before and after a Spring of Discontent," in *The Los Angeles Riots: Lessons for the Urban Future,* ed. Mark Baldassare [Boulder, Colo.: Westview, 1994], 125.)

Percent

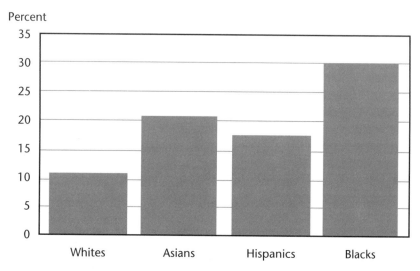

Figure 8.6. Average Level of Objection to Racial Intermarriage among Out-Group Members, Los Angeles County, 1992. (Based on data in Lawrence Bobo, Camille L. Zubrinsky, and Melvin L. Oliver, "Public Opinion before and after a Spring of Discontent," in *The Los Angeles Riots: Lessons for the Urban Future,* ed. Mark Baldassare [Boulder, Colo.: Westview, 1994], 125.)

the base of the positive change in racial attitudes. In short, the structural need for Jim Crow ideology disappeared. Correspondingly, though slowly and only in response to aggressive and innovative challenge from the black civil rights movement, political and ideological supports for Jim Crow institutions yielded. The defeat of Jim Crow ideology and the political forms of its institutionalization (e.g., segregated schooling and public facilities, voting hindrances) was the principal accomplishment of the civil rights movement.

We submit that there are inevitable connections between economic and political structures, on the one hand, and patterns of individual thought and action, on the other hand. As the structural basis of long-standing patterns of social relationships changes, there is a corresponding potential for change in the ways of thinking, feeling, and behaving that had previously been commonplace.

Our argument is similar to Myrdal's. His optimism about the future course of race relations in the United States rested explicitly on a set of ideas about economic interests and needs, demographic trends, and the wartime mobilization, which he thought would all work in the direction of more fully integrating blacks into American society. We part company with Myrdal, however, when he argued that the American creed was a fundamental impetus to changing conceptions of the place of African Americans. Instead, we are impressed with how long many white Americans have been comfortable with conditions in the black community and in the daily lives of African Americans that constitute profound violations of the high moral purposes articulated in the American creed.

Our analysis of the sources of change in racial attitudes rests principally on three important sociological works analyzing the emergence, dynamics, and impact of the civil rights movement. Doug McAdam's *Political Process and the Development of Black Insurgency, 1930–1970* provides a rich analysis of how socioeconomic and demographic shifts fundamentally altered the power resources in the black community, opening the door to a sustained, innovative, and potent social movement.[62] Aldon Morris's *Origins of the Civil Rights Movement* reveals in detail the internal organizational dimensions of strategies used by black communities and leadership as they set about mobilizing the growing resource base in their own communities for political and economic gain.[63] Jack Bloom's *Class, Race, and the Civil Rights Movement* helps pinpoint that the great success of the civil rights movement was the political defeat of the old planter aristocracy, whose economic fortunes were most dependent on the Jim Crow strictures that kept blacks a poor, indebted agricultural labor force.[64] Taken together, these works provide a detailed picture of how the interweaving of the economy and the polity resulted in changes in the status of blacks and set the stage for the emergence of a new American ideology on race.

Economics, Demographics, and Black Institutional Development

Four factors, according to McAdam, set the stage for the emergence of a sustained and potent civil rights movement: (a) a series of reinforcing socioeconomic and demographic changes that led to (b) expanded political opportunities for blacks, which in turn (c) increased the potential for developing strong internal indigenous organizations and thus stimulated a larger (d) cognitive transformation of consciousness within the black population. So long as blacks were a severely oppressed, poorly educated, predominantly southern, and mainly rural agricultural labor force, they were unlikely to be able to mount effective political resistance.

During the Jim Crow era, core institutions of the black community that would later become engines of the civil rights movement—the black church, black colleges and universities, and such organizations as the NAACP—were fledgling versions of what they would become. From roughly 1880 through 1930, the black church tended to espouse an "other worldly" theology of waiting for better treatment in the afterlife, and black congregations tended to be small, financially strapped units headed by poorly educated ministers. Black colleges were sorely underfunded, and many provided little more than the equivalent of a high school education. The NAACP, founded in 1909–10, was principally a northern organization, focused on crafting its long-term legal strategy for change.

The position of blacks as an impoverished and acutely oppressed agricultural labor force began to shift decisively with the decline of "king cotton." Increasing foreign competition, the introduction of new technologies and synthetic fibers, the boll-weevil infestation, and the declining centrality of cotton to the American export economy began to push more blacks out of the rural South to earn a living.

The importance of the decline of cotton in laying the foundations for black insurgency cannot be underestimated. Indeed, according to McAdam, "the factor most responsible for undermining the political conditions that, at the turn of the century, had relegated blacks to a position of political impotence . . . would have to be the gradual collapse of cotton as the backbone of the southern economy."[65] When measured by the amount of cotton acreage harvested and the average seasonal price of cotton per pound, the decline in cotton was enormous. Examining data from the U.S. Bureau of the Census, McAdam reports that the price of raw cotton took a nose dive "from a high of 35 cents per pound in 1919 to less than 6 cents in 1931."[66] From 1931 to 1955, the price of raw cotton actually rose, but during this same period, the total amount of cotton harvested significantly decreased as planters attempted to increase the demand for cotton.

In addition, with World War I and the cessation of heavy European immigration, there was a growing need for black labor in the industrial North. The combination of these and other forces created one of the greatest internal migrations of all time. Upwards of about 200,000 blacks migrated to the North in the 1900–1909 period, while the next decade witnessed the greatest amount of black out-migration, at over 500,000.[67] The migration of blacks out of the South subsequently affected the total number of southern black farm operators, which had reached a high in 1920, at just over 915,000, only to plummet to a low of 267,000 by 1959.[68] Blacks shifted from a largely rural and southern population to a heavily urban and increasingly northern population.

These changes, in turn, had a series of effects that altered the resource base for the critical black institutions of the church, black colleges and universities, and the NAACP. The rise in the number of blacks in urban settings had the effect of increasing their economic resources and reducing the level of intimidation and violence used to repress blacks. Urban black church congregations tended to be much larger and have much more substantial financial support. This facilitated hiring better-trained and better-educated ministers. These forces, coupled with greater political latitude in urban areas, contributed to a shift in the theological emphasis in many black churches toward an increasing concern for justice in the here and now.

At the same time, the growing success of the NAACP legal strategy, which initially sought to force southern states to live up to the "separate but equal" doctrine, had led to important increases in the resource base at historically black colleges and universities. More blacks thus began to receive better college educations. Moreover, the number and size of NAACP chapters in southern states rose as the number of blacks in the urban South rose. In short, according to McAdam, formidable changes in the power resources within black communities took place, particularly between the early 1900s and the early 1950s. The economic footing of black communities improved, and the institutional base for political action increased dramatically.

Indigenous Resource Mobilization

Morris carefully documents the patterns of social networks and organization building in black communities. For example, he shows the lines of communication among the newer, better-educated group of black ministers, epitomized by Dr. Martin Luther King Jr. He also reviews the high level of internal financing that supported such organizations as the Montgomery Improvement Association (MIA), which directed the historic 1955–56 bus boycott. Networks, a new indigenous leadership cadre, and internal financial support were essential to the type of "local movement center," such as the MIA, which became a politicized umbrella organization linking black ministers and their congregations. Morris also points to the mass base of the protest movement that King came to spearhead and the extent to which targeted nonviolent social protest became a genuine power resource in the struggle for racial change. Critically, Morris documents how the increasing persecution directed at the NAACP in much of the South impelled the development of such new organizational forms as the MIA and, subsequently, the Southern Christian Leadership Conference (SCLC). To forge the link to McAdam's analysis more directly, Morris documents how larger trends in the economy and the resource base of critical black institutions discussed by McAdam were, in turn, translated into organization building and sustained, effective mass protest at the grassroots level in black communities.

The ability to mount effective protest campaigns at the grassroots level in southern black communities reached its pinnacle after the Montgomery bus boycott of 1955. The boycott gave blacks a sense that they could effect political change through insurgent actions spearheaded and organized by existing black institutions and community organizations.

Following success in Montgomery, a series of interlocking networks linking several existing institutions and protest organizations coalesced and became the launching pad for targeted protest efforts designed to dramatize the second-class citizenship status of blacks. Using the black church as the central "coordinating unit," such groups as the SCLC, MIA, NAACP Youth Councils, the Congress of Racial Equality (CORE), the Student Nonviolent Coordinating Committee (SNCC), and black fraternities and sororities worked together to challenge Jim Crow segregation in the South.

Morris's discussion of the emergence and rapid spread of the sit-in strategy in the South during the late 1950s and early 1960s provides a clear picture of the intricate and deliberate formation of the networks. Disputing "myths" that the sit-in tactic was a spontaneous, independently conducted, and student-run operation originating in Greensboro, North Carolina, in 1960, Morris shows how such efforts actually grew out of existing institutions and organizations (e.g., the black church) composed of both veteran civil rights workers and student members in the late 1950s. The church served as the core of the network. Church ministers often wore more than one hat. On Sundays they not only preached the gospel but also often, as members and leaders of SCLC, CORE, and the activist wing of the NAACP, served as political activists, encouraging their congregations to donate to and participate in local protest activities to improve their standard of living in the here and now. Morris writes, "These ministers were not only in a position to organize and commit church resources to protest efforts, they were also linked to each other and the larger community via ministerial alliances. In short, between 1955 and 1960 a profound change in Southern black communities had begun. Confrontational politics were thrust to the foreground through new direct-action organizations closely allied with the church."[69]

Included in this new alliance were black colleges, fraternities, and sororities. According to Morris, the emergence and proliferation of the sit-in movement cannot be understood without acknowledging the interaction between black colleges and such local movement centers as the church. Many of the student leaders were also church members and had learned whatever they knew about the civil rights movement and nonviolent protest from their local churches even before sit-ins were instituted as a protest strategy. The organizational base to launch and coordinate sit-ins thus stemmed from the church—with black college students, through their fraternities and sororities, serving as the foot soldiers. The actual organization, financing, and spread of sit-ins followed an elaborate pattern of coordination among a variety of groups. Morris describes the sequence:

> organizers from SCLC, NAACP, and CORE raced between sit-in points relaying valuable information. Telephone lines and the community "grapevine" sent forth protest instructions and plans. These clusters were the sites of numerous midday and late night meetings where the black community assembled in the churches, filled the collection plates, and vowed to mortgage their homes to raise the necessary bail-bond money in case the protesting students were jailed. Black lawyers pledged their legal services to the movement and black physicians made their services available to injured demonstrators. Amidst these exciting scenes, black spirituals calmed and deepened the participant's commitment.[70]

Collectively throughout the South, such activities served to create, sustain, and develop a mass church-based movement designed to dramatize the second-class citizenship status of blacks.

Defeat of the Planter Class

To this picture, Bloom adds critical information concerning the old white planter aristocracy.[71] He maintains that the principal political accomplishment of the civil rights movement was the defeat of the power of the old planter elite. This group benefited most directly from Jim Crow ideology and practices. Correspondingly, it was this group that played a pivotal role in first launching the White Citizens' Councils (WCC) in reaction to the *Brown* decision's call for an end to the doctrine of "separate but equal." In speaking of the WCC, Bloom notes:

> The impetus, the organization, the leadership, and the control of this movement rested in the hands of the traditional black-belt ruling class that had emerged after Reconstruction. That class was still centered in the black belt, though in most cases now in small towns. Its members were businessmen and bankers in these areas, as well as merchants and landlords. . . . It was the old Southern ruling class that set state policy. It was, moreover, the Deep South states of Georgia, Mississippi, Alabama, Louisiana, and South Caro-

lina that, in addition to Virginia, made up the core of the resistance. In these states the old Southern ruling class remained the strongest. In almost every single case where the White Citizens' Council emerged, they were led and organized from the black belt.[72]

As Bloom points out, the WCC drew their leadership "primarily from the ranks of the white community's business, political, and social leadership. . . . these are the same people who made up the 'courthouse cliques' that ran the South, the 'banker-merchant-farmer-lawyer-doctor-governing' class."[73] The WCC used a variety of tactics to dissuade blacks who supported desegregation, for it was this old planter elite, still located in the cotton-producing "black-belt" areas, that most depended on the Jim Crow social order for their livelihoods. So vested were they in maintaining the racial status quo that they engaged in numerous acts of economic coercion, political manipulation, and ruthless violence. Only when these failed were efforts made to compromise with black leaders.

Economic coercion was one of the most common tactics used by the White Citizens' Councils. Any black who attempted to register to vote, sign petitions favoring school desegregation, or was a member of the NAACP faced economic pressures. According to Bloom, "Bankers would deny loans; black merchants couldn't get credit from wholesale houses or sometimes could not get supplies even with cash; insurance policies were canceled; employees were dismissed; renters evicted from their homes; mortgages recalled." Blacks were also forced to apply economic pressure to other blacks. "Blacks dependent on whites for employment or credit were often forced to boycott black ministers or doctors or craftsmen who were violating the racial etiquette."[74]

Another tactic took the form of political manipulation, where members of the WCC regularly redivided voting districts in an effort to limit the black vote. When redistricting was not enough, in several counties in Alabama, for example, blacks were summarily removed from voter registration rolls for such trivial excuses as spelling errors.[75] As if economic and political pressure were not enough, violence was readily perpetrated and became the most effective and oppressive force used against blacks.

Structural Change and Changing Attitudes

The declining importance of cotton to the U.S. economy and as a source of livelihood for blacks opened the door to tremendous economic and political opportunity for blacks. The product of these opportunities, stronger churches, colleges, and political organizations, culminated in a sustained movement of protest for racial justice. The movement and the organizations it created had indigenous leadership, financing, and a genuine mass base of support. Through creative, carefully designed, and sustained social protest, this movement was able to topple a distinct, epochal form of racial oppression that was no longer essential to the interests and needs of a broad range of American political and economic elites.

Widespread cultural attitudes endorsing elements of the Jim Crow social order, quite naturally then, began to atrophy and wither under a steady assault by blacks and their white allies. Segregationist positions were under steady assault and increasingly lacked strong allies. The end product of these forces, the decline of Jim Crow racism, is the broad pattern of improvement seen in whites' racial attitudes in the United States.

The effectiveness of the NAACP's legal strategy challenging segregation, the passage of the Civil Rights Act of 1964, and the passage of the Voting Rights Act of 1965 amounted to an authoritative legal and political rebuke of the Jim Crow social order. This rebuke, however, did not directly alter the socioeconomic status of blacks, especially those living in the northern urban areas. This rebuke also did not directly alter entrenched patterns of racial residential segregation that existed nationwide.[76] Nor did widespread attitudes of hostility toward blacks suddenly disappear.[77] The enormous and far-reaching successes of the civil rights movement did not eliminate stark patterns of racial domination and inequality that existed above and beyond the specific dictates of the distinctly southern Jim Crow system. Instead of witnessing genuine racial comity, we saw the rise of laissez-faire racism.

The Sense of Group Position and Changing Racial Attitudes

Students of prejudice and racial attitudes may have misunderstood the real "object" of racial attitudes. The attitude object, or perceptual focus, is not really the social category "blacks" or "whites," whether as groups or individuals. It is not neighborhoods or schools of varying degrees of racial mixture. Instead, as Herbert Blumer argued forty years ago,[78] the real object of "prejudice," what we are really tapping with our questions, is attitude toward the proper relation between groups: that is, the real attitude object is relative group positions. This sense of group position is historically and culturally rooted, socially learned, and modifiable in response to new information, events, or structural conditions so long as these factors contribute to or shape contexts for social interaction among members of different groups.

What does this "group position" view of racial attitudes mean in the context of all that we have reviewed to this point? First, attitudes toward "integration" or toward "blacks" are, fundamentally, statements about preferred positional relations among groups. They are not simply or even mainly emotional reactions to groups, group symbols, or situations. Nor are they best understood as statements of simple feelings of like or dislike of minority groups and their members. Nor are they simply perceptions of group traits and dispositions. Instead, racial attitudes capture preferred group positions and those patterns of belief and feeling that undergird, justify, and make understandable a preference for relatively little group differentiation and inequality under some social conditions or for a great deal of differentiation and inequality under others.

In the case of changing white racial attitudes in the United States, increasing openness to the principle of integrated education does not mean a desire for greater contact with blacks or even an attachment to integrated education. From the vantage point of group position theory, it means declining insistence on forced group inequality in educational institutions. Declining support for segregated public transportation does not signal a desire for more opportunities to interact with blacks on buses, trains, and the like. Instead, it means a declining insistence on compulsory inequity in group access to this domain of social life.

Second, the group position view sees change in political and economic structures as decisively shaping the socially constructed and shared sense of group position. The sources of change in attitudes—changes in preferred group positions—are not found principally in changing feelings of like and dislike. Changes in the patterns of mass attitudes reflect changes in the structurally based, interactively defined and understood needs and interests of social groups. To put it differently, to have meaning, longevity, and force in people's everyday lives, the attitudes individuals hold must be linked to the organized modes of living in which people are embedded.[79] A demand for segregated transportation, segregated hotels, and blanket labor market discrimination increasingly rings hollow under an economy and polity that have less need for—in fact may be incurring heavy costs because of—the presence of a super exploited, black labor pool. When the economic and political needs of significant segments of a dominant racial group no longer hinge on a sharp caste system for effective functioning, the ideology that explained and justified such a caste system should weaken. It becomes vulnerable to change; its costs should become increasingly apparent—and be rejected.

Third, a key link between changing structural conditions and the attitudes of the public are those prominent social actors who articulate, and frequently clash over and debate, the need for new modes of social organization.[80] The claims and objectives of leaders presumably spring from their conceptions of the interests, opportunities, resources, and needs of the group at a particular point in time. Readily appreciated examples of the role of leaders include the justices' 1954 *Brown* decision, President Kennedy's speech following the effort to enroll two black students at the University of Mississippi, President Johnson's invocation of the civil rights slogan "We shall overcome," and perhaps most memorably Dr. Martin Luther King's "I have a dream" speech.

Of course, not all leadership statements and actions were supportive of positive change. There were White Citizens' Councils, Ku Klux Klan rallies, and a wide variety of other forms of resistance to change. Indeed, Kennedy's speech, which the historian Carl Brauer credits with launching the Second Reconstruction,[81] followed on the heels of Alabama governor George Wallace's "Segregation now! Segregation tomorrow! Segregation forever" declaration. In addition, there were powerful voices and forces on the Left activated by the civil rights movement that were demanding greater change than either Kennedy or Johnson was ready to accept. Our point is that the direction and tenor of change is shaped in the larger public sphere of clashes, debate, political mobilization, and struggle.

Conclusion

Racism Old and New

Can we now share the faith and optimism that Gunnar Myrdal expressed in 1944? Or are the bleak depictions offered by Andrew Hacker and Derrick Bell more accurate analyses? We cannot share Myrdal's optimism, although we resist pessimism and despair.

The long and unabated record of sweeping change in racial attitudes that national surveys document cannot be read as a fundamental breakdown in either racialized thinking or antiblack prejudice. Instead, we have witnessed the disappearance of a racial ideology appropriate to an old social order, that of the Jim Crow South. A new and resilient laissez-faire racism ideology has arisen in its place. As a result, America largely remains "two nations," with African Americans all too often viewing the world from the "bottom of the well."

Jim Crow racism went into decline partly because of a direct and potent assault on it by the civil rights movement. Jim Crow practices and ideology were weakened by an interlocking series of social changes—the declining importance of cotton production to the U.S. economy, limited immigration from Europe, black migration to urban and northern areas—which dramatically increased the power and resources available to black communities. The economic basis for Jim Crow racism had eroded; its political underpinnings were gradually undone by the *Brown* decision, the Civil Rights Act of 1964, the Voting Rights Act of 1965, and other political successes of the civil rights movement.

If racial attitudes reflect the structural conditions of group life,[82] then it is no surprise that Jim Crow attitudes in the public, such as near consensual support for strict segregation and open discrimination—all premised on the assumed biological inferiority of blacks and necessary for the Jim Crow cotton economy—would eventually and steadily ebb in popular acceptance. Jim Crow racism was no longer embedded in American economic or political institutions, and because of the civil rights movement, most of its ideological tenets came to be widely understood as inconsistent with American values.

Despite these monumental changes, blacks and other people of color remain racially segregated and economically disadvantaged. These social conditions continue to prompt many white Americans to feel that they stand to loose something tangible if strong efforts are made to improve the living conditions of people of color. Persistent socioeconomic inequality and residential segregation provide the kernel of truth needed to regularly breathe new life into old stereotypes about putative black proclivities toward crime, violence, and welfare dependency. Viewed in this light, the gap between increasingly egalitarian racial principles and resistance to strong forms of affirmative action is not paradoxical at all. Both are products of changes in the American social structure and politics that successfully deposed Jim Crow institutions but left large numbers of blacks victims of discrimination and residents of poor, isolated ghetto communities.

The end product of these conditions and processes is a new racialized social order with a new racial ideology—laissez-faire racism. Under this regime, blacks are blamed as the cultural architects of their own disadvantaged status. The deeply entrenched cultural pattern of denying societal responsibility for conditions in many black communities continues to foster steadfast opposition to affirmative action and other social policies that might alleviate race-based inequalities. In short, many Americans have become comfortable with as much racial segregation and inequality as a putatively nondiscriminatory polity and free-market economy can produce. Such individuals also tend to oppose social policies that would substantially improve the status of blacks, hasten the pace of integration, or aggressively attack racial discrimination. Enormous racial inequalities thus persist and are rendered culturally palatable by the new laissez-faire racism.

Waiting for the Next Myrdal, King, and Third Reconstruction

The current historical juncture is one of unclear trajectory. A number of conditions, the positive legacy of the civil rights movement and the Second Reconstruction, are salutary. The black middle class is larger and has more resources than at any previous point in American history.[83] It also has the potential of accomplishing greater residential mobility.[84] These positive accomplishments can be seen most clearly in the cultural realm, where black writers, artists, musicians, entertainers, and movie makers have risen to prominence. At the same time, the movement has had a limited impact on the economic conditions of large segments of urban black communities. The circumstances of many poor ghetto communities are difficult at best and are even deteriorating.[85] Along with this deterioration comes the potential to intensify popular negative images of blacks as a dangerous male criminal element or as female welfare cheats exploiting overly generous social programs and wasting the hard-earned tax dollars of working middle Americans.[86]

Because of these conflicting trends, it is not possible to make a simple forecast about the next stage of race relations. On the one hand, the positioning and accomplishments of the black middle class can be read as foreshadowing an era when it would no longer be appropriate to describe the United States as racist or perhaps even as a racialized social order. On the other hand, the social and political response to signs of pathology in poor black communities foreshadows a hardening of both social outlooks and social policy in ways that have an unmistakable racial component. The sharp turn against affirmative action in California and Texas also signals a hardening climate of race relations.

Yet we do not believe that positive change in the future is impossible. Given all that we have argued above, however, another major wave of positive change in racial attitudes and ideology in the United States will hinge on four types of factors. First, economic conditions must favor chances for redistribution. An expanding economy has been an essential ingredient of black progress in the past, and that pattern is likely to hold true in the future.[87] If most white Americans view the economic pie as shrinking, they are less likely to welcome any form of pressure to share that pie more generously with others.[88] Second, a sympathetic and widely shared interpretation of the conditions and dynamics of the status of African Americans must take root, at least at the level of cultural elites. In the absence of a convincing analysis of both the social barriers black communities face and appropriate responses to them that a wide spectrum of social and political elites take seriously, the cultural climate is much less likely to be receptive to another wave of large-scale change. Necessary changes in attitudes and opinions among the mass public will therefore be much harder to accomplish.

Third, new forms of organizing, directing, and applying the political resources of black communities are likely to be needed. In short, another Martin Luther King and the dynamic social forces he came to spearhead and symbolize may be needed. Whether the charismatic leadership, lofty rhetoric, and protest politics seen during the civil rights era will be necessary is unclear at best. What is clear is that institutionalized inequalities and the patterns of thinking and behaving that reconstitute them each day are likely to be undone only when challenged directly and in a sustained manner. Fourth, if economic conditions, predominant outlooks among elites, and the political strategies of black communities and their allies meet these conditions, we may witness a "third reconstruction." Another wave of relatively coordinated political reform involving the judicial, legislative, and executive branches of government may emerge under this scenario and thereby open the way to profound changes in the status of African Americans.

We have sketched an extraordinarily complex and improbable sequence of events. Furthermore, even if these events were to come about, they might result in the emergence of a "new racism" tied to some future configuration of race, economy, and politics. Only if racial identities, racialized social conditions (e.g., segregation), and the commitment to group position that such identities and conditions foster are directly reshaped would we avoid merely reconstituting racial inequality in a fashion that parallels the shift from Jim Crow racism to laissez-faire racism. Two encouraging trends in this direction are the rising rate of black-white intermarriages and the growing critical examinations of whiteness and white identity.[89]

Notes

1. Walter A. Jackson, *Gunnar Myrdal and America's Conscience* (Chapel Hill: University of North Carolina Press, 1990).

2. Gunnar Myrdal, *An American Dilemma: The Negro Problem and Modern Democracy*, 2 vols. (New York: Random House, 1944).

3. David W. Southern, *Gunnar Myrdal and Black-White Relations: The Use and Abuse of "An American Dilemma," 1944–1969* (Baton Rouge: Louisiana State University Press, 1994), xvi.

4. Jackson, *Gunnar Myrdal and America's Conscience*, xviii.

5. Carl M. Brauer, *John F. Kennedy and the Second Reconstruction* (New York: Columbia University Press, 1977); C. Vann Woodward, *The Strange Career of Jim Crow*, 3d rev. ed. (New York: Oxford University Press, 1974).

6. See Southern, *Gunnar Myrdal and Black-White Relations*, 155–86.

7. U.S. President's Committee on Civil Rights, *To Secure These Rights* (New York: Simon and Schuster, 1947).

8. National Advisory Commission on Civil Disorders, *Report of the National Advisory Commission on Civil Disorders* (New York: Bantam Books, 1968), 1.

9. Andrew Hacker, *Two Nations: Black and White, Separate, Hostile, Unequal* (New York: Macmillan, 1992).

10. Derrick Bell, *Faces at the Bottom of the Well: The Permanence of Racism* (New York: Basic Books, 1992).

11. Hacker, *Two Nations*, 219.

12. Herbert Blumer, "Race Prejudice as a Sense of Group Position," *Pacific Sociological Review* 1, no. 1 (1958): 3–7.

13. Howard Schuman, Charlotte Steeh, and Lawrence Bobo, *Racial Attitudes in America: Trends and Interpretations* (Cambridge, Mass.: Harvard University Press, 1985).

14. Donald R. Kinder and David O. Sears, "Prejudice and Politics: Symbolic Racism versus Racial Threat to the Good Life," *Journal of Personality and Social Psychology* 40, no. 3 (1981): 414–31; John B. McConahay, "Modern Racism, Ambivalence, and the Modern Racism Scale," in *Prejudice, Discrimination, and Politics*, ed. John F. Dovidio and Samuel L. Gaertner (New York: Academic, 1986), 91–124; David O. Sears, "Symbolic Racism," in *Eliminating Racism: Profiles in Controversy*, ed. Phyllis A. Katz and Dalmas A. Taylor (New York: Plenum, 1988), 53–84.

15. Sears, "Symbolic Racism"; Donald R. Kinder, "The Continuing American Dilemma: White Resistance to Racial Change Forty Years after Myrdal," *Journal of Social Issues* 42 (Summer 1986): 151–71; David O. Sears, Colette Van Laar, Mary Carillo, and Rick Kaslerman, "Is It Really Racism? The Origins of White American's Opposition to Race-Targeted Policies," *Public Opinion Quarterly* 61 (Spring 1997): 16–53.

16. Blumer, "Race Prejudice as a Sense of Group Position."

17. Compare Myrdal, *American Dilemma*.

18. Prominent legal scholars have pointed to the persistence of racism despite the enactment of antidiscrimination law. See Charles R. Lawrence, "The Id, the Ego, and Equal Protection: Reckoning with Unconscious Racism," *Stanford Law Review* 39

(January 1987): 317–52; and Kimberle W. Crenshaw, "Race, Reform, and Retrench-ment: Transformation and Legitimation in Antidiscrimination Law," *Harvard Law Review* 101 (May 1988): 1331–87.

19. Gerald D. Jaynes, "The Labor Market Status of Black Americans: 1939–1985," *Journal of Economic Perspectives* 4, no. 4 (1990): 9–24; Franklin D. Wilson, Marta Tien-da, and Lawrence Wu, "Race and Unemployment: Labor Market Experiences of Black and White Men, 1968–1988," *Work and Occupations* 22 (Summer 1995): 245–70.

20. Daniel T. Lichter, "Racial Differences in Unemployment in American Cities," *American Journal of Sociology* 93 (January 1988): 771–92; Roderick J. Harrison and Claudette E. Bennett, "Racial and Ethnic Diversity," in *State of the Union: America in the 1990s*, vol. 2, ed. R. Farley (New York: Russell Sage, 1995), 141–210.

21. Reynolds Farley, *Blacks and Whites: Narrowing the Gap?* (Cambridge, Mass.: Harvard University Press, 1984), 80.

22. Joleen Kirschenman and Kathryn M. Neckerman, "We'd Love to Hire Them, But . . . : The Meaning of Race for Employers," in *The Urban Underclass*, ed. C. Jencks and P. E. Peterson (New York: Brookings Institution, 1991), 203–31; Margery A. Turner, Michael Fix, and Raymond J. Struyk, *Opportunities Denied, Opportunities Diminished: Racial Discrimination in Hiring*, Urban Institute Report 91-9 (Washington, D.C.: Urban Institute Press, 1991); Roger Waldinger and Thomas Bailey, "The Continuing Significance of Race," *Politics and Society* 19 (September 1991): 291–329.

23. Joe R. Feagin and Melvin P. Sikes, *Living with Racism: The Black Middle-Class Experience* (Boston: Beacon, 1994).

24. John P. Fernandez, *Black Managers in White Corporations* (New York: John Wiley, 1975); Edward W. Jones, "Black Managers: The Dream Deferred," *Harvard Business Review* 64 (May–June 1986): 84–93; Ryan A. Smith, "Race, Income and Au-thority at Work: A Cross-Temporal Analysis of Black and White Men (1972–1994)," *Social Problems* 44 (February 1997): 19–37.

25. Richard L. Zweigenhaft and G. William Domhoff, *Blacks in the White Estab-lishment: A Study of Race and Class in America* (New Haven, Conn.: Yale University Press, 1990).

26. Gerald D. Jaynes and Robin M. Williams. *A Common Destiny: Blacks and American Society* (Washington, D.C.: National Academy Press, 1989); Melvin L. Ol-iver and Thomas M. Shapiro, *Black Wealth/White Wealth: A New Perspective on Ra-cial Inequality* (New York: Routledge, 1995).

27. Paul Starr, "Civil Reconstruction: What to Do without Affirmative Action," *American Prospect* (Winter 1992): 12.

28. Lawrence Bobo and Camille L. Zubrinsky, "Attitudes on Residential Integra-tion: Perceived Status Differences, Mere In-group Preferences or Racial Prejudice?" *Social Forces* 74 (March 1996): 883–909; Camille L. Zubrinsky and Lawrence Bobo, "Prismatic Metropolis: Race and Residential Segregation in the City of Angels," *So-cial Science Research* 25 (December 1996): 335–74; Martin Sanchez Jankowski, "The Rising Significance of Status in U.S. Race Relations," in *The Bubbling Cauldron: Race, Ethnicity, and the Urban Crisis*, ed. M. P. Smith and J. R. Feagin (Minneapolis: Uni-versity of Minnesota Press, 1995), 77–98.

29. Douglas S. Massey and Nancy S. Denton, *American Apartheid* (Cambridge, Mass.: Harvard University Press, 1993).

30. Diana M. Pearce, "Gatekeepers and Homeseekers: Institutional Patterns in Racial Steering," *Social Problems* 26 (February 1979): 325–42; Margery A. Turner, "Discrimination in Urban Housing Markets: Lessons from Fair Housing Audits," *Housing Policy Debates* 3, no. 2 (1992): 185–215.

31. D. S. Massey, A. B. Gross, and M. L. Eggers, "Segregation, the Concentration of Poverty, and the Life Chances of Individuals," *Social Science Research* 20 (December 1991): 397–420.

32. General Accounting Office, *Death Penalty Sentencing: Research Indicates Patterns of Race Disparities*, Report to the Senate and House Committees on the Judiciary (Washington, D.C.: Government Printing Office, 1990), 5–6.

33. Herbert Blumer, *Symbolic Interactionism* (Los Angeles: University of California Press, 1969).

34. R. T. LaPiere, "Attitudes vs. Actions," *Social Forces* 13 (December 1934): 230–37.

35. Howard Schuman and Michael P. Johnson, "Attitudes and Behavior," *Annual Review of Sociology* 2 (1976): 161–206.

36. Russell H. Weigel and Lee S. Newman, "Attitudes-Behavior Correspondence by Broadening the Scope of the Behavioral Measure," *Journal of Personality and Social Psychology* 33, no. 6 (1976): 793–802.

37. Robert Brannon, Gary Cyphers, Sharlene Hesse, Susan Hesselbart, Roberta Keane, Howard Schuman, Thomas Viccaro, and Diana Wright, "Attitudes and Action: A Field Experiment Joined to a General Population Survey," *American Sociological Review* 38 (October 1973): 625–36.

38. David O. Sears and Jack Citrin, *Tax Revolt: Something for Nothing in California* (Cambridge, Mass.: Harvard University Press, 1985).

39. Thomas M. Begley and Henry Alker, "Anti-Busing Protest: Attitudes and Actions," *Social Psychology Quarterly* 45 (December 1982): 187–97; Garth D. Taylor, *Public Opinion and Collective Action: The Boston School Desegregation Conflict* (Chicago: University of Chicago Press, 1986); Bert Useem, "Solidarity Breakdown Model and the Boston Anti-Busing Movement," *American Sociological Review* 45 (June 1980): 357–69.

40. Edward G. Carmines and James A. Stimson, *Issue Evolution: Race and the Transformation of American Politics* (Princeton, N.J.: Princeton University Press, 1989); Jack Citrin, Donald P. Green, and David O. Sears, "White Reactions to Black Candidates: When Does Race Matter?" *Public Opinion Quarterly* 54 (Spring 1990): 74–96; T. Edsall and M. Edsall, "When the Official Subject Is Presidential Politics, Taxes, Welfare, Crime, Rights or Values . . . the Real Subject Is Race," *Atlantic Monthly*, May 1991, 53–86; Hacker, *Two Nations;* Thomas F. Pettigrew and Diane Alston, *Tom Bradley's Campaign for Governor: The Dilemma of Race and Political Strategies* (Washington, D.C.: Joint Center for Political Studies, 1988).

41. Schuman, Steeh, and Bobo, *Racial Attitudes in America.*

42. George M. Fredrickson, *The Black Image in the White Mind: The Debate on Afro-Americans' Character and Destiny, 1817–1914* (New York: Harper and Row, 1971); Winthrop D. Jordan, *White over Black: American Attitudes toward the Negro, 1550–1812* (Baltimore, Md.: Penguin Books, 1968).

43. Jonathan Turner and Royce Singleton, "A Theory of Ethnic Oppression: Toward a Reintegration of Cultural and Structural Concepts in Ethnic Relations The-

ory," *Social Forces* 56 (June 1978): 1001–18; Lawrence D. Bobo, "Group Conflict, Prejudice, and the Paradox of Contemporary Racial Attitudes," in *Eliminating Racism,* ed. Katz and Taylor, 85–119.

44. Schuman, Steeh, and Bobo, *Racial Attitudes in America,* 78.

45. A. Wade Smith, "Racial Tolerance as a Function of Group Position," *American Sociological Review* 46 (October 1981): 558–73.

46. Robert Blauner, *Black Lives, White Lives: Three Decades of Race Relations in America* (Berkeley: University of California Press, 1989), 317.

47. Richard G. Niemi, John Mueller, and Tom W. Smith, *Trends in Public Opinion: A Compendium of Survey Data* (New York: Greenwood, 1989), 167.

48. Howard Schuman and Lawrence Bobo, "Survey Based Experiments on Whites' Racial Attitudes toward Residential Integration," *American Journal of Sociology* 94 (September 1988): 273–99.

49. James R. Kluegel and Eliot R. Smith, *Beliefs about Inequality: Americans' View of What Is and What Ought to Be* (New York: Aldine de Gruyter, 1986); Seymour Martin Lipset and William Schneider, "The Bakke Case: How Would It Be Decided at the Bar of Public Opinion?" *Public Opinion* (March/April 1978): 38–48.

50. Lawrence Bobo and James R. Kluegel, "Whites' Stereotypes, Social Distance, and Perceived Discrimination toward Blacks, Hispanics, and Asians: Toward a Multiethnic Framework" (Paper presented at the annual meetings of the American Sociological Association, Cincinnati, August 25, 1991); Lawrence D. Bobo and James R. Kluegel, "Opposition to Race-Targeting: Self-Interest, Stratification Ideology and Racial Attitudes," *American Sociological Review* 58 (August 1993): 443–64.

51. Glenn Firebaugh and Kenneth E. Davis, "Trends in Anti-Black Prejudice, 1972–1984: Region and Cohort Effects," *American Journal of Sociology* 94 (September 1988): 251–72.

52. Charlotte Steeh and Howard Schuman, "Young White Adults: Did Racial Attitudes Change in the 1980s?" *American Journal of Sociology* 98 (September 1992): 340–67.

53. Herbert H. Hyman and Paul Sheatsley, "Attitudes toward Desegregation," *Scientific American* 195 (December 1956): 35–39; R. Williams, *Strangers Next Door: Ethnic Relations in American Communities* (Englewood Cliffs, N.J.: Prentice Hall, 1964).

54. Frank Westie, "The American Dilemma: An Empirical Test," *American Sociological Review* 30 (August 1965): 527–38.

55. S. Cummings and C. W. Pinnel III, "Racial Double Standards of Morality in a Small Southern Community: Another Look at Myrdal's American Dilemma," *Journal of Black Studies* 9 (September 1978): 67–86.

56. Irwin Katz, Joyce Wackenhut, and R. Glen Hass, "Racial Ambivalence, Value Duality, and Behavior," in *Prejudice, Discrimination, and Racism,* ed. Dovidio and Gaertner, 35–60.

57. Lawrence D. Bobo, "Attitudes toward the Black Political Movement: Trends, Meaning, and Effects on Racial Policy Preferences," *Social Psychology Quarterly* 51 (December 1988): 287–302.

58. Bobo and Kluegel, "Whites' Stereotypes, Social Distance, and Perceived Discrimination toward Blacks, Hispanics, and Asians."

59. See figure 4 in Lawrence Bobo, James H. Johnson, Melvin Oliver, James Sidanius, and Camille Zubrinsky, "Public Opinion before and after a Spring of Discontent: A Preliminary Report on the 1992 Los Angeles County Survey" (Occasional Working Paper Series 3, no. 1, Center for the Study of Urban Poverty, University of California, Los Angeles, 1992).

60. Mary R. Jackman and M. S. Senter, "Different Therefore Unequal: Beliefs about Trait Differences between Groups of Unequal Status," in *Research in Social Stratification and Mobility*, vol. 2, ed. Donald J. Treiman and Robert V. Robinson (Greenwich, Conn.: JAI, 1983), 309–35.

61. Bobo, "Group Conflict, Prejudice, and the Paradox of Contemporary Racial Attitudes," 105–6.

62. Doug McAdam, *Political Process and the Development of Black Insurgency, 1930–1970* (Chicago: University of Chicago Press, 1982).

63. Aldon D. Morris, *The Origins of the Civil Rights Movement: Black Communities Organizing for Change* (New York: Free Press, 1984).

64. Jack M. Bloom, *Class, Race, and the Civil Rights Movement* (Bloomington: Indiana University Press, 1987).

65. McAdam, *Political Process and the Development of Black Insurgency*, 73.

66. Ibid., 75.

67. Ibid., 74.

68. Ibid., 95.

69. Morris, *Origins of the Civil Rights Movement*, 753.

70. Ibid., 759.

71. Bloom, *Class, Race, and the Civil Rights Movement*.

72. Ibid., 101–2.

73. Ibid., 102.

74. Ibid., 99.

75. Ibid., 100.

76. Karl E. Taeuber and Alma F. Taeuber, *Negroes in Cities: Residential Segregation and Neighborhood Change* (Chicago: Aldine, 1965).

77. Paul B. Sheatsley, "Whites' Attitudes toward the Negro," *Daedalus* 95 (Winter 1966): 217–38.

78. Blumer, "Race Prejudice as a Sense of Group Position."

79. Earl Raab and Seymour Martin Lipset, "The Prejudiced Society," in *American Race Relations Today*, ed. Earl Raab (New York: Doubleday, 1962), 29–55.

80. Blumer, "Race Prejudice as a Sense of Group Position."

81. Brauer, *John F. Kennedy and the Second Reconstruction*, 259–64.

82. Raab and Lipset, "Prejudiced Society."

83. Jaynes and Williams, *Common Destiny*; Bart Landry, *The New Black Middle Class* (Berkeley: University of California Press, 1987).

84. Reynolds Farley and William H. Frey, "Changes in the Segregation of Whites from Blacks during the 1980s: Small Steps toward a More Integrated Society," *American Sociological Review* 59 (February 1994): 23–45.

85. William J. Wilson, *The Truly Disadvantaged: The Inner City, the Underclass, and Public Policy* (Chicago: University of Chicago Press, 1987); William J. Wilson, *When Work Disappears: The World of the Urban Poor* (New York: Alfred A. Knopf, 1996).

86. For images of blacks as dangerous criminals, see Elijah Anderson, *Streetwise: Race, Class, and Change in an Urban Community* (Chicago: University of Chicago Press, 1990), 163–89. For images of blacks as welfare cheats, see Lawrence Bobo and Ryan A. Smith, "Anti-Poverty Policy, Affirmative Action, and Racial Attitudes," in *Confronting Poverty: Prescriptions for Change*, ed. Sheldon Danziger, Gary Sandefur, and Daniel Weinberg (Cambridge, Mass.: Harvard University Press, 1994), 365–95; and Martin Gilens, "Racial Attitudes and Opposition to Welfare," *Journal of Politics* 57 (November 1995): 994–1019.

87. Jaynes and Williams, *Common Destiny*.

88. James E. Blackwell, "Persistence and Change in Intergroup Relations: The Crisis upon Us," *Social Problems* 29 (November 1982): 325–46.

89. On black-white rates of intermarriage, see Harrison and Bennett, "Racial and Ethnic Diversity," 164–67. On critical examinations of white identity, see Cheryl I. Harris, "Whiteness as Property," *Harvard Law Review* 106 (June 1993): 1710–91; Noel Ignatiev, *How the Irish Became White* (New York: Routledge, 1995); David R. Roediger, *The Wages of Whiteness: Race and the Making of the American Working Class* (New York: Verso, 1991).

First let us face what the Negro question is. It is an economic question; it is a political question; yes, so it is; but it is primarily a question of human relations, but not in the common sense of those words. . . . That is where we must begin. There is involved here a revolution in relations comparable only to the revolution which will emancipate labor and the revolution which will emancipate women.
—C. L. R. James, *American Civilization*

A belief in humanity is a belief in colored men.
—W. E. B. Du Bois, *Darkwater: Voices from within the Veil*

9   Toward an Effective Antiracism

Nikhil Pal Singh

At the dawn of the twentieth century, in the shadow of the failure of Reconstruction in the United States, W. E. B. Du Bois stood before the first Pan-African Congress in London and presented a startling formulation, one that established racial hierarchy and colonial domination as aspects of the same historical condition. "The problem of the twentieth century," he stated, "is the problem of the color line."[1] A few years earlier, in front of the American Negro Academy, Du Bois delivered what became his celebrated and widely known paper "The Conservation of Races" (1897). Addressing his audience in unequivocally nationalist accents, Du Bois spoke for "his people," those with whom he was "bone of the bone and flesh of the flesh"; those he would later describe as living within the Veil.[2] Without attacking the global problems of racism and empire directly, Du Bois emphasized another point, that "the Negro people *as a race*, have a contribution to make to civilization and humanity which no other race can make."[3]

As he composed his most famous work, *The Souls of Black Folk* (1903), a few years later, Du Bois deftly combined these two distinct appeals in his searching examination of the racial condition of the United States in the post-emancipation era. Advocating neither assimilation, and conse-

quent erasure of "Negro" distinctiveness, nor the preservation of an ab-
solutist and damaging conception of black difference, he doggedly attacked the color line, while refusing to denigrate those who had lived their
lives within it and had been defined by it. Subtly weaving the civilizationist
appeals of nineteenth-century black nationalism with an insistence on
what Albert Murray has called the "incontestably mulatto" character of
American culture, Du Bois effectively negotiated the double bind presented by American racism at the turn of the century.[4] Resisting both the segregationist implications of insisting on black autonomy and self-activity
and the assimilationist tendency to denigrate the cultural practices and
history of ex-slaves, Du Bois instead asked that the nation and the world
recognize the freedman as a "co-worker in the kingdom of culture."[5]

   This work of nearly a century ago marks the beginning of one man's
immense discursive labor of racial reconstruction, spanning the decades
of post-emancipation disenfranchisement and imperial conquest, as well
as the subsequent era of decolonization and the modern civil rights
movement. Yet today, as we sit on the threshold of the twenty-first century, the condition of poor communities of color, particularly black communities, is as dire as at any time in recent history. Standing in the shadow of the failure of the Second Reconstruction in the United States, do
we take courage from Du Bois's observations and insights about the First
Reconstruction, or do we simply despair?[6] To whom do we address ourselves today, when calling for solutions to the crisis of black politics and
theory, black life in America? Where is the color line? Where are the empires? How do we identify, and how do we confront the calamity that
befalls this generation of "black folk"? Most important, what do we make
of the fact that the "crisis" of which we speak—one of Du Bois's preferred
metaphors for describing what it meant to be black at the turn of the
century—today appears not as an exception but as the rule?[7]

   We have many answers to these questions, most of them unsatisfacto-
ry, if not misleading. Commentators of diverse political stripes, for example, have seized upon the argument that the explicit politics of racial
redress and the struggle for racial justice makes less and less sense due to
race's declining significance in the face of deepening class oppression and
(intraracial) class polarization.[8] Others, more disingenuous, have argued
that to gain influence again, American liberals and leftists must put aside
racial questions altogether, since by aligning progressive ideas under the
banner of antiracism, liberalism has done little more than alienate itself
from a "silent majority" of Americans and has initiated a backlash that
has pushed this country on a more or less continuous rightward course

since the late 1960s.[9] Finally, and perhaps most ingeniously, on the ascendant right it is imagined that the legacies of antiracism (i.e., antipoverty programs, affirmative action, and voting rights legislation) are now the real obstacles to achieving a truly "color-blind" America, as well as being the crutch that continues to hinder black bootstrap self-discipline and progress.[10]

Despite their differences, these positions constitute what amounts to a quite remarkable consensus, indicating that we may have entered a neo-racist, if not a *postracist*, age in the United States, which may hold some keys to understanding the current difficulties of black politics and theory.[11] The range of arguments outlined above represents the dissolution and perhaps even the appropriation of the political gains of *antiracist* theory and practice partially sedimented over the past fifty years, if not longer. Although enlightened elites (especially in the academy) may pay homage to a hollow multiculturalism or denounce the most egregious manifestations of hate speech and overt discrimination, contemporary politicians invariably fashion their appeals to justice, fairness, and expansive neutrality by consistently repudiating even the slightest suggestion that "race" might be a matter of public concern. The 1995 omnibus crime bill, for example (one of the few issues related to poor people of color where the state is still willing to spend money), could not even bear a whisper on behalf of racial justice in its repudiation of the justice-in-sentencing provision for death-row prisoners, who are disproportionately black. Meanwhile, the state of California, already in the forefront of anti-immigrant hysteria, now stands poised to overturn all forms of affirmative action to the applause of America's pundits. In a stunning turnabout, today *antiracism* is depicted as something akin to the boy who cried wolf, while *anti-antiracism* has become the sheep's clothing of "common sense" and fair play.

In the face of these influential and popular formulations, even our most articulate and empowered spokespersons have been reduced to making tepid pleas to what is left of the liberal conscience that "race matters."[12] I do not necessarily fault these efforts. They are an attempt, however insufficient, to hold the line against the combined assaults of neoliberal social policy and neoracist common sense that have accumulated over the past two decades. Nonetheless, it is quite clear that a great deal more needs to be said and done. In Harold Cruse's words, "the crisis in black and white" is still a crisis of social theory, although today it is also a crisis of politics and memory.[13] The political demand for color blindness, heard from all quarters of American public opinion today, is a demand to erase the memory of the struggles against racism; it is also an inadvertently apt description of how racism itself persists in all its forms, but in ways we often have difficulty identifying. Let us make no mistake, however. Right now we are in the midst of what Mike Davis correctly views as the most "drastic devaluation" of the citizenship of poor people of color in the United States since the end of the First Reconstruction, as what is left of the welfare state is slowly absorbed "by the police state."[14] In the face of this, there is little in the way of an effective antiracist challenge in sight.

I argue that the racial "crisis" that characterizes our own moment should be understood, at least in part, as an impasse of antiracism as a political project. Such an impasse should not be understood as a historically unique circumstance or as an unexpected setback in the long march of historical progress toward racial justice and equality in the United States during the twentieth century. Instead, it should be understood as a structural and recurrent dimension of a national formation that continues to be coded by a tortured dialectic of color and democracy. The question of why the ostensibly "color-blind," Enlightenment-based traditions of constitutional democracy in the United States have failed to resolve the persistence of racism and racial difference, in other words, cannot be answered by a simple reaffirmation of these traditions or by an argument that claims the virtues of a consistent theory of universal citizenship against the supposedly inconsistent practice of discrimination. A theory of U.S. history constructed from the standpoint of those subjected to the social practice of racism, for example, would have to probe more deeply—and with fewer illusions—the apparent contradiction itself, namely the American condition of racialized citizenship. The contours of such a theory, first outlined by Du Bois in *The Souls of Black Folk*, already exist in the century-long tradition of black reflection and resistance in the face of America's unfulfilled democratic revolution. The continuing excavation of such a theory, as I argue below, just might be a precondition for constructing an effective antiracism in the United States.[15]

It is useful to consider the ubiquity of the word *crisis* as a way of discussing America's racial predicament. *Crisis* generally refers to a moment of exceptional or extraordinary danger. Yet when we recognize just how regularly it appears as the defining term in discussions of "race" in America—Du Bois's, Cruse's, or our own—we must ask ourselves how it can effectively define or differentiate any one of these moments. The term *crisis* implies that a situation of normality exists in comparison, either as a precedent or as an expected resolution lying in wait in the future. Racism, however, as something that disrupts, dismembers, and disfigures black lives in America is, as Derrick Bell puts it, a "permanent" feature of U.S. society, constituting its normal reality and its normative history.[16] Paradoxically, the term *crisis* as one that denotes a historically exceptional circumstance is a remarkably antihistorical way of depicting the dilemmas of black politics and theory. Here, again, the crisis is not the exception but the rule.

Yet while racism and the racial "crisis" are not exceptional, they have not been unchanging. Rather, they have been shaped by both organic and conjunctural historical processes that have produced dramatic changes in the nature and scope of racial ideologies and significant changes in the social relations of "dominant and subordinate social groups who recognize themselves in terms of 'race.'"[17] The point that needs emphasizing is that racism, and hence the notion of race itself, is historically produced. Contemporary racial discourse binds together the legacies of racism *and* antiracism in structuring racial identities and the forms and horizons of social struggle. Antiracism in this sense must also be understood as a "permanent" feature of American life, constituting a history of continuous struggle, beginning with the efforts to abolish slavery, against the just as continuous and perhaps more forceful reinventions of racism in the twentieth century. As C. L. R. James suggested in 1950 in his fascinating and, until recently, unpublished cultural study of America, antiracism may actually be the one indispensable feature of every important progressive social struggle that has occurred in the United States. It was, for example, central to every significant invention and reinvention of American radicalism in the nineteenth century, including abolitionism, feminism, and populism, and in various ways it helped to pave the way for the rise of the CIO, the Popular Front, the New Left, and the cultural struggles for radical democracy in our own time.[18]

In its current incarnation, however, antiracism is an increasingly inadequate frame, too thinly descriptive and too narrowly construed to encompass the ways in which the struggles against racism have informed emancipatory politics over the past two centuries.[19] In its contemporary guise, antiracism is presented simply as the negation of the juridical structures of discrimination and the tangle of prejudicial "attitudes" that are thought to constitute a given racist complex, frequently in the name of "color-blind" universalism, citizenship, and equality. This form of antiracism, which I call *antiracist universalism*, tends to prematurely dissolve "race" in its earnest desire to transcend racism. Indeed, this form of antiracism has frequently had great difficulty distinguishing its attacks on

the color line from its discomfort and even antipathy toward the real
objects of racial discrimination. What antiracist universalism has had the
hardest time coming to terms with is the legacy of racially coded difference itself. Failing to eradicate this difference once and for all, its bewil-
dered idealism often turns into vengeful resentment against those who
initially evoked concern. Thus, in the end, even the most well-intentioned
proponents of this position have turned against it, implicitly or explicitly reproducing the oppressive interrogative that, as Du Bois noted, has
long been at the center of America's relation to its black people, namely,
"How does it feel to be [the] problem?"[20]

The bind that is presented to those who remain committed to antiracist politics is that antiracist universalism today has passed into anti-antiracism and even postracism. When an archconservative such as Newt
Gingrich, for example, can announce (in the past tense of course) that
"the one real success of modern liberalism was its opposition to segregation, and its support of the civil rights movement and decolonization,"[21]
then it should be clear that the resources of antiracist universalism have
been largely exhausted and deprived of their critical power.[22] Indeed, this
was prophesied over forty years ago by Ralph Ellison in his incisive critique of Gunnar Myrdal's *American Dilemma: The Negro Problem and
Modern Democracy,* still the definitive articulation of contemporary antiracist universalism. As Ellison pointed out, Myrdal and others who proposed that the "American Creed" held all the solutions to the problem
of racism and racial subjection operated under the arrogant delusion of
what Frantz Fanon called unilateral decrees of universality.[23] As a result,
they could scarcely apprehend the fact that black people, in Ellison's
words, had "made a life on the horns of the white man's dilemma."[24]

Myrdal, for example, argued that the "Negro problem" was a great stain
on the American democratic fabric, echoing earlier critiques of slavery
as a "peculiar" rather than the defining institution of the Republic. Further, he maintained that the postwar situation made it imperative that the
United States finally complete "the main trend in its history," or "the
gradual realization of the American Creed," in order to assume its proper role as world leader.[25] According to Myrdal, the "American Creed" was
the Americanization of the Enlightenment legacy, or the defense of human universality, equality, and formal freedom. Far from disproving the
notion that the Enlightenment had entered a glorious new incarnation
with the advent of the "American Century,"[26] the "Negro problem" was
the single glaring exception to the United States' otherwise justifiable
claim that it was, as Myrdal put it, "humanity in miniature."[27] Ironically,

while mounting what was at the time a remarkably comprehensive critique of segregation and discrimination, *An American Dilemma* was intended to prove that the United States contained its transcendence.[28] At the same time, and this was what irked Ellison, the (Hegelian) reading of U.S. history as essentially integrationist completely elided the complex and enduring centrality of black presence and expressive culture in the United States *in spite* of American racism, not to mention the American creed.

As T. V. Reed suggests, Ellison recognized that "double vision [w]as the necessary antidote to the double-consciousness imposed on African-Americans" by racism.[29] As Du Bois demonstrated so powerfully in 1903, American racism has always presented a double bind for black people, negating black humanity in both assimilationist and segregationist accents: today's appeal to be color blind and yesterday's enforcement of the color line. Ellison understood that to be effective, antiracism could not rely on strategies of transcendence but needed to subvert and transform the structure of the double bind itself. At his most subversive, he saw that antiracism had to develop an immanent critique of the American claim to universality and of the implicit and explicit forms of racism that it upheld. Ellison's insights can thus lead to a more radical conception of antiracism skeptical of antiracist universalism, especially its promise of color-blind citizenship. While not necessarily renouncing the practical, humanist goals associated with the antiracist universalism, radical antiracism addresses itself to what Ellison called "the blackness of blackness" and the problem that the color line invariably raises about human emancipation in its broadest, most universal aspects.[30]

Ironically, Ellison's cultural elitism, his embrace of American exceptionalism, and the official canonization of his great novel *Invisible Man* during the 1950s have helped marginalize accounts of his radical vision and one-time radical politics. In what is an all-too-common formula in the history of black politics and intellectuals, Ellison thus becomes a figure of moderation, who is then contrasted with more politically militant black writers before and after him. Certainly, in his own bid for cultural authority in the 1950s, Ellison helped create this eventuality by his widely publicized political and aesthetic disagreements with the left-wing and more overtly political writer Richard Wright. The juxtaposition of Ellison and Wright, however, has tended to obscure the fact that each of them presented a profound and devastating critique of the ascendancy of antiracist universalism in cold war America. At the height of the cold war, when such black radicals as Paul Robeson and W. E. B. Du Bois were held in a virtual state of internal exile and under strict surveillance because of their communist affiliations, it was not Ellison but Wright who most thoroughly developed the political implications of the critique and the "double vision" necessary to uphold it.[31] "Isn't it clear to you," Wright asked defiantly from his self-imposed exile in France, "that the American Negro is the only group in our nation that consistently and passionately raises the question of freedom?" "The voice of the American Negro," he added, "is rapidly becoming the most representative voice of America and of oppressed people anywhere in the world."[32] In an ironic formulation of his own, Wright ultimately inverted the emphasis of *An American Dilemma*, casting the problem of universality from the vantage point of the black, the oppressed, and the unfree. "The history of the Negro in America is the history of America written in vivid and bloody terms. . . . the history of Western Man *writ small.* . . . *The Negro is America's metaphor.*"[33]

Wright's and Ellison's midcentury (re)formulations of antiracist universalism are important because they come at perhaps the most significant juncture in the history of the modern American "racial formation" and are sophisticated reflections on the problem of antiracism in our own time.[34] It is worth remembering that in its current, dominant form, antiracist universalism is primarily a product of the immediate post–World War II period and the cold war that followed it. The postwar period as a whole might be characterized by the combined and uneven efforts on the part of the corporate-liberal state, in dialogue and in struggle with antiracist movements, to (re)construct American nationality on a nonracial basis. The postimperial, geopolitical ambitions of the "American Century" and the domestic imperative to eradicate the "American Dilemma," as Wright argued (and as Newt Gingrich has astutely recognized), have in this sense been intimately bound up with one another. This period marks the formal dismantling of American apartheid, in law and in official state practice, as well as the mass organization of black and white Americans in antiracist social movements. The last fifty years have witnessed an expenditure of immense psychic, political, and intellectual energy in an effort to make the "Negro problem" and hence "the Negro" disappear.[35] The unstable, nominal fulfillment of this process, emblematized in the achievement of the preferred, ostensibly "ethnic" rather than "racial" name, "African American," telescopes a profoundly complex and ambiguous series of transformations.[36]

The current impasse of antiracism as a political project therefore is not simply a result of the explicit Reagan-era attacks on the legacies of the racial liberalism of the 1960s but an outgrowth of the initial, highly contradictory efforts of the Keynesian welfare state to resolve the so-called American dilemma between the 1940s and the late 1960s. The fact is that post–World War II social policy around "race" was a mass of failures and contradictions. The national symbolic impetus toward desegregation in the military and the schools, for example, coexisted with the state's underwriting of a geography of apartheid (euphemistically called suburbanization), which provided one of the important material underpinnings for the contemporary racist complex.[37] Meanwhile, despite the pressure the cold war exerted to end European colonialism and to reform the national image abroad, it also acted as a screen for instituting the global political and economic prerogatives of the United States and for (re)imposing domestic hierarchies.[38] Not the least of the effects of this was the pacification of militant trade unionism and the dissolution of the promise that the unparalleled, sustained economic growth of this period would result in the permanent integration of a black working-class population into the productive and distributive circuits of the U.S. economy.[39]

In this context, Wright's conclusion that "the Negro is America's metaphor" contains a profound insight, namely, that the symbolic and thematic centrality of "race" in the United States consistently underwrites the characteristic forms of political domination in American society, not to mention the concrete marginalization of actual black people. Indeed, as recent work on blackface minstrelsy shows, the elaborate appropriation and consumption of the signs of blackness in American popular culture by white performers and audiences is actually a long-standing homeopathic mechanism enabling racial hierarchy, social distance, and economic accumulation to be secured and recognized and, at the same time, disavowed.[40] Ironically, the rendering of the "Negro problem" in the United States as the "American dilemma" possesses a similar structure, reenacting what may be the most characteristic form of American racism since the early Republic, in which the "Negro" becomes simultaneously the embodiment and the disfiguration of America's democratic dreams and pretensions.[41] The figuration of the "dilemma" (like the aforementioned "crisis") thus paradoxically shores up and even consolidates America's (implicitly white) self-identity, while the "Negro" (recalling Fanon once again) exists as the degraded currency of the "comparison."[42] This remains as true today as at any other time in American history—in spite of formal equality—as an unmistakably racial discourse about crime and welfare is at the center of political reflections and judgments about the state of American society, even for those who loudly proclaim that race does not matter. To such arguments, Wright would have offered the following rejoinder: "There has never been a 'Negro problem' in America, only a 'white problem.'"[43]

What might be most important about the 1960s is that it represented a series of attempts to transform the normative staging of "race" in American culture. As Wright anticipated, the extension of the metaphorical valences of black struggles beyond the United States had strained the nation-form, and with it the self-assurance that American self-identity was something that effectively transcended and subsumed racial difference. For a time at least, it seemed as though black people-in-struggle had seized control of "racial" assets, the fund of metaphor, symbolism, and imagery that have always been central to the construction of the dominant senses of American peoplehood, wrenching, if not rupturing, the self-containing, self-perpetuating logic of America's "dilemma." From James Brown's galvanizing "Say It Loud, I'm Black and I'm Proud" to the redolent phrase "Black is Beautiful," the startling imagery of bare feet and of black fists raised in protest at the Mexico City Olympic Games, and the oxymoronic saliency of the "black power" concept itself, the cultural politics of the 1960s was centered on a series of dramatic and potentially liberatory transvaluations of the signifying content of "blackness."[44] Policy elites and official commentators, for example, noted with alarm that the 1960s "black movement had as surprising a resonance abroad as at home."[45] At home, black struggles were the basis for a different kind of comparison, becoming the "trigger struggle," or switch point, for a host of other minority discourses and contestations and a relay station for emancipatory impulses of decolonization from around the world.[46] In the end, it is this uniquely subversive, insistently traumatizing legacy that has been the least understood and most devalued in the revisionism that characterizes the current conjuncture. At the same time, this legacy remains to a greater and lesser degree most alive in the racial politics of cultural performance and in the critical reworking of antiracist theory and practice today.[47]

Of course, I do not want to completely downplay the immense struggles against Jim Crow in the South during this period, but I think it is important to acknowledge that the central achievement of the civil rights movement, namely, the formal conquest of citizenship rights for African Americans, appears in retrospect as something of a Pyrrhic victory. This was recognized by civil rights activists working in the South relatively early on as nonviolent efforts to expand black voting power were thwarted in Birmingham and Albany and by the actions of the national Democratic party machine.[48] It became even more apparent once the movement began to confront the more durable and immovable obstacles of de facto apartheid in northern cities and suburbs. This has become even clearer today as whatever value accrues to formal citizenship is depreciated under the pressures of inegalitarian deficit reduction and remanded under the auspices of excessive policing and punishment. If the civil rights era was characterized by struggles over the terms of black assimilation into the American polity and its public spheres (including various black nationalist and revolutionary positions that contested the unilateral lure of assimilation as a ruse and a trap), the post–civil rights era has given way to a set of contradictory processes. On the one hand, the past thirty years have seen the growth of a sizable (if not entirely materially stable) black "middle class," constituting anywhere from 30 percent to 50 percent of America's black population.[49] At the same time, this period has witnessed the structural and political reconstitution of racial alterity through the decimation of urban aid programs and the concomitant expansion of a prison-industrial-complex.[50] Perhaps most consequential, the latter processes have been ideologically mirrored and justified by the full replenishing of the age-old national fantasy of the black "anti-citizenry," today populated by criminals, drug-users, predatory youth, teen mothers, and "welfare queens."[51]

The most far-seeing theoreticians of "black power" envisioned many of these developments. They understood that symbolic equality would provide little genuine sustenance for working-class racial migrants and would do little to counteract the ravages of "racial capitalism" that had already systematically "underdeveloped" black America.[52] Even as the legal edifice of segregation was being dismantled by government decree (beginning as early as the end of World War II), a much more enduring and pervasive structure of spatial apartheid was being inscribed into the social landscape as the divide between urban ghettos and suburban idyll.[53] As Jim Crow subjugated blacks in the South, the approximately three million black migrants who came north between 1900 and 1950 had their life-chances curtailed and confined by "a hardening color line in employment, education and especially housing," a division violently enforced by the riot, pogrom, and hate strike.[54] While white communal violence has been central to the construction of black ghettos in urban areas, the perpetuation and extension of ghetto conditions for the millions of black migrants that followed in the 1950s and 1960s was carried out by "civilized" means and with possibly greater consequences. I am referring to the familiar story of redlining, block-busting restrictive covenants, and "neighborhood improvement associations," the impact of which has never been sufficiently calculated. What might even be more startling about the post–World War II period, however, is the degree to which the federal government through the actions of such New Deal agencies as the Federal Housing Administration and the Veteran's Administration promoted and subsidized the massive expansion and elaboration of the racial geography that defines the United States today.[55]

The current tendency to dismiss or repudiate what are often deemed the excesses of black power in the 1960s occurs without an attempt to adequately theorize or historicize the black radicalism of the 1960s in the light of the social transformations characteristic of the post–World War II racist complex.[56] The most radical instances of black power rhetoric, for example, such declarations as "the city is the black man's land" or variations on the idea of the black ghetto as an "internal colony" of the United States, might actually be seen as entirely prescient and real responses to an existing situation.[57] No migrant group has experienced the depth and duration of residential segregation that has been imposed on black internal migrants in the United States. Although black militants during the 1960s may have seemed contradictory when they demanded that the state underwrite greater black inclusion in the polity by enlarging the black share of the social surplus, while at the same time emphasizing their own categorical opposition and apartness from the dominant public sphere (black power's "double vision" perhaps), it seems clear (especially in the light of the sorry tale of "urban renewal" and black-led city government) that the most interesting and creative instances of black power grew out of a justified and widespread feeling that formal state-sanctioned channels of racial redress had been exhausted.

Take the Black Panther party as an example. While it may be that it was the very possibility of state-aided integration and assimilation into the polity (i.e., the Civil Rights and Voting Rights acts and the war on poverty) that gave such a powerful charge to their refusals and contestations,[58] the Panthers dramatic performance of their own noncitizenship and even anticitizenship (especially their open resistance to policing) necessarily implied a wholly different region of identification. The emphases on "power," "community control," and the like, as vague and ill-defined as these notions often were, were nonetheless meaningful responses to what Eldridge Cleaver cleverly disparaged as the hypocritical, halfhearted attempt "to citizenize the Negro."[59] More than anything else the Panthers and others resignified "blackness" in all its geopolitical and intrapsychic density. Indeed, I would argue that the party's much discussed and often criticized emphasis on "violence" may actually have more to do with its repudiation of the "violence" that came with the imperative of black assimilation itself, namely, the idea that black people must internalize the frontiers of the nation and "inhabit the space of the state" as a place where they "have always been—and always will be at home."[60] This was essentially the argument of *An American Dilemma* and the intellectual foundation of a modern civil rights discourse that has posited the end of racism as the telos of American history. This kind of faulty historicism, however, cripples efforts to grasp "the time of the now" or to recognize how a spatialized racist complex continues to hollow out the meaning and substance of black nationality and citizenship in the United States today, in spite of formal equality.[61]

If there is a flaw in the notion that the ghetto is an internal colony, it is that its prospects for "liberation" and "self-determination" seem slim, if not already co-opted by New Right discourses about "enterprise zones," tight discipline, and low-wage austerity as the preconditions for urban aid and future development. As James Blaut suggests, the structural ghettoization of racial and colonial migrants in the United States might be more fruitfully considered as a kind of internal *neocolonialism,* or perhaps more accurately as the internalization of neocolonialism. Although ghettoized areas, in contrast to "real" colonies, fundamentally lack the ability to press for self-determination as autonomous politico-geographic units, the actual achievement of self-determination by former colonies has itself provided few, if any, answers to the exploitation and oppression that continue to underdevelop some parts of the world and overdevelop others.[62] What the internalization of neocolonialism reveals is that the nation-states of the Enlightenment are places where the idea of common citizenship no longer seems to hold sway (if indeed it ever did). The world today, as Etienne Balibar writes, is "traversed by a shifting frontier—irreducible to the frontier between states—between *two* humanities which seem incommensurable, namely the humanity of destitution and that of 'consumption,' the humanity of underdevelopment, and that of overdevelopment."[63]

I would emphasize that just as there was an ongoing relationship between decolonization and antiracist universalism during the cold war heyday of the "American Century," there is currently a relationship between the reconstruction of forms of neocolonial and postcolonial domination in the world system and neoracist and postracist domination in the United States. The entire period since 1945 might be usefully conceptualized in terms of the general extension of a new model of American imperialism that has been built from the outset on the premise of free trade, open universal markets, nationhood, and internal colonization—one of the reasons why it has been and remains so difficult to name.[64] The advantage of the internal colonization perspectives developed during the 1960s is not that they are accurate in every historical or sociological detail but that they accurately depict a world in which state-managed uneven development and racially defined subordination and oppression coincide. The resulting relations of unequal development, moreover, are spatially and temporally defined, as "ghettoized" areas are excluded from sharing in social surpluses, are the sites of superexploitation and underemployment, and are loci for the maximum concentration of official and unofficial forms of social violence. Du Bois himself recognized this connection at the onset of the American Century when he argued that Europe's own colonies were in effect "the slums of the world."[65]

The shift to various terrains of cultural politics and the intensification of the "culture wars" since the 1960s are at least partly the result of the profound disorganization and disaggregation of progressive political forces and a reflection of widespread despair about meaningful political options at the end of the American Century, which is also the era of full-blown transnational capitalism. Progressive cultural politics and cultural struggle, however, must be theorized in relation to the many insights of the black power period. It has primarily been through the agency of feminist and antihomophobic critiques of black power, for example, that it is once again possible to understand black liberation in the terms offered in different ways by Du Bois, James, Ellison, and Wright, namely, not as an isolated or self-contained political struggle but as a universal one.[66] The effort to reinvent an effective antiracism today out of the ample insights of the past, in other words, must draw from the resources inherent within those universalities that present themselves as alternatives to the unilateral declarations of the universality of capitalism that for its victims at least continues to radiate disaster triumphant.[67] In the face of this, there can be no retreat into the narrow politics of nationalism. Black nationalism in particular, while providing what are in many ways the simplest responses to the sustained attack on "race" as a meaningful political category, holds few answers to the complexities of racial subordination today.

Effective political struggles, in other words, must relink antiracist theory and practice to the rethinking of the *thresholds* of citizenship and "nationality," in the international arena, through a politics of human rights, and in subnational, local, and institutional spaces of the nation-state: the housing project, school, and prison. At the same time, we must recognize that the contemporary racist complex appears not only as a spatial order but also as a crisis of public spending, one that consistently presents itself in racial guises as questions of "illegality" and "welfarism." Today a line is being drawn through the very concept of citizenship itself, and black people are not the only ones represented as subcitizens—so are newer immigrants, poor women, the homeless, the sick, and the "deviant." In keeping with the call for double and redoubled vision, then, we must also fight today for a robust concept of social citizenship, one that is dictated not by imagined fiscal constraints and finance capital but by and for ourselves. In this struggle, the intellectual and political resources of antiracism are indispensable and still requisite to a belief in humanity.

Notes

This essay was originally published in *Race and Reason* 3 (Fall 1996): 62–70, and appears here, with slight modifications, by permission of *Race and Reason*.

1. This statement was later used by Du Bois to open his chapter "The Dawn of Freedom," in *The Souls of Black Folk* (New York: Vintage, 1990), 16. The initial context for this prophetic utterance, however—an international congress addressing questions of imperialism and racism—is often forgotten. See George Sheperson, "Notes on Negro American Influences on the Emergence of African Nationalism," *Journal of African History* 1, no. 2 (1960): 307.

2. Du Bois, *Souls of Black Folk*, 4.

3. W. E. B. Du Bois, *W. E. B. Du Bois Speaks: Speeches and Addresses, 1890–1919*, ed. Philip Foner (New York: Pathfinder, 1970), 84 (emphasis added).

4. Albert Murray, *The Omni Americans: Black Experience and American Culture* (New York: Da Capo, 1970), 22.

5. Du Bois, *Souls of Black Folk*, 4.

6. Manning Marable, *Race, Reform and Rebellion: The Second Reconstruction in Black America, 1945–1982* (Jackson: University Press of Mississippi, 1984).

7. Here I am paraphrasing Walter Benjamin's "Theses on the Philosophy of History." "The tradition of the oppressed," Benjamin writes, "teaches us that the 'state of emergency' (i.e., the 'crisis') in which we live is not the exception but the rule. We must attain to a conception of history that is in keeping with this insight. . . . The current amazement that the things we are experiencing are 'still' possible in the twentieth century is *not* philosophical. This amazement is not the beginning of knowledge—unless it is the knowledge that the view of history which gives rise to it is untenable." Walter Benjamin, "Theses on the Philosophy of History," in *Illuminations*, ed. Hannah Arendt (New York: Schocken Books, 1969), 257.

8. William Julius Wilson, *The Declining Significance of Race: Black Politics and Changing American Institutions* (Chicago: University of Chicago Press, 1980).

9. Thomas Byrne Edsall and Mary D. Edsall, *Chain Reaction* (New York: W. W. Norton, 1991). See also David Roediger's useful critique of these positions in "The Racial Crisis of American Liberalism," in his *Towards the Abolition of Whiteness: Essays on Race, Politics, and Working-Class History* (London: Verso, 1994), 122.

10. As Antonin Scalia put it in his opinion overturning state-based redistricting efforts to ensure black political representation: "In the eyes of government, we are just one race here. It is American." This formulation is equal to the most forceful Americanization rhetoric of the twentieth century. Quoted in Jeffrey Rosen, "The Color-Blind Court," *New Republic*, July 31, 1995, 19.

11. The notion of *postracism* is alluded to but not fully explained in a provocative aside by Balibar in Etienne Balibar and Immanuel Wallerstein, *Race, Nation, Class: Ambiguous Identities* (London: Verso, 1991), 9. Manning Marable, *The Crisis of Color and Democracy: Essays on Race, Class and Power* (Monroe, Maine: Common Courage, 1992), has also attempted to describe this phenomenon under the rubric "nonracist racism." See also David Hollinger, "Postethnic America," in this volume. Writing in the tradition of Gunnar Myrdal, Hollinger claims that U.S. history has been based on a "nonethnic" and "universalist" ideology of the nation, which has been coupled uneasily with its "ethnic history," including a history of inequalities defined in terms of ancestry. His argument, however, that we should strive for "a postethnic future," in which group differences are embraced voluntarily instead of being in any way ascribed by the state or other powerful social agents, is "color blind" in a manner that is similar to the arguments adumbrated above. Hollinger, in other words, wants to relativize racial difference as simply *one form* of group difference or ethnic particularity, instead of understanding it as the form of difference that has coded and contradicted all American claims to universality. An elaborated critique of this position is developed further below.

12. Cornel West, *Race Matters* (Boston: Beacon, 1993).

13. Harold Cruse, *Rebellion or Revolution* (New York: William Morrow, 1968), 27.

14. Mike Davis, "Who Killed L.A.? Political Autopsy," *New Left Review* 197 (January/February 1993): 25.

15. More than any other contemporary theorist, Etienne Balibar has developed the argument that an "effective anti-racism" is a central precondition to any project of political emancipation today, including and perhaps especially the reinvention of properly class-based struggles. Readers of Balibar will find much of his influence in what follows. Balibar and Wallerstein, *Race, Nation, Class*, 13.

16. Derrick Bell, *Faces at the Bottom of the Well: The Permanence of Racism* (New York: Basic Books, 1992).

17. Paul Gilroy, "One Nation under a Groove," in *Anatomy of Racism*, ed. David Theo Goldberg (New York: Routledge, 1990), 263.

18. C. L. R. James, *American Civilization* (London: Basil Blackwell, 1994).

19. See, for example, Paul Gilroy's powerful critique of a simple form antiracism has taken in England, "The End of Anti-Racism," in *"Race," Culture, and Difference*, ed. James Donald and Ali Rattansi (Newbury Park, Calif.: Sage, 1992). As Gilroy writes (in a formulation that echoes James in remarkable ways), "The anti-racism I am criticising trivialises the struggle against racism and isolates it from other political antagonisms—from the contradiction between capital and labour, from the battle between men and women. It suggests that racism can be eliminated on its own because it is readily extricable from everything else" (193).

20. This is, of course, the famous query with which Du Bois begins *The Souls of Black Folk*.

21. Newt Gingrich, "New York City Address" (Presented at the Hilton Hotel, March 24, 1995).

22. I do not, however, mean to suggest that overt forms of formal white supremacy and racial hatred have disappeared. If anything, the racist wing of the burgeoning militia movement and the recent round of black church bombings suggest the contrary. The point is that the "official" condemnations of this sort of activity are now always already in place.

23. Frantz Fanon, *Toward the African Revolution: Political Essays* (New York: Grove, 1967), 31.

24. Ralph Ellison, *Shadow and Act* (New York: Signet Books, 1963), 301.

25. Gunnar Myrdal, *An American Dilemma: The Negro Problem and Modern Democracy* (New York: Pantheon Books, 1944), 1:3.

26. The "American Century" in my usage essentially applies to the brief but explosive decades after World War II that were dominated by an expanding, globally influential, and domestically prosperous corporate-liberal state. In my view the American Century lasts roughly from 1945 to 1973. The reasons for its eclipse are too complex to detail here. Suffice it to say, this period is marked by the global ascendancy of U.S. monopoly capitalism, the dismantling of most of the old European colonial empires, and the "virtuous circle" of intensive accumulation and domestic economic growth and prosperity in the United States. The term was first coined by Time, Inc., chairman Henry Luce in 1941 as the name for the dawning of U.S. global hegemony. See also Michel Aglietta, *A Theory of Capitalist Regulation: The U.S. Experience* (London: Verso, 1979).

27. Myrdal, *American Dilemma*, 2:1022.

28. Frederick Keppel, representing the Carnegie Foundation, the sponsors of the study, argued that "to review the most serious race problem in the country is an idea singularly American." Ibid., 1:xlviii (emphasis added).

29. T. V. Reed, *Fifteen Jugglers and Five Believers: The Literary Politics of Social Movements* (Berkeley: University of California Press, 1993), 58.

30. One of the most succinct articulations of "double-vision" during this period was offered by the great black composer Duke Ellington, who in 1944 called on black people to embrace "a strategy of dissonance." As Ellington put it, "Dissonance is our way of life in America, we are something apart; yet an integral part." Mark Tucker, ed., *The Duke Ellington Reader* (New York: Random House, 1994), 150.

31. The idea of double vision, as Paul Gilroy tells us, was actually Wright's reformulation of Du Bois's notion of double-consciousness. Paul Gilroy, *The Black Atlantic: Modernity and Double-Consciousness* (Cambridge, Mass.: Harvard University Press, 1994), 161. I am suggesting, however, that in spite of Ellison's Americocentrism and his desire to distance himself from Wright, the two men were in many ways much closer than is apparent today.

32. Richard Wright, *White Man Listen!* (New York: Anchor Books, 1957), 101.

33. Ibid., 72 (emphasis added).

238 NIKHIL PAL SINGH

34. The concept of racial formation comes from Michael Omi and Howard Winant, *Racial Formation in the United States* (New York: Routledge, 1986).

35. I am indebted here to Cedric Robinson's felicitous phrasing, used in a different context to describe the historical creation of blackness: "The creation of the Negro was obviously at the cost of immense expenditures of psychic and intellectual energies in the West. . . ." Cedric Robinson, *Black Marxism* (London: Zed, 1983), 5.

36. The ascendancy of *African American* as a substitute for *Negro* or *Black* is a part of a normative post–World War II process of ethnicization. In other words, it is an attempt (however fraught) to fold "racial" difference into a concept of ethnicity by substituting a signifier of geographic/national difference for signifiers of "racial" difference. A uniquely American neologism, ethnicity in this sense should be understood as the preferred concept for describing relative difference, a kind of difference that ultimately does not threaten the overall integrity and coherence of properly national belonging or contradict the imperative of assimilation. Of course, the designation "African" as it is placed in front of the dominative "American" still only satisfies this imperative in partial and ambivalent ways because of the centuries of stigmatization attached to and the ongoing underdevelopment of Africa in the world system.

37. Douglas Massey and Nancy Denton, *American Apartheid: Segregation and the Making of the Underclass* (Cambridge, Mass.: Harvard University Press, 1993); Mike Davis, *City of Quartz: Excavating the Future of Los Angeles* (London: Verso, 1990). It is probably time to define what I mean by racist complex. Following Balibar, three interdependent phenomena constitute a given racist complex: a conception of history, or what Balibar calls a "historiosophy"; a social and material structure of discrimination; and a set of relations to identity-constituting institutions (i.e., the nation-state). Modern suburbia encompasses all three with its "there goes the neighborhood" rationalization of white flight; its concrete forms of racial value-coding or discrimination (homeownership, taxation subsidies, infrastructural investment, and zoning restrictions); and its ongoing, vexed relationship with central state authority whenever the state does not uphold the interests of what is imagined to be the "suburban nation" (e.g., spending tax dollars on the urban poor, in other words, blacks, Latinos, and so forth). Etienne Balibar, "Es Gibt Keinen Staat in Europa: Racism and Politics in Europe Today, *New Left Review* 186 (March/April 1993): 11.

38. Among the many useful works I have relied on for thinking about cold war hierarchies, domestic and global, are Mike Davis, *Prisoners of the American Dream: Politics and Economy in the History of the U.S. Working Class* (London: Verso, 1984); George Lipsitz, *A Rainbow at Midnight: Class and Culture in the 1940s* (Urbana: University of Illinois Press, 1994); L. S. Stavrianos, *Global Rift: The Third World Comes of Age* (New York: William Morrow, 1981); Joel Kovel, *Red Hunting in the Promised Land* (New York: Basic Books, 1994); and Gerald Horne, *Black and Red: W. E. B. Du Bois and the Afro-American Response to the Cold War* (Albany: State University of New York Press, 1986).

39. In the light of this, C. L. R. James's insight from 1948 can only be viewed as prophetic. "The independent Negro Movement," James writes, "must find its way to the proletariat. . . . if the proletariat is defeated, if the CIO is destroyed, then there

will fall upon the Negro people in the US such repression, such persecution, comparable to nothing they have seen in the past. We have seen in Germany and elsewhere the barbarism that capitalism is capable of in its death agony." C. L. R. James, "The Revolutionary Answer to the Negro Question in the United States," in *The C. L. R. James Reader*, ed. Anna Grimshaw (London: Basil Blackwell, 1992), 188.

40. Eric Lott, *Love and Theft: Blackface Minstrelsy and the American Working Class* (New York: Oxford University Press, 1993); David Roediger, *The Wages of Whiteness: Race and the Making of the American Working Class* (London: Verso, 1991); Alexander Saxton, *The Rise and Fall of the White Republic* (London: Verso, 1990).

41. As Balibar argues (following Jacques Derrida), racism is the *supplement* of nationalism. Hence my argument, glossing Wright, is that the "Negro" is America's supplement, which is to say that which makes possible, and yet at the same time threatens to undo, the position of the dominative citizen-subject of the United States. Blackness in America, in other words, has been constituted as the boundary of hegemonic citizenship, serving as both its limit and condition. This is what Balibar defines under the rubric of the "paradoxes of universality," which is something that Ellison, Du Bois, James, and Wright (not to mention Fanon), all grasped in their own ways, at different times. See Balibar and Wallerstein, *Race, Nation, Class*, 97.

42. Frantz Fanon, *Black Skins, White Masks* (New York: Grove, 1967), 211. I am indebted to David Lloyd, "Race Under Representation," *Oxford Literary Review* 13 (1991): 63–94, for this insight.

43. Wright, *White Man Listen!* 99.

44. Kobena Mercer, "1968: Periodizing Politics and Identity," in *Cultural Studies*, ed. Lawrence Grossberg and Cary Nelson (New York: Routledge, 1992), 424–49. As James Brown recalls, "In 1968, after I came out with 'Say It Loud, I'm Black and I'm Proud,' it was all over. The dark-skinned man had all of a sudden become a cosmopolitan." James Brown and Bruce Tucker, *James Brown: The Godfather of Soul* (London: Fontana and Collins, 1988), 124. Following on this, we might see 1968 as a moment when "blackness" as a sign of oppositionality and resistance "travels" literally and figuratively in unprecedented ways. Yet, as Mercer cautions, the circulation of a revalued blackness was by no means restricted to the province of oppositional politics. 1968, after all, was also the year that James Brown accepted an invitation to play at Richard Nixon's inauguration, assented to Nixon's description of black power as "black capitalism," and allied himself with the state's own engagement in the struggle to define difference, so as to relocate, and in effect domesticate, its potentially insurgent movement.

45. These are the words of then policy analyst and scholar-pundit Daniel Patrick Moynihan, who may have done more than any other public figure to lay the public policy groundwork for the racist reaction that effectively ended the Second Reconstruction. Quoted in Sheila Collins, *The Rainbow Challenge: The Jackson Campaign and the Future of U.S. Politics* (New York: Monthly Review, 1986), 57.

46. R. Radhakrishnan, "Toward an Effective Intellectual—Foucault or Gramsci," in *Intellectuals, Aesthetics, Politics and Culture*, ed. Bruce Robbins (Minneapolis: University of Minnesota Press, 1990), 59. Radhakrishnan credits Jesse Jackson with formulating the idea that black struggles in America are "trigger struggles." Accord-

ing to him, Jackson's vision of a "Rainbow Coalition" pointed to the possibility of moving beyond a politics of discrete representation and alliance to the articulation of a new "oppositional bloc," which is close to my view of a robust antiracism at the center of the reinvention of political radicalism in the United States. Clearly, there are also more explicit links to the late 1960s contained in this idea, especially considering that the first notion of a "Rainbow Coalition" was not Jackson's but Black Panther leader Fred Hampton's. Hampton developed a coalition between the Puerto Rican Young Lords, the Young Patriots (a white youth gang), SDS, and the Black Panther party in Chicago—a promising moment in the late 1960s worth reconsidering. Hampton was murdered by the Chicago police a few months later. Nikhil Pal Singh, "The Black Panthers and the 'Undeveloped Country' of the Left," in *The Black Panther Party Reconsidered: Reflections and Scholarship,* ed. Charles E. Jones (Baltimore, Md.: Black Classic, forthcoming).

47. I am thinking of the work of scholars who focus on innovative efforts at rethinking questions of "race" that have emerged from cultural studies. Following on the pathbreaking work of Stuart Hall and the so-called Birmingham School, they include Paul Gilroy, Andrew Ross, Eric Lott, Patricia Rose, Hazel Carby, bell hooks, and many others.

48. Clayborne Carson, *In Struggle: SNCC and the Black Awakening of the 1960s* (Cambridge, Mass.: Harvard University Press, 1981).

49. For the statistics and outlook of the new black middle class, see the special issue of the *New Yorker,* "Black in America," April 29 and May 6, 1996. See also Manning Marable, "The Paradox of Integration: Black Society and Politics in the Post-Reform Period, 1982–1990," in his *Race, Reform and Rebellion,* 185–219.

50. Davis, "Who Killed L.A.?" 14.

51. The concept of national fantasy is developed by Lauren Berlant in *The Anatomy of National Fantasy: Hawthorne, Utopia, and Everyday Life* (Chicago: University of Chicago Press, 1991). The notion of black people as "anti-citizens. . . . enemies rather than members of the social compact" comes from Roediger, *Wages of Whiteness,* 57.

52. See Robinson, *Black Marxism,* for the notion of racial capitalism. See also Manning Marable, *How Capitalism Underdeveloped Black America: Problems in Race, Political Economy and Society* (Boston: South End, 1983).

53. Mike Davis points out that the 64 percent cutback in federal aid to cities since the 1980s, combined with the post-1960s white flight, suburbanization, and the production of so-called edge-economies, has intensified conditions of unemployment and underdevelopment affecting black urban dwellers, producing conditions of "spatial apartheid." Davis, *City of Quartz,* chapter 3.

54. Massey and Denton, *American Apartheid,* 30.

55. George Lipsitz, "The Possessive Investment in Whiteness: Racialized Social Democracy and the White Problem in American Studies," *American Quarterly* 47 (September 1995): 369–427. I have also relied on Massey and Denton, *American Apartheid,* especially 17–59.

56. One of the most egregious examples of this is Hugh Pearson, *In the Shadow of the Panther: Huey Newton and the Price of Black Power in America* (New York: Addison-Wesley, 1994).

57. James Boggs and Grace Lee Boggs, "The City Is the Black Man's Land," in *Racism and Class Struggle*, ed. James Boggs (New York: Monthly Review, 1971), 39–51; Robert Allen, *Black Awakening in Capitalist America* (1970; reprint, Trenton: Africa World, 1990).

58. Davis makes this point in *City of Quartz*, chapter 5.

59. Eldridge Cleaver, *Post-Prison Writings and Speeches* (New York: Vintage Books, 1970), 61.

60. Balibar and Wallerstein, *Race, Nation, Class*, 95.

61. Benjamin, "Theses on the Philosophy of History," 263; Singh, "Black Panthers and the 'Underdeveloped Country' of the Left."

62. James N. Blaut, *The National Question: Decolonizing the Theory of Nationalism* (London: Zed, 1987).

63. Balibar and Wallerstein, *Race, Nation, Class*, 44 (emphasis added).

64. See "Imperialism: A Useful Category of Historical Analysis?" special issue, *Radical History Review* 57 (Spring 1995).

65. W. E. B. Du Bois, *Color and Democracy: Colonies and Peace* (New York: Harcourt Brace, 1945), 17.

66. For a brilliant historical account of this dimension of black liberation, see Gilroy, *Black Atlantic*.

67. Here, of course, I am glossing the famous dictum of Adorno and Horkheimer. "The fully enlightened earth," they write, "radiates disaster triumphant." Theodore Adorno and Max Horkheimer, *The Dialectic of Enlightenment*, trans. John Cummings (New York: Continuum, 1982), 3.

It is, of course, true that the African identity is still in the making. There isn't a final identity that is African. But, at the same time, there *is* an identity coming into existence. And it has a certain meaning. Because if somebody meets me, say, in a shop in Cambridge he says "Are you from Africa?" which means that Africa means something to some people. Each of these tags has a meaning, and a penalty and a responsibility.

—Chinua Achebe, *Times Literary Supplement,* February 26, 1982

Afterword: How Shall We Live as Many?

Kwame Anthony Appiah

There is an Akan proverb from my home in Asante in Ghana that says, "Aban bεgu a, εfiri yam." Proverbs are notoriously difficult to interpret and thus to translate, but this one means, roughly, that if the state is going to collapse, it will be from the belly.[1] The idea, of course, is that states collapse from within. The proverb is used to express the sentiment that people suffer as a result of their own weaknesses, not from the attacks of others. It is a rhetoric familiar enough these days here in the United States. In the latest episodes of American jeremiad—truly the longest-running series in our history—it is being suggested that having "won the cold war," we have set out to destroy ourselves from within. American society is being destroyed not by drugs and poverty and political bungling but, allegedly, by multiculturalists intent on schism. Here, then, is a society collapsing from the belly.

I do not believe this. In a world that contains Bosnia-Hercegovina, Belfast, Beirut, East Timor, and Sri Lanka, events such as the reported multicultural riots in Los Angeles do not convince me that the United States is being destroyed by an excess of ethnicity.[2] Those of us born and reared elsewhere but happy to be living here in the United States often find one thing above all else odd in our adopted home: this country's imagination of itself as so new a creature on God's earth that it cannot learn from others. This exceptionalism flows, in part, from a general ignorance of others, which one part of the multicultural movement aims to correct. In this essay, I focus on pluralism and identity in Africa and urge some lessons (both positive and negative) of the way that continent has dealt with its ethnoregional complications.

* * *

The cultural life of most black Africa remained largely unaffected by European ideas until the last years of the nineteenth century. Most black African cultures began the nineteenth century with ways of life that were formed without much direct contact with Europe. Deliberate attempts at change—through contact with explorers and colonizers in the interior and trading posts on the coasts—produced small enclaves of Europeanized Africans, but the major cultural impact of Europe is largely a product of the period since World War I.

To understand the variety of Africa's contemporary cultures, we need to recall the variety of its precolonial cultures. Differences in colonial experiences have also played their part in shaping the continent's diversities, but even identical colonial policies similarly implemented would surely have produced widely varying results.

No doubt we can find generalizations that hold true for most of black Africa before European conquest. A familiar idea in African historiography is that Africa was the last continent in the Old World with an "uncaptured" peasantry, which was largely able to use land without the supervision of feudal overlords and able, if it chose, to market its products through a complex system of trading networks.[3] While European ruling classes were living off the surplus of peasants and the newly developing industrial working class, African rulers were essentially living off taxes on trade. But if we could have traveled through Africa's many cultures in those years—from the small groups of Bushman hunter-gatherers with their Stone Age materials to the Hausa kingdoms rich in worked metal—we would have observed many different ways of life. To speak of an African identity in the nineteenth century—if an identity is a coalescence of mutually responsive (if sometimes conflicting) modes of conduct, habits of thought, and patterns of evaluation or, more concisely, a coherent kind of human social psychology—would have been to give "to airy nothing a local habitation and a name."

* * *

Yet there is no doubt that now an African identity is coming into being. I have argued elsewhere that this identity is a new thing, in part the product of a colonial history, and that the bases through which this identity has largely been theorized—race, a common historical experience, a shared metaphysics—presuppose falsehoods too serious to be ignored.[4] Every human identity is constructed and historical and has its share of false presuppositions, of the errors and inaccuracies that courtesy calls "myth," religion "heresy," and science "magic." Invented histories, invented biologies, and invented cultural affinities come with every identity; each is a kind of role that has to be scripted, structured by conventions of narrative to which the world never quite manages to conform.

Often those who say this or who deny the biological reality of races or the literal truth of our national fictions are treated by nationalists and "race-men" as if they are proposing genocide or the destruction of nations; as if in saying that there is literally no Negro race, they are obliterating all those who claim to be Negroes; as if in doubting the story of Okomfo Anokye, they are repudiating the Asante nation.[5] While this is an unhelpful hyperbole, it is certainly true that there must be contexts in which a statement of these truths is politically inopportune. I am enough of a scholar to feel drawn to truth-telling, though the heavens fall, yet enough of a political animal to recognize that there are places where the truth does more harm than good.

So far as I can see, however, we do not have to choose between these impulses. There is no reason to believe that racism is always—or even usually—advanced by denying the existence of races; and, though there is some reason to suspect that those who resist legal remedies for the history of racism might use the nonexistence of races to argue in the United States, for example, against affirmative action, that strategy is, as a matter of logic, easily opposed. The existence of racism does not require the existence of races; and, we can add, nations are real enough, however invented their traditions.[6]

To raise the issue of whether these truths are truths to be uttered is to be forced, however, to face squarely the real political question of when we should endorse the noble lie. In the real world of practical politics, everyday alliances, and popular mobilization, a rejection of races and nations in theory can be part of a program for coherent political practice only if we can show more than that the black race—or the Shona tribe or any of the other modes of self-invention that Africa has inherited—fits the common pattern of relying on less than the literal truth. We would need to show not that race and national history are falsehoods but that they are useless falsehoods at best, or at worst dangerous ones, and that another set of stories will build us identities through which we can make more productive alliances.

The problem is that group identity seems to work best when it is seen by its members as natural or "real." Such concepts as Pan-Africanism or black solidarity can be important forces with real political benefits, but they do not work without their attendant mystifications. (To turn to the other obvious example, feminism does not work without its occasional risks and mystifications either.) Recognizing the constructed nature of the history of identities has seemed to many incompatible with taking these new identities as seriously as do those who invent or (as they would no doubt rather say) discover and possess them.[7] In the real world of politics, the demands of agency always seem to entail a misrecognition of the genesis of identity; alliances cannot be built without mystifications and mythologies. I am interested in considering the ways in which what is productive in African forms of identity politics can be fruitfully understood by intellectuals—and other searchers after truth—who find it impossible to live through the falsehoods of race and tribe and nation and who believe at the same time that nationalism and racial solidarity can do good without the attendant evils of racism, nationalism, and other particularisms.

* * *

I have often argued against the forms of racism implicit in much Pan-Africanist talk,[8] but such objections to a biologically rooted conception of race may still seem too theoretical: if Africans can get together around the idea of the "Black Person" and can create through this notion productive alliances with African Americans and people of African descent in Europe and the Caribbean, surely these theoretical objections should pale in the light of the practical value of these alliances. But there is every reason to doubt that they can. Within Africa—in the Organization of African Unity (OAU), in the Sudan, in Mauritania[9]—racialization has produced arbitrary boundaries and exacerbated tensions; in the diaspora, alliances with other peoples of color as victims of racism—people of South Asian descent in England, for example, or Hispanics in the United States, Arabs in France, Turks in Germany—have proved essential. In short, a biologically rooted conception of race is both dangerous in practice and misleading in theory. African unity and African identity need more secure foundations than race can provide.

The passage from Achebe with which I began this essay continues in these words: "All these tags, unfortunately for the black man, are tags of disability."[10] To me, however, they are not so much labels of disability as disabling labels. Consider, for example, the identity of Alexander Crummell and W. E. B. Du Bois and the older Pan-Africanists in comparison with the identity of the "Afrocentrists" who speak of a shared metaphysics or a fancied past of shared glories. My complaint can be briskly summarized. "Race" disables us because it proposes as a basis for common action the illusion that black (and white and yellow) people are fundamentally allied by nature and, thus, without effort; it therefore leaves us unprepared to handle the "intraracial" conflicts that arise from the very different situations of black (and white and yellow) people in different parts of the economy and the world.

A retreat to African metaphysical traditions (exemplified, for example, in the powerful rhetoric of Wole Soyinka)[11] disables us because it founds our unity in gods that have not served us well in our dealings with the world. Soyinka never defends what he calls the "African World" against the charge made by the Ghanaian philosopher Kwasi Wiredu that since people die daily in Ghana because they prefer traditional herbal remedies to Western medicines, "any inclination to glorify the unanalytical [i.e., the traditional] cast of mind is not just retrograde; it is tragic."[12] Soyinka has proved the Yoruba pantheon a powerful literary resource, but he cannot explain why Christianity and Islam have so widely displaced the old gods or why an image of the West has so powerful a hold on the contemporary Yoruba imagination; nor can his myth-making offer us the resources for creating economies and polities adequate to our various places in the world.

Similarly, the Afrocentrists—like all who have chosen to root Africa's modern identity in an imaginary history—require us to see the past as the moment of wholeness and unity and to tie us to the values and beliefs of the past, thus diverting us from the problems of the present and the hopes of the future. If the goal of achieving an African identity is empowerment, what is required is not so much throwing out falsehood but acknowledging, first of all, that race and history and metaphysics do not enforce an identity. We must choose, within broad limits set by ecological, political, and economic realities, what it will mean to be African in the coming years.

* * *

I do not want to be misunderstood. We are Africans already. There are numerous examples from multiple domains of what our being African means. We have, for example, the OAU and the African Development Bank, as well as such regional organizations as the Southern African Development Coordination Conference (SADCC) and the Economic Community of West African States (ECOWAS), and African caucuses of the agencies of the United Nations and World Bank. At the Olympics and the Commonwealth games, athletes from African countries are seen as Africans by the world—and, perhaps, more important, by each other. Being "African" already has a certain context and a certain meaning.

But, as Achebe suggests, that meaning is not always one with which we can be happy, and that identity is one we must continue to reshape. In thinking about how we are to reshape it, we would do well to remember that the African identity is, for its bearers, only one among many. Like all identities institutionalized before anyone has permanently fixed a single meaning for them—for example, the German identity at the beginning of this century, the American identity in the latter part of the eighteenth century, or the Indian identity at the moment of independence so few years ago—being African is for its bearers one among other salient modes of being, all of which have to be constantly fought for and rethought. Indeed, in Africa, it is another of these identities that provides one of the most useful models for such rethinking, namely, the constantly shifting definition of "tribal" identities to meet the economic and political exigencies of the modern world.

Once more, let me quote Achebe:

> The duration of awareness, of consciousness of an identity, has really very little to do with how deep it is. You can suddenly become aware of an identity which you have been suffering for a long time without knowing. For instance, take the Igbo people. In my area, historically, they did not see themselves as Igbo. They saw themselves as people from this village or that village. In fact, in some places *Igbo* was a word of abuse; they were the "other" people, down in the bush. And yet, after the experience of the Biafran War, during a period of two years, it became a very powerful consciousness. But it was *real* all the time. They all spoke the same language, called Igbo, even though they were not using that identity in any way. But the moment came when this identity became very very powerful . . . and over a very short period.[13]

A short period it was, and also a tragic one. The Nigerian Civil War defined an Igbo identity. It did so in complex ways that grew out of the development of a common Igbo identity in colonial Nigeria and created the Igbo traders in the cities of northern Nigeria as an identifiable object of assault in the period that led up to the invention of Biafra.

Recognizing Igbo identity as a new thing is not a way of privileging other Nigerian identities. Each of the three central ethnic identities of modern political life—Hausa-Fulani, Yoruba, Igbo—is a product of the rough-and-tumble of the transition from colonial to postcolonial status. David Laitin has pointed out that "the idea that there was a single Hausa-Fulani tribe . . . was largely a political claim of the NPC [Northern Peoples' Congress] in their battle against the South," while "many elders intimately involved in rural Yoruba society today recall that, as late as the 1930s, 'Yoruba' was not a common form of political identification."[14] Nnamdi Azikiwe, one of the key figures in the construction of Nigerian nationalism, was extremely popular in Yoruba Lagos, where, as Laitin points out, "he edited his nationalist newspaper, the *West African Pilot*. It was only subsequent events that led him to be defined in Nigeria as an *Igbo* leader."[15] Yet Nigerian politics—and the more everyday economy of ordinary personal relations—is oriented along such axes. Only very occasionally does the fact float into view that even these three problematic identities account for at most seven out of ten Nigerians.

The story is repeated, even in places where it was not drawn in lines of blood. As Johannes Fabian has observed, the powerful Lingala- and Swahili-speaking identities of Zaire existed "because spheres of political and economic interest were established before the Belgians took full control, and continued to inform relations between regions under colonial rule."[16] Modern Ghana witnesses the development of an Akan identity, as speakers of the three major regional dialects of Twi—Asante, Fante, and Akuapem—organize themselves into a corporation against an (equally novel) Ewe unity.[17]

When it is not the "tribe" that is invested with new uses and meanings, it is religion. Yet the idea that Nigeria is composed of a Muslim North, a Christian South, and a mosaic of "pagan" holdovers is as inaccurate as the picture of three historic tribal identities. Two out of every five southern Yoruba people are Muslim. As Laitin writes, "Many northern groups, especially in what are today Benue, Plateau, Gongola, and Kwara states, are largely Christian. When the leaders of Biafra tried to convince the world that they were oppressed by northern Muslims, ignorant foreigners (including the pope) believed them. But the Nigerian army . . . was led by a northern Christian."[18] It is as useless here as it is in the case of race to point out that in each case the tribe or the religion, like all social identities, is based on an idealizing fiction, for life in Nigeria or in Congo has come to be lived through the idealization. The Igbo identity is real because Nigerians believe in it, and the Shona identity is real because

Zimbabweans have given it meaning. The rhetoric of a Muslim North and a Christian South structured political discussions in the period before Nigerian independence, but it was equally important in the debates about instituting a Muslim court of appeals in the draft constitution of 1976, and it could be found, for example, in many articles in the Nigerian press as electoral registration for a new civilian era began in July 1989.

*   *   *

There are three crucial lessons for the United States in these cases. First, identities are complex and multiple and grow out of a history of changing responses to economic, political, and cultural forces, almost always in opposition to other identities. Second, identities flourish, despite what I earlier called our "misrecognition" of their origins—despite, that is, their roots in myths and in lies. The third lesson is that there is, consequently, no large place for reason in the construction—as opposed to the study and the management—of identities. One temptation, then, for those who see the centrality of these fictions in our lives, is to leave reason behind—to celebrate and endorse those identities that seem at the moment to offer the best hope of advancing our other goals, and to keep silence about the lies and the myths. However, intellectuals do not easily neglect the truth, and, all things considered, our societies profit from the institutionalization of this imperative in the academy. It is therefore important for us to continue to try to tell our truths. But the facts I have been reviewing should imbue us all with a strong sense of the marginality of such work to the central issue of the resistance to racism and ethnic violence—and to sexism and other structures of difference that shape the world of power. These facts should force us to realize that the real battle is not being fought in the academy. As the fires raged in Los Angeles a few years ago, it seemed oddly irrelevant to fuss about racial ideologies. The solutions are the conquest of drugs and despair, new jobs, better education, more credit, and so many other more practical steps. Yet, as we all know, the shape of our world (and the shape of modern Africa) is in large part the product, often unintended and unanticipated, of theories; even the most vulgar of Marxists will have to admit that economic interests operate *through* ideologies. We cannot change the world simply by evidence and reasoning, but we surely cannot change it without them either.

What the academy *can* contribute—even if only slowly and marginally—is a disruption of the discourse of "racial" and "tribal" differences, for the reality of these many competing identities in Africa today plays into the hands of the very exploiters whose shackles we are trying to escape. "Race" in Europe and "tribe" in Africa are central to the way in which the objective interests of the worst-off are distorted.[19] The analogous point for African Americans was recognized long ago by Du Bois, who argued in *Black Reconstruction* that racist ideology had essentially blocked the formation of a significant labor movement in the United States,[20] for such a movement would have required the collaboration of the nine million ex-slave and white peasant workers of the South.[21] It is, in other words, because the categories of difference often cut across our economic interests that they operate to blind us to them. What binds middle-class African Americans to their dark-skinned fellow citizens downtown is not economic interest but racism and the cultural products of resistance to it that are shared across (much of) African American culture.

I have been arguing, in effect, that the political meanings of identities are historically and geographically relative. Because the value of identities is thus relative, we must argue for and against them case by case. Given the current situation in Africa, I think it remains true that Pan-Africanism—as the project of a continental fraternity and sorority, *not* as the project of a racialized Negro nationalism—however false or muddled its theoretical roots, can be a progressive force. It is as fellow Africans that Ghanaian diplomats (my father among them) interceded between the warring nationalist parties in Rhodesia under Unilateral Declaration of Independence (UDI), as fellow Africans that OAU teams can mediate regional conflicts, as fellow Africans that the human rights assessors organized under the OAU's Banjul Declaration can intercede for citizens of African states against the excesses of African governments. If there is to be hope for a Pan-Africanism of the African diaspora, once it is released from bondage to racial ideologies (alongside the many bases of alliance available to Africa's peoples in their political and cultural struggles), it is crucial that we recognize the independence (once "Negro" nationalism is gone) of the Pan-Africanism of the diaspora and the Pan-Africanism of the continent. It is in the exploration of these issues and possibilities that the future of an intellectually reinvigorated Pan-Africanism lies.

* * *

Informed by these African histories, I am impressed by a simple point of contrast. Ethnic variety in the United States is simply not the real resource for resistance to the state and its processes of unification that it can be in my homeland of Ghana and most other parts of Africa and Asia. Africa's societies are multicultural in a much stronger sense than the United States is, and that makes it interesting to compare the reality of Africa with the rhetoric of American multiculturalism.

I am not much one for "isms," and talk of multiculturalism makes me nervous, as does much of the other talk of "isms" that surround us. Multiculturalism sounds like the name of an ideology with a single agenda or a unified political vision. If there is such a unified ideology out there, I do not know what it is. What I do know is that in at least one sense of the much-abused word *culture,* we live in a society of many cultures, a multicultural society.

The idea of "culture" is much abused because it is so elastic. We can, however, identify a spectrum that begins with the most basic anthropological sense of the term, in which *culture* means all the ideas and practices that are shared by a social group, and ends with what we call "high" culture, the critical notion of culture that picks from among those ideas and practices a subset that requires in both producers and consumers the greatest training or the most individual skill. The habit of shaking hands at meetings belongs to culture in the anthropological sense; Sandro Botticelli and Martin Buber and Count Basie belong to culture in the critical sense.

No one is likely to make much fuss about the fact that a society is multicultural in the critic's sense, for, in this sense, most large-scale societies have been multicultural. Once a division of labor and social stratification exist, there will be people who do and people who do not know about music and literature and pottery and painting. If we call all these specialized spheres together "high" culture, then everyone will participate in the high culture to varying degrees, and there are likely to be subgroups (opera-lovers, say, or dedicated moviegoers, or lovers of poetry or rap) who share significant practices and ideas with each other that are not shared with everyone else.

If being multicultural is a problem, it is because societies are multicultural in the anthropological sense, referring to what a social group has in common: it is what we teach our children; and in teaching them, we make them members of our social group. By definition, therefore, culture in this sense is shared; it is the social bottom line that includes language and table manners, religious ideas, moral values. With this idea of culture goes the idea of a subculture: people who share not just the common ideas and practices of the whole social group but also more specific practices and values.

I say "social group" because a single society, a group of people living together in a common state under common authorities, need not have a common culture. There is no single shared body of ideas and practices in most contemporary African states; there is, as we have learned so sadly in recent years, no such shared culture in Bosnia and Hercegovina. I think it is fair to say also that there is not now and never has been such a shared culture in the United States.

The reason is simple. The United States has always been multilingual and has always had minorities that did not speak or understand English. It has always had a plurality of religious traditions, beginning with Native American, Puritan, and Catholic religions and now including many varieties of Judaism, Islam, Buddhism, Jainism, Taoism, Rahai, and others. Further, even among those who do speak English, Americans have always differed significantly, based on their region, from North to South and East to West, and from country to city, in customs of greeting, notions of civility, and a whole host of other ways.

At the same time, it has also always been true that there was a dominant culture in the United States that was Christian, spoke English, and identified with the high culture traditions of Europe, particularly England. Until recently, when people spoke approvingly of American culture, it was this Christian, Anglo-Saxon culture to which they referred. (When they spoke disapprovingly of American culture, especially in Europe, they meant the popular culture of Hollywood, Coca-Cola, and bubble gum.)

As public education has expanded in the United States, its citizens, especially those educated in public elementary schools in this country, have come to share a body of historical knowledge and an understanding of the U.S. political system. It is increasingly the case that whatever other languages children in this country speak, they speak and understand English, and they watch many of the same television programs and listen to much of the same music. In that sense, most young Americans have a shared culture based in a whole variety of kinds of English, but it is no longer that older Christian, Anglo-Saxon tradition that used to be called American culture.

The outline of this common culture is somewhat blurry, but it includes, for example, in its practices, baseball; in its ideas, democracy; in its arts, rap music videos and many movies. This culture is to a large extent the product of schools and the media, yet even those who share this common culture—the shared cultural literacy of E. D. Hirsch, let us say—live in subcultures of language, religion, family organization, and political assumptions. More than this, most who are black and Hispanic have, irrespective of their incomes, radically different experiences and expectations of the state. If anyone did not believe this before, surely every sane person recognized this after the Rodney King verdict and the responses to it in Los Angeles in the spring of 1992.

Now I take it that multiculturalism is meant to be the name of a response to these familiar facts. The word signifies an approach to education and to public culture that acknowledges the diversity of cultures and subcultures in the United States and that proposes to deal with that diversity in some other way than by imposing the values and ideas of the hitherto dominant Anglo-Saxon cultural tradition. That, I think, is the common core of all the things that been called multiculturalism.

I think this common idea is a good one for several reasons. First, the old practice of imposing Christian, Anglo-Saxon tradition was rooted in—and to that extent expresses—racism and anti-Semitism. Second, making the culture of one subculture the official culture of a state privileges its members and gives them advantages in public life in ways that are profoundly antiegalitarian and thus antidemocratic.

Yet agreeing to this idea does not reveal much about what should be done in schools and public culture. It indicates that we must try to impose certain practices and ideas, but it does not assert what should be done affirmatively. I want to suggest that one of the affirmative strategies in this area is a bad idea for public education and that there are other strategies that are better. I also want to reflect on why living together in a multicultural society is bound to turn out to be difficult.

Many multiculturalists seem to think that the way to deal with the fact of our many cultures in the public education system is to teach each child the culture of the child's group. This is the strategy of many Afrocentrists and of some (but by no means all) of those who have favored bilingual education for Hispanics. This is the strategy I oppose.

To explain my first basis for objection, I need to elicit a paradox in this approach, which I can do by considering the Afrocentric answer to the question, Why should we teach African American children something different from what we teach other children? The Afrocentric answer comes in two parts. The first part contends that we should do so because they already come from a different culture; the second part argues we should do so because we should teach all people about their own traditions.

It is the first part of the answer that is paradoxical: it proposes to solve the problems created because children have different cultures by emphasizing and entrenching those differences, not by trying to reduce them.[22] I have no difficulty with the argument that children's home cultures need to be taken into account in deciding how to teach them (there is no point in talking to children in languages or dialects they do not understand or punishing them for behavior that they are being taught at home). But to admit *that* is to admit only that culture may sometimes make a difference in *how* we should teach; it should not make a difference in *what* we should teach. To defend teaching children different histories (e.g., Afrocentric history) or different forms of speech or writing (e.g., Black English) on the ground that this is already their culture simply begs the question. If we teach African American children a different history, then it will become true that knowing that history and not knowing any other history will be part of the culture of African Americans. But the fact is that if we do not enforce cultural differences by means of Afrocentric education in the schools, surely they will largely disappear.

The contrast here with the multicultural realities of a country like Ghana could not be more striking. There, substantial differences in language and culture are created outside the state, independently of the media and the schools, and the schools need to work hard to create a shared culture. In the United States, schools are increasingly central in articulating cultural differences. What that means is that the only serious argument for Afrocentricity that survives is the second part of the answer I considered earlier: the claim that we must teach each child the culture of the child's group because that is the right thing to do, because we should.

* * *

That idea is much more powerful. It is presumably at the basis of the thought that many nonobservant Jews share with observant Jews (who have other reasons for believing this), namely, that it is good to teach their children Jewish history and customs because they are Jewish children. It is the argument—"we have Plato to our father"—that led to the sense of exclusion that many African Americans felt when the history and culture of the United States were taught to them as the continuation of a white Western tradition. Much Afrocentrism is a reaction to this argument. I am skeptical of all arguments of this form. Traditions are worth teaching because they are beautiful and good and true, never because they are ours or yours, mine or thine. After going to my first seder, I was struck by the thought that this was a tradition worth teaching to everybody, Jew or Gentile; similarly, I have always valued the experience of family community among my Moslem cousins at Ramadan. Even if teaching children "their" history were "good," it is not something that would be practical for American public schools to do. If carried to its ultimate, this policy would require segregation into cultural groups, either within or between public schools, in ways that would be plainly unconstitutional in the United States. Moreover, if we did have segregated classes teaching Jewish, African American, Anglo, Hispanic, and Chinese history in our schools, by what right would we forbid children from going to the "wrong" classes?

There are things that we surely all believe that we should teach all American children. In particular, we should teach them something of the history of the American political system. This raises another reason why we cannot hope to teach each child only the child's cultural tradition, for understanding the American constitutional system and its history requires knowledge of slavery and immigration, the Civil War and Reconstruction, the underground railroad and Ellis Island. If there is a sense in which each of these experiences belongs to the history of one social group more than to another, there is also a clear sense in which they belong to us all.

That idea motivates the approach to dealing with our multicultural society that I favor, and it undergirds my notion of multiculturalism, whose affinities with an older pluralism will, I hope, be obvious. What is ideal in a multicultural society, whose multicultural character is created outside the state in the sphere of civil society, is that the state's education systems should try to make these multiple subcultures known to one other. A multicultural education should be one that leaves individuals not only knowing and loving what is good in the traditions of their own subculture but also understanding and appreciating the traditions of others (while critically rejecting the worst of all traditions). This approach has its practical problems; a curriculum filled with the history of Korean Americans, African Americans, Anglo-Americans, Jewish Americans, and others risks imparting only a shallow appreciation of all of them. But the principle of selection is clear. We should try to teach about those many world traditions that have come to be important at different stages of American history. This means that we begin with Native American and Protestant Dutch and English and African and Iberian cultures, adding voices to the story as they were added to the nation. Because different elements are important to different degrees in different places today, the balance should be struck differently in different places.

I have a final argument against Afrocentricity and similar movements, which relates to the danger they represent to the difficult task of managing multicultural—plural—societies. As I indicated previously, no one is likely to be troubled by the variety of subcultures in high culture because however important our participation in high culture is, it is unlikely to be at the heart of our ethnicity. High culture crosses ethnic boundaries to an extraordinary degree. (The boundaries that it crosses with less ease are those of class.) The result is that subdivisions of high culture are not likely to become central to the organization of political life. The United States is not threatened by the cultural autonomy of the American Philosophical Association or even the American Medical Association. In this respect, the associations of high culture are like many elements of popular culture. The next New York mayoral election is not going to be a battle between followers of the Mets and of the Yankees.

In contrast, differences in subcultures—in the anthropologist's sense of culture—run deep. We pass on our language to the next generation because we want to communicate with our young ones; we pass on religion because we care about its vision and endorse its values; we pass on our folkways because we value people with those folkways. Even when these values are not explicitly articulated, they lie at the heart of our self-conceptions and our conceptions of community. Culture in this sense is the home of what we care about most. If other people organize their solidarity around cultures different from ours, this makes them, to that extent, different from us in ways that matter to us deeply. The result, of course, is not just that we have difficulty understanding across cultures—this is an inevitable result of cultural difference, for much of culture consists of language and other shared modes of understanding—but also that we end up preferring our own kind; and if we prefer our own kind, it is easy enough to slip into preferring to vote for our own kind, to employ our own kind, and so on. In sum, culture undergirds loyalties. To the extent that these loyalties matter, they will be mobilized in politics, unless a civic culture can be created that explicitly seeks to exclude them. That is why my multiculturalism is so necessary. It is the only way to reduce the misunderstanding across subcultures, the only way to build bridges of loyalty across the ethnicities that have so often divided us. Multiculturalism of this sort—pluralism, to use an older word—is the only way of making sure we care enough about people across ethnic divides to keep those ethnic divides from destroying us.

The task is not to replace one ethnocentrism with many or to reject old ideals of truth and impartiality as intrinsically biased. Rather, it is to recognize that those ideals have yet to be fully lived up to in our scholarship, that the bias has derived not from scholars who took Western standards (which often turn out to be everybody's standards) of truth for granted but from those who did not take them seriously enough.

The old way of dealing with the problem of many cultures was to make us *e pluribus unum*. Out of many cultures, mold one. Anyone who appreciates the vibrancy of American popular culture and high culture, the splendid variety of our literatures, music, and cuisines, is likely to balk at such a project. At the same time, anyone who has looked at our history and seen how often the one into which we were to be made was white, Anglo-Saxon Protestant will be skeptical that it could be anything other than the cover for the domination of our other cultures. These are legitimate skepticisms. The only alternative that does not threaten perpetual schism is the hard work of a multiculturalism that accepts America's diversity while teaching each of us the ways and the worth of others.

Notes

Portions of this essay are based on chapter 9 of Kwame Anthony Appiah, *In My Father's House: Africa in the Philosophy of Culture* (New York: Oxford University Press, 1992).

1. My father would never have forgiven the solecism of trying to explain a proverb.

2. About half of those arrested in the Los Angeles riots were Latino; a little over a third were black. This is probably not a "fair" representation of the rates of participation in the unrest, since there is some evidence that the police were more likely to arrest Latinos. But the point is that these figures do show (what many people saw on their televisions) that the riots were not monoracial.

3. See, for example, Robert Harms, *Times Literary Supplement*, November 29, 1985, 1343.

4. Appiah, *In My Father's House*, chapters 1, 2, and 9.

5. Okomfo Anokye is the name of the priest who helped the first of the Asante kings, Osei Tutu, form the nation from the various Akan kingdoms that it united. He is said to have brought the golden stool, symbol of Asante kingship, down from heaven.

6. Tzvetan Todorov, "'Race,' Writing and Culture" in *"Race," Writing and Difference*, ed. Henry Louis Gates Jr. (Chicago: University of Chicago Press, 1986), 370–80. One does not have to believe in witchcraft, after all, to believe that women were persecuted as witches in colonial Massachusetts.

7. Gayatri Spivak recognized these problems when she spoke of "strategic" essentialism. See G. Spivak, *In Other Worlds: Essays in Cultural Politics* (New York: Routledge, 1988), 205.

8. See, for example, K. Anthony Appiah, "The Uncompleted Argument: Du Bois and the Illusion of Race," in *"Race," Writing and Difference*, ed. Gates, 21–37; and K. Anthony Appiah, "Alexander Crummell and the Invention of Africa," *Massachusetts Review* 31 (Autumn 1990): 385–406.

9. The violence between Senegalese and Mauritanians in the spring of 1989 can be understood only when we recall that the legal abolition of racial slavery of "Negroes," owned by "Moorish" masters, occurred in the early 1980s.

10. Chinua Achebe, "Interview with Anthony Appiah, D.A.N. Jones and John Ryle," *Times Literary Supplement*, February 26, 1982, 209.

11. See, for example, Wole Soyinka, *Myth, Literature and the African World* (Cambridge: Cambridge University Press, 1976).

12. Kwasi Wiredu, *Philosophy and an African Culture* (Cambridge: Cambridge University Press, 1980), 38.

13. Chinua Achebe, unpublished transcription of the full interview with Chinua Achebe that was edited for the *Times Literary Supplement*, February 26, 1982.

14. David Laitin, *Hegemony and Culture: Politics and Religious Change among the Yoruba* (Chicago: University of Chicago Press, 1986), 7–8.

15. Ibid., 8.

16. This passage continues: "Increasingly also Lingala and Swahili came to divide functions between them. Lingala served the military and much of the administration in the capital of the lower Congo; Swahili became the language of the workers in the mines of Katanga. This created cultural connotations which began to emerge very early and which remained prevalent in Mobutu's Zaire. From the point of view of Katanga/Shaba, Lingala has been the undignified jargon of unproductive soldiers, government clerks, entertainers, and, recently, of a power clique, all of them designated as *batoka chini*, people from down-river, i.e., from Kinshasa. Swahili as spoken in Katanga was a symbol of regionalism, even for those colonials who spoke it badly." Johannes Fabian, *Language and Colonial Power* (Cambridge: Cambridge University Press, 1986), 42–43. The dominance of Swahili in certain areas is already itself a colonial product (ibid., 6).

17. Similarly, Shona and Ndebele identities in modern Zimbabwe became associated with political parties at independence, even though Shona-speaking peoples had spent much of the late precolonial period in military confrontations with each other.

18. Laitin, *Hegemony and Culture*, 8. I need hardly add that religious identities are equally salient and equally mythological in Lebanon or in Ireland.

19. That "race" operates this way has been clear to many African Americans. It shows up, for example, in a fictional context as a central theme of George Schuyler's *Black No More* (New York: Negro Universities Press, 1931); see, for example, 59.

20. W. E. B. Du Bois, *Black Reconstruction: An Essay toward a History of the Part Which Black People Played in America, 1860–1880* (New York: Russel and Russel, 1935). Du Bois provides a body of evidence that remains relevant. Echoing Du Bois, Cedric Robinson writes, "Once the industrial class emerged as dominant in the nation, it possessed not only its own basis of power and the social relations historically related to that power, but it also had available to it the instruments of repression created by the now subordinate Southern ruling class. In its struggle with labour, it could activate racism to divide the labour movement into antagonistic forces. Moreover, the permutations of the instrument appeared endless: black against white; Anglo-Saxon against southern and eastern European; domestic against immigrant; proletarian against share-cropper; white American against Asian, Black, Latin American, etc." Cedric Robinson, *Black Marxism: The Making of the Black Radical Tradition* (London: Zed, 1983), 286.

21. Robinson, *Black Marxism*, 313.

22. I think of this as the "WASPS have Christmas, Jews have Hanukkah, so Blacks should have Kwanzaa" approach.

Commentary:
Race and the American City

Senator Bill Bradley

My purpose is to offer some thoughts on the subject of race and the American city. Slavery was this country's original sin, just as race remains our unresolved dilemma. The future of American cities is inextricably bound to the issue of race and ethnicity. By the year 2000, only 57 percent of the people entering the work force in America will be native-born whites. That means that the economic future of the children of white Americans will increasingly depend on the talents of nonwhite Americans. If we allow them to fail because of penny-pinching or timidity about straight talk, America will become a second-rate power. If they succeed, America and all Americans will be enriched. As a nation, we will either find common ground and move ahead together or each of us will be diminished.

I grew up in a small town located on the banks of the Mississippi River; it was a multiracial, multiethnic factory town in which most of the people were Democrats. My father was the local banker and a nominal Republican. The town had one stoplight, and there were ninety-six students in my high school graduating class. The "Big City," St. Louis, Missouri, was something we were not.

I left that small midwestern town and went to college in New Jersey in another small town, spending most of my time in an even smaller town, the campus, except to travel to such places as Philadelphia, New York, or Providence to play basketball. I graduated, spent two years in England at a slightly larger college town, and then went to New York, where for the first time I lived in a big city.

The city for me was always about race, as much as it was about class or power or fashion. Maybe that was because I was a professional basketball player in New York and was working in a kind of black world. This was before I had any real knowledge about the welfare system, the courts and prisons, the nature of an urban economy, or the sociology of neighborhoods. But if I paid attention, I saw the city through the eyes of my black teammates, as well as through my own.

Above all, the city to me was never what I heard my liberal friends say it was. In their world, people of color were all victims. But while my teammates had been victimized, their experience and their perception of the experience of black Americans could not be reduced to victimization. To many, what the label "victimization" implied was an insult to their dignity, discipline, strength, and potential.

Life in cities was full of more complexity and more hope than the media or the politicians would admit, and part of getting beyond color was not only attacking the sources of inequity but also refusing to make race an excuse for failing to pass judgment about self-destructive behavior.

Without a community, there could be no commonly held standards, and without some commonly held standards, there could be no community. The question is whether in our cities we can build a set of commonly accepted rules that enhances individuality and life chances but also provides the glue and the tolerance to prevent us from going for one another's throats.

It is important to remember that urban America is not only divided by a line between blacks on one side and whites on another. Increasingly, it is a mixture of other races, languages, and religions, as new immigrants arrive in search of economic promise and freedom from state control. Just think: over four and a half million Latinos and nearly five million Asian Pacifics have arrived in the United States since 1970.

In New Jersey, school children come from families that speak 120 different languages at home. In Atlanta, managers of some low-income apartment complexes that were once virtually all-black now need to speak fluent Spanish. Detroit is a city that has absorbed over 200,000 people of Middle Eastern descent. In the San Jose, California, phone book, residents with the Vietnamese surname Nguyen outnumber the Joneses by nearly 50 percent. In Houston, one Korean immigrant restaurant owner oversees Hispanic immigrant employees who prepare Chinese-style food for a predominately black clientele.

Unfortunately, even though our American future depends on finding common ground, many white Americans resist relinquishing the sense of entitlement skin color has given them throughout our national history. They lack an understanding of the emerging dynamics of one world, even in the United States, because to them nonwhites always have been the "other." On top of that, people of different races often do not listen to each other on the subject of race. It is as if we are all experts locked into our narrow views who prefer to be wrong rather than risk changing those views.

Black Americans ask of Asian Americans, "What is the problem? You are doing well economically." Black Americans believe that Latinos often fail to find common ground with their historic struggle, and some Latino Americans agree, questioning whether the black civil rights model is the only path to progress. White Americans continue to harbor absurd stereotypes about all people of color, and black Americans take white criticism of individual acts as an attempt to stigmatize all black Americans. We seem to be more interested in defending our racial territory than in recognizing that we could be enriched by another race's perspective.

In politics for the last twenty-five years, silence or distortion has shaped the issue of race and urban America. Both political parties have contributed to the problem. Republicans have played the race card in a divisive way to get votes. The Willie Horton ads were a prime example. At the same time, Democrats have suffocated discussion of self-destructive behavior among the minority population in a cloak of silence and denial. The result is that yet another generation has been lost. We cannot afford to wait longer. It is time for candor, time for truth, and time for action.

America's cities are poorer, sicker, and more violent than at any period in my lifetime, and their populations are less educated. The physical problems are obvious: old housing, deteriorated schools, aging infrastructure, diminished manufacturing base, a health care system short of doctors that fails to immunize against measles, much less educate about AIDS. The jobs have disappeared, and many neighborhoods have been gutted. A genuine depression has hit cities, with unemployment in some areas at the levels of the 1930s. Yet just as Americans found solidarity then in the midst of trauma and just as imaginative leadership moved us through the darkest days of the Great Depression, so today the physical conditions of our cities *can* be altered. What it takes is collective will, greater accountability, and sufficient resources.

What is less obvious in urban America is the crisis of meaning. Without meaning, there can be no hope. Without hope, there can be no struggle. Without struggle, there can be no personal betterment. Absence of meaning derives from overt and subtle attacks from racist quarters over many years, and, furthered by an increasing pessimism about the possibility of justice, it offers a context for chaos and irresponsibility.

Development of meaning starts from the very beginning of life. Yet over 40 percent of all births in the twenty largest cities of America are to women living alone. Among black women, out-of-wedlock births account for over 65 percent of all births. While many single women do heroic jobs in raising children, millions of others get caught in a life undertow that drowns both them and their children. Many of these children live in a world without love and without a father or any other male supportive figure besides the drug dealer, the pimp, or the gang leader. They are thrown out on the street early without any frame of reference, except survival. They have no historical awareness of the civil rights movement, much less of the power of American democracy. I remember a substitute teacher in New York who once told me that he was assigned *The Autobiography of Malcolm X* when he learned to read and write. Hoping that his students would feel the same excitement in reading the book that he did as a youngster, he assigned it to his students; when he did, they wanted to know why he had assigned a book about Malcolm Ten.

To say to young people who have no connection to religious faith, no family outside a gang, no sense of place outside the territory, no imagination beyond the cadence of rap or the violence of TV that government is on their side rings hollow. Their contact with government has not empowered them but diminished them. To them, government at best is incompetent—as evidenced in their schools, the streets, the welfare department—and at worst, corrupt—as epitomized by the cops and building inspectors on the take, the white-collar criminal who gets only a suspended sentence, or the local politician with gross personal behavior. Moreover, replacing a corrupt white mayor with a corrupt black mayor will not make the difference.

In such a world, calls to "just say no" to drugs or to study hard for sixteen years in order to get an $18,000-a-year job are laughable. Instead of desires rooted in the values of commitment and service to community as expressed through black churches and mosques, desires, such as commodities, become rooted in the immediate gratification of the moment. TV bombards these kids with messages of conspicuous consumption, and they want it now. They become trapped in the quicksand of American materialism. The market sells images of sex, violence, and drugs, regardless of their corrosive effects on hard work and caring—values formerly handed down from an older generation. With no awareness of how to change their world through political action and no reservoirs of real self-knowledge, they are buffeted by the winds of violence and narcissism.

The physical conditions of American cities and the absence of meaning in more and more lives come together at the barrel of a gun. If one
were to identify the one factor that has changed in cities since the 1960s,
it would be the pervasiveness of fear. Fear covers the streets like a sheet
of ice. Everyday the newspaper tells of another murder. The numbers of
both murders and violent crimes have doubled in the twenty largest cities since 1968. Ninety percent of all violence is committed by males, and
they are also its predominant victims. Indeed, murder is the highest cause
of death among young black males. In 1968, there were 394,000 security
guards in America. Today it is a growth industry, with nearly 700,000
guards.

For African Americans in cities, the violence is not new. You do not have
to see *Boyz N the Hood* to confirm it. Just visit public housing projects
where mothers send their children to school dodging bullets; talk with
young girls whose rapes go uninvestigated; listen to elderly residents express their constant fear of violation; and remember the story of a former
drug dealer who told me that he quit only after he found his partner shot,
with his brains oozing onto the pavement.

What is new is whites' fear of random violence. No place in the city
seems safe. Walking the streets seems to be a form of Russian roulette. At
the core is a fear of young black men. The movie *Grand Canyon* captures
the feeling. It sends the message that if a person is white and gets off the
main road into the wrong territory, that person becomes a target because
he or she is white. Furthermore, whites are targets for death, not just rob-
bery. If they stay on the main road, they still might be shot for no apparent reason. Guns in the hands of the unstable, the angry, and the resent-
ful are used. As the kid in *Grand Canyon* says, "You respect me only
because I have a gun."

Never mind that in a society insufficiently color blind, all black men
have to answer for the white fear of violence from a few black men. Never mind that Asian Americans fear both black and white Americans or
that in Miami and Los Angeles some of the most feared gangs are Latinos and Chinese. And never mind that the ultimate racism was whites'
ignoring the violence when it was not in their neighborhoods or that black
Americans have always feared certain white neighborhoods. Never mind
all that.

There are two phenomena here. There is white fear, and there is the
appearance of black emboldenment. Today, many whites, responding to
a more violent reality heightened by sensational news stories, see young
black men traveling in groups, cruising the city, looking for trouble, and
they are frightened. Many white Americans, whether fairly or unfairly,

seem to be saying of some young black males, "You litter the street and deface the subway, and no one, black or white, says stop. You cut school, threaten a teacher, 'dis' a social worker, and no one, white or black, says stop. You snatch a purse, you crash a concert, break a telephone box, and no one, white or black, says stop. You rob a store, rape a jogger, shoot a tourist, and when they catch you, if they catch you, you cry racism. And nobody, white or black, says stop."

It makes no difference whether this white rap is the exact and total reality in our American cities; it is what millions of white Americans feel is true. In a kind of ironic flip of fate, the fear of brutal white repression felt for decades in the black community and the seething anger it generated now appear to be mirrored in the fear whites have of random attack from blacks and the growing anger it fuels. The white disdain grows when a frightened white politician convenes a commission to investigate the charges of racism, and the anger swells when well-known black spokespersons fill the evening news with threats and bombast.

What most politicians want to avoid is the need to confront the reality that causes the fear. They do not want to put themselves at risk by speaking candidly about violence to blacks and whites and saying the same things to both groups. Essentially, they are indifferent to black self-destruction, and violence only hardens that indifference, not only to the perpetrator but to all African Americans.

Physically, increasing numbers of white Americans leave the city and in numbers far greater than blacks. From 1970 to 1990, over four million white Americans moved out of big cities. Psychologically, white Americans put up walls to the increasing desperate plight of those, both black and white, who cannot leave. Those Americans who cannot leave remain, trying to raise children in a war zone, to hold jobs in a Third World economy, and to establish a sense of community in a desert where there is no water of hope and where people are mostly out for themselves.

It is not that there is no racism; racism, unfortunately, is alive and well. It is not that the police brutality does not exist; it does. It is not that police departments give residents a feeling of security; few do. But when politicians do not talk about the reality that everyone knows exists, they cannot lead us out of our current crisis. Institutions are no better than the people who run them, and because very few people of different races make real contact or have real conversations with one other, white vigilante groups and the black TV spokesperson educate the uneducated about race. The result is that the division among races in our cities deepens, with white Americans becoming more and more unwilling to spend the money to ameliorate the physical conditions or to see why the absence of meaning in the lives of many urban children threatens the future of their own children.

Yet, even in this atmosphere of disintegration, the power of the human spirit comes through. Heroic families do overcome the odds, sometimes working four jobs to send their children to college. Churches are peopled by the faithful who do practice the power of love. Local neighborhood leaders have turned around the local school, organized the health clinics, or rehabilitated blocks of housing. These islands of courage and dedication still offer the possibility of local renewal, just as the U.S. system of government offers and makes possible national rebirth.

Urban America will take one of three paths in the future: abandonment, encirclement, or conversion. Abandonment means recognizing that in the current circumstances, with billions of dollars invested in the national highway system that led to suburbia, corporate parks, and the malling of America and with communications technology advancing so fast that the economic advantages of urban proximity are being replaced by the computer screens, the city has outlived its usefulness. Like the small town whose industry leaves, the city will wither and disappear. Like empires of ancient days, urban America has reached a point of no return and will crumble from within, giving way to new and different forms of social arrangement. "Massive investment in urban America would be throwing money away," the argument goes, "and to try to prevent the decline will be futile."

Encirclement means that people in cities will live in enclaves. The racial and ethnic walls will go higher, the class lines will be reinforced by ever increasing security forces, and communal life will disappear. What will replace a sense of communities will be deepening divisions, with politicians splitting up a shrinking economic pie into ever smaller ethnic, racial, and religious slices. There will be a kind of clockwork-orange society in which the rich will pay for their security, the middle class will continue to flee as they confront violence, and the poor will be preyed upon at will or join the army of violent predators. What will be lost for everyone will be freedom, civility, and the chance to build a common future.

Conversion means winning over all segments of urban life to a new politics of change, empowerment, and common effort. Conversion is as different from the politics of dependency as it is from the politics of greed. Its optimism relates to the belief that every person can realize his or her potential in an atmosphere of nurturing liberty. Its morality is grounded in the conviction that each of us has an obligation to another human being, simply because that person is a human being.

There will not be a charismatic leader in this envisioned city, but there will be many leaders of awareness who champion integrity and humility over self-promotion and command performances. Answers will not come from an elite that has determined in advance what the new society will look like. Instead, the future will be shaped by the voices from inside the turmoil of urban America, as well as by those who claim to see a bigger picture.

Conversion requires listening to the disaffected, as well as to the powerful. Empowerment requires seizing the moment. The core of conversion begins with a recognition that all of us will advance together or everyone of us will be diminished, that American diversity is not our weakness but our strength, and that this country will never be able to lead the world by the power of our example until we have come to terms with one another and overcome the blight of racial division that has been our history.

The first concrete steps are to bring an end to violence. This entails intervening early in a child's life, reducing child abuse, establishing rules, remaining unintimidated, and involving the community in its own salvation. As a young man in dredlocks said at a recent town meeting, "What we need is for people to care enough about themselves, so that they won't hurt anyone else." That is the essence of community policing—getting a community to respect itself enough to cooperate and support the police so that together security is ensured. The 5 percent of children who do not want to learn can not be allowed to destroy the learning environment for the 95 percent who do want to learn. In addition, we need gun control, draconian punishment for drug kingpins, mandatory sentences for crimes committed with guns, and reinvestment of some defense budget savings into city police departments, schools, and hospitals.

The second step is to bolster families in urban America. That effort begins with the recognition that the most important year in a child's life is the first. Houses must be established for women who are pregnant and want to spend the first year of their child's life in a residential setting with other mothers. Young fathers would be encouraged to participate, too. These houses would reduce parental neglect and violence by teaching teenage mothers how to parent. By offering a program of cognitive stimulation, these houses would prepare a child for a lifetime of learning. These houses need to be combined with full funding for WIC (Women, Infants, and Children) and Head Start, more generous tax treatment of children, one-year parental leave, tough child support enforcement, and welfare reform that encourages marriage, work, and assumption of responsibility, instead of more children born to parents who cannot afford them.

But there is a hard truth here. No institution can replace the nurturing of a loving family. The most important example in a child's life is the parent, not celebrities, however virtuous or talented they might be. A child might want to play golf like Nancy Lopez or play basketball like Michael Jordan or skate like Kristi Yamaguchi or display the wit of Bill Cosby, but above all the child should want to be like his or her father or mother. In a world where few fathers are involved, mothers have a particularly big burden. There are no shortcuts here—only life led daily.

The third step is to create for those who can work jobs that promise to last; an essential ingredient for this is a growing economy. It is only through individual empowerment that we can guarantee long-term economic growth. Without growth, scapegoats will be sought, and racial tensions will heighten. Without growth, hopes will languish. How do we get growth? Enterprise zones, full funding of jobs corps, more investment in low-income housing, help in financing small businesses, and technical assistance in management. Investment in urban infrastructure, such as ports, roads, and mass transit, will become a source of jobs and training for urban residents at the same time it builds part of the foundation for private investment. Allowing pension funds to be invested in real estate and assessing a very low capital gains tax on the sale of assets that have generated five hundred urban jobs for ten years will attract more investment.

No targeted program can overcome the drag of a sluggish national economy. Reducing the deficit, consuming more wisely, increasing public investment in health and education, and avoiding protectionism are essential for long-term growth. Combined with ensuring economic opportunity for all, long-term growth can save American cities, while taking all Americans to the higher economic ground.

Finally, the political process holds the ultimate key. It has failed to address this country's urban prospects because politicians feel accountable mainly to those who vote. Urban Americans have voted in declining numbers, so politicians have ignored them. Voter registration and active participation remain the critical empowerment link. The history of American democracy is a history of broadening the vote: when the Constitution was adopted, the only Americans who had the vote were white males with property. In the 1830s, voting rights were extended to white males without property, in the 1860s to black males, in the 1920s to women, and in the 1970s to young people, ages eighteen to twenty-one. That is the history. Yet today if one-third of the voting-age population in the United States woke up on election day and wanted to vote, they would not be allowed to because they are not registered. Again, what is needed is not so much charismatic leadership but day-to-day leadership, truthful leadership, dedicated to real and lasting change. In other words, we require leadership that has the power within the community by virtue of the community's *knowing* the leaders and having confidence that they can get things done. For change to come, decisions have to be made, work has to get done, and some group of individuals has to accept collective responsibility for making change happen.

Stephen Vincent Benét once said about American diversity, "All of these you are"—all of these racial ethnic, religious, groups you are—"and each is partly you, and none is false, and none is wholly true."

Another way of saying out of many, one. Benét was describing America. Whether the metaphor we use to define America is the melting pot or a tossed salad, when one becomes an American citizen he or she professes a creed. Citizenship in the United States entails forswearing allegiance to a foreign power and embarking on a journey of development in liberty. For those who came generations ago, there is a need to reaffirm this country's founding principles—liberty, equality, democracy—principles that have always eluded complete fulfillment. The American city is where all these ideas and cultures have always clashed, sometimes violently. But all, even those brought here in chattel slavery and subsequently freed, are not African or Italian or Polish or Irish or Japanese. They are Americans.

What we lose when racial or ethnic self-consciousness dominates are tolerance, curiosity, and civility—precisely the qualities we need to allow us to live side by side in mutual respect. The fundamental challenge is to understand the suffering of others, as well as to share in their joy. To sacrifice that sensitivity on the altar of racial chauvinism is to lose our future. We will lose our future unless urgency informs our action, passing the buck stops, scapegoating fails, and excuses disappear. The American city needs physical rejuvenation, economic opportunity, and moral direction, but, above all, it needs the same thing every small town needs: the willingness to treat a person of another race or ethnicity with the respect you show a brother or sister and the belief that together you will build a better world than you would have done alone, a world in which all Americans stand on common ground.

Note

This essay is based on a speech entitled "Race and the American City," which Senator Bill Bradley delivered on the Senate floor on March 26, 1992.

Contributors

Kwame Anthony Appiah is a professor of Afro-American studies and philosophy at Harvard University. He is the author of *In My Father's House: Africa in the Philosophy of Culture* (1992) and, with Amy Gutmann, of *Color Conscious: The Political Morality of Race* (1996). Among his other works are the novel *Another Death in Venice* (1995).

Lawrence D. Bobo is a professor of sociology and Afro-American studies at Harvard University. He is the coauthor of the award winning book *Racial Attitudes in America* (1988). His research has appeared in the *Public Opinion Quarterly, Social Psychology Quarterly, American Journal of Sociology, American Sociological Review,* and *Journal of Personality and Social Psychology.*

Bill Bradley is a former U.S. senator from New Jersey. In 1995, Senator Bradley announced that he would not seek a fourth term, citing his belief that both political parties have moved away from his concept of service and his vision of what the United States can be. He has continued to speak out on issues central to his work in the Senate.

David A. Hollinger is a professor of history at the University of California at Berkeley. His books include *In the American Province: Studies in the History and Historiography of Ideas* (1985), *Postethnic America: Beyond Multiculturalism* (1995), and *Science, Jews, and Secular Cultural: Studies in Mid-Twentieth Century American Intellectual History* (1996).

Matthew Frye Jacobson is an assistant professor of American studies and history at Yale University and the author of *Special Sorrows: The Diasporic Imagination of Irish, Polish, and Jewish Immigrants in the United States* (1995) and *Becoming Caucasian: The Vicissitudes of Whiteness in American Politics and Culture* (forthcoming).

Wendy F. Katkin is the associate provost for Educational Initiatives at the State University of New York at Stony Brook. She has written numerous articles on the social aspects of contemporary life, Asian immigration at the turn of the century, and women in science, math, and education.

Stanley N. Katz is president of the American Council of Learned Societies. Formerly Class of 1921 Bicentennial Professor of the History of American Law and Liberty at Princeton University, Katz is a leading expert on American legal and constitutional history and the author and editor of numerous books and articles.

Ned Landsman is a professor of history at the State University of New York at Stony Brook. He is the author of *Scotland and Its First American Colony, 1683–1765* (1985) and numerous articles on ethnicity, society, and culture in early America and on Scotland and Scottish emigration in the early modern period.

Nikhil Pal Singh is an assistant professor in the American Studies Program and the Department of History at New York University. He received his Ph.D. in American Studies at Yale University in 1995 and is working on a book on the Black Panthers and the Left.

Ryan A. Smith is an assistant professor in the School of Management and Industrial Relations at Rutgers University–New Brunswick. His research focuses on group differences in access to job authority and the consequences of job authority for income and trends in racial attitudes in America.

Werner Sollors teaches English and Afro-American studies at Harvard University. He is the author of *Beyond Ethnicity: Consent and Descent in American Culture* (1986) and *Neither Black nor White yet Both: Thematic Explorations of Interracial Literature* (1997) and the editor of *Theories of Ethnicity: A Classical Reader* (1996), the Penguin Classics edition of Mary Antin's autobiography *The Promised Land* (1997), and *Multilingual America* (1998).

John Kuo Wei Tchen is the director of the Asian/Pacific/American Studies Program and Institute at New York University. His most recent books are *Monkey Spirits in the Devil's Box: Reimag(in)ing "The Orient" and "The Occident"* (1997) and *New York before Chinatown: Orientalism and the American Quest for Wealth and Destiny, 1776–1882* (forthcoming).

Andrea Tyree is a professor of sociology at the State University of New York at Stony Brook. As a social demographer, she has worked primarily on issues of social stratification, status attainment, international migration, and ethnicity. She was a collaborator on *The American Occupational Structure* (winner of the Sorokin Award).

Mary C. Waters is a professor of sociology at Harvard University. She is the coauthor of *From Many Strands: Ethnic and Racial Groups in Contemporary America* (1988) and the author of *Ethnic Options: Choosing Identities in America* (1990) and numerous articles on immigration and ethnicity in the United States.

Index

Achebe, Chinua, 243, 248
Adler, Mortimer, 66
Affirmative action, 19, 36, 63, 74, 194–97, 212–13, 245; quotas, 196
African Americans: and assimilation, 89, 93–95; attitudes toward, 5–6, 182–214; and Constitution, 11, 23*nn*9, 11; death penalty rates for, 189; diversity of, 53, 115; ethnicization of, 228, 238*n*36; intermarriage rates of, 33; and jury duty, 24*n*15, 25*n*37; legal protection of, 14–15, 16, 18; middle-class, 94–95, 213, 231, 240*n*49, 251; others' perceptions of, 126–27, 199–200; outside of history, 5–6, 255–56; slaves, 110–11; status of, 182–84, 188–90; and urban violence, 265–66, 268. *See also* Black nationalism; Black Panthers; Black power; Black radicalism; Black-white divide; Civil Rights Act of 1965; *Civil Rights Cases;* Civil rights movement; Constitution
Afrocentrism, 50, 60*n*10, 77, 255
Alba, Richard, 35
Alonso, William, 46*n*28
American Century, 226–28, 233–34, 237*n*26
American creed, 183, 184, 188, 203, 226

American Dilemma, An (Myrdal), 182–83, 226–27, 228, 233
"American Farmer," 106–17; and slavery, 112
Ancestry: lineal, 115
Andrew the Hebridean, 115
Anokye, Okomfo, 245, 258*n*5
Antiracism, 221–35
Appiah, Kwame Anthony, 9, 72
Armento, Beverley, 59*n*9
Arnold, Matthew, 80–83
Asante, Molefi Kete, 66
Asian Americans: boycott of businesses of, 145, 148*n*14; courses on, 74; as a demographic bloc, 53; histories of, 151*n*39; intermarriage rates of, 33; outside of history, 6; others' views of, 199, 263; representations of, 8, 52, 126–47. *See also* Chinese Americans; Japanese Americans; Korean Americans
Azikiwe, Nnamdi, 249

Bailyn, Bernard, 113
Balibar, Etienne, 233
Baraka, Amiri, 94
Beddoe, John, 134
Begley, Adam, 70

Bell, Derrick, 184, 187, 211, 225
Benét, Stephen Vincent, 270
Benjamin Cardozo High School, 126
Bensonhurst, 145
Berlin, Isaiah, 67
Berman, Paul, 66, 70
Bernstein, Richard, 65
Bérubé, Michael, 69
Beyond the Melting Pot (Glazer and
    Moynihan), 2
Bill of Rights, 12
Birth certificates: identities on, 34
Black nationalism, 234
Black Panthers, 232–33, 240*n*46
Black power, 232
Black radicalism, 232
Blacks. *See* African Americans
Black-white divide, 146
Blauner, Robert, 193
Blaut, James, 233
Blood quantum, 32
Bloom, Allan, 63, 69, 75, 96
Bloom, Jack, 207–8
Blumer, Herbert, 185, 189, 209
Bobo, Lawrence D., 5, 8, 185, 193, 196
Bourne, Ralph, 56
Bowery, 137–38
Bradley, Bill, 9
Brauer, Carl M., 211
British aspects of American culture, 3
British West Indies, 111
Brown, James, 230
Brown v. Board of Education, 14, 18, 25*n*26,
    83, 207, 211, 213
Buchanan, Patrick, 21
Bureau of Indian Affairs, 32
Butterfield, Fox, 140

Cabezas, Amado, 140
Callahan, Bob, 61*n*20
Canon: academic, 4; semantics of, 78
Caribbean, 111
Carolene Products case, 17–18
Carton, Evan, 59*n*7
Catholics: and American pluralism, 53,
    108–9, 113; and politics, 121*n*7; prejudice
    against, 108–9

Census Bureau: identifications by, 34; and
    mixed-race people, 37–42
Ceremony: and community building, 119
Charlestown, S.C., 112
Chinatown, 141–43
Chinese: attitudes toward, 5–6
Chinese Americans: and American plu-
    ralism, 125–53; images of, 142; immigra-
    tion of, 141; intermarriage rates of, 33;
    and labor, 145–46; representations of,
    143, 130–39. *See also* Chinatown
Chinese Exclusion Act, 129, 140–41, 144
Chinese Immigration (Coolidge), 129
Chinese Staff and Workers Association,
    144
Choi, Mina, 126–27
Christopher, Robert, 73
CIO, 225
Citizenry, 2, 22; in Constitution, 23*nn*9–
    11
Citizenship, 13, 14
City of Richmond v. J. A. Croson, 21
Civil Rights Act of 1964, 19, 32, 209, 212
Civil Rights Cases, 15
Civil rights movement, 203–9, 211, 213–14,
    230–31, 264
Classical republicanism, 13
Cleaver, Eldridge, 232
Cole, Mildred Wiese, 88, 92
Cole, Stewart, 88, 92
Constitution: and Catholics, 109; and citi-
    zenry, 23*nn*9–11; and groups, 11; and
    rights, 11; and slaves, 11, 23*nn*9, 11; and
    suffrage, 23*nn*9–11
Coolidge, Mary Roberts, 129
Corporations: rights of, 15
Cosmopolitanism, 50–52, 56, 60*n*11; com-
    pared with multiculturalism, 55; com-
    pared with pluralism, 51–52, 61*n*6;
    compared with postethnicity, 52, 55–56;
    compared with universalism, 51
Cowling, Mary, 134
Crèvecoeur, J. Hector St. John de, 2, 7, 8,
    86, 106–17, 121*n*2, 124*n*33
Crime bill of 1995, 223
Crummell, Alexander, 247
Cruse, Harold, 223

Cureton, Jean, 74
Curtis, Lewis Perry, 134

"Dan Mulligan," 138
Dasenbrock, Reed Way, 60*n*13
Davis, James W., 199
Davis, Kenneth, E., 197
Davis, Mike, 223
Death penalty, 189
Debs, Victor Eugene, 60*n*15
de Lepervanche, Marie, 72
Denominations: religious, 108
Denton, Nancy, 189
Deutsch, Monroe, 79–80
Devereux, George, 71
Devisee, Jean, 77
Dickstein, Morris, 81, 83
Dot-Busters, 145
Douglas, William, 20
Dred Scott v. Sandford, 23*n*9
D'Souza, Dinesh, 59*n*7, 70, 75, 78, 80
Du Bois, W. E. B., 50, 221–22, 224, 226, 227, 247, 251, 259*n*20
Dutch Americans, 110, 114, 115, 117–18, 124*n*35
Dutch language, 118
Dutch Reformed church, 118
Dutch West Indies, 111

Early, Gerald, 69
East Brunswick, N.J., 145
Educational systems: Asian, 141
Eggers, M. L., 189
Ehrenreich, Barbara, 75
Eisen, Arnold, 61*n*21
Ellison, Ralph, 83, 226–28
Enlightenment, 108, 120, 226
Epistles II in *Satires, Epistles and Ars Poetica* (Horace), 79
E Pluribus Unum: origin of phrase, 79–80; use of, 78, 257–58, 270
Ethnicity, 118; and ethnocentrism, 50, 72, 77, 257; origin of "ethnic identity," 71; postethnic perspective, 52–53, 58*n*3; as social construct, 28; symbolic, 55; variability of, 35. *See also* Identity
Ethnics, 55, 120, 123*n*28

Fabian, Johannes, 249
Federal Housing Administration, 232
Federalism, 12, 13
Federalist, No. 10 (Madison), 25*n*31
Feuer, Lewis S., 60*n*12, 64–65
Fields, Barbara, 53–54
Firebaugh, Glenn, 197
First Amendment, 12
Fish, Stanley, 70
Fitzpatrick, Joseph, 33
Fourteenth Amendment, 14–16
Fox-Genovese, Elizabeth, 71, 80
Frame of Government of Pennsylvania, 120
Freud, Sigmund, 77–78, 99*n*47
Fromm, Erich, 86
Fundamental law, 120

Gans, Herbert, 55
Gates, Henry Louis, Jr., 75, 78, 85
Gaubard, Stephen G., 127–28
Gender: and American pluralism, 117
General Trades Union, 120
German Lutherans, 113
German-speakers, 110
Ghettoization, 231–32
Gingrich, Newt, 228
Giroux, Henry, 66, 80
Gitlin, Todd, 78
Glazer, Nathan, 2, 96
Gleason, Philip, 88
Golden Venture (freighter), 143–45
Goodman, Walter, 84
Gordon, Milton, 30, 93
Gordon, Ted, 65
Gordon riots, 108
Grand Canyon (film), 265
Griggs v. Duke Power Company, 19
Group relations, 90–92. *See also* MacIver, Robert M.; Social Science Research Council; Williams, Robin M., Jr.
Group rights, 13
Guruk, Douglas, 33

Hacker, Andrew, 184, 185, 187, 211
Haley, Alex, 29, 42
Happiness: in eighteenth century, 13

Harper's Weekly, 130–31
Harrigan, Edward, 130, 137–39, 144
Hart, Tony, 138
Haskell, Edward F., 64–64
Hass, R. Glen, 198
Henretta, James, 115
Hentoff, Nat, 85
Heritages, 114–15
Hierarchy: racial, 134
Higham, John, 67, 71, 88, 90
Himmelfarb, Gertrude, 80, 82
Hispanics: courses on, 74, 256; definition
    of 31, 32; identity of, 36, 38, 53; increase
    in, 35, 68; intermarriage rates for, 33;
    whites' views of, 199
"Hog-Eye," 138
Hollinger, David A., 7, 8, 9, 12, 22, 23n7, 29,
    35, 37, 72, 236n11
Horowitz, Irving Louis, 78
Hout, Michael, 36
Hughes, Robert, 72–73
Huguenots, 110
Hurh, W. M., 140

Identity: African, 244–50; African Ameri-
    can, 228; American, 2, 52–53 257; Asian
    American, 41; on birth certificates, 34;
    choice of, 28–44; competing identities,
    47–48; construction of, 52, 53–55,
    99n47, 245–50; ethnic, 71; gender, 39;
    group, 76, 106, 111, 246; Indian, 35; Irish,
    36; Jewish, 52–53, 61n21, 62n30, 90, 94–
    95, 99n47; of mixed-ethnic people, 35;
    of mixed-race people, 34–37; politics,
    71, 246; racial, 90, 210–11, 251; religious,
    249–50, 258n18; shifting nature of, 52–
    53, 73; and social factors, 58; tribal, 248–
    50. *See also* Self-identification
Immigrants: voluntary, 31
Immigration: Chinese American, 141; as
    model of American development, 6,
    113–14; restriction of, 21
Immigration Act of 1965, 32
Indian. *See* Native Americans
Indifference: religious, 107
Industriousness, 113–15
Inheritance: partible, 118

Intermarriage: and identity, 36, 37–42;
    and pluralism, 30, 43; rates of, 28, 31,
    32–33, 36, 43, 197, 214, 220n89; results of,
    29, 30, 35, 37, 42, 119, 134; as a social
    process, 28, 54; studies of, 45n10
International Covenant on Civil and Po-
    litical Rights, 12
International Covenant on Economic,
    Social and Cultural Rights, 12
Invisible Man (Ellison), 83, 227
Irish, 110
Irish Americans: and Chinese, 137–39,
    152n58; identity of, 36; images of, 134;
    and Irish nationalism, 157, 159, 160; and
    politics, 177n34; and U.S. military, 161,
    162, 169
Isaacs, Harold, 140

Jackson, Jesse, 239n46
Jackson, Walter, 183
Jacobson, Matthew Frye, 5, 8
James, C. L. R., 225
Japanese Americans: discrimination
    against, 15, 25n24, 196; identity of, 32,
    53, 54; intermarriage rates of, 33
Jim Crow. *See* Racism
"John Confucius," 131
Jones, LeRoi. *See* Baraka, Amiri
Journal of American Ethnic History, 3

Kallen, Horace M., 52, 61nn16–17, 65, 83
Katz, Irwin, 198
Katz, Stanley N., 2, 5, 6, 36
Kearney, Denis, 144
Keppler, Joseph, 130, 135–37
Kerner Commission, 184, 185
Kikumura, Akemi, 33
Kim, Kwang Chung, 140
Kimball, Roger, 66, 69, 75, 80, 85
Kinkead, Gwen, 141–43
Kitano, Harry, 33
Korean Americans, 33
Kurlansky, Mark, 83

Labor unions, 16
Laitin, David, 249
Landsman, Ned, 2, 7, 8

LaPiere, R. T., 190
Lerner, Robert, 84
Letter on Toleration (Locke), 113
Letters from an American Farmer (Crève-
coeur), 106–17
Levine, Arthur, 73, 74
Liberal individualism, 22
Liberalism, 12–13
Lichter, Daniel T., 188
Lieberson, Stanley, 33, 35
Lineal family, 115, 116, 117
Locke, John, 13, 108, 113, 121*n*4, 129–30
Lubiano, Wahneema, 65
Lum, Joann, 144

MacIver, Robert M., 56, 88–90
Mackintosh, Cameron, 146
Madison, James, 12
Malcolm X, 93–94, 264
Mann, Arthur, 88
Mannheim, Karl, 66
Marshall, Thurgood, 11
Massey, Douglas S., 189
Maternal descent, 39
McAdam, Doug, 203–6
McKinnell, Trudy, 33
Melting pot, 2–3, 53, 67, 78, 79, 107, 270
Menand, Louis, 59*n*7, 73
Mexicans: and American pluralism, 117;
and assimilation, 31
Meyer v. Nebraska, 16
Mid-Atlantic region, 110–11
Middle class, 267; black, 94–95, 213, 231,
240*n*49; Jewish, 94–95; white, 55
Minorities: classification of, 28, 31–32, 34,
36–37, 43; concept of, 88, 89; involun-
tary, 31; in law, 17, 20; protection of, 17,
19, 26*n*37. *See also* Model minorities
Miss Saigon (play), 146
Mitchell-Kernan, Claudia, 33
Mixed-ethnic peoples: identification of,
35
Mixed-race peoples: census data on, 37–
42; children of, 36; identities of, 34–37
Model minorities, 6
Moose Lodge No. 107 v. Irvis, 20
Moretum (ascribed to Virgil), 79–80

Morris, Aldon, 205–7
Moynihan, Daniel P., 2, 239*n*45
Mueller, John, 193–94
Mulligan Guard Chowder (Harrigan), 138
Multiculturalism: compared with cosmopolitanism, 49–51, 52; compared with
pluralism, 51, 65–66, 92; compared with
universalism, 51; debates over, 49–51,
52, 58, 59*n*7, 63, 65–67, 69–70, 75, 77–96,
256; definitions of, 49–50, 51, 60*nn*10–
14, 65–66, 92, 121*n*1, 252–54, 257–58; and
education, 63, 66, 71, 73, 74, 80, 92–93,
95–96, 254–56; origin of word, 64–65,
88; as social policy, 73; U.S. compared
with African, 252–53, 255; U.S. compared with European, 88
Murray, Albert, 222
Myrdal, Gunnar, 50, 182–84, 185, 197–98,
201, 202–3, 211, 213, 226–27, 228, 233

Nash, Gary B., 49–50, 59*n*9, 60*nn*10–11
Nast, Thomas, 130–35
National Advisory Commission on Civil
Disorders. *See* Kerner Commission
National Center for Health Statistics, 34
Nationality, 114–16; mixed, 116
Native Americans: courses on, 74; defined
as a minority, 31, 32; as demographic
bloc, 52, 53; distinctions among, 53, 54;
growth rate of, 35; and history, 6, 10*n*11,
31, 256; identity of, 29, 31, 32, 35, 38, 40,
41, 42
Nativism, 21
Near v. Minnesota, 12
Nehamas, Alexander, 61*n*19, 80
Neocolonialism, 233
Netherlands, 116, 118
New Jersey corridor, 118
New Left, 225
Newton, Christopher, 67
New York: and American pluralism, 129–
47
New Yorker, 141–43
New York Times, 126–28, 140
Niemi, Richard G., 193
Njeri, Itabari, 78
Novak, Michael, 84–85

Ogbu, John, 31
Oliver, Melvin L., 200, 201
One drop rule, 29, 42
Orwell, George, 83–88
Ostendorf, Berndt, 67, 77–78

Paglia, Camille, 85
Pan-Africanism, 246–47, 251
Patai, Daphne, 86
Paternal descent, 39
Patronage: and ethnic groups, 115
Patterson, Orlando, 57
Penn, William, 109, 116
Pennsylvania: commerce of, 111; Frame of
    Government of, 120; opportunity in,
    110; and pluralism, 109–13; population
    of, 110; settlement of, 110
Perlez, Jane, 126
Perry, Ruth, 83
Philadelphia Yearly Meeting, 112
Phrenology, 134
Physiognomy, 134, 137
Pierce v. Society of Sisters, 16
Plessy v. Ferguson, 16, 18
Pluralism: in Africa, 244; alternative ver-
    sions of, 117; American, 2–5, 105–24;
    compared with cosmopolitanism, 51;
    compared with multiculturalism, 65–
    66, 88, 256; cultural, 30; definitions of,
    30, 105–6, 121n1; and diversity, 110; eth-
    nic, 118; functions of, 5; as historical
    creation, 4; and intermarriage, 43; le-
    gal framework of, 11–22; in Pennsylva-
    nia, 109–13; prosperity and, 111; Prot-
    estant, 108; settler, 111, 117; structural,
    30; varieties of, 129–30; working class
    and, 138
Polenberg, Richard, 88
Political correctness, 63, 83–87
Popular Front, 225
Porter, John, 74
Postethnic, 37, 42
Postethnicity, 22, 23n7, 48–58, 72; com-
    pared with cosmopolitanism, 52, 56;
    compared with pluralism, 52; defini-
    tion of, 48, 52, 54, 55, 57, 59n4
Postracism, 223

Prejudices: national, 116
Proposition 13, 191
Protestant: aspects of American culture,
    3; pluralism, 108–9, 129–30

Quakers, 109, 112
Quebec Act, 108
Queenie (miniseries), 42

Race, 5; Americans as, 114, 115; Anglo-Sax-
    on, 114, 117; intermixing of, 30; white,
    114, 117
Racialism, 117
Racism: and assimilation, 89; biological,
    198–99, 245–46; changing attitudes and
    patterns of, 57, 185–87, 191–201, 214; Jim
    Crow, 186, 201–2, 203–4, 209, 211–12,
    214; laissez-faire, 186–87, 211–13; persis-
    tence of, 184–85, 224–25; socioeconom-
    ic and political factors of, 90, 188–90,
    202–9, 210, 211–12, 213–14, 245, 250, 263–
    66, 268–70; and stereotyping, 200, 213–
    14, 263, 265; symbolic, 186–87. See also
    Antiracism; Postracism
Rainbow Coalition, 240n46
Rainbow Republicanism, 22
Ravitch, Diane, 50, 60n10, 77, 78
Reed, Ishmael, 47, 58n1, 66–67, 87
Reed, T. V., 227
Religion: redefinition of, 108–9
Republicanism: classical, 13
Rights: under Constitution, 11–12
Robbins, Bruce, 60n11
Robeson, Paul, 227
Robinson, Cedric, 259n20
Rodden, John, 87
Rorty, Richard, 96
Rothenbert, Paula, 84
Rothman, Stanley, 84

Sahlins, Marshall, 77–78
Salter, Christopher L., 59n9
Sandefur, Gary, 33
Schlesinger, Arthur M., Jr., 50, 60n10, 65,
    69, 75, 78
Schuman, Howard, 185, 192, 193, 194–95,
    196, 197

Schuyler, George, 259*n*9
Scots, 110; in Mid-Atlantic, 118–19
Scottish Presbyterian church, 119
Searle, John, 76–77, 85
Sears, David O., 186
Seceders: Scots, 107, 113
Self-identification, 29; and Census
    Bureau, 34
Separate but equal, 18
Settler society, 118–19
Shanker, Albert, 70, 76
Shelley v. Kraemer, 17–18
Silverman, Kenneth, 79
Singh, Nikhil Pal, 6, 8
Skokie, Ill., 12
Slavery, 13; in Constitution, 23*nn*9, 11
Slaves, 110–11. *See also* Constitution
Smith, Roger B., 59*n*5
Smith, Ryan A., 5, 8, 220*n*86
Smith, Tom W., 194
Snowden, Frank M., 57
Social Science Research Council, 88–90
Sollors, Werner, 4, 7, 59*n*4, 61*n*18
Souls of Black Folk, The (Du Bois), 221–22,
    224
Southern, David W., 183
Soyinka, Wole, 247
Spivak, Gayatri, 258*n*7
Steeh, Charlotte, 185, 192, 193, 194–95, 197
Steele, Shelby, 75–76, 78
Stimpson, Catherine, 77
Stone, Harlan Fiske, 17
Strict scrutiny, 18
Sullivan, Kathleen M., 22

Tchen, John Kuo Wei, 5, 6, 8
Thernstrom, Stephan, 68, 75
Three-fifths compromise, 23*n*11
Todorov, Tzvetan, 72, 85
Toleration, 4, 5, 6, 7, 108–9; 113–14, 130
Toll, Robert, 138

Trudeau, Pierre, 64
Tucker, M. Belinda, 33

U.S. News and World Report, 128
United Nations, 12
Universalism, 51–52; antiracist, 225

Vaughan, Leslie J., 52
Veteran's Administration, 232
Voting Rights Act of 1965, 19, 32, 36, 209,
    212

Wackenhut, Joyce, 198
Walzer, Michael, 65
Warner, W. Lloyd, 65
Wartime Civil Control Administration, 32
Washington v. Davis, 19–20
Waters, Mary, 5, 6, 7, 9, 33, 35, 54–55
Weber, Donald, 67
West, Cornel, 67
West Indies. *See* Caribbean
Westinghouse Science Talent Search, 126
Wexler, Natalie, 102*n*128
Will, George, 59*n*7, 84
Williams, Patricia, 85
Williams, Richard, 146
Williams, Robin M., Jr., 88, 90–91, 95
Winthrop, Chris, 57
Wiredu, Kwasi, 247
Wisconsin v. Yoder, 20
Wixson, Karen K., 59*n*9
Women: as group, 19
Wong, Morrison, 140
Wright, Richard, 227–30

Yarbrough, Larry, 66
Young, Donald R., 89–90, 92, 93

Zangwill, Israel, 88
Zenner, Walter P., 61*n*21
Zubrinsky, Camille L., 200, 201